# Foreword

Ever since our first cook book, published more than fifty years ago, Canadian homemakers have come to regard the Purity Cook Book as the authority on food. We feel certain that this all new edition will achieve the same recognition in the years to come.

The recipes reflect the trend toward easier preparation, increased interest in foreign specialties and party foods, and a tendency toward more unusual yet subtle flavours. In each section the recipes vary from the quick-and-easy or cook-by-themselves ideas to the dramatic show-offs that impress guests.

May this all new Purity Cook Book bring many pleasurable meals with the satisfaction of accomplishment inherent in cooking.

*Anna Lee Scott*

# COOKING SECRETS

## COOKING SECRETS

The secret of home cooking requires the assembling of perfectly balanced recipes that have been developed using consistent measuring techniques and that are written in a precise, easy to follow manner. In The Purity Cook Book we have striven to do just that.

For you to have perfect results, simply follow the same measuring procedures using the recommended measuring equipment. The fundamental aim of any measuring technique is to ensure consistent results by homemakers right across the country.

Specific measuring techniques for ingredients appear on this page but briefly we will review the measurement of flour.

### Pre-Sifted Flour

Advances in milling techniques now enable a homemaker to accurately measure Purity All-Purpose Flour without prior sifting. On the basis of extensive measurement studies, it has been determined that consistency of measurement can be achieved without this extra step.

The purpose of the former method of once sifting flour prior to spooning into the measuring cup was to ensure that all homemakers had about the same weight of flour in each cup, the vital factor in flour measurement. With to-day's Purity All-Purpose Flour, a closely consistent weight per cup of flour can be achieved without prior sifting.

For all the recipes in The Purity Cook Book we recommend that you simply spoon the flour into the cup and level off. These recipes are based on measuring without prior sifting. For your own favourite recipes, we recommend that you continue to measure Purity All-Purpose Flour as has been your custom.

Actually, this time-saving method of measuring flour has been used by many homemakers for years. By survey, more homemakers measure flour without prior sifting than sift once before measuring.

## MEASURING EQUIPMENT

### Liquid Measuring Cups

The cup line is a little below the rim so that a cup of liquid will not spill over.

### Dry Measuring Cups

The cup line is right at the rim.

### Measuring Spoons

## HOW TO MEASURE

### Flour

Spoon flour directly from the bag or canister into a dry measuring cup to fill to overflowing. With a straight-edged spatula or knife, push off the flour that rises above the rim. Cups in the fraction sizes can be filled and levelled in the same way.

For some purposes, you will want flour by the tablespoonful. In such cases, dip the tablespoon into the flour bag or canister and lift up a lightly mounded spoonful, and level off with a straight edge.

### Granulated Sugar

Follow the same method as for flour. Spoon granulated sugar into a dry measuring cup to fill to overflowing. With a straight-edged spatula or knife, level off.

### Brown Sugar

All the recipes in this book call for "lightly packed" brown sugar. Spoon brown sugar into a dry measuring cup, pressing down slightly to ensure there are no hollows underneath. Level off in the usual way. When turned out of the cup, the brown sugar should hold its shape but crumble if lightly touched.

### Solid Fat

The simplest method is to press butter, shortening or lard into a dry measuring cup. Press firmly to ensure there are no hollows underneath. Remove from cup. It is possible to measure solid fat by the water displacement method: Fill liquid measuring cup to ⅓ or ½ cup level with cold water. Drop fat into water, making certain it is completely immersed, until water level is at the 1 cup mark. If you started with ⅓ cup water, then you have measured ⅔ cup of fat. If you started with ½ cup water, you have measured ½ cup of fat.

### Liquid Fat

Measure vegetable oil or melted fat like any other liquid. Note that if recipe reads 1 tablespoon butter, melted—the butter would be measured before melting. If, however, the recipe reads 1 tablespoon melted butter, the butter would be measured after melting. For economy sake, solid fats to be melted are generally measured when solid.

### Liquids

Place measuring cup on table. Pour in liquid until, when you stoop to see the mark at eye level, the liquid is at the required line. To measure a spoonful, lift what the spoon holds naturally—it is more than level. (That is why there are 12 tablespoons liquid to the cup and 16 tablespoons dry measure.)

### Other Dry Ingredients

Such things as baking powder, baking soda, and cocoa sometimes have a tendency to pack down in their containers. To measure, stir the product to loosen, then lift a spoonful and level off in the usual way.

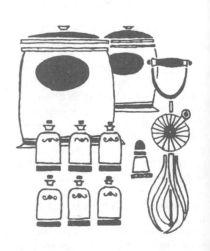

# COOKING TERMS

## Almonds

To Blanch. Drop almonds into boiling water and when skins are loosened, cool in cold water; then rub briskly with a rough cloth, squeezing off stubborn skins.

## Bake

To cook by dry heat, usually in an oven at a temperature suited to the food.

## Barbecue

To roast slowly on a rack or spit, over coals or a free flame, usually basting with a highly seasoned sauce. The term is popularly applied to foods cooked in or served with barbecue sauce.

## Baste

To spoon a liquid over a solid, is to baste it. Generally used in connection with the roasting of meats, when hot fat is spooned over lean meat surfaces at intervals to keep it juicy and flavourful. Sometimes fruit, and fruit desserts are basted with the syrup in the pan, during baking.

## Batter

A combination of flour and liquid, (along with other ingredients) to make a soft mixture which is (1) thin enough to pour as in pancake batter; (2) thick enough to make a batter suitable for muffins, cakes, etc.

## Beat

To make a mixture smooth or to introduce air by using a brisk, regular motion that lifts the mixture over and over.

## Blanch (precook)

To preheat in boiling water or steam. Generally used with vegetables prior to freezing. It is also used to aid in removal of skins from nuts, fruits and some vegetables (see Almonds).

## Blend

To combine thoroughly, until individual ingredients have lost their own identity, each being merged with the other.

## Boil

To heat a liquid, or mixture with considerable liquid in it, until it bubbles rapidly.

## Braise

To brown floured and seasoned meat etc., richly in a little fat in a frypan—then add a small amount of liquid and simmer gently, in a tightly covered pan on top of the stove or in the oven.

## Bread

To coat with bread crumbs alone, or to coat with bread crumbs, then with diluted slightly beaten egg, and again with crumbs.

## Broil

To cook with dry heat, by exposing surfaces of food to direct heat, at a suitable distance. A method frequently used for tender meat, young poultry or fish.
Pan-broiling is an adaptation of true broiling. Cook the food in an ungreased or lightly greased frypan or grill, pouring off any free fat as it may appear.

## Cake Pan

To Prepare—Brush bottom and sides of pan with shortening or other unsalted fat. Cut a piece of waxed paper to fit the bottom and brush again. Cake pans for light coloured cakes (other than chocolate) may be floured instead of the waxed paper lining. To do this, brush bottom and sides of pan with shortening, sprinkle with about a tablespoon of flour and shake pan to coat the inside, invert pan and shake out excess flour.

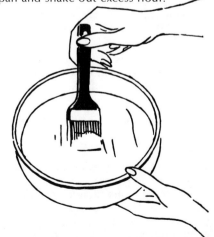

Homemakers who frequently bake cakes may wish to keep a container of a mixture of equal measures of flour and shortening (blended until smooth). In this way one brushing provides both greasing and flouring steps.

### Caramelize

To heat sugar or foods containing sugar until a brown colour and characteristic flavour develop.

### Chocolate

To Melt—Melt squares of chocolate over hot, not boiling, water. This applies to all types of chocolate used in cooking—unsweetened, semi-sweet and sweet.

### Chop

To cut into small pieces with a knife or chopper or other chopping tool.

### Cream

To stir and beat an ingredient until soft and smooth—and if more than one ingredient, until "blended".

### Cut

To divide food materials with a knife or scissors.

### Cut in

Usually used when cutting firm fat into a dry mixture of flour, etc. May be done (1) with a wire pastry blender, each wire of which cuts through the fat or (2) with two knives used scissor fashion. Cut cleanly, sharply, without twisting (which softens the fat). Reduce the fat to size indicated—generally, "until the consistency of coarse meal with a few larger pieces".

### Dice

To cut into small cubes.

### Double Boiler

Two saucepans, one of which fits into the other in such a way that water in lower pot circulates freely below and around the narrower upper pot. Temperature of food in upper pot remains below boiling point. Frequently new gas and electric ranges have a thermostatic element which can be regulated to keep the heat below boiling temperature in a regular saucepan.

### Dough

A mixture of flour and liquid, with other ingredients, which is thicker than the batters—thick enough to hold its shape in varying degrees. Doughs vary from "drop" (dumplings) to "soft" (tea biscuits) to "stiff" doughs (cookies and pastry).

### Drain

(1) To completely pour off such liquid as water, juices, etc. from solids. (2) To place fried food on paper towelling or other absorbent paper, to remove the fat from the surface of the food.

### Dredge

To sprinkle food evenly and generously with such things as flour or sugar.

### Drippings

The fat which melts from meat, during roasting, broiling or pan-broiling.

### Eggs

To Beat to Given Degree—If whole eggs are to be beaten "slightly" that means just until whites and yolks are sufficiently intermingled that neither can be seen alone. If to be beaten "well", yolks and whites together should be beaten with a rotary beater (electric or hand-turned) until very light—lots of air beaten in.

To Separate—Over a bowl, crack shell of egg on one side with a knife, then with thumbs, pull half shells apart, allowing white to drop into bowl beneath, and holding yolk in half the shell. Slip yolk from one half shell to the other to drain off all the white possible. Should you get a tiny streak of yolk in the white, use a piece of shell to remove it cleanly.

## Egg Whites

To Beat Stiff—In several recipes it says to beat egg whites "to form stiff but moist peaks". This means to beat them until they hold their shape and the bowl could be turned upside down without the whites slipping out. The surface of the beaten whites must still be glossy.

## Fat

A very broad term, used to cover all foods which are largely or altogether fat such as butter, shortening, lard, vegetable oil, meat drippings and suet.

## Flame

To set alight during cooking. To flame, warm specified amount of brandy or liqueur, pour over food and light with match. Alcohol burns with a blue flame so turn lights low for it to be visible.

## Flour

A product milled from grain—chiefly wheat. Flour ranges from white to whole wheat according to what parts of the grain have been retained.

## Fold

Generally used with regard to combining whipped cream or stiffly beaten egg white with another mixture. The purpose is to blend it in without losing any of the air incorporated in the whipped cream or beaten egg white. With a rubber spatula or wooden spoon (upside down),

touching bowl all the time, carry spatula or spoon down one side, across the bottom of bowl and up the opposite side

turning to have right or other side up. Turn bowl slightly and repeat until no blobs of egg white or whipped cream are visible.

## Fricassée

To cook by braising; usually applied to fowl or veal cut into pieces.

## Fry

To cook food with fat. (1) Pan-frying calls for just a little fat in a shallow pan, primarily to prevent food from sticking to pan. (2) Deep-frying is to immerse and cook, plain or coated food in deep fat at suitable temperature.

## Glaze

A film over the surface of food such as a syrup or sugar glaze on ham, a thickened transparent sweet coating over fruit in pies and tarts, or a clear coating that forms on candied fruits and nuts.

## Grill

See Broil.

## Grind

To reduce to particles by cutting, crushing, or grinding.

## Knead

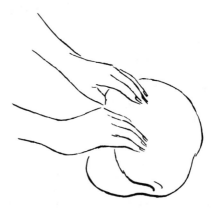

A folding over and pressing together of dough to make it more elastic. Generally used for yeast doughs and some quick breads. Lift one half of dough with fingertips and fold over to give a double thickness; then press together with heels of the hands. Give dough a quarter turn and repeat.

## Lard

The rendered and purified fat of the pig.

## Leavening Agent

A product or procedure which gives lightness to flour mixtures. Examples of products are baking powder, baking soda and yeast. Examples of procedures are beating eggs or egg whites until very light, and creaming fat and sugar in cake making.

## Marinate

To steep a solid food for a time in a flavourful liquid. The flavours of the "marinade" or liquid penetrate the food before it is served (as in a salad) or before it is cooked (as in a steak or pot roast).

## Melt

To heat a firm or "set" product, such as a solid fat, chocolate, etc. until it reaches a liquid or flowing state.

## Meringue

Beaten egg white into which sugar or syrup has been beaten.

## Milk

To Sour—When you want to use sour milk as an ingredient to replace buttermilk, for each cup of sweet milk replace 1 tablespoon milk with 1 tablespoon lemon juice or vinegar and allow to stand a few minutes.

## Mince

To grind or chop very fine.

## Mix

To combine ingredients in a way that produces an even distribution.

## Oven

To Preheat—Turn on oven, setting automatic heat control at specified temperature, or placing oven thermometer in centre of oven for checking temperature. To Reduce Temperature of—When oven heat is to be quickly reduced, open oven door for a few moments.

## Pan-broil

To cook uncovered on a hot surface, usually a frypan. The fat is poured off as it accumulates.

## Panfry

To cook in small amount of fat (see Fry).

## Pan Sizes

Recipes give recommended pan sizes based on inside top measurements. If

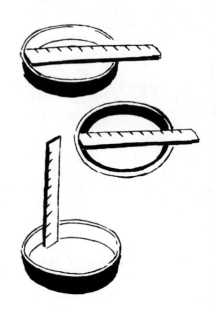

unavailable, use pan with as nearly as possible the same volume. Remember to fill pans for butter-type cakes and muffins ⅔ full and one-bowl cakes ½ full.

## Parboil

To partially cook a food by boiling or simmering in a liquid.

## Pare

To cut off the outside covering.

## Pastry Cloth

A piece of canvas used for rolling out pastry, cookie doughs and tea biscuits. The advantage is that flour can be rubbed into cloth to prevent dough sticking but dough itself absorbs a minimum amount of the flour.

## Peel

To strip off the outside covering.

## Poach

To cook gently in simmering liquid.

## Pot Roast

To brown meat on all sides with high heat and then finish cooking in covered pan with small amount of liquid.

**Roast**

To cook naturally tender meat or poultry by dry heat in the oven using an uncovered pan.

**Sauté**

To brown or cook in a small amount of fat (see Fry).

**Scald**

To make hot, but not to the point of boiling. Liquid has reached "scalding point" when bubbles form a ring against side of pan, but do not appear across surface of liquid.

**Seasoning**

Salt is the primary seasoning for food—used to bring out natural flavours of all other ingredients. For additional flavour, add pepper, mustard and any other spices, herbs, onion (and all its kin, from delicate chives to pungent garlic), salts that have been given the special flavour of celery, onion, garlic, etc., vinegars of various flavours and bottled sauces.

**Shortening**

As commonly used, this term applies to a commercially processed blend of vegetable, and sometimes including some animal fats, that is hydrogenated to be made solid. Preservatives and emulsifying agents are generally added. The resulting fat is then aerated.

**Simmer**

To cook over gentle heat just below boiling point.

**Soufflé**

A very airy mixture consisting chiefly of very lightly beaten egg. It may be baked, in which case it must be served immediately it comes from the oven. Cold soufflés generally contain gelatine and the puffy appearance is contrived through extending the sides of the dish with waxed paper which is later removed when set.

**Steam**

To cook food in a covered perforated container set over a pot of boiling water.

**Stew**

To cook any desired combination of meat, poultry and vegetables in liquid at a gently simmering temperature. The liquid may be thickened before serving.

**Stir**

To mix food materials with a circular motion for the purpose of blending or securing a uniform consistency.

**Stock**

The liquid in which meat, fish, poultry or vegetables have been cooked.

**Syrup and Candy Tests**

In addition to temperature on a candy thermometer, a description of syrup

when dropped from a spoon into very cold water is generally given.

**Toast**

To brown by means of dry heat.

**Whip**

To beat rapidly to produce expansion due to incorporation of air as applied to heavy cream, eggs and gelatine dishes.

*Recipes in this cook book are all based on the large size eggs. In those that call for several eggs you may wish to do a little arithmetic to convert to other sizes. Use the following as a guide: 5 large eggs = 4½ extra large eggs = 5½ medium eggs = 7 small eggs*

# Appetizers and Snacks

## CHEESE WAFERS

Preheat oven to 350°F.
Combine
 **½ cup thick dairy sour cream**
 **¼ cup soft butter**
 **2 cups grated cheddar cheese**
 **¼ teaspoon Worcestershire sauce**
 **¼ teaspoon salt**
Gradually blend in
 **1 cup PURITY Flour**
Knead in last of flour. Shape dough into a roll 2-inches in diameter. Cut into ¼-inch thick slices.
Bake on ungreased baking sheet in preheated 350° oven for 12 to 15 minutes or until light golden.
TO FREEZE: Wrap cheese roll and freeze. Partially thaw (about 1 hour) and just before serving slice and bake. Makes 2 dozen.

ONION-CHEESE WAFERS: Prepare Cheese Wafers following basic recipe but blend 2 tablespoons dried onion flakes into butter mixture.

BACON-CHEESE WAFERS: Prepare Cheese Wafers following basic recipe but blend 4 slices cooked side bacon, crumbled, into butter mixture.

## NUTS & BOLTS

Preheat oven to 300°F.
Combine and bake on ungreased baking sheet in preheated 300° oven until warmed through
 **2 cups crisp shredded wheat cereal**
 **2 cups corn cereal or croutons**
Remove from oven and stir in
 **2 cups (1 pound) salted peanuts**
 **1 cup (5-ounce package) pretzel sticks, broken into small pieces**
Pour over and stir to coat evenly
 **¾ cup melted butter or margarine**

Season with a mixture of
 **½ cup grated powdered cheddar cheese**
 **1 teaspoon garlic salt**
 **1 teaspoon onion salt**
Return to 300° oven for 8 to 10 minutes. This may be stored for several weeks in an air-tight container.
Makes 7 cups

BAR-B-Q NIBBLERS: Prepare Nuts and Bolts following basic recipe but substituting 1 package Bar-B-Q dip mix for cheese mixture.

ONION NIBBLERS: Prepare Nuts and Bolts following basic recipe but substituting 1 package dried onion soup mix for cheese mixture.

## ESCARGOTS À LA BOURGUIGNONNE

Preheat oven to 350°F.
Sterilize in boiling water
 **24 snail shells**
Cream together
 **½ cup soft butter**
 **3 cloves garlic, finely chopped**
 **2 tablespoons finely chopped fresh parsley**
 **2 tablespoons finely chopped green onion**
 **1 tablespoon dry white wine**
 **Pinch of pepper**
Drain
 **1 can snails (24)**
In each shell put about ½ teaspoon of butter mixture, one snail, and then fill with remaining butter mixture.
Bake in preheated 350° oven for 10 minutes or until piping hot.
Serve with crusty French bread as an appetizer.
Makes 4 servings.

## CHEESE BOMBE

Let cheese warm to room temperature.
Cream together with a wooden spoon,
or beat at low speed of electric mixer
until smoothly blended
**4 ounces cream cheese**
**4 ounces blue cheese, crumbled**
**½ cup cheese spread**
**2 tablespoons brandy**
Cover and chill until firm enough to
mould.
Shape into a cone or ball.
Gently press into surface
**½ cup chopped nuts.**
Cover with plastic wrap and chill.
To serve, place in centre of serving plate,
and allow cheese to come to room temperature. Surround with pumpernickel,
rye-bread slices, or crackers.
Makes 2 cups.

CHRISTMAS BOMBE: Prepare Cheese
Bombe as in basic recipe. Criss cross two
1-inch strips of wax paper over the ball,
and press chopped nuts into the rest of
the surface. Remove the wax paper and
fill strips with chopped parsley. Garnish
with strips of red pimiento.

SMOKY CHEESE BOMBE: Prepare
Cheese Bombe following basic recipe but
substituting 8 ounces cream cheese, 4
ounces grated smoked cheese, and 1 tablespoon sesame seeds for cheese mixture.

### CHILI CORN TARTS

Preheat oven to 375°F.
Prepare PURITY Pastry (See page 154) following basic recipe but stir into shortening-flour mixture
**1 egg, beaten**
**1 (3-ounce) package corn**
**chips, finely crushed**
Add water as directed. Roll out dough
¼-inch thick and with cookie cutter, cut
into 2½-inch circles. Line 16 medium-sized muffin pans but do not prick.
Blend together and spoon into tart shells
**1 (15-ounce) can chili con carne**
**Pinch of chili powder**
**Pinch of garlic powder**
Bake in preheated 375° oven for 18 to
20 minutes or until piping hot.
Serve immediately.
Makes 16 tarts.

## HEARTY CHILI DIP

In a small saucepan heat together
**1 (15-ounce) can chili with beans**
**Dash of garlic salt**
**Dash of chili powder**
Mash beans with fork.
Blend in
**½ cup condensed tomato soup**
Serve in a chafing dish as a hot dip with
corn chips, crispy crackers, or bread
sticks.
Makes 2 cups.

CHILI-CHEESE: Prepare Chili Dip following basic recipe but substituting ½
cup processed cheese for tomato soup,
and heat until cheese is melted.

### MARINATED SHRIMP

In a large saucepan, combine
**8 cups water**
**¼ cup chopped onion**
**1 clove garlic, chopped**
**1 bay leaf**
**2 stalks celery with leaves**
**1¼ tablespoons salt**
**Pinch of cayenne**
Bring to boil and simmer for 5 minutes.
Add
**2 pounds frozen, cleaned shrimps**
**½ lemon, thinly sliced**
Bring to boil and simmer for 5 minutes
or until shrimps are fully cooked. Allow
to cool in liquid.
Rub a bowl with
**garlic**
Mix together in bowl
**½ cup chopped celery**
**1 green onion, chopped**
**1 tablespoon chopped chives**
**6 tablespoons olive oil**
**3 tablespoons lemon juice**
**¼ teaspoon Tabasco sauce**
**2 tablespoons chili sauce**
**2 tablespoons catsup**
**2 tablespoons horseradish**
**1 tablespoon prepared mustard**
**¾ teaspoon salt**
**¼ teaspoon paprika**
Stir in drained shrimps and let stand for
at least 24 hours before serving.

*There is no difference between white and
brown eggs. They are alike in flavour,
yolk colour and nutritive value.*

## CURRIED SHRIMP

In a saucepan, combine
**1 (10-ounce) package frozen
shrimps
¾ cup water
⅓ cup chopped fresh parsley
1 tablespoon dried onion flakes
½ teaspoon garlic salt
¼ teaspoon curry powder
¼ teaspoon Tabasco sauce**
Bring to boil and cook, stirring occasionally for 5 minutes or until shrimps are tender.
Chill in this liquid for at least 4 hours.
Serve on toothpicks.
Makes about 4 dozen small shrimp.

## TEMPTING MUSHROOM SHRIMP

In a saucepan, heat until foamy
**2 tablespoons butter or margarine**
Add and cook until onion is transparent
**2 tablespoons finely chopped
onion
1 cup sliced mushrooms
2 teaspoons finely chopped green
pepper
1 teaspoon chopped fresh parsley**
Blend in a mixture of
**2 tablespoons PURITY Flour
½ teaspoon salt
¼ teaspoon paprika
¼ teaspoon pepper**
Gradually, stir in
**¾ cup milk**
Cook, stirring constantly, until thickened.
Mix in
**1 (7-ounce) can shrimps, drained
1 tablespoon dry white wine
1 teaspoon grated cheddar cheese
¼ teaspoon Worcestershire sauce**
Heat thoroughly.
Serve on toasted points or fill tiny cream puff or patty shells and serve as an hors d'œuvres.
Makes 4 servings or 5 dozen bouchées.

## MARINATED MUSHROOMS

Marinate
**1 (10-ounce) can button
mushrooms, drained**
In a mixture of
**⅓ cup wine vinegar
⅓ cup olive oil
½ teaspoon onion salt
¼ teaspoon celery salt
¼ teaspoon marjoram
2 tablespoons chopped parsley, or
1 teaspoon dried parsley flakes**
Cover and chill for at least 4 hours.
(These will keep in refrigerator for several days.)
Serve on toothpicks as hors d'œuvres

---

*Cover fresh mushrooms with a dampened paper towel to retain moisture and store in the refrigerator. They will keep several days.*

---

## CRAB-STUFFED MUSHROOMS

Preheat oven to 400°F.
Grease a baking sheet.
Finely chop stems off
**2 dozen large, fresh mushrooms**
In a frypan, heat until foamy
**1 tablespoon butter or margarine**
Blend in stems with
**¼ cup finely chopped green onion**
Cook until tender. Remove and set aside.
To frypan add an additional
**2 tablespoons butter or margarine**
When melted, blend in
**2 tablespoons PURITY Flour**
Gradually, stir in
**¼ cup dry sherry
2 tablespoons cream
½ teaspoon Tabasco sauce
¼ teaspoon garlic salt**
Cook, stirring constantly, until thickened.
Stir in mushroom-onion mixture with
**1 (5½-ounce) can crabmeat**
Reduce heat and simmer for 5 minutes or until desired consistency.
Spoon mixture into mushroom caps.
Bake on greased baking sheet in preheated 400° oven for 8 minutes or until delicately browned.
Makes 2 dozen.

## QUICKIE STUFFED MUSHROOMS

Preheat oven to 400°F.
Grease a baking sheet.
Finely chop stems from
**2 (10-ounce) cans whole
mushrooms**
Combine
**1 package sour cream mix**

¼ cup milk
3 tablespoons dry sherry
(optional)
Stir in
1 tablespoon dried onion flakes
½ teaspoon dried parsley flakes
Blend in chopped mushrooms with
1 (5½-ounce) can crabmeat
Spoon into mushroom caps.
Bake on greased baking sheet in a preheated 400° oven for 6 minutes, or until
delicately browned.

## CHEESE FONDUE

Rub inside of a fondue dish with
1 peeled, cut garlic clove
Mix together in dish
1 pound grated Swiss cheese
¼ cup PURITY Flour
Stir in
2 cups dry white wine
1 tablespoon Kirsch
1 teaspoon lemon juice
Pinch of nutmeg
Pinch of pepper
Slowly heat, stirring constantly, until
cheese is melted. Remove from heat and
beat with rotary beater until smooth. Set
over a table warmer and simmer, but do
not boil.
Cut into bite size pieces
1 loaf Italian or French bread
(Each piece must have a crusty side.)
With a long handled fork spear a bread
cube and twirl to coat evenly in the simmering fondue.
If the fondue becomes too thick stir in
a tablespoon of heated wine.
Makes 4 to 6 servings.

## TUNA MORSELS

Mix together
1½ cups finely chopped tuna
or chicken
1 (4-ounce) package cream cheese
Stir in
2 tablespoons finely chopped
pimiento
¼ teaspoon salt
Pinch of pepper
Shape into 1-inch balls. Roll in
½ cup finely chopped almonds
Chill. Serve on toothpicks.
Makes 3 dozen.

## SWEDISH MEATBALLS & DIP

MEATBALLS:
Mix together
1 pound ground beef
1 (4-ounce) package cream cheese
1 cup fine, dry bread crumbs
¼ cup dry onion soup mix
½ teaspoon nutmeg
Dash of cayenne
Shape into 1-inch balls. In a large frypan,
heat until foamy
1 tablespoon shortening
Add meatballs and cook until evenly
browned. Cover, reduce heat and cook,
stirring occasionally, for about 20 minutes
or until thoroughly cooked. Remove from
pan and set aside.
SAUCE:
Blend into fat in pan a mixture of
¼ cup PURITY Flour
2 tablespoons dry onion soup mix
¼ teaspoon nutmeg
Gradually, stir in
2½ cups milk
Cook, stirring constantly, until thickened.
Serve in a chafing dish as a hot dip for
the meatballs, or use as a sauce with
meatballs.
Makes 6 servings or 36 meatballs.

## SLIMMERS' DIP

With a fork, mix together until smooth
or press through sieve
1 cup cottage cheese
¼ cup yoghurt or low calorie
mayonnaise
Blend in
2 tablespoons dried onion soup
mix
½ teaspoon dried parsley flakes
Serve as dip with raw vegetables (radish
roses, celery sticks, cucumber fingers,
cauliflowerets, carrot sticks, cabbage
wedges, tomato wedges or cherry tomatoes) or cooked brussel sprouts, asparagus, or broccoli spears.
Makes about 1 cup.

SHRIMP DIP: Prepare Slimmers' Dip
following basic recipe but substituting ½
cup chopped cooked or canned shrimp,
2 tablespoons chopped green pepper and
pinch of pepper, for onion soup mix and
parsley flakes.

## LIVERWURST PATE

Lightly oil a 4-cup mould.
Blend together
**1½ pounds liverwurst**
**½ cup soft butter or margarine**
**¼ cup chopped fresh parsley**
**¼ cup finely chopped**
**green onion**
**¼ cup brandy**
Sprinkle into mould
**1 tablespoon fresh chopped**
**parsley**
Press liver mixture into mould and chill at least 3 hours.
To unmould, partially immerse in hot water for a few seconds and turn out onto serving plate. Garnish with fresh parsley and surround with crackers or buttered bread.
Makes 4 cups.

## COFFEE SLICES

Slice
**1 (8-ounce) can date-nut**
**bread, or fruit and nut loaf**
Combine
**1 (4-ounce) package whipped**
**cream cheese**
**3 tablespoons marmalade**
Spread mixture on date-nut slices.
If desired, sprinkle with
**cinnamon**
Arrange on baking sheet and broil until mixture starts to bubble.
Serve hot.
Makes 8 slices.

## ZIPPY SNACK

Cut in half and spread with butter
**6 English muffins**
Mix together
**2 cups (½ pound) grated processed**
**cheese**
**½ cup tomato catsup**
**¼ cup chopped green olives**
**1 tablespoon finely chopped**
**green onion**
Spread two heaping tablespoons of cheese mixture on each muffin.
If desired, sprinkle with
**Pinch of oregano**
Place on ungreased baking sheet and broil until piping hot.
Makes 12 sandwiches.

## TINY TARTLETS

These may be prepared several hours ahead and baked just before serving.
Preheat oven to 425°F.
Prepare PURITY Pastry (See page 154).
Roll out, cut with cookie cutter and line tiny muffin pans.
Fill with a mixture of
**smoked salmon and**
**cream cheese**
**or**
Sprinkle in bottom any of the following:
**diced ham**
**or**
**cooked side bacon, crumbled**
**or**
**finely chopped onion or dried**
**onion flakes**
**or**
**flaked tuna and diced pimiento**
**or**
**tomato catsup**
Season with
**Pinch of garlic powder**
**Pinch of oregano**
Fill tart shells with
**grated cheddar or Mozzarella**
**cheese**
Press down slightly.
Bake in preheated 425° oven for 10 minutes or until cheese is melted and delicately golden.
Remove from pans immediately.
Serve hot.

## TEATIME SANDWICHES

**RIBBON SANDWICHES:**

Make four-layer sandwiches, alternating ½-inch slices of buttered white and brown bread, and using three kinds of fillings, e.g. tinted cream cheese, devilled ham and finely chopped egg salad. Press slices firmly together and trim crusts from each "stack". Wrap individually, and chill for several hours. At serving time, cut each stack into ½-inch slices, and each slice into three ribbon bars.

**ROLLED SANDWICHES:**

Start with a fresh loaf of unsliced fine-textured bread. Cut crusts off lengthwise on three sides, leaving one crust as a base for slicing. Remove one of the end crusts, leaving the other to hold while slicing. With a very sharp knife, slice loaf as thinly as possible, lengthwise, keeping slices moist by covering with a damp towel. Spread each slice with soft butter or margarine, and then with a colorful creamy sandwich filling (cheese, peanut butter, date and nut mixture, etc.). Wrap each slice tightly around a peeled banana, a dill pickle, a cooked wiener, a row of stuffed olives or a row of gherkins. Fasten end of roll firmly with extra filling. Wrap each roll tightly in waxed paper or plastic wrap, and chill thoroughly. At serving time, slice circles off rolls, being careful to slice through centres.

## SANDWICH LOAF:

Remove top and bottom crusts from an unsliced loaf of sandwich bread. Slice loaf lengthwise into 4 or 5 slices of even thickness. Remove side and end crusts from all slices. Spread butter or margarine on one side of top and bottom slice, and on both sides of other slices.

Build slices back into a loaf by spreading a different kind of filling on each layer. Choose a combination of sandwich fillings with flavours which blend well together, e.g. ham salad, egg salad, chicken salad, and cheese and pimiento. Remove any excess filling from sides.

Frost top and sides of loaf with softened white cream cheese mixed with cream so that it is light and fluffy. If desired, the frosting may be tinted a very pale pastel shade for special occasions. Chill loaf for several hours and just before serving, decorate top and sides with an attractive garnish. Slice loaf with a sharp knife into 1-inch slices. Using individual plates, serve each on a crisp leaf of lettuce with a salad fork.

## PINWHEEL SANDWICHES

Trim crusts from the top and sides of a fresh 24-ounce loaf of unsliced sandwich bread. (Chill loaf for easier cutting.) With loaf of bread on side and bottom crust to your left, cut 8 to 10 lengthwise slices, ¼-inch thick, using a ruler as a guide and a long thin sharp knife. To help reduce "cracking", roll each slice once with rolling pin, starting at the narrow edge.

Spread bread slices with butter or margarine to the edges. Cover with a well seasoned sandwich filling which is not too moist.

Place a row of stuffed olives or gherkins at the narrow edge. Roll up tightly being careful to keep the sides in line. Wrap rolls individually in waxed paper, twisting the ends securely.

Chill for several hours or overnight.
Cut each roll into 6 slices.
Makes: 4 dozen pinwheels per loaf of bread.

## CHEESE AND WIENER PINWHEELS

Spread bread slices with cheese spread; place wiener at narrow edge and roll up as directed.
Wrap and chill.

## EGG AND GHERKIN PINWHEELS

Spread bread slices with butter and then with egg salad filling. Place whole gherkins at narrow edge and roll up as directed.
Wrap and chill.

## CHEESE AND CHERRY PINWHEELS

Spread bread slices with soft plain or pineapple cream cheese. Place well drained whole red or green maraschino cherries in a row at narrow edge. Roll up as directed.
Wrap and chill.

## DANISH SANDWICH WHEEL

Cut a horizontal slice from a round loaf of
**rye, or pumpernickel bread**
Spread with a mixture of
**1 tablespoon butter or margarine**
**½ teaspoon prepared mustard**
Top with and spread to edges
**¼ cup whipped cream cheese**
Around outer edge of circle overlap
**paper thin slices of salami**
**or ham**
Close to middle arrange a circle of
**thinly sliced cucumber**
In centre spoon
**corn relish**
To serve, place on a wooden board and cut in pie-shape wedges.
Makes 6 servings.

# Meat-Fish-Poultry

## MEATS

### PURCHASING

The number of servings in a pound of meat depends on the amount of bone, fat and gristle; the size of servings; added ingredients or extenders; and the shrinkage during cooking. Generally, boneless meat will give three to four servings per pound, bone-in meat two to three servings.

When buying beef look for creamy white fat of moderate thickness and the lean should be well marbled (tiny flecks of fat evenly distributed throughout). Tender meat has a fine-grained velvety texture. The bones of young animals are more porous and tinged with red.

With pork, lamb and veal look for meat that is firm, fine-grained, smooth and velvety. All are lighter in colour than beef: pork and veal should be light greyish pink and lamb varies from a light to dark pink.

Take time to learn the various cuts and how they are best prepared. The cost of meat varies with the demand and less popular cuts can mean a real saving. Consider the cost per serving when comparing one cut to another.

### STORING

Remove butcher's wrapping, wipe meat with a clean damp cloth and cover loosely with wax paper. Store in refrigerator and use within a day or two—minced beef should be used within one day. Meats may be wrapped securely in freezer wrap and frozen. Thaw before cooking. Cured meats may be kept in store wrappings for up to a week. Cooked meats should be cooled quickly, then tightly wrapped and refrigerated.

### COOKING

Low temperature cooking reduces shrinkage and gives better flavour. Only tender cuts should be cooked without liquid or roasted uncovered. Only less tender cuts should be browned or seared first, as the high temperature increases the shrinkage markedly; with less tender cuts liquid is absorbed during braising or stewing to compensate for this shrinkage.

If cooking meat from the frozen state, determine the total cooking time for that particular cut of fresh meat and increase the amount by half as much again. For example a roast that would normally take two hours to cook, would require three hours, if frozen.

**The photograph features Stuffed Pork Tenderloin garnished with Apple Rings, Indonesian Bitterballen and Chicken Supreme, only three of the temptingly different recipes found in this section ▶**

16

# BEEF Cooking Chart

| Tender Cuts | Size | Cooking Time Rare Medium | | DIRECTIONS |
|---|---|---|---|---|
| **Steaks** | **(Thickness)** | **Minutes** | | |
| | | | | **BROIL**—Slash fat edge of meat to prevent curling. Place meat on cold rack, 4-5″ below heat source, in an oven preheated to 325°F. Broil for half prescribed time on one side, season with salt and pepper. Using tongs, turn meat and broil other side until meat is done. |
| Sirloin Steak | ½-¾ | 10-12 | 14-16 | |
| | 1¼ | 15-20 | 20-25 | |
| Porterhouse or | ½-¾ | 9-10 | 12-15 | |
| T-Bone Steak | 1-1¼ | 14-16 | 18-20 | |
| Wing or | ½-¾ | 5 | 6-7 | **PANBROIL**—Slash fat edge of meat to prevent curling. Lightly grease a heavy frying pan and set over moderate heat. Place meat in pan and cook, turning frequently to insure even cooking. Pour off excess fat as it accumulates. |
| Club Steak | 1-1¼ | 9-10 | 12 | |
| Tenderloin | 1-1¼ | 9-10 | 12 | |

| Roasts | Lbs. | Min. Per Lb. | | DIRECTIONS |
|---|---|---|---|---|
| Standing Rib | 7-8 | 18-20 | 22-24 | **ROAST**—Place meat on rack in open pan, fat side up. Cook uncovered in a slow oven 300°F. Do not sear the meat or add water. Cook till meat thermometer registers internal temperatures: |
| Rolled Rib | 6-8 | 32-34 | 36-38 | |
| Rump | | | | |
| (High Quality) | 5-7 | 20-22 | 25-30 | |
| Sirloin | 5-6 | 20-22 | 25-30 | |
| Porterhouse | | | | Rare         140°F. |
| and Wing | 5-6 | 18-20 | 22-24 | Medium    160°F. |
| Round | 5-6 | 20-22 | 25-30 | Well Done 170°F. |
| (High Quality) | | | | |

| Less Tender Cuts | Lbs. | Min. Per Lb. | DIRECTIONS |
|---|---|---|---|
| Shoulder | 5-6 | 30-35 min. per lb. | **POT ROAST**—Rub meat with well seasoned flour. Brown in a heavy pan or Dutch oven with a small amount of fat. Add 1 cup water, tomato juice, soup stock or other liquid. Cover pan tightly and cook slowly in a 300°F. oven or on top of the stove until tender. More liquid should be added as required. |
| Chuck | 5-6 | | |
| Blade | 5-6 | | |
| Rolled Plate | 5-6 | 10 min. extra per lb. for rolled cuts | |
| Rump | 5-6 | | |
| Brisket | 4-5 | | |
| Swiss Steak | 1½-2 | 2-2½ hours (total time) | **BRAISE**—Dip meat in well seasoned flour. Brown on both sides in a heavy frying pan with a small amount of fat. Add ½ cup water, tomato juice, soup stock, or other liquid. Cover pan tightly and cook slowly in a 300°F. oven or on top of the stove until tender. More liquid should be added as required. |
| Short Rib | 2½-3 | | |
| Round Steak | 2 | | |
| Brisket | 2 | | |
| Neck-Boneless | 1½-2 | 3 hours (total time) | **STEW**—Cut meat in small pieces. Dip in seasoned flour and brown quickly in fat. Cover meat with warm water. Simmer until tender. Do not boil. Measure the time from the moment the liquid begins to simmer. Add vegetables and seasonings about 30 min. before the meat is done. The gravy may be thickened with flour, if desired. |
| Shank Meat | 1½-2 | | |
| Stewing Beef | 1½-2 | | |
| Brisket | 1½-2 | | |
| Flank | 1½ | | |

# LAMB-PORK-VEAL Cooking Charts

## TENDER CUTS

| LAMB | PORK | VEAL | SIZE | COOKING TIME | DIRECTIONS |
|---|---|---|---|---|---|
| Leg<br>Loin Roast<br>Crown Roast<br>Rolled Front<br>Front (bone in)<br>Shoulder Roast | Loin Roast<br>Crown Roast<br>Fresh Ham<br>Fresh Pork Butt<br>Tenderloin<br>Rolled Shoulder | Leg Roast (Fillet).<br>Loin Roast (Stuffed)<br>Rump Roast | 4-7 lbs. | **Lamb—**<br>30-35 min. per lb.<br>45 min. per lb. (rolled cuts)<br>**Pork—**<br>40-45 min. per lb.<br>**Veal—**<br>35-40 min. per lb.<br>45 min. per lb. (rolled cuts) | **Roast:** Place meat, fat side up, on a rack in an open pan and insert meat thermometer in centre of largest muscle. Cook uncovered in a slow oven, 325°F. Do not sear the meat or add water. Cook till meat thermometer registers internal temperature of<br>**Lamb**—180°F.<br>**Pork**—185°F.<br>**Veal**—180°F. |
| Rib Chops<br>Loin Chops<br>Shoulder Chops | Loin Chops<br>Rib Chops<br>Tenderloin (Frenched)<br>Butt Chops<br>Spareribs (Braise) | Sirloin Steak<br>Loin Chops<br>Veal Cutlet | **Lamb**—½"-¾" thick<br>**Pork**—½"-¾" thick<br>**Veal**—½"-¾" thick | 10-12 mins. (total)<br>20-25 mins. (total)<br>15-20 mins. (total) | **Broil**—(See Beef Chart opposite.)<br>**Panbroil**—Slash fat edge of meat to prevent curling. Place meat in a lightly greased frypan over medium heat. Turn frequently to ensure even cooking. Pour off fat as it accumulates.<br>**Braise**—Brown meat quickly in hot fat. Lower heat and cook slowly, covered, until tender. A small amount of water or vegetable juice may be added to keep the meat moist. |

## LESS TENDER CUTS

| LAMB | PORK | VEAL | SIZE | COOKING TIME | DIRECTIONS |
|---|---|---|---|---|---|
| Neck<br>Flank<br>Breast<br>Shoulder<br>Shank | —<br>—<br>—<br>—<br>Neck<br>Shank<br>Flank<br>Breast | Front (Rolled) | 3-6 lbs.<br><br>2½-3½ hours (total) | 40-45 mins. per lb. | **Roast**—As for tender cuts.<br>**Braise**—Brown meat on both sides in a heavy baking pan or frypan with a small amount of fat. Add ½ cup water. Cover pan tightly and cook slowly in a 325°F. oven or on top of stove, until tender. More liquid should be added as required.<br>**Stew**—Cut meat in small pieces. Dip in seasoned flour and brown in hot fat. Cover with warm water and simmer gently until tender. Do not boil. Add vegetables and seasoning about 30 minutes before meat is done. The gravy may be thickened with flour if desired.<br>**Soup**—Cook meat with bones in gently simmering water. Celery leaves, onion slices and parsley may be added 30 minutes before meat is done. Season well before serving. |

## FILET PRINCE IGOR

Split, horizontally, leaving ¼-inch uncut
**4 slices of filet mignon
(3-inch thick)**
Open to form butterfly and sandwich each between wax paper. Pound flat with a rolling pin.
In a frypan, heat until foamy
**2 tablespoons butter or
margarine**
Add and cook until transparent
**½ onion, finely chopped**
Stir in
**⅔ cup finely chopped mushrooms
2 green onions, finely chopped
1 clove garlic, finely chopped
2 tablespoons chopped fresh
parsley
½ teaspoon salt
½ teaspoon grated lemon rind
1½ teaspoons lemon juice
Pinch of pepper
Pinch of nutmeg**
Cook until tender and liquid evaporates. Cool. Remove top layer of wax paper from meat and spread both halves of butterflied filet with
**pâté de foie gras**
Spoon mushroom mixture on one half. Flip other half over top and press to seal.
In a frypan, heat until foamy
**1 tablespoon butter**
Add the prepared filets, a few at a time, and cook for 2 minutes on each side.
Add to frypan
**2 tablespoons dry red wine**
Heat thoroughly and pour over filets as a sauce.
For a variation, leave filets in frypan and flame with ¼ cup warmed brandy.
Makes 4 servings.

## BEEF STROGANOFF

Cut into ¼-inch x 1-inch strips
**1½ pounds sirloin steak**
Dredge in
**1½ tablespoons PURITY Flour**
In a heavy frypan, heat until foamy
**¼ cup butter or margarine**
Add meat and cook until browned on one side.
Turn meat, stir in and cook until transparent
**1 medium onion, thinly sliced**
Remove meat and onions from pan and set aside.

Blend into drippings in frypan
**2 tablespoons PURITY Flour**
Stir in
**1 (10-ounce) can undiluted
consommé
2 tablespoons tomato paste
1 teaspoon salt
½ teaspoon dry mustard**
Cook, stirring constantly, until thickened.
Add meat and onions and
**1 (10-ounce) can sliced
mushrooms, undrained
3 tablespoons dry sherry (optional)**
Continue cooking until meat is tender. Then stir in
**1 cup thick dairy sour cream**
Heat thoroughly but do not boil.
Serve on cooked rice or noodles.
Makes 6 servings.
MEATBALLS STROGANOFF: Prepare Beef Stroganoff as in basic recipe but for sirloin steak substitute meatballs made from a mixture of 1 pound ground beef, ½ cup fine, dry bread crumbs, ¼ cup finely chopped onion, 1 egg, ½ teaspoon salt, and ¼ teaspoon pepper.

## SUKIYAKI

In a frypan heat until foamy
**½ cup shortening**
Brown quickly on both sides
**½ pound sirloin steak, cut in
⅛-inch thick slices**
Remove from pan and set aside.
To frypan add
**2 onions, coarsely chopped
2 bunches green onions, cut in
3-inch pieces
3 stalks celery, cut diagonally
1 (15-ounce) can water chestnuts,
drained and thinly sliced
½ pound mushrooms, sliced**
Cook, stirring occasionally, for 5 mins.
Stir in
**3 tablespoons sugar
½ cup soya sauce**
Cook slowly stirring frequently, for about 15 minutes or until almost tender.
Add cooked beef slices and
**1 cake soya bean curd,
sliced (optional)
1 cup undiluted consommé**
Simmer 5 minutes, then serve with rice.
Makes 3 to 4 servings.

## SWISS STEAK

Cut into 6 portions
**1½ pounds round steak**
Dredge in a mixture of
**½ cup PURITY Flour**
**1 teaspoon salt**
**¼ teaspoon pepper**
In a frypan (with lid), heat until foamy
**3 tablespoons bacon drippings**
Add floured meat and cook until browned on one side.
Turn meat and then add
**1 large onion, finely chopped**
Continue cooking until meat is browned on second side.
Stir in
**1 (10-ounce) can undiluted consommé**
**1 soup can water**
**½ cup chopped celery**
**1 green pepper, chopped**
Bring to boil, cover, reduce heat and simmer about 2 hours or until meat is tender.
Makes 6 servings.

## BEEF ROLL-UP

Cut into 6 rectangular slices
**3 pounds round steak (½-inch thick)**
Spread each with
**prepared mustard**
Sprinkle on top of each slice
**¼ cup finely chopped onion**
**1 slice cooked side bacon, crumbled**
**1 dill pickle, finely chopped**
Roll up and tie with string.
In a frypan, heat until foamy
**2 tablespoons bacon fat**
Add meat and cook until browned on all sides.
Stir in
**2 cups beef broth or diluted consommé**
Bring to boil, cover, reduce heat and simmer for one hour or until meat is tender.
Remove meat and stir in a mixture of
**2 tablespoons PURITY Flour**
**1 tablespoon cold water**

Cook, stirring constantly, until thickened.
Add meat and heat thoroughly.
Serve with Dumplings (See page 200).
Makes 6 servings.

## HUNGARIAN POT ROAST

Dredge
**1 beef pot roast (4 pounds round or chuck)**
in a mixture of
**¼ cup PURITY Flour**
**1 teaspoon salt**
**¼ teaspoon pepper**
In a large saucepan or Dutch oven, heat until foamy
**3 tablespoons butter or margarine**
Add roast and cook until browned on all sides.
Add
**2 cups tomato juice**
**2 onions, peeled and quartered**
**1 tablespoon paprika**
**1 teaspoon caraway seeds**
Bring to boil, cover tightly, reduce heat and simmer 3½ hours or until meat is tender. Add water during cooking if necessary.
Remove meat to hot serving platter.
Mix together and stir into hot liquid
**2 tablespoons PURITY Flour**
**1 tablespoon cold water**
Cook, stirring constantly, until thickened.
Serve with cooked noodles or Hungarian Dumplings (See this page).
Makes 8 servings.

---

*A dash of any of the following seasonings will enhance the flavour of pork: bay leaf, caraway, cloves, fennel, marjoram, mustard, onion, oregano, sage, or savory.*

---

## HUNGARIAN DUMPLINGS

Beat together until smooth
**2 eggs**
**2 tablespoons water**
**1 cup PURITY Flour**
**1 teaspoon salt**
In a 3-quart saucepan bring to boil
**6 cups water**
**1 teaspoon salt**
Using edge of a teaspoon and cutting into batter against side of bowl, spoon ¼ teaspoon at a time into boiling water. Repeat to use all of batter. Simmer uncovered for 10 minutes. Drain and keep warm.
To serve, spoon Goulash (See page 22) into serving dish, surround with dumplings and sprinkle with chopped parsley.
Makes 6 servings.

## HUNGARIAN GOULASH

Cut into 1-inch cubes
  **2 pounds boneless stewing beef**
Dredge in a mixture of
  **½ cup PURITY Flour**
  **¼ teaspoon pepper**
In a deep frypan heat until foamy
  **⅓ cup shortening**
Add meat and cook until lightly browned
on all sides.
Stir in remaining flour mixture with
  **1 green pepper, thinly sliced**
  **1 medium onion, thinly sliced**
Continue cooking until onion is transparent.
Blend in
  **2 teaspoons salt**
  **1½ teaspoons paprika**
  **1 teaspoon caraway seeds**
  **1 tablespoon Worcestershire**
    **sauce**
  **3 cups water**
Bring to boil, cover, reduce heat and
simmer for 2 hours or until meat is
tender.
Serve with Hungarian Dumplings (See
page 21) or broad noodles.
Makes 6 servings.

---

*"Whenever possible roast meat fat side
up to keep it moist and tender."*

---

## STUFFED FLANK STEAK

Preheat oven to 325°F.
Prepare half recipe Bread Stuffing (See
page 48) OR prepare according to package directions
  **1 cup herb-seasoned stuffing**
    **mix**
Stir in
  **½ cup finely chopped onion**
Use this mixture to stuff
  **1 flank steak (about 1 pound)**
Roll up and tie with string, or skewer.
Bake in small roasting pan or casserole,
uncovered, in preheated 325° oven for
30 minutes or until browned.
Pour over top a mixture of
  **1 (10-ounce) can condensed**
    **golden mushroom soup**
  **2 tablespoons catsup**
Bake covered for about 1½ hours or until
tender.
Makes 3 to 4 servings.

## BRAISED HAMBURGER

In a saucepan, lightly brown
  **1 pound ground beef**
Then stir in and cook until onion is
transparent
  **2 onions, finely chopped**
  **1 green pepper, coarsely chopped**
  **½ cup chopped celery**
Season with
  **¼ cup catsup**
  **1 teaspoon Worcestershire sauce**
  **½ teaspoon salt**
  **¼ teaspoon pepper**
Stir in
  **1½ cups water**
Bring to boil, reduce heat and simmer
uncovered for 30 minutes or until desired
consistency.
Serve over cooked rice.
Makes 6 servings.

ITALIAN STYLE HAMBURGER: Prepare
Braised Hamburger following basic recipe but substituting 1 (19-ounce) can tomatoes for water. Cook as directed.

GOLDEN BRAISED HAMBURGER:
Prepare Braised Hamburger following
basic recipe but substituting 1 (10-ounce)
can condensed golden mushroom soup
for 1 cup water. Cook as directed.

HAMBURGER À LA TOMATE: Prepare
Braised Hamburger following basic recipe but substituting 1 (10-ounce) can
condensed tomato soup for 1 cup water.
Cook as directed.

QUICK CURRIED HAMBURGER: Prepare Braised Hamburger following basic
recipe and add 2 teaspoons curry powder
to seasonings. Cook as directed.

SOUTH AMERICAN HAMBURGER:
Prepare Braised Hamburger following
basic recipe and add ½ teaspoon garlic
salt and ½ teaspoon chili powder to seasonings. Before serving, stir in ⅓ cup
thick dairy sour cream. Heat thoroughly.

---

*To thicken stews, pot roast gravies, etc.,
estimate the amount of liquid left at the
end of the cooking time. For each cup,
combine 2 tablespoons flour and ¼ cup
water. Stir into the simmering liquid and
bring to a full boil, stirring briskly.*

---

## BOUILLI CANADIEN
### (Boiled Dinner)

In a large saucepan, combine
**1½ pound beef brisket**
**½ pound salt pork, sliced**
**½ teaspoon pepper**
**1 bay leaf**
**3 whole cloves**
**3 cups water**
Bring to boil, cover, reduce heat and simmer for about 4 hours or until meat is almost tender.
Add
**6 carrots**
**6 onions**
**¼ turnip, cut in 6 portions**
**1 celery stalk, cut in 6 portions**
Continue cooking for 15 additional minutes.
Then add
**1 cabbage, cut in 6 wedges**
**½ pound green beans**
Cook 15 minutes longer and then remove cloves and bay leaf.
Traditionally this is served in soup bowls with meat, vegetables and broth. If desired, serve broth separately as soup and then a main course of meat and vegetables.
Makes 6 servings.

## SHEPHERD'S PIE

Preheat oven to 350°F.
Grease a 1½-quart casserole.
In a frypan, heat until foamy
**¼ cup butter or margarine**
Add and cook until transparent
**2 large onions, finely chopped**
Then stir in and cook until lightly browned
**1 pound ground beef**
Season with
**1 teaspoon salt**
**1 teaspoon thyme**
**¼ teaspoon pepper**
Blend in
**½ cup undiluted consommé**
Turn into prepared casserole.
Spoon over top
**2 cups mashed potatoes**
Bake in preheated 350° oven for 30 minutes or until potatoes begin to brown.
Serve with a tossed salad.
Makes 4 servings.

## MEAT PIE

Preheat oven to 425°F.
Sift together
**1½ cups PURITY Flour**
**3 teaspoons baking powder**
**½ teaspoon salt**
**¼ teaspoon pepper**
**¼ teaspoon paprika**
Cut in with a pastry blender or two knives
**¼ cup shortening**
Add
**¾ cup milk**
Stir with a fork to make a soft dough.
Roll out dough into an 8-inch circle.
In a saucepan, heat until foamy
**2 tablespoons butter or margarine**
Add and cook until transparent
**1 onion, finely chopped**
Then, stir in and cook until lightly browned
**½ pound ground beef**
Blend in
**1 (28-ounce) can tomatoes**
**2 tablespoons PURITY Flour**
**½ teaspoon salt**
**½ teaspoon oregano**
Turn meat mixture into a 1½-quart casserole.
Cover with prepared pastry.
Bake in preheated 425° oven for 25 minutes or until golden brown.
Makes 6 servings.

## TANGY MEAT LOAF

Preheat oven to 350°F.
Combine
**1½ pounds lean ground beef**
**½ cup grated cheddar cheese**
**¼ cup PURITY rolled oats**
**2 onions, finely chopped**
**2 tablespoons chopped parsley**
Mix together and blend in
**⅓ cup catsup**
**1 egg**
**1 teaspoon salt**
**1 teaspoon Worcestershire sauce**
**½ teaspoon pepper**
Press into a 9 × 5 × 3-inch loaf pan.
Top with
**3 slices side bacon**
Bake in preheated 350° oven for one hour.
Makes 6 servings.

## ITALIAN MEAT LOAF

Preheat oven to 350°F.
Grease an 8½ × 4½ × 3-inch loaf pan.
In a saucepan, heat until foamy
**1 tablespoon butter or margarine**
Add and cook until onion is transparent
**1 onion, finely chopped**
Combine onion with
**1 pound ground raw beef**
**1 cup cooked spaghetti**
**1 teaspoon salt**
**1 teaspoon poultry seasoning**
**1 teaspoon sage**
**Pinch of pepper**
**1 egg**
Turn into prepared pan.
Bake in preheated 350° oven for 1 hour or until desired doneness.
Serve with Tomato Mushroom Sauce (See page 213).
Makes 4 servings.

## BEEF À L'ITALIEN

In a saucepan, heat thoroughly
**2 tablespoons vegetable oil**
Add and cook until transparent
**1 clove garlic, finely**
**chopped**
Blend in
**1 (19-ounce) can tomatoes**
**1 (7½-ounce) can**
**tomato sauce**
**¾ teaspoon salt**
**¼ teaspoon oregano**
**¼ teaspoon pepper**
**2 cups cubed cooked beef**
Bring to boil, reduce heat and simmer uncovered 15 minutes or until desired consistency.
Serve as sauce with cooked spaghetti or noodles and garnish with chopped parsley.
Makes 6 servings.

## PLANKED STEAK

Preheat broiler.
Arrange on wooden board
**1 sirloin steak (2-inches thick)**
Dust top side lightly with
**PURITY Flour**
Broil 5 minutes, or until lightly browned.
Remove from oven and turn browned side down on board.
Preheat oven to 250°F.

With pastry tube or spoon, surround edge of steak with a thick layer of
**mashed potatoes (about 3 cups)**
Bake in preheated 250° oven for about 2 hours.
Cut into wedges
**1 tomato**
Insert attractively in potato border about twenty minutes before end of cooking time. Continue baking 20 minutes longer or until meat is tender.
Serve immediately cutting steak into vertical slices.
Makes 8 servings.

## CHEDDAR BURGERS

In a large bowl, combine
**⅔ cup undiluted evaporated milk**
**1 egg**
**1 teaspoon salt**
**½ teaspoon prepared mustard**
**Pinch of pepper**
Stir in
**1 cup grated cheddar cheese**
**½ cup fine dry bread or**
**cracker crumbs**
**¼ cup chopped onion**
Add and blend thoroughly
**1½ pounds ground beef**
Shape into 8 to 12 patties.
Panfry in a small amount of fat.
Patties may be broiled or barbecued over moderate heat for about 25 minutes if desired.
Makes 6 to 8 servings.

## PORK CHOPS WITH ONIONS

In a frypan, heat thoroughly
**2 tablespoons vegetable oil**
Add and cook until browned on both sides
**6 pork chops, ½-inch thick**
Sprinkle with
**1 envelope onion soup mix**
**¼ teaspoon pepper**
Place on chops
**6 peeled orange slices**
Pour over top
**1 cup orange juice**
Bring to boil, cover, reduce heat and simmer for 30 minutes or until chops are tender.
Makes 6 servings.

## BARBECUED SPARERIBS

Preheat broiler.
Cut into 4 portions
  **3 pound spareribs**
Arrange in a 13 × 9 × 2-inch pan.
Grill in preheated broiler for 30 minutes
turning occasionally.
In a saucepan, combine
  **½ cup finely chopped
    onion**
  **¼ cup finely chopped
    green pepper**
  **¼ cup lightly packed
    brown sugar**
  **¼ cup vinegar**
  **1 tablespoon Worcestershire
    sauce**
  **1 (14-ounce) can tomato
    sauce**
  **1 (10-ounce) can
    pineapple juice**
Bring to boil, reduce heat, and simmer
uncovered for 20 minutes or until desired
consistency.
Pour sauce over spareribs and bake in
350° oven for 20 to 30 minutes or until
tender. Baste with sauce occasionally.
Makes 4 servings.

## SAUERKRAUT AND PORK
## DINNER

Preheat oven to 375°F.
Dredge
  **2 pounds cubed pork shoulder**
In a mixture of
  **¼ cup PURITY Flour**
  **1 teaspoon salt**
  **¼ teaspoon pepper**
In a frypan, cook until crisp
  **2 slices side bacon**
Remove bacon and crumble.
Heat bacon fat thoroughly. Add floured
pork and cook until evenly browned.
Combine with bacon
  **1 (28-ounce) can
    sauerkraut, drained**
  **1 cup chopped onion**
  **1 cup peeled, chopped
    apple**
  **1 cup dry white wine**
  **1 cup water**
  **1 clove garlic, finely
    chopped**
  **1 tablespoon dill seeds**

Turn into a 2-quart casserole (with lid).
Top with browned pork cubes. Cover and
bake in preheated 375° oven for 1 hour
or until meat is tender. Remove meat and
keep warm. Strain sauerkraut and keep
warm on serving platter reserving broth.
In a saucepan, blend with the broth a
mixture of
  **2 tablespoons PURITY Flour**
  **2 tablespoons cold water**
Bring to boil and cook, stirring constantly, until thickened.
To serve, arrange meat over sauerkraut
and top with sauce.
Makes 6 servings.

---

*The brown "CANADA APPROVED"
stamp on wholesale cuts of meat is your
guarantee that the meat has met Federal
Government standards for health, clean-
liness and wholesomeness. Shop for meat
only where all meat sold has been properly inspected to ensure your family's
good health.*

---

## TOURTIÈRE—(MEAT PIE)

Preheat oven to 425°F.
In a saucepan, combine
  **1½ pounds ground pork**
  **1 cup finely chopped onion**
  **½ cup water**
  **1 bay leaf**
  **1½ teaspoons salt**
  **½ teaspoon thyme**
  **¼ teaspoon cloves**
  **¼ teaspoon pepper**
Bring to boil and cook, stirring constantly
until meat loses red colour.
Cover, reduce heat, and simmer for 45
minutes or until very tender. Remove bay
leaf.
Meanwhile, make PURITY Pastry (See
page 154).
Roll out half of pastry and line a 9-inch
pie plate. Fill with meat mixture and
cover with top crust made from remaining pastry. Seal and flute edges. Slash top.
Bake in preheated 425° oven for 15 minutes or until golden. Then reduce heat
to 350° and bake an additional 15 minutes or until thoroughly heated.
Serve with tomato catsup or pickled
beets.
Makes 6 servings.

# RAGOUT

In a large saucepan, combine
**6 pork hocks**
**2 onions, finely chopped**
**2 bay leaves**
**1 tablespoon allspice**
**4 teaspoons salt**
**1 teaspoon pepper**
Add enough cold water to completely cover meat. Bring to boil, cover, reduce heat and simmer for 2 hours or until meat is tender.
Meanwhile, make 1-inch meatballs from a mixture of
**1 pound ground pork**
**⅓ cup cracker crumbs**
**¼ cup finely chopped onion**
**1 egg**
**½ teaspoon salt**
**½ teaspoon thyme**
**¼ teaspoon pepper**
Bone and skin cooked pork hocks and remove bay leaves. Skim off fat.
Mix together and stir in
**½ cup PURITY Flour***
**½ cup cold water**
**Few drops gravy colouring**
Cook, stirring constantly, until thickened.
Add meatballs and
**5 potatoes, peeled and halved**
Continue cooking until potatoes and meat are tender, about 30 minutes longer.
* Traditionally in French Canada this is thickened with 1 cup browned flour made by cooking in heavy pan until golden brown.
Makes 8 to 10 servings.

## INDONESIAN BITTERBALLEN

Preheat oven to 375°F.
Drain, reserving ¼ cup juice from
**1 (28-ounce) can peach halves**
Blend juice with
**1½ teaspoons curry powder**
Brush peach halves with curried juice and bake in preheated 375° oven for 30 minutes, brushing occasionally.
In a 2-quart casserole (with lid) combine
**5 cups boiling water**
**2 cups long-grained rice**
**2 tablespoons butter or margarine**
**2 teaspoons salt**
Cover and bake in preheated 375° oven for 30 minutes or until rice is tender.

Meanwhile, mix together
**¾ pound ground pork**
**¾ pound ground veal**
**⅓ cup PURITY rolled oats**
**⅓ cup finely chopped onions**
**⅓ cup milk**
**1 teaspoon salt**
**¼ teaspoon pepper**
Shape into 36 small balls.
In a large frypan, heat thoroughly
**2 tablespoons vegetable oil**
Add meatballs and cook thoroughly.
Mix together, stir in and heat
**2 (10-ounce) cans beef gravy**
**¼ cup dry red wine**
**1 tablespoon curry powder**
To serve, top rice with meatballs and garnish with peach halves.
Makes 6 to 8 servings.

## STUFFED PORK TENDERLOIN

Preheat oven to 325°F.
Slit horizontally in half leaving ½-inch uncut
**1 pork tenderloin (about one-pound)**
Mix together
**¼ cup fine, dry bread crumbs**
**¼ cup finely chopped onion**
**3 tablespoons butter or margarine, melted**
**½ teaspoon salt**
**¼ teaspoon sage**
**¼ teaspoon pepper**
Fill tenderloin with stuffing. Tie with cord and wrap in aluminium foil. Bake in preheated 325° oven for 1 hour. Loosen and fold back foil. Bake an additional 30 minutes or until meat is browned and tender.
Makes 4 servings.

## PORK CHOPS PARMESAN

Dredge
**6 loin pork chops, (1-inch thick)**
In a mixture of
**¼ cup PURITY Flour**
**½ teaspoon salt**
**¼ teaspoon pepper**
Dip in
**2 eggs, slightly beaten**

Then, coat in a mixture of
**1½ cups fine, dry bread crumbs**
**½ cup grated Parmesan cheese**
In a frypan, heat until foamy
**⅓ cup butter or margarine**
Add breaded chops and cook until browned on both sides. Cover, reduce heat, and continue cooking for 20 minutes or until meat is tender.
Garnish with lemon slices.
Makes 6 servings.

## VEAL MARSALA

In a large saucepan, heat until foamy
**¼ cup butter or margarine**
Add and cook until browned on all sides
**1 veal roast (about 3 pounds)**
Stir in
**1 cup Marsala wine**
**1 cup beef broth, or diluted**
**consommé**
**½ teaspoon salt**
**Pinch of cayenne**
Bring to boil, cover, reduce heat, and simmer for 1½ to 2 hours or until meat is tender.
Mix together and blend in
**¼ cup PURITY Flour**
**¼ cup cold water**
Cook, stirring constantly, until thickened. Slice and serve meat with sauce, garnished with mushroom caps.
Makes 6 to 8 servings.

## VEAL RAGOÛT

Preheat oven to 375°F.
Cut into ½-inch slices
**1 boneless veal shoulder**
**(3 pounds)**
Pound each slice and cut into 1-inch strips.
Dredge in a mixture of
**¼ cup PURITY Flour**
**1 teaspoon salt**
**Pinch of pepper**
In a frypan, heat until foamy
**3 tablespoons butter or margarine**
Add floured meat and cook until evenly browned. Remove meat and arrange in a 2-quart casserole (with lid).
Stir into remaining fat in frypan
**1 cup chopped onion**
**2 cloves garlic, finely chopped**
Cook until transparent.

Then blend in
**1 (19-ounce) can tomatoes**
**1 cup dry red wine**
**¾ cup chopped fresh parsley**
**1 teaspoon salt**
**½ teaspoon granulated sugar**
**½ teaspoon oregano**
**½ teaspoon basil**
Pour over meat in casserole.
Cover and bake in preheated 375° oven for 1 hour or until meat is tender.
Makes 6 to 8 servings.

## BREADED VEAL CUTLETS

Dredge
**6 veal cutlets**
In a mixture of
**½ cup PURITY Flour**
**1 teaspoon salt**
**¼ teaspoon pepper**
Dip in
**2 eggs, slightly beaten**
Then coat in
**2 cups fine dry bread crumbs**
In a frypan, heat until foamy
**2 tablespoons shortening**
Add breaded cutlets and brown on both sides. Reduce heat and cook for 10 minutes or until meat is tender.
Sprinkle with
**2 tablespoons lemon juice**
Serve immediately.
Makes 6 servings.

## HUNGARIAN VEAL CASSEROLE

In a frypan, heat until foamy
**⅓ cup butter**
Add and brown
**2½ pounds cubed veal**
Blend in
**2 (10-ounce) cans condensed**
**cream of mushroom soup**
**½ cup water**
**¼ cup dry sherry**
**½ teaspoon salt**
**¼ teaspoon pepper**
**Dash of Tabasco sauce**
Bring to boil, cover, reduce heat and simmer for 1½ hours or until meat is tender.
Stir in
**⅔ cup thick dairy sour cream**
Heat thoroughly but do not boil.
Serve over rice or noodles.
Makes 6 to 8 servings.

## VEAL QUEBEC STYLE

In a large saucepan, heat until foamy
**3 tablespoons butter or margarine**
Add and brown on all but one side
**1 veal shoulder roast
(3 pounds)**
Turn meat to brown remaining side and add
**2 onions, thinly sliced**
Cook until onion is transparent and meat browned.
Stir in
**2 cups water
1 (6-ounce) can tomato paste
1 teaspoon salt
¼ teaspoon pepper
1 bay leaf
2 cloves garlic, finely
chopped**
Bring to boil, cover, reduce heat, and simmer for 2½ hours or until tender. Trim meat, remove bones and bay leaf.
Divide in portions and serve with boiled potatoes.
Makes 6 servings.

## EASY VEAL STEW

Cut into 1-inch cubes
**1 pound veal**
Dredge in a mixture of
**3 tablespoons PURITY Flour
1 teaspoon salt
Pinch of pepper**
In a saucepan, heat thoroughly
**2 tablespoons vegetable oil**
Add floured meat and cook until lightly browned on all but one side.
Stir in and cook until onion is transparent and meat evenly browned
**¼ cup coarsely chopped onion
1 clove garlic, finely chopped**
Add
**1½ cups water**
Bring to boil, cover, reduce heat and simmer for 1 hour or until meat is tender.
Then mix in
**1 (12-ounce) package frozen
green beans
1 (15½-ounce) can beef
ravioli in sauce
1 teaspoon dried parsley
flakes
¼ teaspoon oregano**
Heat thoroughly.
Makes 4 servings.

## ROAST LEG OF LAMB

Preheat oven to 325°F.
Slash fat covering of
**1 leg of lamb (about 4 pounds)**
Insert in cuts
**2 cloves garlic, slivered**
Cover with
**2 slices side bacon**
Secure with toothpicks.
Roast in preheated 325° oven for 2½ hours or to desired doneness.
In a frypan, heat until foamy
**2 tablespoons butter or margarine**
Add and cook until tender
**1¼ cups sliced mushrooms
3 green onions, finely
chopped
2 cloves garlic, finely chopped
1 tablespoon chopped
fresh parsley**
Transfer meat from roasting pan to heated serving platter. Remove toothpicks. Blend mushroom mixture into meat drippings and serve as a sauce.
Makes 8 servings.

## QUICKIE BAKED LAMB CHOPS

Preheat oven to 400°F.
In a frypan, heat until foamy
**2 tablespoons shortening**
Add and cook until browned on both sides
**8 lamb chops (1-inch thick)**
Remove chops from pan and set aside.
Stir into remaining fat in frypan
**½ cup chopped onion
½ cup fresh or canned whole
mushrooms
2 tablespoons chopped green
pepper**
Continue cooking until onion is transparent. Allow two chops per person and place each portion on a 15-inch square sheet of heavy aluminum foil. Top with mushroom mixture.
On each portion, arrange
**2 small onions, peeled
2 small potatoes, peeled
1 tomato, peeled and halved**
Season with salt and pepper and seal tightly.
Bake in shallow pan in preheated 400° oven for 1 hour or until meat is tender.
Makes 4 servings.

## STUFFED LAMB SHOULDER

Preheat oven to 325°F.
In a frypan, cook until evenly browned
**½ pound sausage meat**
Stir in
**½ cup fine, dry bread crumbs**
**2 green onions, finely**
**chopped**
**1 clove garlic, finely chopped**
**2 tablespoons tomato paste**
**½ teaspoon salt**
**¼ teaspoon pepper**
**Pinch of cloves**
Use sausage mixture to stuff
**1 boned lamb shoulder**
**(about 3 pounds)**
Tie with cord.
Roast in preheated 325° oven for 2 hours
or to desired doneness.
Makes 6 servings.

## PARSLEY LAMB CHOPS

In a frypan, heat until foamy
**2 tablespoons butter or margarine**
Add and cook until browned on both
sides
**12 lamb chops (½-inch thick)**
Stir in
**2 onions, thinly sliced**
**½ cup undiluted consommé**
**¼ cup dry sherry (optional)**
**1 tablespoon finely chopped**
**fresh parsley**
**¼ teaspoon salt**
**Pinch of pepper**
Bring to boil, cover, reduce heat and
simmer for 40 minutes or until meat is
tender.
Makes 6 servings.

## CURRIED LAMB

Cut into 1-inch cubes
**2 pounds boneless lamb**
In a saucepan, heat until foamy
**2 tablespoons butter or margarine**
Add meat and cook until browned on all
but one side.
Turn meat to brown remaining side and
add
**1½ cups finely chopped onion**
Cook until onion is transparent and meat
browned.
Stir in
**4 cups beef broth or**
**diluted consommé**
**2 tablespoons coconut**
**2 tablespoons curry powder**
**2 tablespoons tomato paste**
**1 teaspoon salt**
**2 bay leaves, crushed**
**1 clove garlic, finely chopped**
**Pinch of thyme**
Bring to boil, cover, reduce heat and
simmer for 2 hours or until meat is
tender.
Combine and stir in
**¼ cup PURITY Flour**
**¼ cup cold water**
Cook, stirring constantly, until thickened.
Blend in
**½ cup table cream (18%)**
Heat thoroughly.
Serve with cooked rice or noodles.
Makes 6 servings.

## LAMB STEW

Dredge
**2 pounds boneless lamb, cubed**
In a mixture of
**¼ cup PURITY Flour**
**1 teaspoon salt**
**¼ teaspoon thyme**
**¼ teaspoon pepper**
In a saucepan, heat thoroughly
**¼ cup vegetable oil**
Add floured meat and cook until evenly
browned.
Stir in
**½ green pepper, finely chopped**
**1 tablespoon chopped fresh**
**parsley**
**1 clove garlic, finely chopped**
**1 bay leaf**
**1½ cups undiluted consommé**
Bring to boil, cover, reduce heat and
simmer for 30 minutes or until meat is
partially tender.
Then add
**2 onions, quartered**
**3 cups cubed potatoes**
Continue cooking for an additional 30
minutes or until tender.
Stir in
**1 (10-ounce) can green**
**beans, drained**
Heat thoroughly. Remove bay leaf.
Serve with sliced tomatoes or a tossed
salad.
Makes 6 servings.

## CURRIED LAMB MORSELS

Combine with a fork
  **2 cups finely chopped
  cooked lamb**
  **2 tablespoons fine, dry
  bread crumbs**
Blend together and stir in
  **¼ cup condensed cream of
  mushroom soup**
  **¾ teaspoon prepared mustard**
  **¼ teaspoon curry powder**
  **¼ teaspoon salt**
  **Pinch of pepper**
Form into 1-inch balls.
Cover and chill until serving time.
Serve with salad or as appetizers.
Makes 2½ dozen rounds.

## CORNED-BEEF DINNER

In a large kettle, cover with cold water
  **1 corned beef (4 to 5 pounds)**
Add
  **1 clove garlic**
  **2 whole cloves**
  **10 whole black peppers**
  **2 bay leaves**
Bring to boil, cover, reduce heat and
simmer about 3 hours or until meat is
almost tender.
Add
  **8 medium carrots**
  **8 small potatoes**
  **8 medium onions**
Continue cooking for 15 minutes and
then add
  **1 small head cabbage, cut in
  8 wedges**
Cook until vegetables are tender, about
15 minutes longer.
Drain and arrange meat in centre of serving dish and surround with vegetables.
Makes 8 servings.

## BAKED COTTAGE ROLL

Preheat oven to 325°F.
Place in a roasting pan (with lid)
  **1 cottage roll (about 5 pounds)**
Pour over top
  **3 cups beer or gingerale**
Cover and bake in preheated 325° oven
for 3 hours, or until tender.
Serve hot or cold.
Makes 8 servings.

## HAM STEAKS

**BAKE:**

Preheat oven to 325°F.
Place steaks in shallow baking pan and
sprinkle with brown sugar or honey, and
mustard. Bake in preheated 325° oven,
allowing 25 to 30 minutes for ½-inch
thick steaks, 50 to 55 minutes for 1-inch
steaks. If desired, during last half of baking time, add ½ cup apple, pineapple or
orange juice.

**BROIL:**

Preheat broiler.
Place steaks on broiler pan and broil 3
inches below heat. Allow 12 to 15 minutes total cooking time for ½-inch thick
steaks, and 18 to 20 minutes for 1-inch
steaks. Turn once and brush with barbecue sauce or herb butter after turning.

**PAN BROIL:**

In a lightly greased pan quickly brown
ham steaks. Reduce heat and cook slowly, turning occasionally. Allow times as
for broiling.

## BAKED HAM STEAK

Preheat oven to 400°F.
Grease a baking dish.
Coat both sides of
  **2 ham steaks (1-inch thick,
  about 1 pound each)**
with
  **2 tablespoons brown sugar**
Stud fat on sides with
  **whole cloves**
Place in prepared dish and bake in preheated 400° oven for 20 minutes.
In a saucepan, melt
  **¼ cup butter or margarine**
Blend in
  **¼ cup PURITY Flour**
Gradually stir in
  **2½ cups apple juice**
Cook, stirring constantly, until thickened.
Stir in
  **⅓ cup raisins**
Continue cooking until raisins plump.
Pour sauce over ham steaks and continue
baking for 30 minutes, or until meat is
tender.
Makes 6 servings.

## GLAZED HAM

Preheat oven to 325°F.
Score in diamond pattern
**1 precooked ham**
Insert in diamonds
**whole cloves**
Bake in preheated 325° oven for 1 hour.
Remove ham from oven and increase
temperature to 450°F.
Combine and pour over ham
**3 cups lightly packed brown sugar**
**3 tablespoons PURITY Flour**
**2 tablespoons corn syrup**
**3 teaspoons dry mustard**
**¼ cup vinegar**
Bake in preheated 450° oven for 30 minutes, or until glaze threads from a spoon.
Remove from oven. Continue basting as
it cools until glaze hardens.

---

*Use browned flour to give a richer colour
and at the same time thicken stews or
gravies. Brown one cup or more of flour
in a heavy frypan over medium heat, stirring continually until evenly coloured.
For each cup of liquid to be thickened,
mix ¼ cup of browned flour in ½ cup
water. Stir into simmering liquid and
bring to a full boil, stirring briskly.*

---

## GLAZED BACK BACON

In a large saucepan, place
**1 piece of sweet pickled back
bacon (1½ to 2½ pounds)**
**1½ cups apple juice**
Bring to boil, cover, reduce heat and
simmer for 25 to 30 minutes per pound,
or until tender. Remove bacon and place
in a lightly greased baking pan.
Preheat oven to 400°F.
Combine and pour over bacon
**1 cup lightly packed brown sugar**
**1 tablespoon PURITY Flour**
**1 teaspoon dry mustard**
**1 tablespoon corn syrup**
**2 tablespoons vinegar**
Bake in preheated 400° oven for 30 minutes, or until glaze threads from a spoon.
Remove from oven. Continue basting as
it cools until glaze hardens.
Slice and serve either hot or cold.
Makes 4 to 6 servings.

## SAUSAGES

Sausages are prepared from pork or pork
and beef, with filler and seasonings
added. They are sold fresh, with casing
or skinless, smoked or cooked. Fresh
sausages are pink in colour. Purchase as
fresh as possible, refrigerate and use
promptly. Cooked sausages are uniformly
grey inside with no pink tinge.

LINK SAUSAGES have a casing that
should not be pricked during cooking.
Place in a lightly greased frying pan. Cook
slowly over moderate heat for 20 to 30
minutes, turning frequently. Drain well.

SKINLESS SAUSAGES are made of fresh
pork sausage meat, shaped like link sausages using artificial casing, then frozen
to permit easy removal of casing. Skinless
sausages are frequently sold frozen. Cook
as for link sausages.

FARMER STYLE SAUSAGE (large sausage, in casing) Place in a frying pan with
½ inch of water. Cook slowly for 35 to
40 minutes. After water evaporates turn
sausage occasionally to brown evenly.

SAUSAGE MEAT may be shaped into
patties. Brown in lightly greased frying
pan. Cook slowly over moderate heat for
about 20 minutes, turning frequently.

Any kind of sausage may be baked or
broiled. Partially cook sausages before
adding to casseroles.

## CREOLE SAUSAGES

Preheat oven to 350°F.
Grease a 1-quart casserole.
In a frypan, heat until foamy
**2 tablespoons shortening**
Add and cook until browned on all sides
**1 pound pork sausages**
In prepared casserole arrange alternate
layers of sausages and
**1 onion, sliced**
**1 cup canned tomatoes**
**1 green pepper, sliced**
Season with salt and pepper.
Bake in preheated 350° oven for 30 min-
utes, or until thoroughly heated.
Arrange on top
**6 slices side bacon**
Broil until bacon is crisp.
Makes 4 to 6 servings.

## SAUSAGE AND CABBAGE BAKE

Preheat oven to 375°F.
Lightly grease a 1½-quart casserole (with lid).
In a frypan, heat until foamy
**2 tablespoons shortening**
Add and cook until evenly browned
**1 pound pork sausages**
Remove sausages from pan and set aside.
Add to remaining fat in frypan and lightly brown
**1 (19-ounce) can potatoes**
Arrange potatoes in prepared casserole.
Sprinkle with
**2 tablespoons chopped parsley**
**½ teaspoon thyme**
Cover with
**½ small cabbage, shredded**
Place sausages on cabbage and pour over top
**1 (10-ounce) can undiluted consommé**
Cover and bake in preheated 375° oven for 30 minutes or until cabbage is tender.
Makes 4 servings.

## CHILI FRANKS

In a frypan (with lid), heat until foamy
**2 tablespoons butter or margarine**
Add and cook until onion is transparent
**½ cup chopped onion**
**½ cup chopped green pepper**
Stir in
**1 pound wieners, cut in ½-inch pieces**
**1 (14-ounce) can tomato sauce**
**1½ teaspoons chili powder**
**¼ teaspoon salt**
**¼ teaspoon oregano**
**Pinch of cayenne**
Bring to boil, cover, reduce heat and simmer for 30 minutes or until thoroughly heated. Serve over cooked noodles or rice.
Sprinkle with
**½ cup grated cheddar cheese**
Makes 6 servings.

---

*A generous sprinkle of paprika will add a note of colour to broiled or roasted meats.*

---

## QUICK FRANK SUPPER

In a large frypan (with lid), heat until foamy
**1 tablespoon butter or margarine**
Arrange in pan
**3 tomatoes, peeled and sliced**
**1 large onion, sliced**
**1 green pepper, sliced**
Sprinkle with
**½ teaspoon salt**
**¼ teaspoon pepper**
Slice in half lengthwise and crosswise
**6 wieners**
Arrange on top of vegetables.
Cover and cook over low heat for 15 to 20 minutes or until heated thoroughly.
Remove from heat and sprinkle over top
**1 cup grated cheddar cheese**
Cover until cheese melts.
Makes 4 servings.

---

*Steaks and chops may be broiled from the frozen state very successfully. Simply position broiler pan one inch further away from the heat than you normally do and allow longer cooking time (approximately half as much more, e.g. 6 minutes a side becomes 9 minutes a side).*

---

## CURRIED HAM À LA MODE

In a frypan, heat until foamy
**1 tablespoon butter or margarine**
Add and cook until onion is transparent
**1 tablespoon chopped onion**
**1 tablespoon chopped green pepper**
Stir in
**2 cups cubed cooked ham**
**1 (10-ounce) can condensed cream of celery soup**
**¾ cup milk**
**⅓ cup mayonnaise**
**⅓ cup canned, sliced mushrooms**
**1 teaspoon curry powder**
Heat thoroughly but do not boil.
Serve over cooked rice or noodles. Garnish with parsley.
Makes 6 servings.

## LIVER CASSEROLE
Preheat oven to 350°F.
Grease a 1½-quart casserole (with lid).
Cut into four portions
**1 pound calves' or baby
beef liver**
Dredge in a mixture of
**⅓ cup PURITY Flour
½ teaspoon salt
Pinch of pepper**
In a large frypan, heat until foamy
**¼ cup butter or margarine**
Add liver and cook until browned on one side.
Turn liver and add
**4 medium onions, thinly sliced
1 (10-ounce) can sliced
mushrooms, drained
¼ cup chopped celery**
Cook until onion is transparent and liver browned. Arrange in prepared casserole.
To frypan, stir in remaining flour mixture together with
**1½ cups tomato juice**
Cook, stirring constantly, until thickened. Strain and pour over liver and vegetables in casserole.
Cover and bake in preheated 350° oven for 25 to 30 minutes or until thoroughly heated.
Makes 4 servings.

---

*Generally, beef is graded as to quality with red brand beef being the top grade and blue brand beef second. The corresponding cuts, of both these grades will be almost equally tender.*

---

## VARIETY MEATS
**Liver:** Remove outer skin and cut away tubes if necessary. Soak beef and pork liver in milk for 2 hours in refrigerator for a milder flavour. Calf and baby beef liver are considered the choicest. Allow ¼ pound per serving.

*To panbroil*—flour liver slices and cook over moderate heat in a small amount of fat for 2 to 3 minutes on each side. Cook until pink colour in centre just disappears. Do not overcook or liver will be very tough. Season.

*To broil*—calf and baby beef liver may be cooked in this way. Brush generously with fat and place 3-inches below heat. Broil 4 to 5 minutes on each side. Season.

**Kidney:** These vary in flavour and tenderness. Before cooking kidney, remove the membrane, fat and tubes. Cut kidney in half lengthwise for panbroiling or broiling. Allow ⅓ pound per serving.

*To panbroil*—brown kidney in a small amount of fat and cook 3 to 5 minutes, turning frequently. For kidney halves, allow 7 to 9 minutes cooking time. Do not overcook. Season.

*To broil*—brush generously with fat and place 3-inches below heat.
Broil 4 to 7 minutes on each side. Season.

*To braise*—beef and pork kidneys are generally cooked in this way. Soak in salted water for 1 hour in refrigerator. Flour and brown in a small amount of fat. Add liquid to about ¼-inch depth, cover and cook slowly 35 to 40 minutes.

**Heart:** All types of heart require long slow cooking at a low temperature. A beef heart that has passed government inspection will be cut in two. Heart is generally stuffed and baked. Allow approximately ½ pound per person; 2 cups stuffing for 6 servings.

Wash thoroughly, wipe dry and cut away coarse tubes and excess fat. Trim out heart cavity and fill with well-seasoned bread stuffing. Fasten with skewers and string, if necessary. Place bacon strips on top. Bake in preheated 325° oven, basting frequently, for following times:
Beef = 2½ to 3 hours;
Pork = 2 to 2½ hours;
Lamb = 1 to 1¼ hours;
Veal = 1½ to 2 hours.

**Tongue:** Tongue requires long, slow cooking in moist heat. Beef, veal and pork tongues are sold fresh. Beef is also sold pickled (which adds greatly to the flavour). Allow ½ pound per serving. Wash tongue thoroughly and cover with water. Simmer in a covered saucepan. Allow time as follows:

Fresh beef . . 60 minutes per pound
Pickled beef . 50 minutes per pound
Lamb, Pork, Veal . . . . . . . . 2 hours

Tongue should be cooked until tender.

Remove skin, excess fat, glands and bones while still hot.

# FISH

## TO KEEP FISH:

**Fresh** fish should be washed in cold water and dried. Wrap securely in waxed paper, store in refrigerator. Use within a day or two.

**Frozen** fish should be kept in freezer in original package until ready to use. Depending upon recipe, frozen fish may be cooked frozen or thawed.

**Smoked** fish should be handled the same as fresh. Smoking retards spoilage in addition to adding a distinctive flavour, but does not preserve fish.

**Salted** dried fish will keep without refrigeration.

## TO COOK FISH:

Cook fish quickly at a high temperature to retain the flavour and juiciness. Fish should be cooked just until the flesh is opaque and flakes readily. An approximate guide is to allow 10 minutes cooking time per inch of thickness. (Double this time for frozen fish.) If fish is covered with a sauce, allow 15 to 20 minutes per inch thickness. Always test for flakiness with a fork to be sure the fish is cooked.

## TO CLEAN FRESH FISH:

**To Scale:** Holding the tail firmly and using the dull edge of a knife held at a 45° angle, loosen the scales from tail to head. This is best done under running water so the scales do not scatter.

**To Clean:** Using a thin sharp knife, or kitchen shears, slit skin from vent to gills. Remove viscera. Wash in running water and brush to clean thoroughly. Remove the fins by cutting the flesh along both sides of the fins, and then pull each fin sharply towards head to remove root bones. Remove the head and tail. Dry thoroughly.

## TO USE CANNED FISH:

**Tuna:** Pour off oil and place in a sieve. Pour boiling water over the tuna.

**Salmon:** Bones may be mashed with a fork and retained with the juices for extra flavour and nutrition.

**Shrimps:** Drain and rinse with cold water. Remove black vein, if necessary.

**Lobster, Crab:** Drain.

**Clams, Oysters:** Most recipes call for use of liquor. Strain to remove sand and small pieces of shell.

## SHELLFISH

**Lobsters** may be purchased alive, cooked and frozen, or canned. The shell of live lobsters varies from dark green to blue, and turns bright red when cooked.

**Crabs** are available cooked—fresh, frozen, or canned. Live crabs are sold only in areas close to fishing centres.

**Oysters** from the Atlantic coast are sold in the shell or shucked. The shells should be tightly closed. Pacific (or Japanese) oysters from the west coast of Canada are larger and always sold shucked. They may be fresh, frozen, canned or smoked.

**Clams** are sold alive in the shell, or shucked in fresh, frozen or canned forms. Like the oyster, the shell of a live clam should be tightly closed.

**Scallops** are always sold shucked, either fresh or frozen. Thaw frozen scallops before using.

**Shrimps** are available fresh, frozen and canned. Most frozen and some canned shrimps have the dark vein removed. If not, it should be lifted out with the point of a knife.

## FILETS DE SOLE BONNE FEMME

Preheat oven to 350°F.
Grease a 1½-quart baking dish and sprinkle in bottom
**1 tablespoon finely chopped chives or green onion**
Cut in serving portions
**2 pounds sole fillets**
Season with
**½ teaspoon salt**
**¼ teaspoon pepper**
Arrange fillets in prepared dish, overlapping if necessary.
Sprinkle with
**1 tablespoon finely chopped chives or green onion**
Dot with
**1 tablespoon butter or margarine**
Pour over top
**¾ cup dry white wine**
Bake in preheated 350° oven for 15 minutes or until fish loses its transparency and flakes easily. Drain reserving 1 cup of liquid.
Meanwhile, in a frypan heat until foamy
**2 tablespoons butter or margarine**
Add and cook until lightly browned
**¾ cup sliced mushrooms**
Season with
**1 teaspoon lemon juice**
**½ teaspoon salt**
**¼ teaspoon pepper**
Keep warm.
In a small saucepan, heat until foamy
**3 tablespoons butter or margarine**
Blend in a mixture of
**3 tablespoons PURITY Flour**
**Pinch of salt**
**Dash of cayenne**
Stir in reserved liquid.
Cook, stirring constantly, until thickened.
Add and heat thoroughly
**¼ cup table cream (18%)**
To serve, cover fish with sauce and scatter mushrooms on top.
Then, garnish top with Hollandaise Sauce (See page 212).
Broil until sauce is golden brown.
Makes 6 servings.

*Frozen fillets may be prepared quickly for frying or baking by cutting a 1-pound block into sections, rather than waiting for the fillets to thaw enough to separate.*

## QUICK SOLE FILLETS

Preheat oven to 400°F.
Grease a 1½-quart baking dish.
Arrange in prepared dish, overlapping if necessary
**4 sole fillets**
In a saucepan, heat thoroughly
**1 (10-ounce) can condensed frozen shrimp soup, thawed**
Pour over fish.
Dot with
**1 tablespoon butter or margarine**
Bake in preheated 400° oven for 15 minutes or until fish loses its transparency and flakes easily.
Makes 4 servings.

## TANGY SOLE FILLETS

Lightly coat
**4 sole fillets**
with
**¼ cup prepared mustard**
Dredge in
**⅓ cup PURITY Flour**
In a frypan, heat until foamy
**2 tablespoons butter or margarine**
Add floured fish and cook on both sides for about 5 minutes or until fish loses its transparency and flakes easily. Keep warm.
Chop the whites of
**2 hard cooked eggs**
Set aside.
Mash yolks and combine with
**¼ cup lemon juice**
**1 tablespoon finely chopped capers (optional)**
**2 teaspoons finely chopped fresh parsley**
**1 teaspoon prepared mustard**
**1 clove garlic, finely chopped**
**½ teaspoon basil**
**¼ teaspoon salt**
**¼ teaspoon pepper**
Stir in
**1 tablespoon vegetable oil**
To serve, spread sauce over warmed sole fillets.
Sprinkle top with reserved chopped egg whites.
Makes 4 servings.

## FILETS DE SOLE DUGLÉRÉ

Preheat oven to 350°F.
Grease a 1½-quart baking dish.
Cut in serving portions
**6 sole fillets**
Season with
**½ teaspoon salt**
**¼ teaspoon pepper**
Brush with
**¼ cup butter, melted**
Dredge in
**fine, dry bread crumbs**
Combine in prepared dish
**3 green onions, finely chopped**
**¼ cup sliced mushrooms**
Arrange fish over top, overlapping if necessary.
Pour over top
**1 (19-ounce) can tomatoes**
Sprinkle with
**¼ cup toasted, slivered almonds**
Mix together and pour over top
**¼ cup heavy cream**
**2 tablespoons lemon juice**
Bake in preheated 350° oven for 30 minutes or until fish loses its transparency and flakes easily.
Makes 6 servings.

## ASPARAGUS SOLE

Preheat oven to 350°F.
Grease a 1½-quart baking dish.
Cut in serving portions
**4 sole filets**
Drain, reserving liquid
**1 (12-ounce) can asparagus tips**
Wrap each portion of fish around one asparagus tip. Secure with toothpicks. Arrange in prepared baking dish.
Bake in preheated 350° oven for 15 minutes or until fish loses its transparency and flakes easily. Remove toothpicks.
Meanwhile, in a saucepan, heat until foamy
**2 tablespoons butter or margarine**
Blend in a mixture of
**1 tablespoon PURITY Flour**
**½ teaspoon salt**
**Pinch of pepper**
**Pinch of basil**
Gradually stir in
**½ cup reserved asparagus liquid**
**1 cup milk**

Cook, stirring constantly, until thickened. Slice and stir in remaining asparagus tips. Heat.
Pour sauce over fish rolls. Garnish with sliced tomatoes and parsley.
Makes 4 servings.

## SALMON SOUFFLÉ

Preheat oven to 375°F.
Grease a 7-inch soufflé dish.
In a saucepan, heat until foamy
**3 tablespoons butter or margarine**
Add and cook until transparent
**¼ cup finely chopped onion**
Mix in
**3 tablespoons PURITY Flour**
Gradually, stir in
**1 cup milk**
Cook, stirring constantly, until thickened. Cool.
Beat in, one at a time
**6 egg yolks**
Stir in
**2 (7¾-ounce) cans salmon, flaked**
**1½ tablespoons lemon juice**
**1 tablespoon tomato paste**
**½ teaspoon salt**
**Pinch of cayenne**
Beat to form stiff but moist peaks
**6 egg whites**
Fold salmon mixture into egg whites.
Turn into prepared dish.
Bake in preheated 375° oven for 50 to 55 minutes or until puffed and set.
Serve with Hollandaise Sauce (See page 212). Makes 6 servings.

SHRIMP SOUFFLÉ: Prepare Salmon Soufflé following basic recipe but substituting 2 (4¼-ounce) cans baby shrimps (drained) for the salmon and 2 tablespoons catsup for tomato paste. Reduce salt to ¼ teaspoon and add ¼ teaspoon chervil. Bake as directed.

TUNA SOUFFLÉ: Prepare Salmon Soufflé following basic recipe but substituting 2 (7-ounce) cans flaked tuna (drained) for the salmon and adding ½ teaspoon oregano. Bake as directed.

LOBSTER SOUFFLÉ: Prepare Salmon Soufflé following basic recipe but substituting 2 (5-ounce) cans lobster (drained) for the salmon and adding ½ teaspoon tarragon. Bake as directed.

## SALMON QUICHE

Preheat oven to 400°F.
Prepare PURITY Pastry (See page 154).
Roll out half and line a 9-inch pie plate.
Trim and flute edges. Do not prick.
Sprinkle in pie shell
**1 cup grated cheddar cheese**
**1 (7¾-ounce) can salmon,**
**flaked**
**4 green onions, thinly sliced**
Beat together
**2 cups milk**
**3 eggs**
**½ teaspoon salt**
**½ teaspoon dry mustard**
Pour into pie shell.
Sprinkle with paprika.
Bake in preheated 400° oven for 30 to 35 minutes or until filling is set around the edge and soft in the centre. Remove from oven and let stand for 15 minutes before serving.
Makes 6 servings.

## BAKED SALMON STEAKS

Preheat oven to 350°F.
Season
**6 salmon steaks**
with
**½ teaspoon salt**
**¼ teaspoon pepper**
In a frypan, heat until foamy
**2 tablespoons butter or margarine**
Add and cook until onion is transparent
**½ cup chopped celery**
**¼ cup chopped onion**
Stir in
**¾ cup fine, dry bread**
**crumbs**
**¼ cup catsup**
**½ teaspoon Worcestershire sauce**
Cover each salmon steak with crumb mixture.
Bake in preheated 350° oven for 15 minutes or until fish loses its transparency and flakes easily.
Makes 6 servings.

CHEESY SALMON STEAKS: Prepare Baked Salmon Steaks following basic recipe but substituting ¾ cup crushed cheese crackers for the bread crumbs. Bake as directed.

## SALMON CROQUETTES

In a saucepan, heat until foamy
**2 tablespoons butter or margarine**
Add and cook until tender
**2 tablespoons finely chopped**
**green onion**
Combine with
**1 (7¾-ounce) can salmon, flaked**
**½ teaspoon salt**
**½ teaspoon oregano**
**Pinch of pepper**
Remove and set aside.
To pan add an additional
**2 tablespoons butter or margarine**
When melted, blend in
**2 tablespoons PURITY Flour**
Gradually, stir in a mixture of
**1 cup milk**
**1 egg yolk**
Cook, stirring constantly, until thickened. Combine with fish mixture and allow to cool. Shape into small rolls, using about 1 tablespoon of mixture.
Roll in
**½ cup PURITY Flour**
then dip in
**1 egg white, slightly beaten**
Coat with
**½ cup fine, dry bread crumbs**
Allow to stand for about 15 minutes.
Preheat deep fat to 375°F.
Fry croquettes for 2 to 3 minutes or until golden brown. Drain on absorbent paper. Garnish with lemon wedges and serve with a salad.
Makes 20 croquettes.

CRAB CROQUETTES: Prepare Salmon Croquettes following basic recipe but substituting 1 (5½-ounce) can crab and 1 cup cooked rice, for salmon and ½ teaspoon dry chives for oregano. Fry as directed.

CLAM CROQUETTES: Prepare Salmon Croquettes following basic recipe but substituting 1 (5½-ounce) can baby clams (drained) for salmon and ½ teaspoon garlic powder for oregano. Fry as directed.

FISH SOUFFLÉ: Prepare Salmon Croquettes following basic recipe but substituting 1¼ cups flaked cooked or canned fish for salmon and ½ teaspoon of basil, tarragon or chives for oregano. Fry as directed.

## DEVILLED FILLETS

Preheat oven to 400°F.
Grease an 8-inch square baking dish.
Arrange in prepared dish
  **6 fish fillets**
In a small bowl, combine
  **¼ cup thick dairy**
    **sour cream**
  **¼ cup mayonnaise**
  **1 tablespoon finely chopped onion**
  **1 tablespoon prepared mustard**
  **½ teaspoon salt**
Spread mixture over fish.
Bake in preheated 400° oven for 15 minutes or until fish loses its transparency and flakes easily.
Meanwhile, arrange on an ungreased baking sheet
  **1 (6-ounce) package frozen**
    **onion rings, thawed**
Heat together with fish during last 10 minutes of baking.
To serve, arrange onion rings around fish. Garnish with parsley and lemon wedges.
Makes 6 servings.

## TARRAGON FISH

Combine
  **¼ cup PURITY Cornmeal**
  **¼ cup PURITY Flour**
  **1 teaspoon tarragon**
  **½ teaspoon salt**
    **Pinch of pepper**
Sprinkle
  **6 fish fillets**
with
  **½ cup lemon juice**
Dredge fish in flour mixture.
In a frypan, heat until foamy
  **2 tablespoons butter or margarine**
Add floured fish and cook until browned on both sides. Reduce heat and continue cooking a few minutes longer or until fish loses its transparency and flakes easily.
Makes 6 servings.

BAKED TARRAGON FISH: Prepare Tarragon Fish as in basic recipe but brush fish fillets with ¼ cup melted butter or margarine before dredging in flour mixture. Arrange in baking dish and sprinkle with lemon juice. Bake in preheated 400° oven for 15 minutes or until fish loses its transparency and flakes easily.

## CRAB PIQUANT

In a saucepan, heat until foamy
  **¼ cup butter or margarine**
Add and cook until onion is transparent
  **½ cup chopped onion**
  **⅓ cup chopped green pepper**
  **1 (10-ounce) can sliced**
    **mushrooms, drained**
Blend in a mixture of
  **¼ cup PURITY Flour**
  **1 teaspoon salt**
Gradually, stir in
  **2 cups milk**
Cook, stirring constantly, until thickened.
Mix in
  **2 (5½-ounce) cans**
    **crabmeat**
  **2 tablespoons brandy**
Serve in pastry shells or on toast points.
Makes 8 servings.

## LOBSTER NEWBURG

Break into bite-size pieces
  **2 (5-ounce) cans lobster**
Melt in a frying pan
  **2 tablespoons butter or margarine**
Add
  **½ pound mushrooms, sliced**
Cook until tender.
Melt in top of double boiler, over direct heat
  **2 tablespoons butter or margarine**
Blend in
  **3 tablespoons PURITY Flour**
  **½ teaspoon salt**
  **¼ teaspoon paprika**
  **¼ teaspoon dry mustard**
Gradually add, stirring constantly
  **1½ cups milk**
Stir and cook until smoothly thickened.
Add
  **⅓ cup grated cheddar cheese**
Add a little of the hot sauce to
  **2 egg yolks, slightly beaten**
Return to double boiler and cook, over boiling water, stirring constantly, for 2 minutes.
Add the lobster meat and cooked mushrooms.
Heat thoroughly, stirring frequently.
If desired, add
  **3 tablespoons dry sherry**
Serve immediately over hot cooked rice.
Makes 5 to 6 servings.

## BOILED LOBSTER

Thrust the live lobsters, head first, into boiling salted water. Cover, simmer 15 to 20 minutes depending on size.

**To Serve Hot:** Remove from boiling water, place lobster on its back and split lengthwise with sharp knife or scissors. Remove dark vein and small sac behind the head. Crack large claws.
Serve piping hot with melted butter and lemon wedges.

**To Serve Cold:** Cool cooked lobster quickly in cold running water. Chill in refrigerator thoroughly, then prepare for serving as above. Serve with vinegar or Tartar Sauce.

For salads and main dishes, remove meat from claws, legs and tail and break into bite-size pieces. Be sure to remove the flat thin pieces of cartilage in the claw meat of both cooked and canned lobster.

## BRAISED FISH

In a saucepan, heat until foamy
  **3 tablespoons butter or margarine**
Add and cook until onion is transparent
  **2 onions, finely chopped**
  **½ cup finely chopped raw carrots**
Blend in
  **3 tablespoons PURITY Flour**
Gradually, stir in
  **2 cups beef broth or diluted consommé**
  **½ cup dry white wine**
Cook, stirring constantly, until thickened.
Add to sauce
  **2 pounds fish fillets**
  **4 tomatoes, quartered**
Bring to boil, cover, reduce heat and simmer for 30 minutes or until fish loses its transparency and flakes easily.
Serve with mashed potatoes.
Makes 8 servings.

## SWEET AND SOUR TUNA

In a saucepan, heat until foamy
  **2 tablespoons butter or margarine**
Add and cook until tender
  **1 cup diagonally sliced celery (½-inch thick)**
  **1 green pepper, cut in strips**

Stir in
  **2 (7-ounce) cans tuna, cubed**
  **1 (10-ounce) can crushed pineapple**
  **1 cup chicken broth**
  **2 tablespoons white vinegar**
  **2 tablespoons soya sauce**
  **¼ teaspoon pepper**
Heat thoroughly.
Blend in a mixture of
  **2 tablespoons PURITY Flour**
  **¼ cup cold water**
Cook, stirring constantly, until thickened.
Serve with rice or fried noodles.
Makes 6 servings.

*When storing foods, keep in mind that, in general, the air in a refrigerator is coldest next to the freezer and warmer at points further from it. (Frost-free refrigerators tend to have less variation in temperature.) Store fresh meat, poultry, and fish nearest the freezing compartment, and fresh vegetables furthest away.*

## HOT TUNA PIE

Preheat oven to 425°F.
Prepare PURITY Pastry (See page 154). Roll out half of dough and line a 1½-quart baking dish. Trim. Roll out top crust.
In a frypan, heat until foamy
  **¼ cup butter or margarine**
Add and cook until onion is transparent
  **1 large onion, coarsely chopped**
  **1¼ cups sliced mushrooms**
In pastry-lined dish, crumble
  **2 (7-ounce) cans tuna, drained**
Spread onion mixture over top together with
  **1 cup cooked spaghetti**
Pour over top
  **1 (10-ounce) can condensed cream of celery soup**
Cover with top crust. Seal and flute edges. Slit or prick top.
Bake in preheated 425° oven for 15 minutes or until golden.
Reduce heat to 350° and continue baking an additional 20 minutes or until heated thoroughly.
Makes 6 servings.

## CREOLE SHRIMP

In a saucepan, heat until foamy
**2 tablespoons butter or margarine**
Add and cook until onion is transparent
**½ cup finely chopped onion**
**½ cup sliced mushrooms**
**¼ cup finely chopped**
**green pepper**
Blend in a mixture of
**2 tablespoons PURITY Flour**
**¼ teaspoon pepper**
**½ teaspoon oregano**
**½ teaspoon salt**
Gradually, stir in
**1½ cups canned tomatoes**
Cook, stirring constantly, until thickened.
Mix in
**1 (4¼-ounce) can shrimps**
Heat thoroughly.
Serve with cooked rice, garnished with parsley.
Makes 4 servings.

## SHRIMP BASIL

In a saucepan, heat until foamy
**¼ cup butter or margarine**
Add and cook until onion is transparent
**2 cups shrimps**
**2 onions, thinly sliced**
**¼ cup coarsely chopped celery**
**¼ cup sliced mushrooms**
**1 tablespoon finely chopped**
**green pepper**
Blend in a mixture of
**2 tablespoons PURITY Flour**
**1 teaspoon basil**
**¼ teaspoon salt**
**¼ teaspoon pepper**
Gradually, stir in
**1 cup beef broth or diluted**
**consommé**
**2 tablespoons dry white wine**
**(optional)**
**1 teaspoon tomato paste**
Cook, stirring constantly, until thickened.
Stir in
**1 cup table cream (18%)**
**3 tablespoons thick dairy**
**sour cream**
Heat thoroughly, but do not boil.
Serve with noodles.
Makes 4 servings.

## COQUILLES ST. JACQUES

Before serving, preheat broiler or oven
(See asterisked paragraphs below).
Grease 6 scallop shells or prepare Toast Cups (See page 184).
In a frypan, heat until foamy
**3 tablespoons butter or margarine**
Add and cook until lightly browned on all but one side
**1 pound scallops**
Turn fish to brown remaining side and add
**½ cup sliced mushrooms**
**¼ cup finely chopped**
**green onion**
**1 clove garlic, finely chopped**
Cook until fish is tender and browned.
Meanwhile in a saucepan, melt
**3 tablespoons butter or margarine**
Blend in a mixture of
**3 tablespoons PURITY Flour**
**½ teaspoon salt**
**Pinch of pepper**
Gradually, stir in
**2 cups milk**
**¼ cup grated Swiss cheese**
**2 tablespoons dry white wine**
**(optional)**
Cook stirring constantly, until thickened.
Blend in scallop mixture and fill shells.
(If desired pipe with cooked mashed potatoes.) Sprinkle with
**¼ cup fine, dry bread crumbs**
Dot with
**1 tablespoon butter or margarine**
*Broil for 1 minute or until top is golden brown. Garnish with parsley and serve as an appetizer or use four large shells and serve as a luncheon dish.
Makes 6 servings.
*Filled shells may be refrigerated until just before serving and then bake in preheated 350° oven until piping hot and golden brown, about 12 minutes.

---

*Do not overcook fish as it will become tasteless and dry. Serve fish as soon as it is cooked, because the flavour and texture deteriorate rapidly on standing.*

*Suggested seasonings for fish are: bay leaf, curry powder, dill, fennell, marjoram, onion, paprika, cayenne pepper, and thyme.*

---

**USE PURITY FLOUR, THE JOLLY MILLER FLOUR, FOR HAPPY BAKING**

## WINNIPEG GOLDEYE

Allow one goldeye per serving. They may be cooked with head and tail on or off.

**TO BAKE:**

Preheat oven to 400°F.
Grease a baking dish.
Arrange goldeyes on prepared baking dish and brush generously with butter or margarine. Bake fish, basting occasionally with butter, in preheated 400° oven for 15 minutes or until fish flakes easily.

**TO POACH:**

Place goldeye on greased foil. Secure edges of foil with double folds to make package watertight. Place package in boiling water. Bring to boil again, cover, and cook for 10 minutes (20 minutes if frozen).
Unwrapped goldeye may be cooked in a steamer for 15 to 20 minutes, or simmered in water for 10 minutes, or until fish flakes easily.
Serve with lemon wedges.

*Good fresh fish has flesh that is firm and elastic, and does not readily pull away from the bones.*

## FISH STICKS ROMANO

Bake according to package directions
   **2 (12-ounce) packages frozen**
    **fish sticks, thawed**
Meanwhile in a saucepan, heat until foamy
   **¼ cup butter or margarine**
Add and cook until transparent
   **½ cup chopped onions**
   **½ cup chopped celery or green**
    **pepper**
Blend in a mixture of
   **¼ cup PURITY Flour**
   **½ teaspoon oregano**
   **½ teaspoon salt**
   **¼ teaspoon sugar**
   **¼ teaspoon garlic powder**
   **Pinch of pepper**
Gradually stir in
   **1 (19-ounce) can tomatoes**
Cook, stirring constantly, until thickened.
Serve over hot fish sticks.
Makes 6 servings.

## SALMON LOAF

Lightly grease a 1½-quart baking dish, fish mould or loaf pan.
In a large bowl, blend thoroughly
   **½ cup milk**
   **2 eggs**
   **2 tablespoons lemon juice**
   **1 tablespoon soft butter**
   **½ teaspoon salt**
   **¼ teaspoon pepper**
Stir in
   **2 (7¾-ounce) cans salmon**
   **1½ cups unsalted cracker crumbs**
   **1 cup mashed potatoes**
Press into prepared dish. Cover with wax paper and foil. Tie tightly.
Steam for 1½ hours.
Serve hot with Blender Hollandaise Sauce (See page 212), or cold with mayonnaise or Cucumber Sauce (See page 212).
Makes 8 servings.

## BAKED COD FONDUE

Preheat oven to 350°F.
Lightly grease a 1½-quart casserole (with lid).
In a saucepan, combine
   **1 pound cod fillets**
   **1½ cups milk**
Cover and simmer until fish flakes easily. Do not boil. Drain, reserving liquid. Flake cod into prepared casserole.
In a saucepan, melt
   **¼ cup butter or margarine**
Blend in a mixture of
   **¼ cup PURITY Flour**
   **½ teaspoon salt**
   **Pinch of basil**
   **Pinch of pepper**
Gradually, stir in reserved liquid and
   **¼ cup dry white wine**
    **(optional)**
Cook, stirring constantly, until thickened. Sprinkle over cod
   **1 cup grated Swiss cheese**
   **1 teaspoon dried parsley flakes**
Pour hot sauce over top and bake in preheated 350° oven for 15 to 20 minutes or until heated thoroughly.
Makes 3 to 4 servings.

*When buying fish, allow ⅓ pound of steak or fillets, or ½ pound whole fish, per person.*

## BAKED STUFFED FISH

Preheat oven to 450°F.
Wash and dry
 **1 whole fish (about 4 pounds)**
Sprinkle inside lightly with salt.
Stuff fish with about
 **¾ cup dressing**
for each pound of fish.
Fasten opening with small skewers or toothpicks and lace with string, or sew opening with coarse thread.
Place fish on greased foil in baking pan and brush with vegetable oil or melted shortening. Measure stuffed fish at the thickest part and bake in preheated 450° oven allowing 10 minutes for each inch of stuffed fish.
Serve immediately with lemon wedges.
Makes 6 to 8 servings.

## LEMON RICE DRESSING

In a frypan, heat until foamy
 **⅓ cup butter or margarine**
Add and cook until transparent
 **½ cup chopped onion**
 **½ cup chopped celery**
Mix in
 **3 cups cooked rice**
 **1 tablespoon grated lemon rind**
 **½ teaspoon salt**
 **¼ teaspoon thyme**
 **Pinch of pepper**
 **¼ cup lemon juice**

## FRENCH FRIED SCALLOPS

Preheat deep fat to 375°F.
Dredge
 **1 pound scallops**
in a mixture of
 **¼ cup PURITY Flour**
 **½ teaspoon salt**
 **Pinch of pepper**
Dip in a mixture of
 **1 egg, slightly beaten**
 **2 tablespoons cold water**
Coat with
 **¾ cup fine dry bread crumbs**
Fry in preheated fat for 3 to 4 minutes, or until golden brown.
Drain on absorbent paper.
Serve with Tartar Sauce (See page 212).
Makes 3 to 4 servings.

## BAKED SCALLOPS

Preheat oven to 450°F.
Grease 4 scallop shells or individual baking dishes.
Dredge
 **1 pound scallops**
in a mixture of
 **½ cup PURITY Flour**
 **½ teaspoon salt**
 **Pinch of pepper**
Divide scallops among prepared dishes. Place on baking sheet for easier handling.
Spoon in each
 **1 tablespoon table cream**
 **1 teaspoon butter, melted.**
Sprinkle with
 **1 teaspoon fine dry bread crumbs**
Bake in preheated 450° oven for 20 minutes or until scallops are cooked.
Serve with lemon wedges.
Makes 4 servings.

---

*Cod, haddock, ocean perch, freshwater perch, pickerel, pike, smelt, sole and all shellfish are low in fat and thus a wise choice for calorie counters.*

---

## LOBSTER STEW

In a large saucepan, heat until foamy
 **¼ cup butter**
Add and cook until pink
 **1 (14-ounce) package frozen**
 **lobster meat, thawed**
Remove meat from pan and set aside.
Add to remaining fat in frypan and cook until transparent
 **1 onion, finely chopped**
Stir in
 **2 cups chopped raw potatoes**
 **2 cups boiling water**
 **1 teaspoon salt**
Bring to boil, cover, and simmer for about 5 minutes or until potatoes are tender.
Stir in lobster and
 **2 cups milk**
 **½ teaspoon salt**
 **¼ teaspoon pepper**
Heat thoroughly, but do not boil.
Pour into individual serving bowls containing
 **broken soda crackers**
Makes 4 to 5 servings.

# POULTRY

Poultry includes all domestic fowl such as chicken, turkey, duck, goose and guinea hen.

## HOW TO BUY POULTRY:

**Fresh poultry** is available in two forms:

**1.** *Eviscerated* (also called oven-ready and ready-to-cook) refers to poultry which has been drawn and is ready for use.

**2.** *Dressed* refers to poultry from which only the blood and feathers have been removed. While this type will cost less per pound, remember that it includes head, feet and entrails which you must remove.

**Frozen poultry** is eviscerated. Thaw frozen poultry before cooking, except for stewing.

Do not refreeze poultry once it has thawed.

*Do not thaw frozen stuffed poultry before cooking. Follow directions on the label.*

**Amount To Buy:** For roasting, allow ½ to ¾ pound eviscerated poultry per serving. For broiling or frying, allow ¾ to 1 pound. Plan for extra servings and some leftovers too.

## HOW TO PREPARE POULTRY FOR COOKING:

If necessary, singe the bird with a candle or gas flame. Remove any large pin feathers. Pull out any large leg tendons by using a heavy metal skewer.

## TO EVISCERATE:

Using a sharp knife, make a 3 or 4 inch cut in the skin from the tail piece up towards the keel or breast bone. Insert the hand, pressing it well up against the breast bone and ribs. Loosen and then draw out the entrails. Be careful not to break the gall bladder (small yellow-green pocket in the liver).

Loosen the skin at the neck and remove the crop and windpipe. Cut the oil sac from the tail.

Be sure the lungs are removed from the upper back and the kidneys from the lower back. Hold the bird under cold running water and wash thoroughly inside and out and then pat dry with a cloth. Stuff and cook immediately or cover loosely and store in refrigerator. Cook within 24 hours.

## TIPS ON BUYING:

*Broiler-Fryers:* small tender birds of 1½ to 3½ pounds ready-to-cook weight, available whole or cut up.

*Roasters:* tender birds weighing over 3½ pounds, usually purchased whole but may be cut up.

*Capons:* exceptionally tender birds weighing 4 to 8 pounds, having a large proportion of white meat.

*Fowl* (or stewing chickens): mature less tender birds, but flavourful for fricassée if simmered slowly.

*Turkey broilers:* young birds weighing 10 pounds or less.

*Young turkeys:* young birds weighing 10 pounds or more with a flexible tip of the breastbone.

## TIPS ON POULTRY STUFFING:

Crumbs may be prepared a day ahead, but do not combine with other stuffing ingredients. Because of the danger of food poisoning, do not stuff poultry until you are ready to cook it. Extra stuffing may be baked in a casserole or open pan. Cover with sliced bacon. Bake for 1 hour in oven with poultry.

## HOW TO MAKE GRAVY:

After roasting, remove poultry to heated platter. Keep warm in oven with heat off.

Pour fat and drippings from pan. For each cup of gravy, measure 1 to 2 tablespoons drippings back into pan. Blend in 2 tablespoons PURITY Flour. Slowly add 1 cup liquid (water, milk, chicken broth or cooking water from giblets). Stir constantly until gravy boils and is smoothly thickened. Season to taste with salt and pepper. For a more flavourful gravy, add a dash of mustard, onion or garlic salt, or Worcestershire sauce.

Allow approximately ¼ cup gravy per serving (remember to allow enough for leftovers).

**Giblet Gravy:** Rinse giblets thoroughly, discarding any yellowish parts of the liver. Place gizzard, heart and neck in a saucepan, cover with salted water and simmer gently for about one hour or until tender. Add liver during the last half hour of cooking time. Then chop giblets finely and add to gravy. Turkey giblets, being larger, will require about 1½ to 2 hours cooking.

## CHICKEN SUPREME

Preheat oven to 375°F.
Skin and bone
**8 half chicken breasts**
Dredge in a mixture of
**¼ cup PURITY Flour**
**1 teaspoon salt**
**Pinch of pepper**
In a frypan, heat until foamy
**½ cup butter or margarine**
Add floured chicken and brown on both sides.
Flame with
**¼ cup warm cognac**
Remove chicken and arrange in 2-quart casserole.
Stir into remaining fat in frypan
**1 cup coarsely chopped onions**
**1 clove garlic, finely chopped**
Cook until transparent and then blend in
**1 (10-ounce) can**
  **sliced mushrooms, undrained**
**1 cup dry red wine**
**¼ cup chopped parsley**
**1 bay leaf, crumbled**
Heat, stirring in browned bits and then pour over chicken in casserole.
Bake uncovered in preheated 375° oven for 20 to 25 minutes, or until thoroughly heated.
Makes 4 servings.

## CHICKEN CHASSEUR

In a frypan, heat until foamy
**¼ cup butter or margarine**
Add and cook until browned
**3 pounds cut-up chicken**
Remove chicken from pan and set aside.
Stir into remaining fat in frypan and cook until transparent
**1 onion, finely chopped**
Blend in
**2 tablespoons PURITY Flour**
Gradually, stir in
**1 (19-ounce) can tomatoes**
**1 (10-ounce) can whole**
  **mushrooms, drained**
**½ cup chicken broth or dry**
  **white wine**
**1 tablespoon finely chopped**
  **parsley**
**1 teaspoon salt**
**¼ teaspoon pepper**
Cook, stirring constantly, until thickened. Add chicken, bring to boil, cover, reduce heat and simmer 45 minutes or until chicken is tender.
Makes 6 servings.

---

*Never partially roast poultry one day and complete it the next. Arrange to roast the bird completely at one time and so avoid the possibility of spoilage.*

---

# POULTRY Cooking Chart

| Oven ready weights in lbs. | Amounts per person drawn or eviscerated | undrawn | Cooking time (hours) | Directions |
|---|---|---|---|---|
| **Chicken** | | | | **ROAST**—Wipe inside with damp |
| 2½-3½ | ½-¾ | ¾-1 | 1½-2 | cloth, and stuff loosely with your |
| 3½-4¾ | pound | pound | 2¼-2½ | favourite dressing. Turn back skin on |
| 4¾-up | | | 2¾-3 | neck, fold wings across back with tops touching. Tie legs together. |
| **Turkey** | | | | Place bird on rack in open roaster. |
| 4-6 | ¾-1 | 1-1¼ | 3 -3¾ | If desired, cover bird with parchment |
| 6-8 | pound | pound | 3¾-4½ | or foil. Use a 325°F. oven and cook |
| 8-10 | ½-¾ | ¾-1 | 4 -4½ | till internal temperature of meat on |
| 10-12 | pound | pound | 4½-5 | the inside of the thigh reaches |
| 12-14 | | | 5 -5¼ | 195°-200°F., or until drumstick twists |
| 14-16 | | | 5¼-6 | easily. |
| 16-18 | | | 6 -6½ | |
| 18-20 | | | 6½-7½ | |
| 20-24 | | | 7½-9 | |
| **Chicken** Broilers | ½ bird or ½-¾ pound | ½ bird or ¾-1 pound | 30-35 min. | Place chicken pieces skin side down on cold broiler rack, 5 inches from broiler, in preheated oven. Brush with butter. Broil underside 18-20 minutes. Turn over, coat with butter, broil 10-14 minutes. |
| **Fryers** | ½ bird or ½-¾ pound | ½ bird or ¾-1 pound | 35-40 min. | Dip pieces in flour or crumbs and seasonings. Brown in hot fat, reduce heat, cover, cook until tender. Remove cover to brown and crisp quickly. |
| **Duck** | ½-¾ pound | 1 pound | 25-30 min. per lb. | Roast uncovered at 325°F., with a small amount of water for 25-30 min. per lb. Pour off excess fat as it accumulates. |
| **Goose** | ½-¾ pound | 1 pound | 25-30 min. per lb. | Roast covered at 450°F., for one hour. Then pour off accumulated fat. Sprinkle with seasoned flour. Add 1 cup water and roast uncovered at 325°F., for 25 minutes per pound. |

**Speedy Method for Roasting Turkey**

Wrap the oven ready bird completely and tightly with aluminum foil. Roast as follows at 450°F. for approximately

|  |  |
|---|---|
| 8-10 lbs. . . . . . . . . . . . . . . . . . . . . . . . . . . . . . . . . . . . . . . . | 3 -3¼ hrs. total time |
| 10-12 lbs. . . . . . . . . . . . . . . . . . . . . . . . . . . . . . . . . . . . . . . | 3½-3¾ hrs. total time |
| 14-16 lbs. . . . . . . . . . . . . . . . . . . . . . . . . . . . . . . . . . . . . . . | 3¾-4 hrs. total time |
| 18-20 lbs. . . . . . . . . . . . . . . . . . . . . . . . . . . . . . . . . . . . . . . | 4 -5¼ hrs. total time |
| 22-24 lbs. . . . . . . . . . . . . . . . . . . . . . . . . . . . . . . . . . . . . . . | 5¼-6 hrs. total time |

Decrease time by 45 minutes if bird is not stuffed.

## CHICKEN À L'ORANGE

In a saucepan, heat until foamy
 **¼ cup butter or margarine**
Add and cook until browned
 **2 pounds cut-up chicken**
Remove chicken and set aside.
Blend into remaining fat in pan a mixture of
 **2 tablespoons PURITY Flour**
 **½ teaspoon salt**
 **Pinch of cinnamon**
 **Pinch of ginger**
Gradually, stir in
 **1½ cups orange juice**
 **1 cup raisins**
Cook, stirring constantly, until thickened.
Add chicken.
Bring to boil, cover, reduce heat and simmer for 45 minutes or until chicken is tender.
Stir in and heat thoroughly
 **1 cup orange sections**
Serve with cooked rice.
Makes 6 servings.

## CHICKEN MARENGO

Dredge lightly with flour
 **2 pounds cut-up chicken**
In a large frypan, heat thoroughly
 **¼ cup vegetable oil**
Add floured chicken and brown on both sides.
Cover and continue cooking until chicken is tender, about 30 minutes.
Remove cooked chicken to serving platter and sprinkle with
 **½ teaspoon salt**
 **⅓ cup chopped fresh parsley**
Keep warm.
To frypan, add and cook until transparent
 **2 cloves garlic, finely chopped**
Stir in
 **1 (10-ounce) can whole**
 **mushrooms, not drained**
 **2 tablespoons dry white wine**
 **1 tablespoon tomato paste**
Cook, stirring constantly, until thickened.
To serve, pour heated sauce over chicken.
Traditionally garnished with fried eggs and crayfish on grilled bread slices, this chicken with sauce suffices most Canadians without such trimmings.
Makes 4 servings.

## MADRAS CHICKEN

In a large saucepan, heat until dissolved
 **4 cups water**
 **2 chicken bouillon cubes**
Add
 **3 pounds cut-up chicken**
Bring to boil, cover, reduce heat and simmer for one hour or until chicken is almost tender. Remove 2 cups of broth and set aside, keeping chicken hot in remaining broth.
In a saucepan, melt
 **¼ cup butter or margarine**
Mix together and blend in
 **3 tablespoons PURITY Flour**
 **1 teaspoon curry powder**
 **½ teaspoon salt**
 **Pinch of pepper**
Gradually stir in reserved chicken broth.
Cook, stirring constantly, until thickened.
Stir in and heat
 **1 (19-ounce) can fruit**
 **cocktail, drained**
 **1 banana, sliced**
To serve, arrange cooked rice on platter with drained chicken pieces in centre and pour fruit sauce over chicken.
Makes 6 servings.

---

*Turkey leftovers can be used in any recipe calling for cooked chicken.*

---

## SWEET AND SOUR CHICKEN

In a frypan, heat until foamy
 **¼ cup butter or margarine**
Add and cook until browned
 **2½ pounds cut-up chicken**
Stir in
 **1 cup water**
Bring to boil, cover, reduce heat and simmer for 45 minutes or until chicken is almost tender.
Mix together and stir in
 **½ cup cider vinegar**
 **⅓ cup sliced gherkins**
 **¼ cup lightly packed brown sugar**
 **2 tablespoons honey**
 **1 tablespoon Worcestershire**
 **sauce**
 **1 tablespoon catsup**
Cover and continue cooking 15 minutes longer or until chicken is tender.
Serve with cooked rice.
Makes 4 servings.

## CHICKEN BOURGUIGNON

Carefully, skin and bone
**8 half chicken breasts**
In a frypan, heat until foamy
**2 tablespoons butter or margarine**
Stir in and cook 2 to 3 minutes
**⅔ cup finely chopped
mushrooms**
**3 slices cooked ham, diced**
**3 tablespoons diced Mozzarella
cheese**
**1 tablespoon chopped chives**
Heat until cheese is melted.
Slit a pocket in thick portion of each half chicken breast and stuff with 1 tablespoon mushroom mixture.
To frypan add an additional
**2 tablespoons butter or margarine**
When foamy, brown chicken breasts on both sides and then flame with
**¼ cup warm brandy**
Remove chicken from pan and set aside.
Stir into pan
**2 tablespoons PURITY Flour**
**1 teaspoon tomato paste**
Gradually add
**¾ cup undiluted consommé**
**¾ cup water**
**¼ cup dry red wine**
Cook, stirring constantly, until thickened.
Season with
**¼ teaspoon salt**
**Pinch of pepper**
Add chicken, bring to boil, reduce heat and simmer uncovered 20 minutes, basting several times.
Serve hot with cooked rice or noodles.
Makes 4 to 6 servings.

## CHICKEN AMANDINE

In a saucepan, heat until foamy
**2 tablespoons butter or margarine**
Add and cook until lightly browned, stirring frequently
**1 cup uncooked rice**
**1 cup sliced mushrooms**
**½ cup slivered blanched almonds**
**1 onion, finely chopped**
**½ green pepper, finely
chopped**
Stir in
**2 cups hot water**
**½ teaspoon salt**

Bring to boil, cover, reduce heat and simmer for 15 minutes, stirring occasionally.
When rice is tender, blend in
**2 cups cubed cooked chicken**
**1 (10-ounce) can condensed
cream of mushroom soup**
**1 (10-ounce) container thick
dairy sour cream**
Heat thoroughly, but do not boil. Garnish with snipped parsley and toasted almonds. Serve with tossed salad.
Makes 6 servings.

## SCALLOP TURKEY STROGANOFF

In a large frypan, heat until foamy
**¼ cup butter or margarine**
Stir in and cook until almost transparent
**¼ cup finely chopped onions**
Mix in and cook until tender
**½ pound mushrooms, sliced**
Blend in
**3 cups cubed cooked turkey**
**8 ounces fresh scallops,
quartered**
**2 (10-ounce) cans condensed
golden mushroom soup**
**¼ teaspoon pepper**
Bring just to boil, cover, reduce heat and simmer gently for 20 minutes, stirring occasionally.
Stir in and heat, but do not boil
**1 cup thick dairy sour cream**
Serve with cooked noodles or rice.
Makes 8 servings.

### LEMONY RABBIT

In a heavy saucepan, heat thoroughly
**1 tablespoon butter or margarine**
**2 tablespoons vegetable oil**
Add and cook until browned
**3½ pounds cut-up rabbit**
**OR**
**3½ pounds cut-up chicken**
Stir in
**½ cup lemon juice**
**6 green onions, finely chopped**
**½ teaspoon salt**
**½ teaspoon thyme**
**Pinch of pepper**
Bring to boil, cover, reduce heat and simmer for 1 hour or until tender.
Before serving, sprinkle with
**chopped parsley**
Makes 6 servings.

## SAUTÉED CHICKEN LIVERS

Dredge lightly with flour
**1 pound chicken livers**
In a saucepan, heat until foamy
**¼ cup butter or margarine**
Add floured chicken livers and cook until evenly browned.
Stir in
**1¼ cups sliced mushrooms**
**1 tablespoon finely chopped**
**green pepper**
**2 green onions, finely**
**chopped**
Continue cooking, stirring frequently, until onion is tender.
Gradually blend in a mixture of
**1 cup chicken broth**
**1 bay leaf**
**1 tablespoon finely chopped**
**parsley**
**½ teaspoon salt**
**¼ teaspoon pepper**
**Pinch of thyme**
Cook, stirring constantly, until thickened. Cover, simmer about 15 minutes longer. Remove bay leaf and serve with cooked rice.
Makes 4 servings.

## CHINESE DUCK

In a frypan, heat until foamy
**¼ cup butter or margarine**
Add and cook until golden brown
**5 pounds cut-up duck**
Remove duck and discard fat.
Stir into frypan
**¼ cup soya sauce**
**¾ cup orange juice**
**2 tablespoons dry sherry**
**(optional)**
**1 cup sliced mushrooms**
**3 cloves garlic, finely**
**chopped**
**1 tablespoon chopped green**
**onions**
**1 teaspoon salt**
**1 teaspoon cinnamon**
**½ teaspoon pepper**
Heat, stirring in browned bits in frypan. Then add duck and bring to boil, cover, reduce heat and simmer about one hour or until duck is tender.
Garnish with sliced orange.
Makes 4 to 6 servings.

## POULTRY STUFFING

Combine
**4 cups soft stale bread crumbs**
**1 onion, finely chopped**
**¼ cup butter or margarine,**
**melted**
**2 teaspoons poultry seasoning**
**½ teaspoon salt**
**Pinch of pepper**
Pack loosely in chicken.
Makes 4 cups stuffing, sufficient for 4 pound chicken.

PORK STUFFING: Prepare Poultry Stuffing following basic recipe but substituting 1 teaspoon sage for the poultry seasoning. Add ½ apple, finely chopped.

LAMB STUFFING: Prepare Poultry Stuffing following basic recipe but substituting ¾ teaspoon thyme for the poultry seasoning. Add 2 tablespoons chopped fresh mint.

## RICE STUFFING

Cook in boiling, salted water until tender
**1 cup rice**
In a frypan, heat until foamy
**¼ cup butter or margarine**
Add and cook until onion is transparent
**½ cup finely chopped onion**
**½ cup finely chopped celery**
**⅔ cup sliced mushrooms**
**1 green pepper, finely chopped**
**1 teaspoon chopped fresh**
**parsley**
Combine with cooked rice.
Season with
**½ teaspoon salt**
**Pinch of pepper**
Pack fairly tightly in chicken.
Makes 3 cups stuffing, sufficient for a 3-pound chicken.

RAISIN & RICE STUFFING: Prepare Rice Stuffing following basic recipe but substituting 1 cup raisins "plumped" for the mushrooms and adding them with the cooked rice. (To plump raisins, cover with boiling water and let stand until edges begin to whiten, then drain.)

BREAD & MUSHROOM STUFFING: Prepare Rice Stuffing following basic recipe but substituting 2 cups fresh bread cubes for rice. Pack loosely in chicken.

## CURRIED CHICKEN OR TURKEY

In a large saucepan, melt
**¼ cup butter or margarine**
Blend in a mixture of
**¾ cup PURITY Flour**
**1 teaspoon salt**
**¼ teaspoon nutmeg**
Gradually, stir in
**3½ cups chicken or turkey stock**
Cook, stirring constantly, until thickened.
In a small saucepan, heat until foamy
**2 tablespoons butter or margarine**
Add and cook until onion is transparent
**1 cup finely chopped onion**
Stir in
**1 tablespoon curry powder**
**¼ teaspoon thyme**
**2 bay leaves**
**½ cup chicken or turkey stock**
**1 teaspoon lemon juice**
Bring to boil and stir into white sauce.
Cover and simmer for 15 minutes but do
not boil. Strain.
Just before serving add and heat thoroughly
**3 cups cubed cooked chicken**
**or turkey**
**½ cup table cream**
Serve over cooked rice.
Makes 4 to 6 servings.

## GLAZED CHICKEN WINGS

Preheat oven to 350°F.
Grease a shallow baking dish.
Wipe with a damp cloth
**2 pounds chicken wings**
Combine in a medium-sized paper or
plastic bag
**1 cup PURITY Flour**
**4 teaspoons paprika**
**2 teaspoons salt**
**1 teaspoon chili powder**
**½ teaspoon pepper**
Coat chicken wings by shaking a few at
a time in bag.
In a frypan, heat until foamy
**¼ cup butter or margarine**
Brown chicken wings until golden and
arrange in prepared baking dish.
Combine and pour over top
**¾ cup orange marmalade**
**¾ cup water**
Bake in preheated 350° oven for 30 minutes or until chicken is tender.
Makes 6 to 8 servings.

## CREAMY CHICKEN AND MUSHROOMS

In a large frypan, melt
**2 tablespoons butter or margarine**
Blend in
**¼ cup PURITY Flour**
**½ teaspoon salt**
**Pinch of nutmeg**
**Pinch of pepper**
Gradually stir in
**1 cup milk**
**1 cup chicken broth**
Cook, stirring constantly, until thickened.
Blend in
**3 cups cubed cooked chicken**
**1 (10-ounce) can sliced**
**mushrooms, drained**
**⅓ cup finely chopped green**
**pepper**
**2 tablespoons diced pimiento**
Heat thoroughly but do not boil.
Serve on hot buttered biscuits, toast or
in patty shells.
Makes 6 servings.

CREAMY EGGS AND MUSHROOMS:
Prepare Creamy Chicken and Mushrooms
as in basic recipe but substituting 6 sliced
hard-cooked eggs for the chicken.

## CHICKEN PIE

Preheat oven to 425°F.
Prepare one-half recipe for PURITY Pastry
(See page 154). Roll out dough into a
9-inch circle.
In a large frypan, heat until foamy
**2 tablespoons butter or margarine**
Add and cook until onion is transparent
**½ cup sliced onions**
Blend in
**1 (10-ounce) can cream of**
**mushroom soup**
**½ cup milk**
**Pinch of marjoram**
Heat thoroughly but do not boil.
Arrange in an 8-inch baking dish or deep
pie plate
**1 cup cubed cooked chicken**
**1 cup canned whole potatoes or**
**cubed cooked potatoes**
Pour the hot mushroom sauce over top.
Cover with prepared pastry. Seal and
flute edges. Slit or prick top.
Bake in preheated 425° oven for 25 minutes or until golden brown.
Makes 4 to 6 servings.

# Barbecue and Main Dishes

## BARBECUE COOKING

The weather, the tantalizing aroma and even the sizzle during cooking all contribute to the popularity of barbecuing. Always plan on extra food to satisfy the whetted appetites.

### EQUIPMENT

The size and variety of barbecues pose a problem when it comes to buying. As a start, a small portable one, such as a Japanese hibachi, might serve. Later, once family enthusiasm necessitates a larger model, the portable one may be used on camping trips or in the fireplace in winter.

The grill-type barbecue permits cooking small cuts of meat. If equipped with hood and fire damper, better control of cooking temperature may be achieved.

Spit barbecues operate best with a hood to reflect the heat around the food, although an aluminum foil tent does serve adequately when it is not too windy.

Small accessories such as long handled tongs, fork and lifter may be purchased as needed. One handy gadget for dousing unwanted flames is a toy water pistol.

### FUEL

Charcoal or charcoal briquets provide the best source of heat. It takes too long for the wood to burn to the desired degree of ash for most enthusiasts. Briquets have the added advantage of being uniform in size and thus easier to give an even heat.

### LIGHTING THE FIRE

Allow 30 to 45 minutes for fire to burn to the right degree for cooking. Charcoal and more particularly charcoal briquets can be hard to light. The slowest method is to build a paper and kindling fire and then gradually add the briquets when it is burning well. For speedier results douse a pyramid of charcoal or briquets with inflammable liquid, allow it to soak in for a few minutes and then ignite. Some experts keep on hand a few briquets that have been soaked in the fluid until bubbling stops. Two or three soaked briquets at the bottom of a pyramid suffice for a quick start. To make a fire chimney remove the top and bottom of a large 48-ounce fruit juice can, punch 8 or 10 wedges around bottom edge with triangle-cut can opener, and bend triangles down to form short legs. To use, fill bottom with wadded paper, a squashed milk carton or soaked briquets, fill chimney with briquets and light. Coals will be ready for cooking in about 30 minutes. Then remove chimney and arrange coals evenly in

**Glowing coals barbecue steaks, fresh corn on the cob, and bananas as nectarines await their turn. Crisply cooked Elegant Potatoes, have just been unwrapped ready for serving ▶**

fire basket. Electric starters may be buried in a pile of coals to start them. Do no use inflammable liquids with these.

## COOKING FIRE

For grilling arrange the hot coals to cover the entire area under the food. The coal should be entirely covered with ash, as the black spots will flare or smoke too muc during cooking. Douse small flare-ups caused from drippings with a well-aimed squir of the water pistol. If fire is too hot, space the coals in an even pattern. Thick piece of meat should be cooked more slowly and for these arrange a drip pan in fire basket surround with hot coals and place food directly above drip pan.

For spit roasting have the bottom of roast turn towards you and the top away from you (the hood should be away from you). Position a foil pan (of the same lengt and width as the roast) near the front of the fire basket and the hot coals near the back under the hooded portion. As the spit rotates the drippings will fall into th foil pan.

During spit barbecuing when extra coals are needed, place them on the outside edge of the fire but touching a hot coal. When ash-covered, move into fire.

## COOKING TIMES

The temperature of both the day and the fire together with the distance the foo is from the heat and the amount of wind blowing will all influence the cooking time The following charts should serve as a guide.

# SPIT BARBECUE Cooking Chart

| Cut | Size lbs. | Fire | Cooking Time—Hours | | |
| | | | Rare 130°-135°F | Medium 140°-145°F | Well-Done 150°-160°F |
| --- | --- | --- | --- | --- | --- |
| **Beef Roasts** | | | | | |
| Standing Rib | 7 to 8 | Hot-medium | 2 to 2½ | 2½ to 3 | 3 to 4½ |
| Rolled Rib | 6 to 8 | Hot-medium | 2¼ to 3 | 2¾ to 3¼ | 3¼ to 5 |
| Rib Eye | 4 to 7 | Hot-medium | 1¼ to 2½ | 2 to 2½ | 2½ to 3½ |
| Rump (high quality) | 4 to 7 | Medium | 2 to 2½ | 2½ to 3 | 3 to 4 |
| Sirloin | 5 to 6 | Hot-medium | 2 to 2½ | 2½ to 3 | 3 to 4 |
| Porterhouse and Wing | 5 to 6 | Hot-medium | 1¾ to 2½ | 2 to 2½ | 2½ to 3½ |
| Round (high quality) | 5 to 6 | Medium | 2 to 2½ | 2½ to 3 | 3 to 4 |
| **Lamb-Pork-Veal (Pork should be well cooked)** | | | | | |
| Leg (Rolled) | 4 to 7 | Medium | — | — | 2½ to 4 |
| Loin | 4 to 7 | Medium | — | — | 2 to 4 |
| Rolled front (lamb) | 4 to 7 | Medium | — | — | 2 to 3 |
| Rolled Shoulder | 4 to 6 | Medium | — | — | 2 to 4 |
| Spareribs (pork) | 2 to 3 | Medium | — | — | 1 to 1½ |
| **Poultry** | | | | | |
| Chicken | 3 to 5 | Medium | — | — | 1¼ to 2½ |
| Cornish Hen | 12 to 16 oz. | Medium | — | — | ¾ to 1 |
| Turkey | 10 to 14 | Medium | — | — | 2 to 4 |
| Turkey | 15 to 25 | Slow | — | — | 6 to 8 |

# GRILL BARBECUE Cooking Chart

| Cut | Size (Thickness) | Fire | Cooking Time (each side)—in minutes | | |
|---|---|---|---|---|---|
| | | | Rare | Medium | Well-Done |
| **Beef** | | | | | |
| Sirloin Steak | ½″-¾″ | Hot | 4 to 5 | 6 to 7 | 9 to 10 |
| | 1″-1½″ | Hot | 5 to 6 | 7 to 8 | 10 to 11 |
| Porterhouse Steak | ½″-¾″ | Hot | 4 to 5 | 6 to 7 | 9 to 10 |
| | 1″-1½″ | Hot | 5 to 6 | 7 to 8 | 10 to 11 |
| Wing or Club Steak | ½″-¾″ | Hot | 4 | 6 | 9 |
| | 1″-1¾″ | Hot | 5 | 7 | 10 to 11 |
| Tenderloin | Whole | Medium | 12 to 15 | 16 to 19 | 19 to 22 |
| | 1″-1½″ | hot | 5 to 6 | 7 to 8 | 10 to 11 |
| Hamburger | 1″ | Medium-hot | 3 to 4 | 4 to 5 | 6 to 7 |
| **Pork-Lamb-Veal** | | | | | |
| Chops | ½″-¾″ | Low to medium | — | — | 10 to 13 |
| | 1″-1¼″ | Low to medium | — | — | 13 to 15 |
| Spareribs | Whole | Very low | — | — | 25 to 30 |
| **Poultry** | | | | | |
| Chicken | Split | Medium | — | — | 20 to 25 |
| Cornish Hens | Split | Medium | — | — | 15 to 20 |
| **Ham** | | | | | |
| Steak | ¾″-1¼″ | Medium | — | — | 10 to 15 |
| Steak | 1½″-2″ | Medium | — | — | 15 to 20 |
| **Fish** | | | | | |
| Whole | | Medium | — | — | 10 to 15 |
| Steak | ½″-¾″ | Medium | — | — | 3 to 5 |

## BAR-B-CUE CHICKEN

In a plastic bag, combine
**1 cup gingerale**
**½ cup orange juice**
**½ cup finely chopped onion**
**¼ cup corn syrup**
**½ teaspoon salt**
**½ teaspoon ginger**
**¼ teaspoon pepper**
Add and then tie bag
**1 broiling chicken (about**
**3 pounds)**
Allow to marinate for 2 hours.
Drain chicken, reserving liquid. Balance on barbecue spit.
Barbecue, rotating spit, over medium hot coals for 1½ hours or until chicken is tender.
Brush occasionally with liquid.
Makes 3 to 4 servings.

## ZESTY STEAK

In a plastic bag, combine
**1 cup malt vinegar**
**1 cup cider vinegar**
**1 clove garlic, finely chopped**
**Pinch of pepper**
Add and then tie bag
**1 flank steak (about 1 pound)**
Allow to marinate for 1 hour.
Drain meat and barbecue over hot coals for about 5 minutes on each side or until meat is tender.
Brush occasionally with liquid.
To serve, slice diagonally across the grain.
Makes 4 servings.

## BUDGET STEAK DIVINE

Cut into 6 portions
**2 pounds round steak**
Barbecue over medium hot coals, about 5 minutes on each side or until browned.
Place meat on a large piece of aluminium foil.
Pour over top
**1 (10-ounce) can condensed**
**onion soup**
**¼ cup dry red wine**
Wrap tightly.
Barbecue over medium hot coals for about 2 hours or until meat is tender.
Makes 6 servings.

## SHISH KABOB BALKANESE

Arrange on 4 skewers
**1 pound boneless lamb cut**
**in 1-inch cubes**
**8 slices side bacon, rolled up**
**8 small onions**
**8 cherry tomatoes**
**4 gherkins**
**4 mushroom caps**
Brush with
**olive oil**
Season with
**salt**
**pepper**
Barbecue over hot coals for about 10 minutes or until meat is tender.
Turn occasionally.
Serve with Curried Rice (See page 56) and add Mushroom Sauce made by removing top from
**1 (10-ounce) can condensed**
**golden mushroom soup**
Set can on barbecue rack to heat.
Makes 4 servings.

---

*Barbecue snacks such as drained cocktail wieners and chunks of bologna may stave off hunger pangs of the watchers and permit the chef of the house to properly cook the "pièce de resistance".*

---

## BARBECUED PORK CHOPS

In a plastic bag, combine
**½ cup dry sherry**
**¼ cup vegetable oil**
**3 green onions, finely**
**chopped**
**1 clove garlic, finely**
**chopped**
**½ teaspoon salt**
**½ teaspoon thyme**
**¼ teaspoon pepper**
Add and then tie bag
**6 loin pork chops (½-inch**
**thick)**
Allow to marinate for 1 hour.
Place meat and liquid in a large piece of aluminium foil along with
**6 apple rings**
Wrap tightly.
Barbecue over hot coals for about 45 minutes or until meat is tender.
Makes 6 servings.

## CARIBBEAN SPARERIBS

Cut into 8 portions
  **4 pounds spareribs**
In a large saucepan, mix together
  **¼ cup soya sauce**
  **¼ cup catsup**
  **¼ cup honey**
  **1¼ cups water**
Add meat, bring to boil, cover, reduce heat and simmer for 30 minutes or until partially tender.
Barbecue spareribs over medium hot coals for 10 minutes on each side, or until meat is tender.
Brush occasionally with barbecue sauce.
Makes 8 servings.

## BARBECUE BURGERS

Combine
  **1 pound ground beef**
  **¼ cup chopped green pepper**
  **1 egg**
  **1 teaspoon salt**
  **½ teaspoon thyme**
  **½ teaspoon Tabasco sauce**
  **¼ teaspoon pepper**
  **1 clove garlic, finely chopped**
  **¼ cup undiluted evaporated milk**
Shape into patties.
Brush with
  **vegetable oil**
Barbecue over medium hot coals for about 5 minutes on each side or until desired doneness.
Makes 8 patties.

## CHEESY BOLOGNA

Split horizontally, leaving ½-inch uncut at one edge
  **1 slice bologna (1-inch thick)**
Insert in slit a slice of
  **cheddar cheese**
Circle with
  **2 slices side bacon**
Secure with toothpicks.
Barbecue over medium hot coals for about 10 minutes or until cheese is melted.
When meat is turned, brush cooked side with
  **2 tablespoons orange marmalade**
To serve, top other side with an additional
  **2 tablespoons orange marmalade**
Makes 2 servings.

## VEAL WHIRLAGIGS

Season
  **6 veal cutlets**
with
  **½ teaspoon salt**
  **½ teaspoon thyme**
  **¼ teaspoon pepper**
Remove wrappers from
  **1 (6-ounce) package sliced Swiss cheese**
  **1 (6-ounce) package sliced cooked ham**
Stack a slice of cheese and a slice of ham on each veal cutlet.
Roll up and skewer.
Barbecue over medium hot coals for about 30 minutes or until meat is tender. Turn occasionally.
Makes 6 servings.

## HERBED SALMON STEAKS

Cream together
  **⅓ cup butter or margarine**
  **2 green onions, finely chopped**
  **1 clove garlic, finely chopped**
  **¼ teaspoon salt**
  **Pinch of pepper**
Spread over
  **6 salmon steaks (1-inch thick)**
Barbecue over hot coals for about 5 minutes on each side or until salmon loses its transparency and flakes easily. Brush occasionally with garlic butter.
Serve with lemon wedges.
Makes 6 servings.

## SUNNY TOPPED FILLETS

Cut in serving portions
  **4 haddock fillets**
Spread with a mixture of
  **1 tablespoon prepared mustard**
  **2 tablespoons finely chopped onion**
  **½ teaspoon salt**
  **Pinch of pepper**
Wrap in aluminium foil.
Barbecue over hot coals for about 10 minutes or until fish loses its transparency and flakes easily.
Serve with lemon slices.
Makes 4 servings.

## ELEGANT POTATOES

Peel and thinly slice sufficient parboiled potatoes to give
**6 cups sliced potatoes**
In an aluminium foil container, arrange one layer of potatoes.
Brush with butter from
**½ cup butter or margarine, melted**
Season with
**Pinch of salt**
**Pinch of pepper**
Repeat until potatoes and butter are used.
Cover with foil and barbecue over medium hot coals for about 30 minutes or until potatoes are tender. Serve with hamburgers.
Makes 6 servings.

## CURRIED RICE

In an aluminium foil container, bring to boil over hot coals
**2 cups water**
Stir in
**1 cup rice**
**1 tablespoon curry powder**
**1 teaspoon salt**
**1 teaspoon dried parsley flakes**
**¼ teaspoon pepper**
Cover with foil and cook over medium hot coals for about 30 minutes or until rice is tender.
Makes 6 servings.

## GLAZED CARROTS

Mix together
**¼ cup butter or margarine, melted**
**2 tablespoons brown sugar**
**¼ teaspoon salt**
**Pinch of pepper**
On a piece of aluminium foil, arrange
**12 whole carrots, parboiled**
Top with butter mixture and wrap tightly. Barbecue over medium hot coals for about 30 minutes or until tender.
Makes 4 servings.

GLAZED ONIONS: Prepare Glazed Carrots following basic recipe but substituting 8 parboiled onions for carrots.

## CRISPY CORN

Cook in boiling salted water for 10 minutes or until partially tender
**husked ears of corn**
Drain and brush corn with
**vegetable oil**
Wrap around each ear securing with toothpicks
**1 slice side bacon**
Barbecue over medium hot coals for about 15 minutes or until corn is tender and bacon is crisped.
Turn occasionally.

## EGGPLANT AU BEURRE

Mix together
**¼ cup butter or margarine, melted**
**¼ teaspoon salt**
**Pinch of pepper**
Brush over
**1 eggplant, sliced 1-inch thick**
Dredge in
**¼ cup PURITY Flour**
Barbecue over medium hot coals for about 10 minutes or until tender, brushing occasionally with remaining butter mixture.
Makes 8 servings.

## GARLIC BREAD

Cream together
**½ cup soft butter or margarine**
**2 cloves garlic, finely chopped**
**or**
**1 teaspoon garlic powder**
Spread mixture on each slice of
**1 loaf French bread, sliced diagonally**
Wrap in aluminium foil and heat over hot coals for about 30 minutes or until piping hot.
Turn bread occasionally.

---

*Of all meats, veal barbecues the least satisfactorily. As it is an especially lean meat it tends to become dry and the delicate flavour of veal is overpowered by the smoky flavour.*

---

PURITY FLOUR GUARANTEES SATISFACTION OR YOUR MONEY BACK PLUS 20%

## SPICY ZUCCHINI

Cut in 4 slices each
**3 zucchini**
Brush with a mixture of
**2 tablespoons butter, melted**
**2 tablespoons lemon juice**
**¼ teaspoon onion salt**
**Pinch of pepper**
Barbecue over medium hot coals for about 15 minutes or until tender.
Turn occasionally.
Makes 4 servings.

## TEA-BISCUITS ON SKEWERS

Prepare Tea-Biscuit dough (See page 193). Cut out biscuits and arrange 1-inch apart on long-handled skewers or individually on forks.
Toast like marshmallows over hot coals for about 10 minutes or until golden.
Turn constantly during cooking.
Brush with
**¼ cup butter or margarine, melted**
Serve hot.

## TOFFEE BANANAS

Barbecue over medium hot coals for about 10 minutes
**6 unpeeled bananas**
Turn occasionally.
Remove from heat. Peel leaving one strip for base.
Slice bananas diagonally.
Brush with a mixture of

**¼ cup lightly packed brown sugar**
**¼ cup lemon juice**
Barbecue 5 minutes longer.
Serve as a dessert or as an accompaniment for meat.
Makes 6 servings.

## BARBECUED APPLES

Core and place each on a piece of aluminium foil
**6 unpeeled apples**
Mix together
**½ cup lightly packed brown sugar**
**2 tablespoons chopped walnuts**
**2 tablespoons butter or margarine**
Fill centre of each apple and wrap tightly.
Barbecue over medium hot coals for 30 minutes or until tender.
Makes 6 servings.

## GOLDEN NECTARINES

On a large piece of aluminium foil arrange
**6 nectarines or peaches,**
**peeled and sliced**
Sprinkle with
**⅔ cup lightly packed brown sugar**
Pour over top
**¼ cup Grand Marnier or rum**
Wrap tightly.
Barbecue over hot coals, 30 minutes or until tender.
Makes 6 servings.

# CASSEROLES AND MAIN DISHES

## CURRIED MACARONI

Preheat oven to 350°F.
Grease a 2-quart casserole.
Cook according to package directions
**2 cups elbow macaroni**
Meanwhile, in a saucepan, combine
**1 (10-ounce) can condensed**
**cream of chicken soup**
**1 (10-ounce) can condensed**
**cream of mushroom soup**
**½ cup milk**
**⅓ cup water**
**2 teaspoons curry powder**
Bring to boil, cover, reduce heat and simmer for 10 minutes.

Stir in
**⅓ cup sliced mushrooms**
**1½ teaspoons finely chopped**
**onion**
**¼ teaspoon thyme**
**Pinch of basil**
**Pinch of oregano**
Simmer an additional 10 minutes.
Combine with macaroni in casserole.
Sprinkle over top
**¼ cup grated Parmesan cheese**
Bake in preheated 350° oven for about 20 minutes or until cheese is melted.
Makes 8 to 10 servings.

## MACARONI AND CHEESE

Preheat oven to 350°F.
Grease a 1½-quart casserole.
In a saucepan, heat until foamy
  **2 tablespoons butter or margarine**
Add and cook until onion is transparent
  **¼ cup chopped onion**
  **¼ cup chopped celery**
Stir in
  **1 (10-ounce) can condensed**
    **cream of mushroom soup**
  **⅓ cup milk**
  **2 cups grated cheddar cheese**
Heat, stirring constantly, until cheese is melted.
Blend in
  **3 cups cooked elbow macaroni**
  **½ cup canned tomatoes**
Turn into prepared casserole.
Bake in preheated 350° oven for 30 minutes or until thoroughly heated.
Makes 6 servings.

MEAT MACARONI: Prepare Macaroni and Cheese following basic recipe but substituting 1 cup cubed cooked ham, chicken or turkey and 2 tablespoons chopped pimiento for the tomatoes. Sprinkle top with 1 tablespoon chopped fresh parsley. Bake as directed.

CHICKEN LUAU: Prepare Macaroni and Cheese following basic recipe but adding 1½ cups cubed cooked chicken, ½ green pepper, sliced, 1 clove garlic, finely chopped to cheese mixture. Garnish top with ¼ cup toasted slivered almonds. Bake as directed.

ITALIAN MACARONI: Prepare Macaroni and Cheese following basic recipe but adding ¼ cup finely chopped green pepper and 1 clove garlic, finely chopped and cook with onion mixture. Substitute 2 (7½-ounce) cans tomato sauce, ½ cup water, 2 tablespoons chopped fresh parsley, ½ teaspoon oregano for tomatoes. Bake in a 2-quart casserole, as directed.

---

*To cook noodles, spaghetti or macaroni, drop into a large amount of boiling, salted water. Cook, uncovered, keeping the water boiling briskly; stir occasionally. When firm but not hard in the centre, it is cooked sufficiently.*

---

## SPANISH RICE À L'AMÉRICAINE

Preheat oven to 350°F.
In a saucepan, heat until foamy
  **¼ cup butter or margarine**
Add and cook until onion is transparent
  **1 onion, thinly sliced**
  **¼ cup chopped celery**
  **1 clove garlic, finely chopped**
Stir in
  **1 cup uncooked rice**
  **1 (28-ounce) can tomatoes**
  **1 green pepper, finely chopped**
  **1 bay leaf, crumbled**
  **1½ teaspoons salt**
  **½ teaspoon pepper**
  **Pinch of thyme**
Bring to boil, cover, reduce heat and simmer for 20 minutes or until rice is tender.
Meanwhile, cut once lengthwise and then crosswise into 1-inch pieces
  **1 pound wieners**
In a 2-quart casserole (with lid), arrange alternate layers of rice and wieners.
Cover and bake in preheated 350° oven for 25 minutes or until thoroughly heated. If desired, sprinkle with grated cheddar cheese and broil until bubbly.
Makes 6 servings.

## HAWAIIAN RICE

In a saucepan, heat thoroughly
  **1 tablespoon vegetable oil**
Add and cook until onion is transparent
  **1 onion, finely chopped**
  **½ cup chopped green pepper**
Stir in and cook slightly
  **1 pound ground, cooked ham**
Blend in
  **1 (19-ounce) can crushed**
    **pineapple**
  **2 cups water**
  **1 cup uncooked rice**
  **2 tablespoons brown sugar**
  **1 teaspoon prepared mustard**
  **¼ teaspoon salt**
Bring to boil, cover, reduce heat and simmer for 20 minutes or until rice is tender.
Serve with Honey'd Onions (See Page 76).
Makes 4 servings.

## RICE AND CHEESE BAKE

Preheat oven to 400°F.
Cook in boiling salted water until tender
**1 cup rice**
In a saucepan, heat until foamy
**¼ cup butter or margarine**
Add and cook until transparent
**1 onion, finely chopped**
Blend in a mixture of
**3 tablespoons PURITY Flour**
**1 teaspoon salt**
**½ teaspoon dry mustard**
**Pinch of pepper**
**1 teaspoon Worcestershire sauce**
Gradually, stir in
**2 cups milk**
Cook, stirring constantly, until thickened.
Stir in and cook until melted
**½ pound diced cheddar cheese**
In a 1½-quart casserole, put half of
cooked rice, then half of sauce mixture
and then another layer or rice and remaining sauce.
Sprinkle with
**3 tablespoons fine, dry bread**
**crumbs**
Dot with
**2 tablespoons butter or margarine**
Bake in preheated 400° oven for 20 minutes or until golden brown.
Makes 4 to 6 servings.

MEAT-CHEESE RICE: Prepare Rice and
Cheese Bake following basic recipe but
adding ½ to ¾ cup chopped luncheon
meat, or cooked ham or tongue to hot
cheese sauce. Bake as directed.

VEGETABLE-CHEESE RICE: Prepare
Rice and Cheese Bake as in basic recipe
but over first rice layer arrange 1 cup
cooked green beans, or cooked asparagus
or canned peas. Bake as directed.

FISH-CHEESE RICE: Prepare Rice and
Cheese Bake following basic recipe but
adding 1 (7¾-ounce) can salmon or tuna,
drained and flaked, to hot cheese sauce.
Bake as directed.

## CHILI CON CARNE

In a saucepan cook until evenly browned
**1 pound ground beef**
**1 cup chopped onion**
**¾ cup chopped green pepper**

Stir in
**1 (19-ounce) can tomatoes**
**1 (7½-ounce) can tomato sauce**
**2 (14-ounce) cans pinto or red**
**kidney beans, drained**
**1 tablespoon chili powder**
**1 teaspoon salt**
**1 teaspoon dried parsley flakes**
**1 bay leaf**
Bring to boil, cover, reduce heat and
simmer for 1 hour. Remove bay leaf.
Serve with hot rolls and a salad.
Makes 6 servings.

## ANCHOVY EGGS ON NOODLES

Preheat oven to 350°F.
Grease a 2-quart casserole.
Cook according to package directions
and turn into prepared casserole
**8 ounces noodles (¾ of a**
**12-ounce package)**
Cut in half
**5 hard cooked eggs**
Remove egg yolks and mash with
**1 tablespoon dried parsley flakes**
**2 tablespoons anchovy paste**
**1 tablespoon mayonnaise**
**1 tablespoon lemon juice**
**1 teaspoon finely chopped onion**
Stuff egg whites and arrange on noodles.
Combine and pour over
**1⅔ cups undiluted evaporated milk**
**1 (10-ounce) can condensed**
**tomato soup**
Bake in preheated 350° oven for 20 to
25 minutes or until thoroughly heated.
Makes 4 servings.

EGGS AND TUNA CASSEROLE: Prepare Anchovy Eggs on Noodles following
basic recipe but substituting 1 (7-ounce)
can flaked tuna for the anchovy paste,
1 (10-ounce) can condensed cream of
asparagus soup for the tomato soup.
Blend leftover egg yolk mixture into soup
sauce and season with 1 finely chopped
onion, 2 teaspoons dried parsley flakes,
½ teaspoon salt, and ½ teaspoon dry
mustard. Bake as directed.

EGG AND OLIVE CASSEROLE: Prepare
Anchovy Eggs on Noodles following
basic recipe but substituting 1 (10-ounce)
can condensed cream of celery soup for
the tomato soup, and 2 tablespoons
finely chopped olives for the anchovy
paste. Bake as directed.

## HAM AND RICE RING

In a saucepan, melt
**3 tablespoons butter or margarine**
Blend in a mixture of
**3 tablespoons PURITY Flour**
**3 tablespoons lightly packed**
**brown sugar**
Gradually stir in 1 cup juice from
**1 (19-ounce) can pineapple chunks**
**3 tablespoons vinegar**
Cook, stirring constantly, until thickened.
Add drained pineapple chunks with
**3 cups cubed cooked ham**
**¾ cup sliced pimiento**
Heat thoroughly.
Meanwhile, preheat oven to 400°F.
In a medium saucepan, heat until foamy
**2 tablespoons butter or margarine**
Add and cook until transparent
**1 tablespoon finely chopped**
**onion**
Stir in
**3 tablespoons PURITY Flour**
**1½ teaspoon salt**
Then add
**1⅓ cups uncooked rice**
**1⅓ cups milk**
**1⅓ cups water**
Cook over low heat, stirring constantly
for 10 minutes or until rice is almost
tender.
Blend in
**1 tablespoon chopped fresh**
**parsley**
Turn into a 9-inch ring mould and bake
in preheated 400° oven for 10 minutes.
Unmould on serving plate.
Spoon ham mixture in centre of rice ring
allowing sauce to drip down sides.
Makes 6 servings.

## POLYNESIAN HAM

Drain, reserving juice
**1 (10-ounce) can**
**pineapple chunks**
Cut sufficient ham into strips like match-
sticks to give
**2 cups cooked ham**
In a saucepan, melt
**2 tablespoons butter or margarine**
Blend in a mixture of
**3 tablespoons PURITY Flour**
**2 tablespoons brown sugar**
**2 teaspoons prepared mustard**
**½ teaspoon salt**

Gradually, stir in reserved pineapple juice
and
**¾ cup water**
**1 tablespoon vinegar**
Cook, stirring constantly, until thickened.
Add drained pineapple chunks and ham
together with
**½ cup coarsely chopped celery**
**½ green pepper, sliced**
Bring to boil, cover, reduce heat and
simmer for 10 minutes or until vegetables
are tender.
If desired, add
**1 (28-ounce) can bean sprouts**
**or**
**1 (10-ounce) can sliced**
**mushrooms, drained**
Serve with cooked rice or a tossed salad.
Makes 4 to 6 servings.

## EGGPLANT AND LAMB CASSEROLE

Preheat oven to 350°F.
Grease a 2-quart casserole (with lid).
In a saucepan, heat thoroughly
**¼ cup vegetable oil**
Add and cook until browned on all but
one side
**1½ pounds lamb shoulder, cubed**
Add
**1 onion, finely chopped**
**½ green pepper, coarsely chopped**
Cook until onion is transparent and meat
browned. Turn into prepared casserole.
Cook in boiling salted water until tender
**½ cup rice**
Drain and stir into meat mixture.
Peel and cut into 1-inch thick cubes
**1 eggplant**
Cover with water, bring to boil, reduce
heat and simmer for 5 minutes or until
partially cooked. Drain on absorbent
paper.
Stir into meat mixture with
**1¼ cups canned tomatoes**
**½ cup dry red wine or broth**
**¼ cup grated cheddar cheese**
**1 clove garlic, finely chopped**
**1 teaspoon salt**
**Pinch of cinnamon**
Cover and bake in preheated 350° oven
for 1 hour or until meat is tender.
Makes 4 to 6 servings.

## SPINACH CASSEROLE

Preheat oven to 350°F.
Grease a 9-inch square casserole.
Cook until just tender in a very small amount of boiling water
**1 (12-ounce) package spinach**
In prepared casserole, arrange
**4 slices bread without crusts**
Top with
**1 (8-ounce) package processed cheddar cheese slices**
Spread drained cooked spinach over top and sprinkle with
**1½ cups cubed cooked ham**
Arrange on top, overlapping slightly
**6 bread slices, halved**
Beat together and pour over top
**1½ cups milk**
**3 eggs**
**½ teaspoon dry mustard**
**¼ teaspoon salt**
Dot with
**1 tablespoon butter or margarine**
Bake in preheated 350° oven for 45 to 50 minutes or until egg mixture is just set. Serve hot.
Makes 4 to 6 servings.

---

*Allow longer cooking time for a refrigerated casserole. Special pyroceram casseroles permit baking from frozen state without thawing; allow double the cooking time.*

---

## BEEF-ZUCCHINI CASSEROLE

In a saucepan, heat thoroughly
**1 tablespoon vegetable oil**
Add and cook until browned
**1 pound round steak, cut into thin strips**
Stir in
**2 cups water**
**1 (7½-ounce) can tomato sauce**
**1 package mushroom gravy mix**
**1 package spaghetti sauce mix with mushrooms**
Bring to boil, reduce heat and simmer for 40 minutes stirring occasionally.
Add
**3 zucchini, cut in 1-inch slices**
Cover and simmer for an additional 5 minutes or until meat is tender.
Serve with cooked noodles.
Makes 4 servings.

## CREAMY TUNA CASSEROLE

Preheat oven to 350°F.
Grease a 2-quart casserole.
Cook according to package directions
**8 ounces noodles (¾ of 12-ounce package)**
Combine
**2 (7-ounce) cans flaked tuna**
**2 (7½-ounce) cans tomato sauce**
Mix together
**2 cups cottage cheese**
**1 (8-ounce) package cream cheese**
**⅓ cup finely chopped onion**
**⅓ cup finely chopped raw carrot**
**½ teaspoon dried parsley flakes**
**¼ teaspoon basil**
Arrange half of cooked noodles in prepared casserole. Cover with half of cheese mixture, then, half of tuna mixture. Repeat layers.
Bake in preheated 350° oven for 45 minutes or until nicely browned.
Makes 8 servings.

## NOODLE CREAM PIE

Preheat oven to 375°F.
Grease a 9-inch pie plate.
In a bowl, combine
**1½ cups cooked large noodles**
**3 wieners, sliced**
**1 cup thick dairy sour cream**
**½ cup cottage cheese**
**3 eggs**
**2 teaspoons dried onion flakes**
**½ teaspoon salt**
**Pinch of pepper**
Turn into prepared pie plate.
Sprinkle with
**⅓ cup cornflake crumbs**
Dot with
**2 tablespoons butter or margarine**
Bake in preheated 375° oven for 20 minutes.
Meanwhile, cut lengthwise and crosswise to give four pieces each
**3 wieners**
Arrange attractively on pie.
Bake an additional 5 minutes or until wieners are thoroughly heated, and filling almost set. Let stand 10 minutes before serving.
Cut in wedges and serve with sliced tomatoes.
Makes 4 to 6 servings.

## BEEF BEER STEW

Dredge
  **2 pounds stewing beef, cut
    in 1-inch cubes**
in a mixture of
  **¼ cup PURITY Flour
  2 teaspoons salt
  ½ teaspoon pepper**
In a frypan, heat thoroughly
  **¼ cup vegetable oil**
Add floured meat and cook until evenly
browned.
In a large saucepan, heat thoroughly
  **¼ cup vegetable oil**
Add
  **2 pounds onions, thinly sliced
  1 clove garlic, finely chopped**
Cook until onion is transparent.
Combine browned meat with onions and
stir in
  **1 (12-ounce) bottle beer
  1 tablespoon soya sauce
  1 tablespoon Worcestershire sauce
  1 tablespoon steak sauce
  2 bay leaves
  ½ teaspoon thyme**
Bring to boil, cover, reduce heat and
simmer for 1½ hours or until meat is
almost tender.
Then add
  **3 potatoes, peeled and quartered**
Simmer covered for an additional 20
minutes or until potatoes are partially
cooked.
Stir in
  **1 (10-ounce) package frozen peas**
Bring to boil, cover, reduce heat and
simmer for 10 minutes or until meat and
vegetables are tender. Remove bay
leaves.
Makes 6 servings.

## STEW SURPRISE

Drain
  **1 (10-ounce) can sliced peaches**
Drain and slice
  **1 (10-ounce) can pears**
Rinse fruit in cold water to remove syrup
and set aside to drain on absorbent
paper.
In a saucepan, heat thoroughly
  **¼ cup vegetable oil**
Add and cook until browned on all but
one side

  **2 pounds stewing beef, cut
    in 1-inch cubes**
Add
  **2 cups coarsely chopped onion**
Cook until onion is transparent and meat
evenly browned.
Stir in
  **1 (10-ounce) can undiluted
    consommé
  ½ cup dry red wine
  1 bay leaf
  1 teaspoon salt
  ½ teaspoon thyme
  ¼ teaspoon pepper**
Bring to boil, cover, reduce heat and
simmer for 1 hour or until meat is almost
cooked.
Then add
  **2 cups cubed sweet potatoes**
Simmer covered for an additional 15
minutes or until potatoes are partially
cooked.
Stir in drained canned fruit with
  **1 (14-ounce) package frozen
    sliced yellow squash
  ½ cup chopped tomatoes**
Bring to boil, cover, reduce heat and
simmer for 5 to 10 minutes.
Serve with cooked rice or noodles and
garnish with chopped parsley.
Makes 6 servings.

## SHORTRIBS CASSEROLE

Preheat oven to 400°F.
Cut into 6 portions
  **3 pounds beef shortribs**
Season with
  **2 teaspoons salt
  ¼ teaspoon pepper**
Arrange meat in a 2-quart casserole (with
lid). Bake uncovered in preheated 400°
oven for 1 hour or until meat is browned.
Reduce oven temperature to 375°.
Stir into meat
  **2 potatoes, peeled and quartered
  1 onion, thinly sliced
  ½ cup chopped celery
  1 (14-ounce) can tomato sauce
  1 (7½-ounce) can tomato paste
  1 cup water
  2 tablespoons horseradish
  1 tablespoon dried parsley flakes**
Cover and bake in preheated 375° oven
for 2½ hours or until meat is tender.
Makes 6 to 8 servings.

## SAUSAGE CASSEROLE

Preheat oven to 400°F.
In a saucepan, bring to boil
**5 cups water**
Stir in
**1 (12-ounce) package dried
split peas
½ teaspoon salt**
Bring to boil, reduce heat and simmer for
30 minutes or until peas are tender. Drain
reserving ½ cup of liquid.
In a frypan, crumble and cook until
evenly browned
**1 pound pork sausage meat**
Combine with cooked split peas and ½
cup of reserved liquid.
Mix in
**2 tablespoons finely
chopped onion
½ teaspoon salt
½ teaspoon Worcestershire sauce
¼ teaspoon pepper**
Turn into a 1½-quart casserole.
Sprinkle top with
**1 cup grated cheddar cheese**
Bake in preheated 400° oven for 30 minutes or until cheese is golden brown.
Makes 6 servings.

---

*To serve your barbecued roast with fin-
esse use the sharpest carving knife available.*

---

## WINTER WARMER

Preheat oven to 350°F.
Mix together
**2 (14-ounce) cans pork and
beans in tomato sauce
1 pound wieners, cut in
1-inch pieces
1 (10-ounce) can condensed
tomato soup
1 teaspoon prepared mustard
1 tablespoon Worcestershire sauce**
Turn into a 2-quart casserole and bake
in preheated 350° oven for 15 minutes
or until thoroughly heated.
Remove from oven and garnish with
**5 unpeeled apple rings**
Sprinkle with
**¼ cup lightly packed brown sugar
Pinch of nutmeg**
Bake an additional 5 minutes or until
apples are tender.
Makes 6 to 8 servings.

## CANCAN CASSEROLE

Preheat oven to 325°F.
Mix together
**1 (5-ounce) can chow mein
noodles
1 (10-ounce) can condensed
cream of mushroom soup
1 (10-ounce) can mushroom
pieces, undrained
1 (10-ounce) can mandarin
oranges, drained
2 (7-ounce) cans tuna, drained
½ cup chopped onion
½ cup chopped celery**
Garnish with cashew nuts or peanuts.
Turn into a 1½-quart casserole.
Bake in preheated 325° oven for 30 minutes or until thoroughly heated.
Makes 6 servings.

## TAMALE DELIGHT

Preheat oven to 350°F.
Grease a 1½-quart baking dish.
In a saucepan, cook until lightly browned
**¼ pound sausage meat
1 pound ground beef**
During cooking mash with a fork to
crumble.
Add
**1 cup finely chopped onion
½ cup finely chopped celery
⅓ cup finely chopped
green pepper**
Cook until onion is transparent.
Stir in
**1 (19-ounce) can tomatoes
1 (12-ounce) can whole kernel
corn, drained
2 teaspoons chili powder
1 teaspoon salt
¼ teaspoon pepper**
Bring to boil, cover, reduce heat, and
simmer for 5 minutes or until piping hot.
Gradually, blend in a mixture of
**½ cup PURITY Cornmeal
1 cup water**
Cook, stirring constantly until thickened.
Mix in
**1 cup sliced olives**
Turn into prepared casserole.
Sprinkle top with
**¾ cup grated cheddar cheese**
Bake in preheated 350° oven for 30 to
35 minutes or until piping hot and cheese
is golden.
Makes 6 servings.

# CASSOULET

In a large saucepan, bring to boil
**2 quarts water**
Add and boil for 2 minutes
**1 (16-ounce) package dried
white pea beans**
Remove from heat and let stand for 1 hour.
Then, add
**2 cups thinly sliced onion
2 cloves garlic, finely
chopped
1 tablespoon salt
1 tablespoon dried parsley
flakes
4 cloves**
Bring to boil, cover, reduce heat, and simmer for 1½ hours. Drain and remove cloves.
Meanwhile, in a large saucepan cook until crisp
**½ pound sliced side bacon,
cut in 1-inch pieces**
Remove bacon and set aside. Discard all but 2 tablespoons bacon fat in saucepan.
Add and cook until browned on all but one side
**2 pounds pork, cut in
1-inch cubes**
Add
**2 cups sliced onion
2 cloves garlic, finely
chopped**
Cook until onion is transparent and meat evenly browned.
Then, stir in
**2 (10-ounce) cans undiluted
consommé
1 (14-ounce) can tomato
sauce
3 bay leaves
1 tablespoon salt
1 teaspoon thyme**
Bring to boil, cover, reduce heat and simmer for 1½ hours or until meat is tender. Remove bay leaves.
Preheat oven to 350°F.
Mix together meat mixture, bacon, and drained beans. Stir in
**½ cup dry white wine or beef
broth or undiluted consommé**
Turn into a 3-quart casserole.
Bake in preheated 350° oven for 45 minutes or until piping hot.
Makes 8 servings.

# ENCHILADAS

**Tortillas:**
In a small bowl, combine
**1 cup PURITY Flour
½ cup PURITY Cornmeal
¼ teaspoon salt
1 egg
1½ cups cold water**
Beat smooth with rotary beater or electric mixer. Spoon 3 tablespoons of batter at a time onto a medium hot ungreased frypan to make a very thin 6-inch pancake. Turn when edges look dry but not browned. Cook other side. Repeat until all batter is used. Set aside while preparing filling.

**Filling:**
In a saucepan, combine
**½ pound ground pork
1 clove garlic, finely chopped
½ teaspoon salt
1 cup buttermilk**
Bring to boil, cover, reduce heat and simmer for 30 minutes.
Drain reserving liquid and combine meat with
**¼ cup finely chopped onion
Pinch of salt
Pinch of cumin seed
Pinch of marjoram**
Chop and stir in
**¼ pound chorizo (Spanish hot
sausage) or pepperoni,
or Italian salami**
Heat thoroughly.

**Sauce:**
In a saucepan, combine reserved liquid with
**1 cup canned tomatoes
2 dry red chillies, crushed
¼ teaspoon salt
1 bay leaf**
Bring to boil, reduce heat and simmer uncovered for 10 minutes, then remove bay leaf.
To serve stuff Tortillas with meat filling rolling into cylinders. Cook in butter until browned, cover with sauce and heat thoroughly.
Makes 12 enchiladas.

## RAVIOLI

**Sauce:**

In a saucepan, heat thoroughly
   ¼ cup vegetable oil
Add and cook until onion is transparent
   1 cup finely chopped onion
   1 clove garlic, finely chopped
Stir in
   1 (28-ounce) can tomatoes
   1 (5½-ounce) can tomato
      paste
   1½ cups water
   1 tablespoon salt
   1 tablespoon dried parsley
      flakes
   2 teaspoons sugar
   1 teaspoon oregano
   ½ teaspoon basil
   ¼ teaspoon pepper
Bring to boil, cover, reduce heat and
simmer for 30 minutes or until flavour
is well blended.

**Filling:**

Meanwhile, mix together
   1 pound cottage cheese
   1 (8-ounce) package Mozzarella
      cheese, grated
   ¼ cup grated Parmesan cheese
   1 egg
   1 tablespoon dried parsley
      flakes
   ½ teaspoon salt
      Pinch of pepper

**Noodles:**

In a bowl beat together
   3 cups PURITY Flour
   4 eggs
   ¼ cup water
Turn onto a floured surface. Knead for
10 minutes or until dough is elastic. Divide into four portions. Roll out one
quarter into a 17 × 13-inch rectangle.
Cover with plastic wrap and put aside.
Repeat with second quarter of dough.
Drop filling by teaspoonfuls in 24 evenly
spaced mounds onto this rectangle.
Cover with first rectangle. Trim edges and
run pastry wheel between mounds of
filling to give 24 ravioli. Seal edges with
a fork. Let stand for 15 minutes or until
dry. Repeat with remaining dough and
filling.

Cook in salted boiling water for 15 minutes. To serve, turn ravioli into a large
heated serving dish. Top with prepared
sauce. Sprinkle with grated Parmesan
cheese.
Makes 8 to 10 servings.

---

*Noodles do not increase in size when
cooked; spaghetti increases about one
and one half times its original size; macaroni doubles in volume when cooked.*

---

## ITALIAN MANICOTTI
## OR LASAGNA

Manicotti is a large, hollow cylindrical
pasta but if unavailable in your area use
Lasagna and sandwich cooked Lasagna
strips together with alternate layers of
cheese filling and sauce.
Preheat oven to 350°F.
In a saucepan, heat thoroughly
   2 tablespoons vegetable oil
Add and cook until it begins to brown
   ½ pound ground beef
Stir in and cook until onion is transparent
and meat is evenly browned
   ½ cup finely chopped onion
   ¼ cup finely chopped green
      pepper
Drain off fat.
Blend in
   1 (14-ounce) can tomato sauce
   1 cup water
   1 tablespoon granulated sugar
   1 teaspoon salt
   1½ teaspoons Italian seasoning
   ¼ teaspoon pepper
Bring to boil, cover, reduce heat and
simmer for 15 minutes or until meat is
tender.
Meanwhile, mix together
   2 cups ricotta or cottage cheese
   1 cup grated Mozzarella cheese
Fill with cheese mixture
   8 cooked manicotti shells
Arrange filled shells into a 10 × 6 ×
2-inch baking dish. Cover with prepared
sauce.
Bake in preheated 350° oven for 20 to
25 minutes or until thoroughly heated.
Makes 4 servings.

## PIZZA

For step-by-step bread making directions see pages 172 to 178.
Dissolve
**1 teaspoon sugar**
in
**½ cup lukewarm water (100°F.)**
Over this, sprinkle
**1 envelope active dry yeast**
Let stand for 10 minutes. Then stir briskly with a fork.
In a large bowl combine softened yeast mixture together with
**¼ cup vegetable oil**
**½ cup lukewarm water**
**1 teaspoon salt**
**1¼ cups PURITY Flour**
Beat vigorously by hand or with electric mixer.

Then gradually beat in with a spoon an additional
**1 to 1¼ cups PURITY Flour**
Work in last of flour with a rotating motion of the hand. Turn dough onto a floured surface and knead 8 to 10 minutes. Shape into a smooth ball and place in a greased bowl, rotating dough to grease surface. Cover with a damp cloth and let rise until doubled (about ¾ hour). Keep in a warm place.
Meanwhile, mix together
**1 (5½-ounce) can tomato paste**
**½ cup water**
**1 teaspoon salt**
**1 teaspoon oregano**
**Pinch of pepper**
Punch dough and divide in half. Form each half into a ball and place on greased baking sheets. Press out with palms of hands into circles about 12 inches in diameter, making edges slightly thicker.
On each circle of dough arrange
**¼ pound thin Mozzarella cheese slices**
**¼ pound cooked Italian sausages (pepperoni and salami)**
**½ cup sliced mushrooms, canned or fried**
**2 tablespoons chopped green pepper**
**2 tablespoons sliced stuffed green olives**
Spread each round with half of the tomato mixture and sprinkle with
**2 tablespoons vegetable oil**

**2 tablespoons grated Parmesan or old cheddar cheese**
Bake in preheated 400° oven for 25 to 30 minutes or until pastry is golden brown.
Makes 2 (12-inch) pizzas.

## CLAM SPAGHETTI

In a saucepan, heat thoroughly
**2 tablespoons vegetable oil**
Add and cook until transparent
**1 clove garlic, finely chopped**
Stir in
**2 (5-ounce) cans baby clams, undrained**
**1 tablespoon dried onion flakes**
**1 teaspoon dried parsley flakes**
**½ teaspoon salt**
**Pinch of pepper**
Bring to boil.
Add and heat thoroughly
**6 cups cooked spaghetti**
Serve with jellied salad.
Makes 6 servings.

## JAMBALAYA

Preheat oven to 350°F.
Grease a 1½-quart casserole (with lid).
In a frypan cook until bacon is crisp
**4 slices side bacon, cut in 1-inch pieces**
**½ cup chopped onion**
**½ cup chopped green pepper**
Drain well.
In prepared casserole stir until dissolved
**3 cups boiling water**
**3 chicken bouillon cubes**
Blend in
**½ cup catsup**
**2 tablespoons brown sugar**
**½ teaspoon salt**
**1⅓ cups precooked rice**
Stir in bacon mixture with
**3 (4¼-ounce) cans shrimp, drained**
**OR**
**2 cups cubed cooked ham**
Cover casserole and bake in preheated 350° oven, stirring occasionally, for 25 to 30 minutes or until rice is tender.
Makes 6 to 8 servings.

## MARTHA'S CASSEROLE

Preheat oven to 350°F.
Grease a 2-quart casserole.
Cook according to package directions and arrange in prepared casserole
**8 ounces noodles**
Meanwhile, in a large saucepan, heat until foamy
**3 tablespoons butter or margarine**
Add and cook until onion is transparent
**1 cup sliced onion**
**½ cup chopped green pepper**
Stir in and cook until evenly browned
**1 pound ground beef**
**½ pound ground pork**
Drain well.
Blend in
**1 (10-ounce) can mushrooms, undrained**
**1 (10-ounce) can condensed tomato soup**
**1 (4-ounce) package cream cheese**
**1 tablespoon Worcestershire sauce**
**½ teaspoon salt**
**¼ teaspoon pepper**
Heat thoroughly, but do not boil.
Pour over noodles in prepared casserole.
Sprinkle with
**1 cup crushed cornflakes**
Bake in preheated 350° oven for 30 minutes or until thoroughly heated.
Makes 8 to 10 servings.

## SALMON CASSEROLE

Preheat oven to 350°F.
Grease a 1½-quart casserole.
Cook according to package directions and turn into prepared casserole
**8 ounces noodles**
Combine with
**1 (7¾-ounce) can salmon, flaked**
Meanwhile, in a saucepan, combine
**1 (10-ounce) can condensed cream of mushroom soup**
**½ cup milk**
**1 cup (¼-pound) grated processed cheese**
Heat, stirring constantly, until cheese is melted and sauce is smooth. Do not boil.
Pour into casserole.
Around the top, arrange a border of
**½ cup chow mein noodles**
Bake in preheated 350° oven for 20 minutes or until thoroughly heated.
Makes 6 servings.

## CHICKEN TETRAZZINI

Preheat oven to 350°F.
Grease a 1½-quart casserole.
Cook according to package directions and turn into prepared casserole
**8 ounces noodles or spaghetti**
In a frypan, melt
**3 tablespoons butter or margarine**
Blend in
**¼ cup PURITY Flour**
**½ teaspoon salt**
**Pinch of paprika**
**Pinch of pepper**
Gradually, stir in
**2 cups milk**
Cook, stirring constantly, until thickened.
Stir in
**1 (10-ounce) can mushrooms, drained**
**1 cup cubed cooked chicken**
**2 tablespoons chopped pimiento**
Pour over noodles in prepared casserole.
Sprinkle with
**⅓ cup grated cheddar cheese**
Bake in preheated 350° oven for 25 to 30 minutes, or until thoroughly heated.
Makes 4 servings.

---

*To cook regular rice use a large amount of boiling salted water. Cook, uncovered, keeping the water boiling briskly. Do not stir. Cook until tender, about 25 minutes, then drain and rinse in cold water. Regular rice at least triples in volume during cooking.*

---

## OYSTER SCALLOP

Preheat oven to 350°F.
Grease a 1½-quart casserole.
In prepared casserole, arrange in alternate layers
**½ pint shelled oysters**
**1¼ cups coarse cracker crumbs**
Combine and pour over oysters
**½ cup butter, melted**
**¼ cup milk**
**½ teaspoon Worcestershire sauce**
**½ teaspoon salt**
**Pinch of pepper**
Cover with a layer of crumbs.
Bake in preheated 350° oven for 25 to 30 minutes, or until thoroughly heated.
Makes 2 to 3 servings.

# Vegetables and Preserving

## VEGETABLES

Most fresh vegetables should be stored in a cool place such as a refrigerator after purchasing and used within two or three days, except for root vegetables which may keep several weeks. Pare vegetables thinly when necessary and avoid soaking, except for vegetables such as broccoli, Brussels sprouts and cauliflower where there might be insects. Soak these in salted water. Vegetables that might be sandy, such as spinach Swiss chard or asparagus should be thoroughly cleansed in cold water.

Cook only enough vegetables for one meal as nutritive value may be lost during storage. In general, cook vegetables in a small amount of water, as quickly as possible and only until crispy tender.

### COOKING METHODS

**Boiling:** Cook vegetables in a deep, heavy saucepan which has a tight fitting lid, using as little water as possible. Add vegetables and salt to boiling water, cover and bring to the boil quickly, reducing heat enough to just keep vegetables boiling. Cook until just tender. Drain, season to taste and serve immediately.

**Pressure Cooking:** This method provides an ideal way of cooking vegetables to help retain colour, flavour and nutritive value. Follow manufacturer's directions carefully.

**Steaming:** This is another excellent method of cooking vegetables. Allow 10-20 minutes more cooking time than for boiling vegetables (see pages 70-72).

**Oven Steaming:** Do this when cooking an oven meal. Cook prepared vegetables in a tightly covered casserole with a small amount of salted water. Allow three times as long as for boiling vegetables.

**Braising:** This is another way to steam vegetables. Allow 2 tablespoons each of butter and water to every 4 cups of shredded or thinly sliced vegetables.

**Baking:** Place prepared vegetables in oven on rack, baking sheet or casserole. Bake along with an oven meal, adjusting cooking time with temperature required for the main dish.

**Frying:** This gives special flavour and crispness to raw or cooked vegetables. Use heavy frying pan and small amount of shortening.

**Canned Vegetables:** Drain liquid from vegetables into saucepan. Boil to reduce liquid to half. Add vegetables, heat gently and season to taste.

**Frozen Vegetables:** For commercially frozen vegetables, carefully follow the directions on the package. See page 96 for cooking home frozen vegetables.

An attractive array of fresh vegetables, jams and pickles surround the featured specialties of Carrot Quiche, Zucchini Broil and Pink n' Pretty Fruit Medley ▶

# VEGETABLE CHART

*Use about 1 inch boiling salted water for mild flavoured vegetables. Use more water for potatoes, strong flavoured vegetables and those which require long cooking times. Cooking times given in the chart are approximate.*

| Vegetable | Amount to Purchase For 4 | Preparation | Boiling Time (Minutes) | Suggestions |
|---|---|---|---|---|
| **Asparagus** | 2 pounds | Cut off tough ends. Wash. Stand in tall saucepan or coffee pot. *Add 2-inch depth of boiling, salted water. Cook covered.* Whole | 15-20 | Drizzle with melted butter. *Sauces:*—Hollandaise, Cheese, Mushroom, Egg. |
| | | Cut in 1-inch pieces | 10-15 | |
| **Beans** Green and Wax | 1 pound | Wash. Snip off ends and remove strings if any. Whole | 20-30 | Sprinkle with slivered toasted almonds, diced pimiento, or grated Parmesan cheese. |
| | | Cut in 1-inch straight or diagonal slices | 10-20 | *Sauces:*—Cream, |
| | | French cut in thin lengthwise strips | 10-20 | Mustard, Mushroom |
| **Beets** | 2 pounds | Cut off tops, and root. Scrub well. *Use boiling, salted water to cover.* Small, whole | 30-60 | Slip off skins under cold water. Leave whole, slice or dice. Reheat with seasonings and butter. |
| | | Large, whole | 1-2 hours | Serve with vinegar or lemon juice. |
| **Broccoli** | 2 pounds | Cut off large leaves and tough ends. Slit thick stems. *Place flat in frypan. Add 1-inch boiling salted water. Cook covered.* | 10-15 | Serve with melted butter, lemon wedges or grated Parmesan cheese. *Sauces:*—Hollandaise, Cheese, Mustard. |
| **Brussels Sprouts** | 1 pound | Remove wilted leaves. Cut off stem end. Wash thoroughly. Whole | 10-25 | Serve with lemon juice, snipped parsley, chives or fresh chopped dill. *Sauce:*—Lemon Butter. |
| **Cabbage** Green and Savoy | | Remove wilted leaves. Wash. | | |
| Wedges | 1¼ pounds | Cut in wedges. Leave enough core to hold shape. | 8-12 | *Sauces:*—Cream, Egg, Mustard, cheese. |
| Shredded | 1 pound | Cut in quarters. Shred with very sharp knife or coarse grater. | 5-10 | |

| Vegetable | Amount to Purchase For 4 | Preparation | Boiling Time (Minutes) | Suggestions |
|---|---|---|---|---|
| Carrots | 1 pound | Scrub, scrape or thinly pare.<br>Small whole<br>Halved or quartered<br>Thin strips or slices | <br><br>20-30<br>15-20<br>10-15 | Sprinkle with snipped parsley, mint or chives.<br>*Sauces:*—Cream, Parsley, Lemon Butter |
| Cauliflower | 1 medium head | Remove outer leaves. Cut off any blemishes. Wash thoroughly. Cut out centre core.<br>Whole<br>Break into flowerets | <br><br><br><br>20-30<br>8-15 | Top with buttered crumbs and grated cheese. Broil.<br>Sprinkle with snipped chives or parsley.<br>*Sauces:*—cheese, Hollandaise. |
| Celery | Allow ⅔ cup diced or sliced raw per serving. | Remove leaves, trim roots. Scrub.<br>Dice or slice diagonally in ½ or 1-inch pieces | <br><br>15-20 | Brown in butter and cook until tender in consommé or bouillon.<br>*Sauces:*—Cream, Parsley, Hollandaise |
| Corn on the Cob | 8 ears | Remove husks, silk and any blemishes just before cooking. *Cook in boiling salted water to cover.* | <br><br><br>5-8 | Wrap in foil and roast or barbecue.<br>Cut fresh corn off cob. Simmer 10 minutes with butter and milk. |
| Onions | 1½ pounds | Cut slices from stem and root ends. Peel and remove loose layers under cold running water. | | Serve whole—boiled, baked, or glazed.<br>*Sauces:*—Cream, Cheese. |
| Yellow<br>Small White | | Whole (2-inch or larger)<br>Whole<br>For slices, cut ¼-½ inch thick. | 30-35<br>20-25<br><br>10 | |
| Spanish *or* Bermuda | | Cut into slices. | | Serve raw or deep fat fried. |
| Parsnips | 1½ pounds | Wash, pare, cut into halves or quarters. Remove woody cores.<br>Halved or quartered<br>Sliced or diced | <br><br><br>20-30<br>8-15 | Mash, pan fry, or cream.<br>Cook with carrots and mash. |
| Peas | 2 pounds | Shell and wash just before cooking. Add 1 teaspoon sugar to water. | 8-20 | Combine with tiny cooked onions, new potatoes, or pan fried mushrooms.<br>*Sauces:*—Cream, Mushroom. |

| Vegetable | Amount to Purchase For 4 | Preparation | Boiling Time (Minutes) | Suggestions |
|---|---|---|---|---|
| **Potatoes** | | | | |
| Sweet *or* Yams | 2 pounds | Scrub well. Remove blemishes. Do not pare. | 30-35 | Boil, bake, mash or candy. |
| White | 2 pounds (1 medium potato = ⅓ pound) | Scrub well, remove blemishes and eyes. Cook in skins, scrape or thinly pare. | | Boil, mash, bake, cream, pan fry, scallop, or deep fat fry. |
| | | Whole | 35-40 | |
| | | Cut in halves or quarters | 20-25 | |
| **Spinach and Greens** | 2 pounds | Discard ends, tough stalks and yellow leaves. Wash in warm water 3-4 times, lifting greens out of water *If greens are young, cook without adding water. Otherwise use ½-inch boiling, salted water.* | | Cut cooked greens before serving. Sprinkle with chopped hard cooked egg, chopped beets, lemon juice or vinegar. |
| | | Spinach | 6-10 | *Sauces:*—French |
| | | Beet tops | 5-15 | Dressing, Cream, Egg |
| | | Swiss Chard | 3-10 | |
| **Summer Squash** Yellow Crookneck | 2 pounds | Scrub well. Cut slices from stem and blossom ends. Do not pare (unless old). Do not remove seeds. Cut into thin slices *Cook in ½-inch boiling, salted water.* | 15-20 | Boil, mash, or use in casseroles *Sauces:*—Tomato, Cheese. |
| **Winter Squash** Pepper | 2 whole | Scrub well. Cut in half lengthwise. Remove seeds and stringy portions. | 25-30 | Bake |
| Hubbard Butternut | 2½ to 3 pounds | Scrub well, cut into pieces. Remove seeds and stringy portions. | 25-30 | Mash or bake |
| **Tomatoes** | 2 pounds | Wash, pare thinly or scald and slip off skins. *Quarter and cook without water.* | 5-15 | Stew, bake, broil or serve in casseroles. |
| **Turnip** Yellow *or* Rutabaga | 2 pounds | Scrub well. Cut into ½-inch slices and pare. Cut into cubes or strips. | 20-30 | Cook with potatoes and onions for flavour and texture. Sprinkle with chopped parsley. |
| White | 2 pounds | Scrub well. Cut into ½-inch slices and pare. Cut into cubes or strips | 15-20 | |

**PURITY FLOUR IS MILLED WITH EXTRA CARE FOR EXTRA GOODNE**

## IRISH APPLES

Bring to a boil in a large saucepan
  **3 cups water**
  **1 tablespoon granulated sugar**
  **1 teaspoon salt**
  **Pinch of pepper**
Add and simmer 15 minutes
  **6 potatoes, peeled and cut**
    **into 1-inch cubes**
Stir in
  **6 apples, peeled, cored and cubed**
Continue cooking until apples and potatoes are tender (about 5 minutes longer).
Meanwhile, fry until crisp
  **8 slices side bacon, diced**
Remove from pan and drain on absorbent paper.
Stir into bacon fat and cook until rings are transparent
  **2 onions, thinly sliced**
Sprinkle with
  **½ teaspoon salt**
Drain potato mixture and toss in heated serving dish with
  **1½ tablespoons butter or margarine**
  **½ teaspoon salt**
Garnish with bacon bits and sautéed onion rings.
Makes 6 to 8 servings.

## STUFFED BAKED POTATOES

Preheat oven to 400°F.
Scrub
  **4 baking potatoes**
Prick with fork. For soft skins rub with shortening.
Bake in preheated 400° oven for 1 hour or until tender.
Cut in half and scoop out cooked potato, reserving skins.
Mix together and stir in
  **1 package sour cream mix**
  **⅓ cup milk**
  **2 tablespoons butter or margarine**
  **¼ teaspoon salt**
Beat until fluffy and spoon into shells.
Bake in preheated 400° oven for 20 minutes or until golden brown.

**CHEESE & CHIVE POTATOES:** Bake potatoes as above, then stuff with a mixture of cooked potato and 1 (4-ounce) package cream cheese and chives, 2 tablespoons milk, 2 tablespoons butter, and a pinch of pepper.
Bake as directed.

## FLUFFY HERBED POTATOES

Preheat oven to 350°F.
Grease a 2-quart casserole.
Prepare according to package directions
  **6 servings (3 cups) instant**
    **mashed potatoes**
Combine and beat with potatoes until smooth
  **1 (8-ounce) container French**
    **onion chip dip**
  **1 cup cream-style cottage cheese**
  **2 egg yolks**
  **1 tablespoon finely chopped**
    **green onion**
  **1 tablespoon dried parsley flakes**
  **Pinch of nutmeg**
  **Pinch of pepper**
Beat to form stiff but moist peaks
  **2 egg whites**
Fold into potato mixture.
Turn into prepared casserole and dot with
  **1 tablespoon butter or margarine**
Bake in preheated 350° oven for 55 to 60 minutes or until set. If desired, broil until top is lightly browned.
Garnish with chopped parsley.
Makes 6 to 8 servings.

---

*For Golden Potato Quickies: combine 1 cup crushed cheese crackers, ½ cup melted butter and pinch of pepper. Coat small whole canned potatoes with crumb mixture and bake in preheated 375°F. oven for 25 to 30 minutes.*

---

## SWEET POTATOES

Preheat oven to 400°F.
Peel
  **4 sweet potatoes**
Cut into ¼-inch vertical slices almost to bottom of potato.
Dot with
  **butter or margarine**
Wrap in aluminium foil.
Bake in preheated 400° oven for 1 hour or until tender.
Unwrap and sprinkle with
  **1 teaspoon brown sugar**
Broil until golden brown.

## TANGY MASHED SWEET POTATOES

Preheat oven to 350°F.
Grease a small casserole dish.
In a small bowl, beat together
**1 (19-ounce) can sweet potatoes, drained**
**2 tablespoons orange marmalade**
**1 tablespoon soft butter or margarine**
**Pinch of pepper**
Turn into prepared casserole.
Bake in preheated 350° oven for 15 to 20 minutes, or until piping hot.
Makes 4 servings.

## CHEESIE-CORN CASSEROLE

Preheat oven to 350°F.
Grease a 2-quart casserole.
Prepare according to package directions
**2 (12-ounce) packages frozen kernel corn**
Core, cut three rings, and chop remainder of
**1 green pepper**
Meanwhile, in a saucepan heat until foamy
**¼ cup butter or margarine**
Stir in chopped green pepper and
**1 small onion, finely chopped**
Cook until onion is transparent.
Remove from pan and set aside.
Blend into remaining fat in pan a mixture of
**¼ cup PURITY Flour**
**½ teaspoon salt**
**¼ teaspoon dry mustard**
**Pinch of pepper**
Gradually, stir in
**1½ cups milk**
Cook, stirring constantly, until thickened.
Remove from heat and stir in drained corn and onion mixture.
Blend in
**1 egg, beaten**
**1½ cups cheese twists (Cheesies) broken into small pieces**
Pour into prepared 2-quart casserole.
Sprinkle over top
**½ cup crushed cheese twists**
Bake in preheated 350° oven for 25 to 30 minutes or until piping hot.
Garnish with reserved pepper rings.
Makes 8 servings.

## SWISS SCALLOP

Preheat oven to 350°F.
Wash, peel and slice
**6 potatoes**
Cover with salted water. Bring to boil and cook for 2 minutes. Drain and rinse with cold water.
Grease a 2-quart casserole (with lid) and rub with
**1 clove garlic, halved**
Mix together
**2 cups (8-ounces) grated Swiss cheese**
**¼ cup PURITY Flour**
Alternate layers of potato slices and cheese mixture in prepared casserole.
Combine and pour over top
**2 cups milk**
**1 tablespoon dried onion flakes**
**1 teaspoon dried pepper flakes, crumbled**
**½ teaspoon salt**
**Pinch of nutmeg**
**Pinch of pepper**
Top with
**¼ cup grated cheddar cheese**
Cover and bake in preheated 350° oven for 30 minutes.
Uncover and bake for an additional 45 to 50 minutes, or until potatoes are tender.
Makes 6 to 8 servings.

## SAVORY HARVARD BEETS

Drain, reserving liquid
**1 (19-ounce) can sliced or diced beets**
In a large saucepan melt
**1 tablespoon butter or margarine**
Blend in
**1 tablespoon PURITY Flour**
Gradually stir in ½ cup reserved beet liquid.
Cook, stirring constantly, until thickened.
Blend in
**2 tablespoons brown sugar**
**1 tablespoon vinegar**
**¼ teaspoon ginger**
**¼ teaspoon salt**
**Pinch of dry mustard**
**Pinch of pepper**
Stir in drained beets and heat thoroughly.
Makes 4 servings.

## CARROT QUICHE

Preheat oven to 425°F.
Prepare PURITY Pastry (See page 154).
Roll out half and line a 9-inch pie plate.
Trim and flute edges. Do not prick.
Prepare and cook in boiling salted water
  **4 cups sliced carrots**
Drain on absorbent paper.
Season with
  **½ teaspoon salt**
  **¼ teaspoon pepper**
  **Pinch of nutmeg**
Beat together
  **4 eggs**
  **¼ cup heavy cream**
Blend in
  **1 cup grated Swiss cheese**
  **½ teaspoon salt**
  **¼ teaspoon nutmeg**
  **Pinch of pepper**
Arrange carrot slices attractively in prepared pie shell and pour egg-cheese
mixture over top.
Bake in preheated 425° oven for 10 minutes or until pastry is golden. Reduce
heat to 350° and continue baking about
30 to 35 minutes or until set around edges
and slightly soft in centre. Let stand 10
minutes before serving.
Makes 6 servings.

*Store eggs either in their carton or cov-*
*ered in the refrigerator as the porous*
*shells permit moisture loss.*

## CHEESE CELERY CASSEROLE

Preheat oven to 350°F.
Grease a 1½-quart casserole.
Cook in boiling water until almost tender
  **4 cups coarsely chopped celery**
Drain and place in prepared casserole.
Combine and pour over celery
  **1 (10-ounce) can condensed**
    **cream of celery soup**
  **1 green pepper, finely**
    **chopped**
  **¾ cup grated cheddar cheese**
  **Pinch of pepper**
Mix together and sprinkle over top
  **½ cup crushed cheese crackers**
  **2 tablespoons butter or margarine,**
    **melted**
Bake in preheated 350° oven for 15 to
20 minutes or until piping hot.
Makes 8 servings.

## ARTICHOKE-MUSHROOM BAKE

Preheat oven to 325°F.
Grease a 1½-quart casserole.
Cover bottom of casserole with
  **1 (10-ounce) can sliced**
    **mushrooms, drained**
Arrange on top
  **1 (14-ounce) can artichoke**
    **hearts, drained**
Beat together and pour over vegetables
  **1 cup milk**
  **2 eggs**
  **½ teaspoon salt**
  **Pinch of pepper**
Bake in preheated 325° oven for 40 to
45 minutes, or until custard is set around
edges and slightly soft in centre. Let
stand 10 minutes before serving.
Makes 4 to 6 servings.

*Use vegetable cooking liquid when mak-*
*ing gravies, soups, and sauces for flavour*
*and nourishment. The liquid contains*
*some vitamins and minerals present in*
*the vegetables.*

## HAWAIIAN ONIONS

Preheat oven to 400°F.
Grease a 12 × 8 × 2-inch baking dish.
Cook in boiling salted water until tender
  **4 large onions, peeled**
Meanwhile, combine
  **1 (15-ounce) can corned beef hash**
  **1 tablespoon brown sugar**
  **¾ teaspoon salt**
  **½ teaspoon dry mustard**
  **½ teaspoon Worcestershire sauce**
  **¼ teaspoon pepper**
Then, slice top of each cooked onion.
Remove centre and chop sufficient to
give ½ cup.
Stir into meat mixture and fill onions.
Arrange in prepared baking dish
  **4 pineapple slices**
Top with stuffed onion and garnish with
  **½ pineapple slice**
Brush with
  **2 tablespoons butter, melted**
Bake in preheated 400° oven for 40 minutes or until onions are golden. Baste
once or twice with pan juices during
cooking.
Serve with cold meats, ham or beef.
Makes 4 servings.

## BARBECUED LIMAS

Following package directions cook until almost tender
**2 (10-ounce) packages frozen lima beans**
Meanwhile, in a large saucepan heat until foamy
**1 tablespoon butter or margarine**
Add and cook until tender
**4 green onions, finely chopped**
Blend in and bring to boil
**1 (10-ounce) can condensed cream of tomato soup**
**\*2 tablespoons barbecue sauce**
**¼ teaspoon celery salt**
**Pinch of pepper**
Stir in drained lima beans.
Cover and simmer for 5 minutes or until heated thoroughly.
Makes 8 servings.
\* Use bottled barbecue sauce or Tomato Barbecue Sauce (See page 212).

## HONEY'D ONIONS

Peel
**2 pounds cooking onions**
In a saucepan, combine
**2 tablespoons honey**
**2 tablespoons butter or margarine**
**2 tablespoons granulated sugar**
**¼ cup lemon juice**
**1 teaspoon Worcestershire sauce**
**1 teaspoon cider vinegar**
**Pinch of salt**
**Pinch of pepper**
Bring just to boil, add onions, and return to boiling point.
Cover, reduce heat and simmer, stirring occasionally, about 20 minutes or until onions are tender and golden.
Makes 4 servings.

## TURNIP-APPLE BAKE

Preheat oven to 350°F.
Grease a 2-quart casserole.
Peel, dice and cook in boiling water for 10 minutes, or until tender
**1 large turnip (5 cups diced)**
Drain and toss with
**1 tablespoon butter or margarine**
**½ teaspoon salt**
**Pinch of pepper**

Combine
**1 (19-ounce) can apple pie filling**
**¼ cup lightly packed brown sugar**
**Pinch of cinnamon**
Beginning and ending with turnip layer, arrange alternate layers of turnip and apple mixture in prepared casserole.
Mix together and sprinkle over top
**⅓ cup PURITY Flour**
**2 tablespoons brown sugar**
**2 tablespoons soft butter or margarine**
Bake in preheated 350° oven for 45 to 50 minutes or until turnip is soft.
Makes 8 to 10 servings.

## MARBLE SPINACH SOUFFLÉ

Preheat oven to 350°F.
Grease a 7-inch soufflé dish.
In a saucepan, melt
**⅓ cup butter or margarine**
Blend in a mixture of
**⅓ cup PURITY Flour**
**Pinch of garlic salt**
**Pinch of pepper**
Gradually, stir in
**1¼ cups milk**
Cook, stirring constantly, until thickened.
Beat
**6 egg yolks**
Gradually blend in flour mixture.
In a large bowl, beat to form stiff but moist peaks
**6 egg whites**
**½ teaspoon salt**
**¼ teaspoon cream of tartar**
Fold in egg yolk mixture.
Divide in half and into one half fold
**1 cup chopped fresh spinach**
**1½ teaspoons chopped parsley**
Into the other half fold in a mixture of
**½ cup grated cheddar cheese**
**¼ teaspoon dry mustard**
Alternately spoon mixtures into prepared soufflé dish. If desired, sprinkle with grated Parmesan cheese.
Bake in preheated 350° oven for 55 to 65 minutes or until puffed and set.
Serve hot with cold roast beef, ham or turkey.
Makes 8 servings.

*For flavour and food value, leave jackets on potatoes during cooking.*

## ZUCCHINI & TOMATOES

Scrub, cut in 1-inch slices, and then quarter
**4 zucchini**
Slice and separate into rings
**2 onions**
In a saucepan, heat until foamy
**2 tablespoons butter or margarine**
Stir in zucchini and onions.
Cover and cook over low heat, stirring occasionally, until tender (about 5 minutes).
Add and heat thoroughly
**1 (19-ounce) can tomatoes**
**1 teaspoon salt**
**Pinch of garlic salt**
**Pinch of oregano**
**Pinch of pepper**
Makes 8 servings.

## ZUCCHINI BROIL

In a saucepan, stir until dissolved
**1 cup boiling water**
**1 chicken bouillon cube**
**½ teaspoon salt**
**Pinch of pepper**

Scrub, cut in ½-inch slices and add
**4 zucchini**
Bring to boil, cover, reduce heat and simmer for 5 minutes or until almost tender.
Drain, and arrange slices in a shallow baking dish.
Sprinkle with
**1 cup grated cheddar cheese**
**Pinch of paprika**
Broil until cheese melts.
Serve immediately.
Makes 4 to 6 servings.

---

*For Crispy Fantail Potatoes: slice partially cooked potatoes almost to opposite side, brush with melted butter and bake in preheated 425° F. oven until golden brown and crispy, about 1 hour. Brush occasionally with butter.*

*For Blushing Potatoes: parboil and pat dry 6 potatoes. Brush with a mixture of ¼ cup vegetable oil and ¼ cup catsup and bake in preheated 350°F. oven for 50 to 60 minutes.*

---

## BACON SQUASH GEMS

Preheat oven to 350°F.
Prepare according to package directions
**1 (2-pound) package frozen diced squash**
Or use
**3½ cups mashed cooked squash**
If necessary, drain and then beat in
**2 tablespoons butter or margarine**
**1 tablespoon dried onion flakes**
**1 teaspoon salt**
**Pinch of pepper**
Stir in
**6 slices cooked side bacon, crumbled**
When cool enough to handle, shape into 1-inch balls and roll in
**¾ cup cornflake crumbs**
Bake in preheated 350° oven for 20 to 25 minutes, or until piping hot.
Makes 6 to 8 servings.

To freeze. Prepare gems but do not bake. Freeze on baking sheet and then remove and store in plastic bag. Bake frozen gems in preheated 350° oven about 30 to 35 minutes.

## VEGETABLE MERRY-GO-ROUND

In a saucepan, combine and stir until dissolved
**1 cup boiling water**
**1 chicken bouillon cube**
Add, bring to boil and cook until almost tender
**1 (10-ounce) package frozen Brussels sprouts**
Meanwhile, in a large frypan, heat until foamy
**3 tablespoons butter or margarine**
Stir in, and heat thoroughly
**1 (19-ounce) can baby whole carrots, drained**
**1 (19-ounce) can whole potatoes drained and halved**
Combine in a warmed serving dish with drained Brussels sprouts and season with
**½ teaspoon salt**
**Pinch of pepper**
**Pinch of caraway seeds**
Makes 6 to 8 servings.

---

# SALADS

## SNOWY GREEN BEAN SALAD

Prepare according to package directions
**2 (10-ounce) packages frozen green beans**
Drain and chill.
Blend together
**1½ cups thick dairy sour cream**
**4 slices cooked side bacon, crumbled**
**1 tablespoon chopped pimiento**
**1 tablespoon dried onion flakes**
**1 tablespoon dry onion soup mix**
**Pinch of pepper**
Combine with green beans. Cover and chill.
Makes 6 to 8 servings.

## FRESH SPINACH SALAD

Thoroughly wash and trim
**1 (12-ounce) package spinach**
Break in pieces.
Chop and mix with spinach
**2 hard cooked eggs**
Combine and put in a jar with tight-fitting lid and shake
**6 tablespoons vegetable oil**
**2 tablespoons wine vinegar**
**1 clove garlic, finely chopped**
**½ teaspoon salt**
**¼ teaspoon pepper**
**Pinch of dry mustard**
When ready to serve, pour dressing over spinach, tossing to coat well.
Makes 6 servings.

## UNTRADITIONAL POTATO SALAD

Cook in boiling salted water until tender
**6 potatoes, peeled and cubed**
Drain and rinse with cold water.
Blend together
**1½ cups thick dairy sour cream**
**¼ cup chopped red pepper**
**¼ cup chopped green pepper**
**2 tablespoons chopped black olives**
**1 teaspoon salt**
**¼ teaspoon paprika**
**Pinch of pepper**
Combine with potatoes and toss gently to evenly coat potatoes. Cover and chill at least 2 hours.
Makes 6 to 8 servings.

## PICNIC POTATO SALAD

In a small bowl, combine
**1½ cups mayonnaise**
**3 tablespoons sweet pickle juice**
**1 tablespoon prepared mustard**
**2 teaspoons salt**
**Pinch of pepper**
Set aside.
In a large bowl, combine
**8 cups cubed cooked potatoes**
**1½ cups thinly sliced celery**
**½ cup chopped green onion**
**¼ cup thinly sliced radishes**
**¼ cup chopped gherkins**
**4 hard cooked eggs, chopped**
Pour dressing over vegetables and toss gently. Season to taste. Chill at least 3 hours.
Makes 10 to 12 servings.

## TRADITIONAL COLESLAW

Combine
**4 cups shredded cabbage**
**½ cup thinly sliced celery**
**½ cup Coleslaw Dressing**

**(See page 82)**
Toss lightly and chill.
Makes 4 servings.

## GOURMET CHICKEN SALAD

In a bowl combine
**3 cups cubed cooked chicken**
**3 cups thinly sliced celery**
**3 tablespoons lemon juice**
Cover and chill at least one hour.
Stir in
**1 cup seedless grapes**
or
**⅔ cup halved seeded grapes**
**1 cup toasted slivered almonds**
Blend together
**1 cup mayonnaise**
**¼ cup table cream (18%)**
**1½ teaspoons salt**
**1 teaspoon dry mustard**
**Pinch of pepper**
Pour over salad ingredients and toss lightly. Serve in lettuce-lined salad bowl and garnish with additional grapes and almonds.
Makes about 6 cups.

PURE, WHITE PURITY FLOUR—THE PERFECTLY PRE-SIFTED FLOUR

# CAESAR SALAD

Wash
**2 heads romaine lettuce**
Dry on absorbent paper.
In a frypan, cook until crisp
**½ pound side bacon, diced**
Remove and set aside.
Fry in bacon fat until golden
**1 cup small bread croutons**
In bottom of large wooden bowl, combine
**6 tablespoons vegetable oil**
**2 tablespoons vinegar**
**1 tablespoon olive oil**
**1 tablespoon lemon juice**
**1 teaspoon salt**
Season with a pinch of each of
**sugar**
**pepper**
**dry mustard**
**tarragon**
Add
**Dash of Tabasco sauce**
**Dash of Worcestershire sauce**
**1 teaspoon finely chopped parsley**
**1 teaspoon finely chopped garlic**
**1 raw egg**
Stir with a wooden spoon until blended. Break lettuce into small pieces and arrange over dressing.
Sprinkle with
**¾ cup freshly grated Parmesan cheese**
Add bacon and croutons and sprinkle with
**½ cup chopped fresh parsley**
Do not mix. Cover and refrigerate until serving time.
At serving time arrange around edge of bowl
**3 hard cooked eggs, quartered**
Toss just before serving.
Makes 8 to 10 servings.

# FUNDY SEAFOOD SALAD

In a small frypan, heat until foamy
**3 tablespoons butter**
Blend in
**2 teaspoons lemon juice**
**1 clove garlic, finely chopped**
Stir in
**1 cup bread croutons**
Cook until golden brown and butter is absorbed.

In a large wooden bowl break into small pieces
**1 large head lettuce**
Arrange over lettuce
**1 (4¼-ounce) can shrimp, drained**
**1 (10 ounce) package frozen lobster tails, cooked, shelled, and sliced**
**1 (2¾-ounce) can crabmeat**
Sprinkle over top
**4 ounces blue cheese, crumbled**
Add the croutons.
Cover and chill.
Just before serving toss with Basil Parmesan Dressing (See page 82).

# GINGERED CITRUS SALAD

Peel, section and remove seeds from
**1 grapefruit**
**3 oranges**
Let stand in sieve or colander to drain well.
In a saucepan, combine
**1 cup orange juice**
**½ cup water**
**1 tablespoon finely chopped crystallized ginger**
Bring just to boiling point and then stir in
**2 (3-ounce) packages lime-flavoured jelly powder**
**1 (3-ounce) package lemon-flavoured jelly powder**
Stir until dissolved.
Blend in
**2 cups gingerale**
When foam subsides, measure 1¼ cups and transfer to small bowl.
Add
**Pinch of ginger**
**Pinch of nutmeg**
Chill until the consistency of unbeaten egg white.
Whip until doubled in volume and fold in
**⅓ cup coarsely chopped pecans**
Pour into 1½ quart mould and refrigerate. Chill remaining jelly mixture until consistency of unbeaten egg white. Fold in well drained fruit. Spoon over almost set whipped mixture. Chill until firm.
Unmould and serve on lettuce garnished with crystallized ginger.
Makes 8 servings.

## RUSSIAN SALAD

Cook separately in boiling salted water until just tender
**1 cup frozen baby lima beans**
**1 cup frozen cut green beans**
**1 cup frozen green peas**
**1½ cups sliced fresh carrots**
**1 small cauliflower, broken into flowerets**
Drain and chill immediately.
Gently combine vegetables in a glass or crockery bowl.
Pour over
**1 cup French dressing**
Cover with plastic wrap and refrigerate overnight. Three hours before serving, drain vegetables and add
**1 cup thinly sliced celery**
**¼ cup finely chopped onion**
**2 tablespoons chopped fresh parsley**
Blend together
**2 cups mayonnaise**
**1 teaspoon prepared mustard**
**1 teaspoon curry powder**
**1 teaspoon salt**
**½ teaspoon chervil**
Combine with vegetables and toss.
To serve, place mound of salad on lettuce-lined serving platter and garnish as desired with devilled egg halves, cooked shrimp, halved cherry tomatoes, sardines or cucumber fingers.
Makes 8 to 10 servings.

## PINK N' PRETTY
## FRUIT MEDLEY

Lightly oil a 4-cup mould.
Dissolve
**1 (3-ounce) package raspberry flavoured jelly powder**
in
**¾ cup boiling water**
Stir in
**⅓ cup cold water**
Chill until partially set.
Then fold in
**¾ cup plain yoghurt**
**½ cup blueberries**
**½ cup cantaloupe balls or sliced peaches**
**½ cup chopped apple**

**½ cup canned pineapple cubes**
**½ cup fresh raspberries**
Pour into prepared 4-cup mould and chill until firm.
Unmould on lettuce greens to serve as luncheon salad, or use as a dessert.
Makes 6 servings.

## SALMON MOUSSE IN ASPIC

Thoroughly chill a fish mould.

**Aspic**
In a large saucepan, combine
**3 cups undiluted consommé**
**2 cups water**
**2 tablespoons tomato paste**
**2 tablespoons dry sherry**
Heat to a full rolling boil.
Meanwhile, beat to from stiff but moist peaks
**3 egg whites**
Stir into hot consommé mixture and allow to cool. Strain through damp cloth. (Egg whites make aspic sparkling clear.)

**Salmon Mousse**
In a saucepan, combine
**⅓ cup PURITY Flour**
**1 envelope gelatine**
**¼ teaspoon salt**
**Pinch of cayenne**
Gradually blend in
**1½ cups milk**
Cook, stirring constantly, until thickened. Pour into a pie plate, cover with plastic wrap and chill.
Then cream until light and fluffy
**¾ cup butter**
Gradually beat in chilled sauce.
Mash finely and gradually beat into whipped mixture.
**2 (16-ounce) cans salmon**
Season with
**salt and white pepper**
Pour a little of aspic into chilled fish mould, tilting to coat. Repeat until aspic layer is about ½ inch thick. Insert half a stuffed olive for eye, and then strips of green pepper for fins. Chill until firm.
Fill with salmon mousse leaving ¼-inch space around edge. Fill space with aspic. Chill until firm.
Unmould and pipe rosettes of remaining salmon mousse to garnish.
Makes 8 to 10 servings.

## FROSTY FRUIT FINALE

Lightly oil a 9 X 5 X 3-inch loaf pan.
Drain, reserving liquid
**1 (10-ounce) can pineapple
    tidbits**
Combine ½ cup reserved liquid with
**2 tablespoons lemon juice**
Sprinkle over liquid
**1 envelope gelatine**
Set in pan of boiling water and stir to
dissolve gelatine. Cool.
Meanwhile, in a large bowl, cream together
**1 (4-ounce) package cream cheese
¼ cup thick dairy sour cream**
Fold in gelatine mixture and drained
pineapple with
**1 cup seedless grapes or mandarin
    orange sections
¾ cup maraschino cherries, halved**
Chill until the consistency of unbeaten
egg white (about 30 to 45 minutes).
Gently fold in
**1 cup heavy cream, whipped**
Turn into prepared loaf pan, and cover
with plastic wrap and freeze until firm
(about 4 hours).
Serve in slices on salad greens and garnish with fruit or sprigs of mint.
Makes 6 to 8 servings.

## SEAFOOD SOUFFLÉ SALAD

Soften
**2 envelopes gelatine**
in
**½ cup cold water**
Dissolve gelatine over boiling water.
Blend into
**2 cups Thousand Island Dressing**
    (See page 82)
Stir in
**¼ cup chili sauce**
Fold in

**½ cup heavy cream, whipped
1 (7¾-ounce) can crabmeat,
    flaked
1 cup cooked cubed lobster**
Turn into 1½-quart mould. Chill until
firm. Unmould on salad greens. Garnish
with lemon.
Makes 6 to 8 servings.

## CROWNED MELON

Lightly oil a 6-cup mould.
Soften
**2 envelopes gelatine**
in
**½ cup cold water**
Add and stir until dissolved
**¾ cup boiling water**
Stir in
**1 (6-ounce) can frozen pink
    lemonade, concentrate**
Slowly add
**1¾ cups gingerale**
Stir until foam subsides and then divide
evenly in two.
To first half stir in
**2 tablespoons maraschino
    cherry juice**
Chill until the consistency of unbeaten
egg white and then fold in
**2 cups honeydew melon balls
2 tablespoons sliced maraschino
    cherries**
Turn into prepared 6-cup mould and
chill.
Leave the second half at room temperature, until the first layer is partially set.
Then chill the second half until the consistency of unbeaten egg white.
Whip slightly and fold in a mixture of
**⅓ cup thick dairy sour cream
¼ cup mayonnaise**
Slowly pour the mixture over set fruit
layer. Chill at least four hours.
Unmould and serve on crisp salad greens.
Makes 8 servings.

# SALAD DRESSINGS

## BLUE CHEESE DRESSING

In a small bowl, mash with a fork
**4 ounces blue cheese**
Stir in until smooth
**¾ cup mayonnaise**
Blend in

**1 tablespoon wine vinegar
1 green onion, finely chopped
½ teaspoon salt
Pinch of pepper**
Cover and chill. Mix well before serving.
Makes 1¼ cups.

## MAYONNAISE

In small mixer bowl, combine
**2 egg yolks**
**1 teaspoon dry mustard**
**1 teaspoon sugar**
**1 teaspoon salt**
**Dash of cayenne**
Using electric mixer, beat in, drop by drop
**¼ cup vegetable oil**
Beat in
**1 tablespoon vinegar**
Then very gradually beat in
**1 cup vegetable oil**
When thick, alternate oil additions with few drops of
**1 tablespoon lemon juice**
Store and chill in tightly covered jar.
Makes 1¾ cups.

CHIVE DRESSING: Prepare Mayonnaise following basic recipe and blend 1 cup with ½ cup heavy cream, whipped, ½ cup chopped chives, 1 tablespoon horseradish, and a pinch of pepper.

SOUR CREAM DRESSING: Prepare Mayonnaise following basic recipe and blend in ½ cup thick dairy sour cream, ½ teaspoon seasoned salt, and if desired add 1 teaspoon celery or dill seeds.

THOUSAND ISLAND DRESSING: Prepare Mayonnaise following basic recipe and blend 1 cup with ¼ cup chili sauce, 1 tablespoon vinegar, ¼ cup chopped stuffed olives, 2 tablespoons finely chopped green pepper and 2 tablespoons finely chopped green onion.

FLUFFY LEMON DRESSING: Blend into ½ cup commercial or homemade mayonnaise, ½ cup heavy cream, whipped, 3 tablespoons lemon juice and 3 tablespoons sifted icing sugar.

ROQUEFORT DRESSING: Blend into ½ cup commercial or homemade mayonnaise, ¼ cup French dressing and 2 tablespoons crumbled Roquefort or blue cheese.

*WARNING: Keep potato salad well chilled until serving time. Serious food poisoning can result if potato salad is allowed to stand in a warm place for any length of time.*

## FRENCH DRESSING

In jar with tight fitting cover combine
**1¼ cups vegetable oil**
**½ cup lemon juice**
**2 tablespoons catsup**
**1 clove garlic, finely chopped**
**2 teaspoons salt**
**1 teaspoon pepper**
**½ teaspoon sugar**
**½ teaspoon paprika**
Cover and shake until thoroughly blended. Chill.
Makes 1¾ cups.

## COLESLAW DRESSING

Combine
**1 cup mayonnaise or cooked salad dressing**
**1 teaspoon prepared mustard**
**¼ cup light cream (18%)**
**½ teaspoon salt**
**Pinch of pepper**
Cover and refrigerate.
Makes about 1¼ cups or enough for 8 cups shredded cabbage.

## BASIL PARMESAN DRESSING

Combine in a jar
**½ cup vegetable oil**
**½ cup lemon juice**
**¼ cup grated Parmesan cheese**
**2 teaspoons grated lemon rind**
**¾ teaspoon salt**
**¼ teaspoon basil**
**Pinch of pepper**
Cover and shake until thoroughly blended. Chill.
Makes 1¼ cups.

## GUACAMOLE DRESSING

Combine
**2 ripe avocados, mashed**
**(about 2 cups)**
**2 tablespoons lemon juice**
**1 teaspoon grated lemon rind**
**1 teaspoon dried onion flakes**
Stir in
**½ cup thick dairy sour cream**
**1 teaspoon salt**
**Dash of Tabasco sauce**
Blend until smooth.
Serve with fruit salads, or use as a chip dip.
Makes 2½ cups.

USE PURITY FLOUR, THE JOLLY MILLER FLOUR, FOR HAPPY BAKING

# PRESERVING

## GHERKINS

Wash and scrub 2 to 3-inch cucumbers. Rinse and drain.
Measure
**10 cups cucumbers**
Place in a clean dry crock.
Mix together
**20 cups boiling water**
**1½ cups coarse salt**
Pour over cucumbers and let stand overnight, covered.
Drain cucumbers thoroughly and leave in crock.
Combine
**8 cups blended vinegar**
**¼ cup coarse salt**
**½ cup granulated sugar**
**¼ cup mustard seeds**
**½ cup mixed pickling spice**
Pour cold pickling mixture over cucumbers.
Each morning for the next 14 days add, stirring to dissolve
**¾ cup granulated sugar**
Drain and rinse pickles and pack into clean, sterilized jars.
Strain pickle mixture to remove spices. Pour over pickles and seal.
Makes 10 pints.

## BREAD AND BUTTER PICKLES

Combine in a crock or bowl
**16 cups thinly sliced cucumbers**
**½ cup coarse salt**
**8 cups sliced onions**
Cover with ice cubes. Let stand 2 or 3 hours or until cucumbers are crisp and cold. Add more ice if necessary. Drain.
In a large kettle combine
**4 cups white vinegar**
**5 cups granulated sugar**
**1 tablespoon celery seeds**
**2 tablespoons mustard seeds**
**1½ teaspoons turmeric**
**½ teaspoon white pepper**
Bring quickly to boil and boil 10 minutes. Add cucumber and onion slices and bring to boiling point. Pack at once in sterilized jars. Seal and store in cool place one month before using.
Makes 5 pints.

## DILL PICKLES

Wash and cut off flower end of
**24 (3 to 4-inch) cucumbers**
Cover with ice water and let stand for 2 hours.
To each hot sterilized quart sealer, add
**1 head of dill**
**½ sweet red pepper, sliced**
**2 cloves garlic, sliced**
**1 teaspoon pickling spice**
**Pinch of alum**
Bring to boil
**1 cup white vinegar**
**2 cups water**
**¼ cup coarse salt**
Pack cucumbers into prepared jars. Fill jars with hot vinegar mixture. Seal.
Makes 2 quarts.

---

*Use coarse salt when making pickles as "free-running" and iodized salt may cause cloudiness and darkening.*

---

## PICKLED ONIONS

Cover with boiling water and let stand for 3 minutes
**2 quarts small white onions**
Drain and cover with cold water, then peel.
Mix together
**8 cups boiling water**
**¾ cup coarse salt**
Pour over onions and let stand overnight. Drain, then rinse thoroughly with cold water.
Combine
**4 cups white vinegar**
**1 cup granulated sugar**
**1 bay leaf**
**1 stick cinnamon**
**½ teaspoon celery salt**
**½ teaspoon tarragon**
Boil for 5 minutes. Remove cinnamon stick and bay leaf. Add onions and bring just to boiling point.
Pack onions in sterilized jars and fill with boiling liquid. Seal.
Makes 4 pints.

## MUSTARD PICKLES

Wash and cut into flowerets
 **2 heads cauliflower**
Wash and cut into chunks sufficient cucumbers to make
 **10 cups cucumber chunks**
Peel and leave whole
 **2 quarts small white onions**
Wash, seed and cut into strips
 **3 green peppers**
 **3 sweet red peppers**
Combine vegetables in a large crock.
Mix together and pour over vegetables
 **1⅓ cups coarse salt**
 **16 cups water**
 **1 teaspoon alum**
Let stand overnight.
Drain off brine and rinse in cold water.
In a large preserving kettle, combine
 **½ cup dry mustard**
 **1 cup PURITY flour**
 **2½ cups granulated sugar**
 **1 teaspoon turmeric**
 **1 teaspoon celery salt**
Blend in
 **2 cups water**
Cook, stirring constantly, until thickened.
Slowly add
 **7 cups cider vinegar**
Bring to boil and then add vegetables.
Cook over medium heat until tender,
about 15 minutes. Ladle into hot sterilized jars and seal.
Makes about 14 pints.

## PICKLED MUSHROOMS

In a saucepan, combine
 **1¼ cups white vinegar**
 **2 cloves garlic**
 **2 tablespoons granulated sugar**
 **½ teaspoon salt**
 **1 bay leaf**
 **1 clove**
Bring to a boil and add
 **2 (10-ounce) cans whole
  mushrooms, drained**
Boil rapidly for 5 minutes.
Strain liquid to remove garlic, bay leaf and clove.
Pack mushrooms in a sterilized jar. Fill with hot liquid. Seal and store for a week.
Makes 1 pint.

## MARINATED GREEN BEANS

Drain into a saucepan
 **1 (14-ounce) can Blue Lake
  whole or cut green beans**
Pack green beans into a sterilized jar.
Combine liquid in saucepan with
 **½ cup malt vinegar**
 **1 small onion, thinly sliced**
 **1 clove garlic**
 **1 bay leaf**
 **½ teaspoon salt**
 **½ teaspoon tarragon**
Bring to boil, reduce heat and simmer uncovered for 10 minutes.
Strain and fill prepared jar with hot liquid. Seal, and store for a week.
Makes 1 pint.

## BETH'S GOURMET BEETS

Drain
 **1 (19-ounce) can whole beets**
Slice into a sterilized jar.
In a small saucepan, bring to boil
 **⅔ cup white vinegar**
 **⅓ cup lightly packed brown sugar**
 **1 teaspoon dried parsley**
Fill prepared jar with hot vinegar mixture.
Seal.
Makes 1 pint.

## CELERY CHUTNEY

In a large saucepan, combine
 **16 cups finely chopped celery
  (6 large heads)**
 **3 cups finely chopped onion**
 **6 ounces dry mustard**
 **3 cups granulated sugar**
 **1½ quarts white vinegar (7½ cups)**
 **2 ounces mustard seed**
 **1½ teaspoons turmeric**
 **2¼ teaspoons salt**
 **¼ teaspoon cayenne**
Bring to boil, reduce heat and simmer uncovered for 3 hours.
Combine to a paste
 **3 tablespoons cornstarch**
 **3 tablespoons cold water**
Stir into hot mixture and cook, stirring constantly, until thickened.
Simmer 20 minutes longer.
Ladle into sterilized jars. Seal.
Makes about 5 quarts.

## TOMATO RELISH

Peel and chop
**12 tomatoes**
Put through meat grinder
**3 large, peeled cucumbers**
**2 green peppers, seeded**
**2 hot red peppers, seeded**
**4 large, peeled onions**
Combine vegetables and sprinkle with
**¼ cup coarse salt**
Let stand 10 minutes and drain.
In a large saucepan or preserving kettle,
combine drained vegetables and
**5 cups cider vinegar**
**4 cups granulated sugar**
Bring to boil and simmer until tender.
Mix together
**½ cup PURITY Flour**
**4 teaspoons dry mustard**
**4 teaspoons turmeric**
**4 teaspoons celery seeds**
Add a little of hot mixture to mustard
mixture, then blend it into remaining hot
vegetable mixture.
Continue cooking, stirring frequently,
until desired consistency.
Ladle into sterilized jars and seal.
Makes about 7 pints.

## HOT CHUTNEY

Put through meat grinder or finely chop
**1½ pounds onions, peeled**
**2 cups seedless raisins**
**8 lemons (remove pits)**
Wrap in a piece of cheesecloth
**10 dried chillies**
In a crock or large bowl, combine ground
mixture, chillies and
**4 teaspoons ground ginger**
**1 teaspoon ground mace**
**1 teaspoon allspice**
**½ teaspoon ground cloves**
**1 tablespoon dry mustard**
**1½ tablespoons salt**
**4 cups cider vinegar**
Allow to stand in a cool place overnight.
Transfer to a saucepan and cook stirring
frequently until tender.
Remove spice bag and blend in
**2 cups cider vinegar**
**4 cups lightly packed brown sugar**
Continue cooking, stirring occasionally
until the desired consistency.
Ladle into sterilized jars and seal immediately.
Makes about 6 pints.

## QUICK CHILI SAUCE

In a saucepan, combine
**1 (19-ounce) can tomatoes**
**1 green pepper, coarsely chopped**
**1 cup coarsely chopped onions**
**¼ cup white vinegar**
**⅓ cup lightly packed brown sugar**
**½ teaspoon salt**
**¼ teaspoon dry mustard**
Wrap loosely in cheesecloth and add
**1 teaspoon pickling spices**
**1 teaspoon celery seeds**
Bring to boil, reduce heat, and simmer
uncovered for 45 minutes or until a good
consistency. Remove spice bag. Pack in
sterilized jars. Seal and store in a cool,
dark place. If desired, wrap jars in brown
paper to retain colour.
Makes 2 pints.

---

*Grandmother added grape leaves when
making pickles and now scientists have
discovered grape leaves contain a sub-
stance that inhibits development of en-
zymes which cause cucumbers to soften
during brining.*

---

## GREEN TOMATO RELISH

Wash and slice sufficient green tomatoes
to give
**8 cups sliced green tomatoes**
Mix with
**3 tablespoons salt**
and allow to stand overnight. Drain.
In a large saucepan, combine
**2 cups cider vinegar**
**2 cups granulated sugar**
**3 tablespoons mustard seeds**
**½ teaspoon celery seeds**
**1 teaspoon turmeric**
**3 cups sliced onions**
Bring to boil and simmer gently 5 minutes.
Stir in drained tomatoes and
**2 large sweet red peppers, chopped**
**1 hot red pepper, chopped**
Bring to boil and simmer gently 5 minutes, stirring occasionally.
Pack into hot sterilized jars, and seal.
Makes about 5 pints.

## SPICED CRABAPPLE JELLY

Wash and remove blossom end and stems from
**1 (6-quart) basket crabapples**
Combine in a large saucepan with enough water to cover.
Bring to boil and simmer uncovered for about 20 minutes or until mushy.
Strain through jelly bag overnight.
Measure
**5½ cups crabapple juice**
Combine in saucepan with
**½ cup white vinegar**
Tie in cheesecloth and add
**1 (4-inch) stick cinnamon, broken**
**1 tablespoon whole cloves**
Bring to boil and boil uncovered for 3 minutes. Remove spices.
Slowly stir in
**5 cups granulated sugar**
Bring to boil and boil uncovered about 30 minutes or until a teaspoonful when chilled quickly has desired consistency.
Stir frequently. Ladle into sterilized jars.
Seal while hot with a thin layer of melted paraffin.
Makes about 8 (6-ounce) glasses.

---

*To extract juice for jelly strain in jelly bag or new diaper or many layers of fine cheesecloth.*

---

## GRAPE JELLY

Wash and stem
**6 quarts fresh Concord grapes**
In a large saucepan or preserving kettle combine with
**1 cup water**
Bring to boil and cook uncovered for 15 minutes, stirring occasionally.
Strain through jelly bag. Allow juice to stand overnight in refrigerator. Measure juice, being careful not to use sediment.
Combine
**4 cups grape juice**
With
**3½ cups granulated sugar**
Bring to boil and boil uncovered for 20 minutes or until a spoonful when chilled quickly has desired consistency.
Ladle into sterilized jars. Seal while hot with a thin layer of melted paraffin.
Repeat until all juice has been made into jelly.
Makes about 16 (6-ounce) glasses.

## GREEN PEPPER JELLY

Put through meat grinder
**8 medium sized green peppers, seeded**
Measure pulp and juice and combine 2 cups in saucepan along with
**5½ cups granulated sugar**
**1 cup white vinegar**
Bring to boil and set aside for 15 minutes, strain.
Mix strained juice with
**⅓ cup lemon juice**
Bring to boil, stirring constantly.
Stir in
**1 (6-ounce) bottle liquid pectin**
**½ teaspoon green food colouring**
Bring to a full rolling boil and boil 1 minute, stirring constantly.
Remove from heat, skim off foam and ladle quickly into sterilized jars.
Seal while hot with a thin layer of melted paraffin.
Makes 6 to 7 (6-ounce) glasses.

## FRESH FRUIT MELANGE

Mix together in a crock (with lid)
**1 (26-ounce) bottle brandy**
**1 tablespoon grated orange rind**
**1 teaspoon thyme**
**1 teaspoon cinnamon**
**1 teaspoon allspice**
**Pinch of cloves**
Stir in
**1 quart strawberries, hulled**
Cover and let stand in a cool place for one week.
Then add
**1 quart sour cherries, pitted**
**1 quart raspberries**
**3 cups granulated sugar**
Cover and continue to store in a cool place. In season, add each of the following together with 2 cups granulated sugar or select your favourite fruit from these
**2 cups seedless grapes, halved**
**2 cups gooseberries**
**2 cups red currants**
**2 cups peeled, sliced peaches**
**2 cups cored, sliced pears**
**2 cups halved honey plums**
**2 cups halved blue plums**
Cover with a plate to hold fruit under syrup. Store for 3 months. Ladle into sterilized jars. Seal and store in cold room.
Makes 7 quarts.

## RASPBERRY JAM

Wash and crush enough berries to give
**8 cups crushed raspberries
(4-quarts)**
Place in a large saucepan.
Bring to boil and cook uncovered for 15
minutes.
Stir in
**6 cups granulated sugar**
Bring to boil and boil uncovered for
about 15 to 20 minutes or until a teaspoon when chilled quickly has desired
consistency.
Ladle into sterilized jars.
Seal while hot with a thin layer of melted
paraffin.
Makes about 12 (6-ounce) glasses.

## FREEZER RASPBERRY JAM

Wash and mash
**2 cups raspberries (1-quart)**
Mix in
**4 cups granulated sugar**
Combine together
**2 tablespoons lemon juice
½ (6-ounce) bottle liquid pectin**
Stir into fruit mixture and continue stir-
ring for 3 minutes.
Ladle into sterilized glasses and seal.
Allow to set at room temperature.
Store in freezer.
Makes 6 (6-ounce) glasses.

## STRAWBERRY JAM

Wash, and hull about 2 quarts strawberries.
Measure
**4 cups strawberries**
In a large saucepan or preserving kettle
alternate layers of strawberries with
**3 cups granulated sugar**
Let stand for 2 hours.
Bring to boil and cook uncovered for 5
minutes. Stir occasionally.
Stir in
**¼ cup lemon juice**
Bring to boil and boil uncovered about
5 minutes longer or until a teaspoonful
when chilled quickly has desired consistency.
Stir frequently.
Remove from heat, stir and skim off foam
by turns for 5 minutes.

Ladle into sterilized jars. Seal while hot
with a thin layer of melted paraffin.
Makes about 11 (6-ounce) glasses.

## FREEZER STRAWBERRY JAM

Wash, stem and crush
**1¾ cups strawberries (1-quart)**
Mix in
**4 cups granulated sugar**
Combine together
**2 tablespoons lemon juice
½ (6-ounce) bottle liquid pectin**
Stir into fruit mixture and continue stir-
ring for 3 minutes.
Ladle into sterilized glasses and seal.
Allow to set at room temperature.
Store in freezer.
Makes 5 (6-ounce) glasses.

## DAMSON JAM

Wash and stem enough damson plums
to give
**8 cups damson plums**
Combine in a large saucepan or preserving kettle with
**3½ cups water**
Bring to boil and cook uncovered for 15
minutes. Stir occasionally.
Stir in
**7 cups granulated sugar**
Bring to boil and boil uncovered about
7 minutes or until a teaspoonful when
chilled quickly has desired consistency.
Stir frequently, removing pits as they rise
to surface.
Ladle into sterilized jars. Seal while hot
with a thin layer of melted paraffin.
Makes about 12 (6-ounce) glasses.

## BRANDIED CHERRIES

Wash and shorten the stems of
**2½ pounds sweet cherries**
Pack 3 sterilized quart jars three-quarters
full and to each add
**¼ cup granulated sugar**
Fill with brandy.
Seal tightly.
Turn the jars upside down and reverse
them end for end every hour for four
hours to mix sugar and brandy. Store for
at least 3 months before using.
Makes 3 quarts.

## CHERRY COMPOTE

In a saucepan, combine and boil for 5 minutes
**2 cups dry red wine**
**1 cup granulated sugar**
**2 tablespoons lemon juice**
**1 teaspoon grated lemon rind**
Stir in and simmer for 15 minutes
**2 quarts sour cherries, pitted**
Remove the cherries and continue cooking until the syrup is reduced to ⅔ of its original volume.
Combine and blend into syrup
**1 teaspoon cornstarch**
**1 tablespoon cold water**
Simmer for five minutes and flavour with
**2 tablespoons Kirsch**
Pour syrup over cherries.
Ladle into sterilized jars. Seal hot with a thin layer of melted paraffin.
Makes 6 (6-ounce) jars.

## APPLE RINGS

In a saucepan, bring to boil
**4 cups water**
**½ cup granulated sugar**
**1 (½-ounce) bottle red food colouring**
Add
**4 peeled cored apples, halved horizontally**
Reduce heat and simmer for 5 minutes or until apples are cooked. Remove apple rings, dry on absorbent paper.
Refrigerate or freeze. Serve as a meat garnish, filling centres with cream cheese.
If desired, you can repeat with more apple rings.
Makes 8 rings.

## SEVILLE MARMALADE

Halve from stem to blossom end and slice very thinly (including rind)
**12 Seville oranges**
**3 large sweet oranges**
**2 lemons**
Measure prepared fruit into a crock and for each cup add
**2¼ cups water**
Cover and let stand for 24 hours.
Bring to boil and simmer uncovered for 1½ hours.
Allow to stand overnight.

Measure 2 cups cooked fruit and add
**2 cups granulated sugar**
Bring to boil and simmer uncovered for about 1 hour or until a teaspoonful when chilled quickly has desired consistency.
Ladle into sterilized jars. Seal while hot with a thin layer of melted paraffin.
Repeat until all fruit is used.
Makes 42 (6-ounce) glasses.

## APPLE BUTTER

Wash and quarter (do not peel or core) sufficient apples to give
**12 cups quartered apples**
In a large saucepan or preserving kettle combine apples with
**5 cups water**
Bring to boil, reduce heat and simmer until very soft. Press through colander or strainer.
In a saucepan, combine apple purée with
**2⅔ cups granulated sugar**
**1½ teaspoons allspice**
**1½ teaspoons cinnamon**
**½ teaspoon cloves**
Boil gently about 20 minutes or until desired consistency.
Ladle into hot sterilized jars and seal.
Makes 3 pints.

## ORANGE CUCUMBER PICKLES

Combine in a crock and let stand overnight
**2 cups peeled, chopped cucumber (large)**
**¾ cup chopped green pepper**
**2 tablespoons salt**
**¼ cup cold water**
In the morning, drain vegetables and discard liquid.
In food chopper, grind peel of
**1½ oranges**
Combine drained vegetables, ground orange rind in a saucepan with
**¼ cup chopped pimiento**
**1 cup malt vinegar**
**1 cup lightly packed brown sugar**
**½ teaspoon mustard seeds**
**½ teaspoon celery seeds**
Bring to boil, reduce heat and boil gently for about 20 minutes or until desired consistency.
Ladle into hot sterilized jars and seal.
Makes 4 pints.

## GINGER RHUBARB PRESERVE

Combine in a bowl or crock and allow to stand overnight
**6 cups rhubarb chunks**
**6 cups granulated sugar**
**½ cup lemon juice**
**1 tablespoon grated lemon rind**
Transfer mixture to a large saucepan. Bring to boil and cook uncovered until thickened about 1 hour.
Stir in
**¼ cup chopped preserved ginger**
Simmer 5 additional minutes.
Ladle into hot sterilized jars. Seal while hot with a thin layer of melted paraffin.
Makes about 12 (6-ounce) glasses.

## BANANA-PINEAPPLE MARMALADE

Mash to a fine pulp enough ripe bananas to give
**1½ cups mashed bananas**
Combine in a large saucepan with
**1 (14-ounce) can crushed pineapple**
**⅓ cup lemon juice**
**6½ cups granulated sugar**
Bring to boil and cook, stirring constantly, for one minute.
Remove from heat and stir in
**1 (6-ounce) bottle liquid pectin**
Return to heat and boil for one minute.
Remove from heat, stir and skim off foam by turns for 5 minutes.
Ladle into sterilized jars. Seal while hot with a thin layer of melted paraffin.
Makes 8 (6-ounce) jars.

## MINTED ONION RINGS

In a saucepan, combine
**4 cups white vinegar**
**⅓ cup granulated sugar**
Tie in cheesecloth and add
**⅓ cup dried mint leaves**
Bring to boil, reduce heat and simmer for 10 minutes, then remove from heat.
Stir in
**few drops green food colouring**
Then add
**4 cups peeled sliced onions**
**½ cup sliced pimiento**
Bring to boil and then remove mint. Ladle into hot sterilized jars and seal.
Makes 2 pints.

## CORN RELISH

In a large saucepan, combine
**4 cups canned whole kernel corn, drained ***
**1 cup chopped celery**
**½ cup chopped onion**
**½ cup chopped green pepper**
**2 cups granulated sugar**
**1½ cups white vinegar**
**½ cup water**
**1½ teaspoons coarse salt**
**1 teaspoon mustard seeds**
**1 teaspoon celery seeds**
Bring to boil, reduce heat, and simmer for 10 minutes.
Smoothly blend together
**¼ cup PURITY Flour**
**1½ teaspoons dry mustard**
**½ teaspoon turmeric**
**½ cup water**
Gradually stir into hot mixture.
Mix in
**¼ cup chopped pimiento**
Continue cooking, stirring frequently, for 10 minutes or until desired consistency.
Ladle into hot sterilized jars and seal.
Makes 3 pints.
*If desired, substitute 4 cups of corn cut from cob for canned corn. Cook 6 to 7 ears in boiling water for 5 minutes, then immerse in cold water and cut from cob.

## STUFFED SPICED APRICOTS

Drain, reserving juice
**2 (28-ounce) cans apricot halves (45% syrup)**
Measure juice and to 3 cups add
**1½ cups malt vinegar**
**¾ cup orange juice**
**1 tablespoon grated orange rind**
**1 teaspoon cinnamon**
**¼ teaspoon ginger**
Bring to boil, reduce heat and simmer 10 minutes.
Stuff apricot halves with
**1 (8-ounce) package glacé chopped mixed fruit**
Fasten two halves together with toothpicks.
Simmer in hot liquid for 10 minutes. Pack apricots tightly in hot sterilized jars and fill with liquid. Seal.
Makes about 3 pints.

# FREEZING

## FREEZING

The complete and intelligent use of a home freezer can add pleasure to your labours as a cook, simplify menu planning and marketing, and enhance your reputation as a hostess.

Most foods can be frozen successfully, either cooked or uncooked, and in combination with other foods. The list of foods which cannot be frozen is very short and quite easy to remember.

### FOODS NOT TO FREEZE

Lettuce, tomatoes, cucumbers, celery and radishes.
Whites of hard cooked eggs.
Custard pies, cream fillings and puddings.
Gelatine salads and desserts unless whipped.
Mayonnaise.
Boiled potatoes, alone or used in potato salad.
Heavy cream. (It can be frozen after it has been whipped.)

Here are some suggestions to help insure success in the freezing of foods:

**Select only foods of good quality:** Freezing does retain the flavour, texture, colour and nutritive value of food, but it does not improve the quality.

**Freeze foods promptly:** Speed in preparing and packaging fresh produce from garden or grower is important. If immediate processing is impossible, refrigerate for a short time. This also applies to meat, fish and prepared foods.

**Freeze suitable quantities of food:** Consult your freezer instruction book to determine the quantities of food to prepare and freeze at a time to avoid overloading the machine.

**Package and wrap foods carefully:** Use only packaging materials designed for freezer use.

**Label and date all packages:** It is important to include the type of food, weight or number of servings and date of freezing.

**Freeze packages quickly:** Do not let packages stand at room temperature before freezing. If a delay is necessary, refrigerate packages.

**Use frozen foods regularly:** Plan to use items from your freezer daily so that you have a complete yearly turnover.

**Do not refreeze thawed foods.** Once a food has been thawed completely, it should not be refrozen. Partially thawed food, which still has ice crystals and is quite firm, can be refrozen. This sometimes happens when there has been a power failure. Re-label and use as soon as possible. *The exception:* You can, of course, cook a completely thawed food and refreeze it.

## PACKAGING

Proper packaging is necessary to protect the food from the cold dry air of the freezer. Therefore, wrapping papers and containers suitable for freezing foods must be moisture and vapour resistant in order to keep the food from becoming dry, flavourless and unattractive. Proper wrapping and sealing is equally important.

### FREEZER WRAPPING PAPERS

**1.** Plastic films—polyethylene, pliofilm, etc.

**2.** Freezer aluminum foil.

**3.** Laminated papers, locker paper, or waxed freezer paper.

If using plastic films or foil on irregular shaped packages, it is sometimes necessary to cover again with heavy paper to avoid puncturing.

**To Wrap:** Place food in centre of paper and bring two ends of paper together over the top of the food. Then fold over two or three times until tight, leaving as little air space as possible. Press out air at the ends and fold under the parcel. This is known as the "drugstore wrap". Aluminum foil is shaped around the food and does not require the drugstore wrap.

**To Seal:** Secure wrappings with freezer tape, rubber or metal bands; or *heat-seal* using a hand iron set at "rayon" or "synthetic". If sealing plastic films, place some paper between the wrapping and the iron.

**Freezer bags**
Assorted sizes of plastic bags are easy to use and are suitable for packaging poultry, dry pack fruits and vegetables, and some prepared foods such as bread, cake and cookies.
To seal, press out as much air as possible, then twist the top several times and secure tightly with paper or metal closures, or rubber bands. After freezing foods in plastic bags, pack like foods in large paper or plastic bags. This will keep similar foods together.

**FREEZER CONTAINERS**
**1. Folding Cartons:** Wax or plastic lined, some with plastic-liner bags. Some liner bags require heat-sealing (see freezer wrappings), others are supplied with metal or elastic closures.

**2. Rigid Containers:** Made of plastic, glass, waxed cardboard, aluminum or aluminum foil. They are available in various shapes and sizes. Square shapes with flat tops and bottoms take up less space in the freezer since they stack easily.

**3. Baking Dishes:** Heat and freezer-proof glassware; aluminum pie, cake and roasting pans; special foil containers and pie plates.

**HEADSPACE**
When using a liquid or sugar pack, allow 1 inch headspace for glass containers and ½ inch headspace for others.

---

**Use only packaging material designed for freezer use.**

---

## FREEZING FRUITS
Freeze only fresh high quality fruit of proper maturity. Choose varieties recommended for freezing, since some freeze better than others. Your Provincial Department of Agriculture will provide you with this information.
Fruits can be packaged in any leak-proof container or carton. Freezer bags can be used for dry packed fruit.

**PACKING FRUITS**
**1. Dry pack:** Pack fruits such as blueberries, raspberries, currants and rhubarb without sugar or syrup. Drain prepared fruit thoroughly on towels, and fill containers or bags. Seal and freeze. Fruits packed in this way can be used for jams, jellies, pies, desserts, or special diets.

**2. Syrup Pack:** Make syrup in advance, choosing the strength of syrup suited to tartness of fruit and personal taste. Recommended strengths are given with each fruit (Table below). Place prepared fruit in containers and cover with syrup, allowing headspace. To keep fruit under syrup, especially peaches and apricots, place crushed cellophane or waxed paper on top of the fruit.

**3. Dry Sugar Pack:** Sprinkle juicy fruits with the required amount of sugar in a shallow bowl or tray. Mix gently, coating

**SYRUPS:** Allow ⅔ to 1 cup of syrup for each 16-ounce container.

| Type | Sugar | Water | Yield | To Make Syrup |
|---|---|---|---|---|
| Thin | 1 cup | 2 cups | 2½ cups | Add sugar to water. |
| Moderately thin | 1 cup | 1½ cups | 2 cups | Stir well to dissolve. |
| Medium | 1 cup | 1 cup | 1½ cups | Chill. |
| Heavy | 1 cup | ¾ cup | 1¼ cups | DO NOT HEAT |

## PREPARATION OF FRUITS FOR FREEZING

| | |
|---|---|
| **APPLES** | Use good tart cooking varieties as soon as they have ripened. Do not use storage apples.<br>**Preparation:** To prevent discolouration while preparing apples, slice peeled, cored fruit into a brine solution made of 2 tablespoons salt to 1 gallon water.<br>**Pack:** Drain off brine solution and pack using thin syrup with ascorbic acid added. |
| **APPLESAUCE** | Prepare as usual. Chill thoroughly, package and freeze. |
| **APRICOTS** | Unpeeled frozen apricots are not satisfactory as a dessert fruit but are very nice when used in pies or puddings.<br>**Preparation:** Wash but do not blanch apricots. Pit and cut into quarters.<br>**Pack:** Use thin syrup with ascorbic acid added. |
| **BLUEBERRIES** | **Preparation:** Sort, wash and drain.<br>**Pack:** Dry Pack—for use in baking.<br>OR<br>Dry Sugar pack—allow 5 pounds fruit to 1 pound sugar. |
| **CHERRIES**<br>**(Sour)** | **Preparation:** Wash, stem and pit.<br>**Pack:** Dry Sugar Pack—allow 4 pounds fruit to 1 pound sugar.<br>OR<br>Syrup Pack—use medium syrup. |
| **CRANBERRIES** | **Preparation:** Sort, wash and drain.<br>**Pack:** Dry Pack. |
| **FRUIT COCKTAIL** | Use 1 part each . . . . . . .green grapes<br>red grapes<br>apples<br>2 parts . . . . . . . . . .cantaloupe<br>6 parts . . . . . . . . . .peaches<br>**Preparation:** Prepare as for fruit cocktail or salad.<br>**Pack:** Use thin syrup with ascorbic acid added. |
| **PEACHES** | **Preparation:** Blanch, remove skins and pit. Slice fruit directly into syrup or dry sugar with ascorbic acid added.<br>**Pack:** Dry Sugar Pack—allow 4 pounds fruit to 1 pound sugar.<br>OR<br>Syrup Pack—use moderately thin syrup. |
| **PLUMS** | **Preparation:** Wash, cut into halves and pit.<br>**Pack:** Dry Sugar Pack—use 4 pounds prepared fruit to 1 pound sugar with ascorbic acid added.<br>OR<br>Syrup Pack—use moderately thin syrup with ascorbic acid added. |

## PREPARATION OF FRUITS FOR FREEZING

| RASPBERRIES | **Preparation:** Sort, wash if necessary.<br>**Pack:** Dry Sugar Pack—use 5 pounds prepared fruit to 1 pound sugar.<br>OR<br>Syrup Pack—use a thin syrup. |
|---|---|
| RHUBARB | **Preparation:** Wash, cut stalks into 1 inch lengths.<br>**Pack:** Dry pack.<br>OR<br>Dry Sugar Pack—use 4 pounds prepared fruit to 1 pound sugar. |
| STRAWBERRIES | **Preparation:** Wash, sort and hull.<br>**Pack:** Sliced Strawberries—Dry Sugar Pack using 4 pounds prepared fruit to 1 pound sugar<br>Whole Strawberries—Syrup Pack using a medium syrup. |

each piece with sugar. Spoon into leak-proof containers, allowing for headspace. Seal and freeze. The specific amount of sugar needed for each fruit is given in the Table on page 91. The ratio of fruit to sugar is roughly 4 pounds fruit to 1 pound sugar.

**To Prevent Discolouration of Fruits:** Light coloured fruits, such as peaches, apricots and apples, will turn brown when exposed to air before completely frozen or while thawing in unopened package. To prevent this, powdered ascorbic acid is added to the fruit before freezing. For syrup pack: Add ½ teaspoon ascorbic acid for each quart of cold syrup and stir to dissolve. To use with dry sugar pack, mix ½ teaspoon ascorbic acid with each pound of sugar.

**STORAGE TIME:**

Frozen fruits may be stored 8 to 12 months.

**TO THAW:**

Leave in unopened container. Allow 6 hours in refrigerator; 2 hours at room temperature; 1½ hours if container is placed in front of an electric fan; or 1 hour if container is placed in a bowl under cold running water. Turn package over occasionally while defrosting to evenly distribute the syrup.

**TO SERVE:**

If using as a dessert fruit or in fruit cocktail, serve when partially thawed.

**Dry packed fruits**—can be used just as fresh fruit.

**Dry sugar packed fruits**—thaw only enough to separate. Add no more sugar unless desired. Use more thickening for pies made with frozen fruits than with fresh fruits.

**Syrup packed fruits**—should be drained if used in pies or puddings. Use amount of syrup necessary for recipe and save remainder for fruit drinks.

---

**FOR BEST RESULTS**

**Prepare, pack and freeze small quantities of fruit at a time.**
**Wash fruit in ice cold water, working quickly, so fruit does not absorb excess water.**

---

If freezing fruits for jams or jellies (dry pack), measure the desired amount of fruit *before* freezing as thawed fruits tend to collapse and are difficult to measure accurately. Use the same recipes for these pre-measured frozen fruits as you would for fresh fruits.

## FREEZING VEGETABLES

Freeze only good quality vegetables which have been freshly picked. Select the varieties recommended for freezing by your Provincial Department of Agriculture.

### TO PREPARE:

Prepare vegetables as you would for table use. In addition, all vegetables must be blanched (scalded) to retard enzyme action and thus retain flavour, texture and colour. (See Table below).

### TO BLANCH:

Heat two gallons of water in each of two large kettles, bringing them to a vigorous boil. Place about a pound of prepared vegetables in a wire basket, colander or cheesecloth bag. Immerse in first kettle of boiling water for 30 seconds. Transfer immediately to second kettle; start to count blanching time when the water returns to a boil after vegetables are added. For blanching times of various vegetables see Table below.
Carefully time the blanching process since over or under blanching can harm the quality of the vegetable. Do not attempt to blanch more than one pound of vegetables at a time.

### TO CHILL:

Cool blanched vegetables quickly in ice water or cold running water. Remove as soon as vegetables are cold—do not leave in water any longer than necessary. Drain on a clean towel or paper towelling placed on a shallow pan or tray. Pack immediately in containers and then freeze.

### TO PACK:

Select suitable size and type of container. A pint package will hold 3 to 4 servings. Since vegetables are dry packed, plastic bags are very popular and after freezing they can be packed in large paper bags for neater storage.
Exclude as much air as possible after filling bag and twist top nearly to vegetable, then seal with proper closure. If you use moulded plastic containers or glass jars, allow ½ inch headspace for expansion. Freeze packed vegetables at once.

---

**Follow directions in the Table below when selecting, preparing and blanching vegetables. Then chill, drain, pack and freeze them as outlined above.**

---

### PREPARATION OF VEGETABLES FOR FREEZING

| | |
|---|---|
| **ASPARAGUS** | Select young tender stalks. Remove tough ends and scales. Wash thoroughly. Cut into uniform lengths to fit containers or into 1 inch pieces.<br>**Blanch small stalks** . . . . . . . . . .3 minutes<br>**Blanch large stalks** . . . . . . . . . .4 minutes |
| **BEANS**<br>**Green or Wax** | Select young tender beans. Wash, trim ends, string if necessary. Leave whole, slice crosswise or cut French-style.<br>**Blanch** . . . . . . . . . . . . . . . . . .3 minutes |
| **BROCCOLI** | Select dark green compact heads. Trim off woody stalk. Cut through heads and stalk lengthwise leaving head about 1 inch across. Immerse in brine solution (1 tablespoon salt to 5 cups water) for ½ hour; drain and rinse thoroughly.<br>**Blanch** . . . . . . . . . . . . . . . . . .3 minutes |

## PREPARATION OF VEGETABLES FOR FREEZING

| | |
|---|---|
| **BRUSSELS SPROUTS** | Select deep green compact sprouts. Trim and immerse in brine solution (1 tablespoon salt to 5 cups water) for ½ hour. Drain and rinse thoroughly.<br>**Blanch . . . . . . . . . . . . . . . . . .3 minutes** |
| **CARROTS** | Wash and scrape. Slice or dice ¼ inch thick.<br>**Blanch . . . . . . . . . . . . . . . . . .3 minutes**<br>**For tiny whole carrots blanch . . . .5 minutes** |
| **CAULIFLOWER** | Select compact, white tender heads. Break into flowerets about 1 inch in diameter. Immerse in brine solution (1 tablespoon salt to 5 cups water) for ½ hour. Drain and rinse thoroughly.<br>**Blanch . . . . . . . . . . . . . . . . . .3 minutes** |
| **CORN**<br>**on the cob** | Select freshly picked corn and prepare immediately. Remove husks and silk; trim cobs to even lengths. Wash. Blanch, allowing 2 quarts boiling water for each medium-sized ear.<br>**Blanch large ears . . . . . . . . . . .11 minutes**<br>**Blanch medium ears . . . . . . . . .9 minutes**<br>**Blanch small ears . . . . . . . . . . .7 minutes**<br>Chill very thoroughly, about 15 minutes in cold water so that the interior of the cob is **cold** before freezing. Freezer foil or wrappings may be used rather than trying to fit cobs into containers. |
| **CORN**<br>**whole kernel** | Choose corn as for corn on the cob. Remove husks and silk, then wash.<br>**Blanch . . . . . . . . . . . . . . . . . .3 minutes**<br>Chill and cut off kernels close to the cob. |
| **PEAS** | Select young tender peas. Shell, sort, and wash.<br>**Blanch . . . . . . . . . . . . . . . . . .2 minutes** |
| **SPINACH**<br>**CHARD**<br>**and other greens** | Use only tender green leaves. Discard tough stems and bruised portions. Wash very thoroughly.<br>**Blanch . . . . . . . . . . . . . . . . . 2 minutes**<br>NOTE: Drain well after chilling so that leaves do not mat. |
| **SQUASH**<br>**PUMPKIN** | Cut or break apart, remove seeds and stringy portion. Cut into small pieces then steam or boil until tender. Cool quickly and remove from rind. Mash or sieve, then pack and freeze. |

NOTE: Broccoli, brussels sprouts and cauliflower are immersed in a brine solution (1 tablespoon salt to 5 cups water) for ½ hour to remove any insects. Drain and rinse thoroughly before blanching.

## TO PREPARE FOR SERVING:

Cook most vegetables while still frozen, allowing a shorter cooking period than for fresh vegetables because they have been partially cooked during blanching. However, corn on the cob should be completely thawed before cooking; spinach and greens should be partially thawed then broken apart before cooking. Pumpkin and squash can be completely thawed and used as you would cooked or canned.

## TO COOK:

Allow ½ cup water and ½ teaspoon salt for 2 cups frozen vegetables. Bring quickly to a boil, reduce heat and boil gently, covered, until tender. Corn on the cob should be cooked in boiling water to cover.

### Approximate Cooking Times:

Asparagus, broccoli, cauliflower, corn on the cob, peas and spinach, allow 3 to 5 minutes. Wax beans, brussels sprouts, whole kernel corn, allow 4 to 6 minutes. Green beans, allow 5 to 7 minutes.

## FREEZING MEATS, FISH, POULTRY

Take advantage of market specials by freezing meats, fish and poultry for year round enjoyment. Package individually in freezer wrapping, padding the bones to avoid puncturing the outer wrapping. Label each package clearly with date, cut and weight. An inventory is recommended.

Poultry and meats should be completely thawed in freezer wrapper for uniform cooking. Use the same cooking methods as for fresh. Fish may be cooked frozen or thawed, although partial thawing may be necessary if the pieces are to be separated. Never refreeze meats, fish or poultry that have been thawed.

## FREEZING BAKED FOODS

Freezing adds much to the joy of baking. It requires the same time to assemble utensils and ingredients, then clean up afterwards for one batch of cookies as it does for a double or triple batch. Therefore, with wise planning and little extra effort, you can stockpile a delightful variety of baked foods to take care of many occasions.

---

It is especially important to package baked goods carefully. Exclude as much air as possible and seal securely.
Wrap in foil those items you plan to heat and serve warm. Plastic bags or film will melt if heated.

---

## YEAST BREADS AND ROLLS:

Prepare and bake breads, rolls and sweet breads as usual. Cool to room temperature, package and freeze.

**To Package:** Wrap in freezer wrappings or bags being careful to exclude as much air from package as possible. Small loaves of bread can be packaged in bags; pan rolls and coffee cakes in aluminum foil containers and covered with sheet wrappings. Package only amounts which will be used quickly. It is better to package bread cut in half or as many rolls as you need for a meal since they soon become stale.

**To Thaw:** Thaw in freezer wrappings at room temperature. Bread requires 2 hours, rolls and sweet breads less time depending upon size. If foil wrapped, place in preheated 300°F oven for 15 to 30 minutes. Do not loosen wrappings.

**Storage Time:** 4 to 6 months for baked bread, rolls and sweet breads.
Commercially baked bread may be frozen in original wrapping and kept for 1 to 2 weeks. For longer storage, place wrapped loaf in a freezer bag. Storage time is 3 months.

## QUICK BREADS:

All baked quick breads (muffins, biscuits, waffles, fruit and nut breads, and cornbread) can be frozen very successfully. Use any recipe you choose; bake, cool, package (see packaging directions for yeast breads above) and freeze.

**To Thaw:** Leave in freezer wrappings at room temperature. Muffins, tea biscuits, scones, etc. will require 1 hour. Loaves and square-shaped quick breads will require 2 hours or more depending upon size. If foil wrapped, place in preheated 300°F oven for 15 to 30 minutes. Waffles and pancakes can be put in the toaster to thaw and warm.

**Storage Time:** 4 to 6 months for baked quick breads.

## STEAMED PUDDINGS:

Prepare and steam as usual; chill, then remove from the mould if you wish. Wrap in freezer wrappings. If you usually allow a ripening period for rich fruit puddings, do so before freezing. If wrapped in foil, the puddings are ready for resteaming.

**To Thaw:** Thaw at room temperature then steam 30 minutes to 1 hour depending upon size of pudding.

**Storage Time:** 4 to 6 months.

## CAKES:

All varieties of baked cakes may be frozen—sponge, chiffon, angel and fruit cakes; also butter cakes in any shape—loaves, layers or cupcakes. It is a good idea to make and bake two round or square cakes at a time, one for immediate use, the other to freeze. Cool baked cakes to room temperature before freezing.

**To Package:** Place cake on a piece of cardboard; wrap in freezer wrapping or bag, then freeze. Since cakes need extra protection during freezer storage, place frozen cake in an ordinary bakery carton, metal or plastic container; seal and return to freezer. Or, place unwrapped cake in container then wrap with freezer wrappings; seal and freeze. It is also convenient to cut cakes into halves, quarters or slices before freezing. Slices are handy for lunch boxes and thawed quarters of cake are excellent for one meal. You can also plan to have two or three varieties of cake halves for party use.

**To Freeze Iced Cakes:** Uncooked butter icings are best for freezing; boiled icings become sticky and fudge icings crumble. Do not use cream fillings in layer cakes.

Bake, cool, then ice the cake. Place unwrapped in freezer for 1 to 2 hours to set the icing.

Package as outlined above and return to freezer.

**To Thaw:** Leave in freezer wrappings at room temperature.

*For uniced cakes* allow 1 to 1½ hours for layers, and 2 to 3 hours for loaves and squares. In an emergency and if foil wrapped, thaw cake in preheated 300°F oven for 15 to 20 minutes.

*For iced cakes* allow 2 to 3 hours. Reduce thawing time one-third by placing package in front of an electric fan.

*For fruit cakes* allow 1 hour per pound of cake.

**Storage Time:** Both iced and uniced cakes can be stored for 4 to 5 months; fruit cakes up to 1 year.

## COOKIES:

Most cookies can be frozen baked or unbaked except macaroons and meringues which do not freeze well. It is best to freeze the dough as this saves space and gives cookies that fresh baked flavour.

However, it is convenient to have a package or so of the baked variety in the freezer. Doughs for drop, moulded or sliced cookies can be frozen successfully, while bar cookies such as brownies should be baked before freezing.

**To Package Cookie Doughs:** Pack drop or moulded cookie dough in bulk in airtight freezer containers; or drop by teaspoonfuls on baking sheet ¼ inch apart and freeze for 1 hour. Package these frozen cookie balls in containers with a double thickness of wax paper between layers. Refrigerator cookie dough can be shaped into rolls as usual and wrapped in freezer foil, plastic film or bags.

**For Baked Cookies:** Cool to room temperature; package in containers with crumpled wax paper between layers. Bakery cartons can be used if overwrapped tightly with freezer wrappings. If preparing for a party, decorated cookies can be arranged on trays or heavy cardboard with freezer paper between layers. Package with freezer wrappings.

**To Thaw:** Thaw cookie dough frozen in bulk in container at room temperature until it can be easily handled. Prepare and bake as usual. Frozen cookie balls can be placed unthawed on baking sheet and baked right away. Refrigerator cookie dough can be sliced as soon as the knife will go through the roll. Bake immediately. Return unused portion of roll to the freezer.

Thaw baked cookies in freezer wrappings at room temperature. The time will depend upon the number of cookies in the container and size of cookie. Bar cookies require longer than others.

**Storage Time:** Baked cookies of all varieties can be stored for 12 months, unbaked cookie doughs for 6 to 8 months.

## PIES:

Pies and pastry freeze easily and with excellent results. In fact, pastry seems to improve with freezing, especially pies frozen before baking. The best pies to freeze are mince and double crust fruit or berry pies. Chiffon pies may also be frozen but never freeze cream or custard pies.

**Unbaked Mince or Fruit Pies:** Prepare as usual using regular pie plates or aluminum foil pie plates. For fruit filled pies allow one-third more flour in each recipe to keep extra juices from running out. Do not slit top crust before freezing. Quick-freeze pie first and then wrap. To protect pastry during storage, place in bakery carton or cover with inverted cardboard pie plate. Wrap with freezer wrappings or place in freezer bag.

**To Thaw:** Remove freezer wrappings, cut slits in top crust and place directly in preheated 425°F. oven and bake for 10 to 20 minutes. (Then bake thawed pie as directed in recipe.)

**Storage Time:** 3 months.

---

Double crust fruit or mince pies can be baked before freezing but the quality is not as good as the frozen unbaked product. Also, there is little time saved by doing it in this way.

---

**Baked Pies:** Chiffon pies are prepared as usual and the fillings allowed to set. Omit whipped cream topping. Quick-freeze pies for 1 hour, then remove for wrapping. Press a circle of foil or plastic film against the surface of the filling and wrap as directed for unbaked pies. Pecan and butter tarts may be prepared and frozen the same as chiffon pies. Wrap as directed, omitting the circle of foil over the filling.

**To Thaw:** Leave in freezer wrappings at room temperature for 20 to 30 minutes.

**Storage Time:** 2 months.

---

*Increase flour or cornstarch used for thickening fresh fruit pies to be frozen, allowing one third more thickener.*

---

## PASTRY:

Since frozen pastry dough requires a long thawing time, it is better to roll dough into rounds for pie shells, top and bottom crusts or tart shells.

Prepare pastry as usual; roll out and cut into rounds of the desired size. Cut a heavy cardboard circle larger than the pastry and cover with freezer wrapping. Place pastry rounds in layers on top with a double thickness of waxed paper between. Place in a freezer bag or wrap securely in freezer wrappings and freeze.

**To Use:** Thaw in freezer wrappings at room temperature until the rounds can be shaped in pie plate.

**Storage Time:** 6 months.

## CREAM PUFFS AND ECLAIRS:

Freeze baked unfilled puffs and éclairs; package in containers or freezer bags. Thaw at room temperature in freezer wrappings 15 to 20 minutes. Fill and glaze as usual.

**Storage Time:** 3 months.

## ICE CREAM PUFFS:

Cream puffs filled with ice cream can be frozen and then packaged. No thawing is required; serve frozen with ice cream sauce.

**Storage Time:** 1 month.

## SANDWICHES:

Picnics, parties, teas and lunch boxes can be taken care of with dispatch when sandwiches are prepared ahead and frozen. Bread of any kind and most fillings freeze well. The ingredients which do not freeze satisfactorily are: Whites of hard-cooked eggs; mayonnaise; fresh celery, lettuce, tomatoes and cucumbers.

Jams and jellies are not suitable for freezing because they tend to soak into the bread.

Meats, poultry, fish, cheese, peanut butter and nuts are good fillings to freeze. Use them separately or in combination with each other or minced and mixed with cream cheese, salad dressing (small amount) or pickle relish. Sliced or chopped olives, dill and sweet pickles may be used with fillings or as garnishes on fancy sandwiches and canapés to be frozen.

Fresh lettuce, tomatoes and cucumbers may be added to the sandwiches when ready to serve.

**Lunch Box Sandwiches:** Spread bread slices (crusts on) with softened butter or margarine, any spread of the salad dressing type will soak into the bread. Fill, wrap and seal.

Package sandwiches singly or in pairs in small freezer bags or freezer wrappings. Be sure to lable the package.

**To Thaw:** Leave in wrappings at room temperature for 3 to 4 hours. They will be ready for noon lunches if taken out in the morning.

**Storage Time:** 3 to 4 weeks.

---

### DO NOT REFREEZE THAWED SANDWICHES

---

**Picnic and Party Sandwiches:** Prepare as for lunch box sandwiches. Arrange sandwiches together in loaf form (about 3 to 4 sandwiches) using crusts at each end for added protection. Use only one kind of filling for each package of sandwiches since flavours tend to intermingle. Wrap securely in freezer wrappings or bags.

**Party sandwich loaves** which are iced with cream cheese freeze well.

**Ribbon, pinwheel, rolled and checkerboard sandwiches** are best frozen unsliced. However, if it is desirable to have them sliced, place on tray or heavy cardboard covered with freezer paper; separate layers of sandwiches with the paper and overwrap the whole tray securely and seal.

**Open-faced tea sandwiches** may be made and spread with suitable filling and frozen on trays as described above. Or, slice and cut desired bread shapes for open-faced sandwiches. Stack and wrap in freezer wrappings.

*To Use:* Spread while still cold and garnish as desired.

**Canapés** may be made as for open-faced sandwiches and packed in layers on trays and frozen. Garnish just before serving.

**To Thaw:** Leave sandwiches in wrappings at room temperature and plan so they will be ready just at serving time. If thawed too soon, store in refrigerator. Trim crusts and cut plain sandwiches; slice ribbon, pinwheel and checkerboard sandwiches; garnish open-faced sandwiches.

Allow ½ hour for thawing small fancy and open-faced sandwiches packed on trays; 2 to 3 hours for ½ loaf of sandwiches (3 to 4 sandwiches) packaged together and 4 to 6 hours for a whole loaf of sandwiches (6 to 8 sandwiches). Canapés thaw very quickly so place in refrigerator 2 hours before serving.

**Storage Time** for party type sandwiches is about 1 week.

### WHAT TO DO WHEN THE FREEZER GOES OFF

A power or motor failure may cause the freezer to go off—for short periods it is sufficient to simply not open the door. In an emergency blocks of dry ice will keep the temperature low enough for several days.

More frequently, it seems, the freezer goes off without being noticed until signs of thawing of the food become visible. First make arrangements to get the freezer operating or rent a locker in a frozen food storage plant.

Then separate the food into four groups:
1. items that may be safely re-frozen
2. those that should be cooked before re-freezing
3. those that should be cooked and eaten
4. those that should be discarded

Examine each package to determine the extent of thawing. The presence of ice crystals indicates that the product should permit re-freezing. If thawed but still cold as when the temperature has not risen above 50°F, discard only the vegetables and re-freeze the rest but be prepared for a slight deterioration in quality. If the temperature of the food has risen above 50°F. discard all vegetables, fish, processed and ground meat, and organ meats. Other meats and poultry that still have a fresh odour should be cooked and eaten or cooked and re-frozen.

Fruits deteriorate by fermenting and for this reason they may be re-frozen even when no ice crystals are present. Later on make jam or jelly from those packages that have suffered too much of a loss in colour, texture or flavour.

Problems may arise in re-freezing fried food particularly when the re-started freezer must endeavour to bring a large quantity of partially thawed food to the proper temperature. Take it to a locker plant or borrow some space in a neighbour's freezer.

## FROZEN APPLESAUCE

In a saucepan, mix together
**1 cup granulated sugar**
**1 cup water**
**¼ cup lemon juice**
Bring to boil, reduce heat and simmer for 5 minutes.
Peel, core and shred into hot syrup
**4 apples**
Cool. ladle into sterilized jars and seal.
Store in freezer
Makes 3 (6-ounce) glasses.

## GLAZED CARROT CASSEROLE

Line a 1-quart casserole with double layers of heavy aluminum foil.
Wash, peel and cut in strips
**1½ pounds carrots**
Cover with boiling salted water. Bring to

boil and cook for 5 minutes. Drain and arrange in foil-lined casserole.
In a saucepan, melt
**2 tablespoons butter or margarine**
Blend in
**2 teaspoons PURITY Flour**
Gradually stir in
**½ cup orange juice**
Cook, stirring constantly, until thickened.
Blend in
**¼ cup lightly packed brown sugar**
**1 tablespoon grated orange rind**
**1 tablespoon vinegar**
**1 tablespoon lemon juice**
**½ teaspoon salt**
Pour over carrots, cool, seal and freeze. When firm remove package from casserole and return to freezer.
To serve: Preheat oven to 350°F. Turn carrot mixture into greased casserole with lid. Cover and bake for 40 minutes. Uncover and bake for an additional 15 to 20 minutes or until carrots are tender.
Makes 6 servings.

## OVEN-FRIED POTATOES

Preheat oven to 450°F.
Wash, peel and cut into ¼-inch slices
**6 potatoes**
Cover with salted water. Bring to boil and cook for 2 minutes.
Drain and rinse with cold water.
Into each of two large shallow baking pans pour half of
**⅔ cup vegetable oil**
Arrange half of slices, one layer deep, in each pan. Turn to coat evenly with oil. Bake in preheated 450° oven turning once, for 20 to 25 minutes or until golden brown. Drain on absorbent paper. Freeze on baking sheets and then remove and store in plastic bags.
To serve: Preheat oven to 400°F. Spread slices on baking sheet and bake in preheated 400° oven for 5 to 10 minutes or until piping hot. Season with salt and pepper.
Makes 6 to 8 servings.

## FREEZER TEA BISCUIT TOPPER

Sift together
**1½ cups PURITY Flour**
**1 tablespoon granulated sugar**

3 teaspoon baking powder
½ teaspoon salt
With a pastry blender or two knives cut in finely
¼ cup butter or margarine
Add a mixture of
1 egg
¼ cup milk
Stir with a fork to make a soft dough. Turn dough onto a lightly floured surface and knead gently 8 to 10 times. Roll out ¼ inch thick and with a floured cookie cutter, cut into biscuits.
On an ungreased baking sheet, arrange biscuits with sides touching to form the same shape as top of casserole dish. Freeze until firm and then wrap in foil. Return to freezer.
To serve: Place frozen biscuit topping on casserole filling and bake in preheated 350°F. oven until casserole is thoroughly heated and biscuits are golden.

## EVER-READY POPOVERS

Grease 14 custard cups.
Blend together
2 cups PURITY Flour
1½ teaspoons salt
Beat together
4 eggs
2 cups milk
2 tablespoons melted shortening
Add liquid to dry ingredients and beat with electric mixer or rotary beater until very smooth. Fill prepared custard cups ½ full.
Place custard cups on tray and freeze until firm. Quickly dip cups in warm water and unmould frozen batter, store in plastic bags in freezer.
To serve: Return to greased custard cups on a baking sheet and put in cold oven. Turn oven on, setting temperature at 400°F. and bake for 55 to 60 minutes or until golden.
Makes 14 popovers.

## FRENCH TOAST POP-UPS

Grease a baking sheet.
Dip to coat both sides
8 slices dry bread
in a mixture of
4 eggs, beaten
1½ cups milk

2 tablespoons sugar
½ teaspoon salt
¼ teaspoon nutmeg
¼ teaspoon vanilla
In a frypan, heat until foamy
2 tablespoons butter or margarine
Brown bread on both sides. Freeze on greased baking sheet. Stack slices, separating with a piece of freezer wrap, then overwrap or put in plastic bag and store in freezer for up to 3 months.
To serve: Pop in toaster and heat through. Serve with butter and maple syrup.
Makes 8 slices.

## BROWN-AND-SERVE ROLLS

Prepare Basic Rolls (See page 187), shape and place in greased muffin cups. Cover with a damp cloth and let rise in a warm place but not until doubled—only to 1½ times their original size.
Bake in preheated 300°F. oven for 40 minutes or until baked through. Do not brown. Cool in pan for 20 minutes. Completely cool before wrapping and freezing.
Makes 4 dozen rolls.
To serve: Allow to thaw at room temperature. Bake in preheated 400° oven for 5 to 7 minutes or until golden brown.

## PINK PARFAIT CAKE

Slice horizontally into 3 slices of even thickness
1 (9×5×3-inch) angel or sponge cake
Stir to soften slightly
1 quart vanilla ice cream
Swirl through ice cream
2 tablespoons frozen pink lemonade concentrate, partially thawed
Quickly spread ice cream between cake layers and freeze.
Whip until stiff
1 cup heavy cream
Spread on top and sides of cake and return to freezer. When firm, store in airtight container or box.
To serve: Remove from freezer 10 minutes before serving and slice.

# Desserts and Sauces

## DESSERTS

Fresh, canned or frozen fruits provide one of the most popular Canadian desserts, served just as is, with little or no preparation. For best quality and price, buy fresh fruits in season and in an amount that can be used without spoilage.

Pears, bananas and avocados usually need to be ripened at room temperature. Fruits that have a smooth firm skin, such as apples, pears and plums should be washed prior to storing in refrigerator. Do not wash berries, cherries or grapes prior to refrigerating but do wash before serving. If you store fruits in a plastic bag in refrigerator, make a few small holes to permit ventilation.

Let the following serve as a guide when buying, as the months specified denote when the greatest percentage of the total annual supply is sold:

| | |
|---|---|
| Apples | September, October, November |
| Apricots | July, August |
| Bananas | year round |
| Blueberries | August, September |
| Cantaloupes | June, July, August |
| Cherries | July |
| Grapes | September, October |
| Grapefruit | January, February, March |
| Limes | July |
| Oranges | February, March |
| Peaches | July, August, September |
| Pears | August, September |
| Pineapples | March, April, May |
| Plums | August, September |
| Raspberries | July |
| Rhubarb | March, April, May |
| Strawberries | May, June, July |
| Watermelons | June, July, August |

**An elegant trio of party desserts to tempt any guest—Almond Chiffon Roll, Strawberry Compote and Cold Praline Soufflé ▶**

## SPEEDY BAVARIAN

Dissolve
 **1 (3-ounce) package lemon
 flavoured jelly powder
 ¼ cup granulated sugar**
in
 **1 cup boiling water**
Stir in
 **¾ cup cold water**
Chill until the consistency of unbeaten egg white.
Meanwhile, whip according to package directions
 **1 (2-ounce) packaged whipped
 dessert topping**
Fold 1½ cups into thickened gelatine along with
 **1½ cups fresh berries**
Turn into a 1-quart jelly mould. Chill until firm. Unmould and garnish with remaining whipped topping.
Makes 8 servings.

## STRAWBERRY BAVARIAN

Wash and hull
 **1 quart fresh strawberries**
Strain through a sieve.
In a saucepan, combine
 **¾ cup granulated sugar
 2 envelopes gelatine**
Blend in and dissolve over boiling water
 **¼ cup water
 2 tablespoons lemon juice**
Stir in the berries and cool until thickened.
Fold in
 **2 cups heavy cream, whipped**
Pour into a 1½-quart jelly mould and chill for at least 4 hours.
Unmould and garnish with whole strawberries.
Makes 8 servings.

## BAVARIAN CREAM

Wash and mash
 **2 cups fresh raspberries**
Stir in and allow to stand for 2 hours
 **1 cup granulated sugar**
In a saucepan, combine
 **1 envelope gelatine
 ⅓ cup granulated sugar
 ¼ teaspoon salt**
Stir in and cook until gelatine is dissolved
 **1½ cups juice from berries**

Chill until the consistency of unbeaten egg white.
Whip with rotary beater or mixer.
Fold in the drained fruit together with
 **½ pint heavy cream, whipped**
Turn into a 4-cup mould.
Chill until set.
Makes 8 servings.

## FRUIT JELLY

In a saucepan, mix together
 **1 envelope gelatine
 ½ cup granulated sugar**
Add and heat until dissolved
 **1 cup boiling water**
Remove from heat and stir in
 **1 cup orange, grape or apple juice
 1 tablespoon lemon juice
 1 teaspoon grated lemon rind**
Pour into 4-cup mould. Chill until firm. Unmould.
Makes 4 servings.

**LEMON JELLY:** Prepare Fruit Jelly following basic recipe but increase sugar to ¾ cup, boiling water to 1½ cups and lemon juice to ¼ cup and omit fruit juice.

**RASPBERRY JELLY:** Prepare Fruit Jelly following basic recipe but increase sugar to ¾ cup, boiling water to 1½ cups and substitute ½ cup strained raspberry purée for fruit juice.

**UNMOULDING JELLY:** With a knife, free edge where jelly touches mould. In ring mould, release centre edge, too. Wrap bottom and sides of mould with warm cloth. Tilt mould on side to allow air to enter. Invert on serving plate.

## STRAWBERRY BAVARIAN CREAM

Thaw
**1 (15-ounce) package frozen
sweetened strawberries**
Drain.
Measure juice and add water to make
**1¼ cups strawberry liquid**
In a saucepan, mix together
**1 envelope gelatine**
**½ cup granulated sugar**
Stir in strawberry liquid and
**1 tablespoon lemon juice**
Bring to boil, stirring to dissolve gelatine.
Chill until the consistency of unbeaten
egg white.
Beat with rotary beater or mixer until
fluffy.
Fold strawberries into jelly mixture to-
gether with
**1 cup heavy cream, whipped**
Turn into 6-cup mould and chill until set.
Unmould.
Makes 6 to 8 servings.

RASPBERRY BAVARIAN CREAM: Prepare Strawberry Bavarian Cream following basic recipe but substituting 1 (15-
ounce) package frozen sweetened raspberries for strawberries. Mash drained
raspberries and press through a strainer
to remove seeds, before folding into
whipped jelly mixture.

## VANILLA BAVARIAN CREAM

Soften
**1 envelope gelatine**
in
**¼ cup cold water**
Dissolve over boiling water.
Scald together
**1¾ cups milk**
**½ cup granulated sugar**
Stir a little of hot milk mixture into
**2 eggs, slightly beaten**
Return to remaining hot milk. Cook, stirring constantly, about 1 minute.
Stir in dissolved gelatine.
Remove from heat and blend in
**1 teaspoon vanilla**
Chill until very slightly thickened.
Fold in
**1 cup heavy cream, whipped**
Turn into a 5-cup mould. Chill until set
(about 2 hours). Unmould.
Makes 4 to 6 servings.

COFFEE BAVARIAN: Prepare Vanilla
Bavarian Cream following basic recipe
but adding 1 tablespoon instant coffee
powder to scalded milk mixture and de-
creasing vanilla to ½ teaspoon. Unmould
and garnish with toasted chopped almonds.

CHOCOLATE BAVARIAN: Prepare Vanilla Bavarian Cream following basic recipe but increasing sugar to 1 cup and
adding 2 squares unsweetened chocolate
to milk mixture before scalding. Chocolate melts while milk is heating and,
when melted, blend smooth with rotary
beater.

---

*If you prefer individual steamed pud-
dings, divide pudding batter among
greased custard cups or small pudding
moulds, filling each about ⅔ full. Cover
each with aluminum foil and tie in place.
Steam for about 1 hour. To reheat the
individual puddings, steam for about 30
minutes.*

---

## LEMON SNOW

Soften
**1 envelope gelatine**
in
**½ cup cold water**
Allow to stand about 5 minutes and then
stir over low heat to dissolve.
Combine with
**¾ cup granulated sugar**
**¼ teaspoon salt**
**1 teaspoon grated lemon rind**
**¼ cup lemon juice**
**¾ cup cold water**
Chill until slightly thickened, then add
**2 egg whites, unbeaten**
Beat with rotary beater until mixture
begins to hold its shape. Spoon into dessert dishes or large bowl. Chill until firm.
Serve with chilled Soft Custard Sauce
(See page 107), using ½ recipe and 2
yolks.
Makes 4 to 6 servings.

ORANGE SNOW: Prepare Lemon Snow
following basic recipe but substituting
grated orange rind for lemon rind and
orange juice for half the water.

## BUTTERSCOTCH PUDDING

Scald
**2 cups milk**
In a saucepan, combine
**3 tablespoons PURITY Flour**
**¾ cup lightly packed dark brown sugar**
**¼ teaspoon salt**
Gradually blend in scalded milk. Cook over medium heat, stirring constantly, until thickened and smooth. Cover and cook, stirring occasionally, for 2 minutes longer.
Stir a little of hot mixture into
**1 egg, slightly beaten**
Then blend into remaining hot mixture and stir and cook 2 minutes longer.
Remove from heat and blend in
**1 teaspoon vanilla**
Chill.
Makes 6 servings.

## CHOCOLATE PUDDING

Scald together
**2½ cups milk**
**2 squares unsweetened chocolate**
When chocolate is melted, beat smooth with rotary beater.
In a saucepan, combine
**3 tablespoons PURITY Flour**
**1 cup granulated sugar**
**¼ teaspoon salt**
Gradually blend in hot milk mixture. Cook over medium heat, stirring constantly, until thickened. Cover and cook, stirring occasionally, for 2 minutes longer.
Stir a little of hot mixture into
**1 egg, slightly beaten**
Pour back into remaining hot mixture and stir and cook 2 minutes longer.
Remove from heat and blend in
**1 teaspoon vanilla**
Chill.
Makes 5 to 6 servings.

## CRÈME BRÛLÉE

Scald
**2 cups heavy cream**
Beat lightly
**7 eggs**
and beat in

**½ cup granulated sugar**
**½ teaspoon vanilla**
Gradually stir in scalded cream.
Cook, stirring constantly, over low heat until mixture thickly coats a metal spoon (about 5 minutes).
Turn into an 8-inch square baking dish and chill overnight or at least 6 hours. When ready to serve, set dish in pan of ice and sprinkle with
**½ cup lightly packed brown sugar**
Broil 1 to 2 minutes in preheated oven, until sugar is melted.
Serve with fresh berries, if desired.
Makes 5 to 6 servings.

## CHERRIES JUBILEE

Wash and pit
**2 cups fresh sweet cherries**
Stir in and let stand for 2 hours
**¼ cup granulated sugar**
**¼ cup cognac or brandy**
In a saucepan, combine
**2 tablespoons PURITY Flour**
**¼ cup granulated sugar**
Stir in cherry mixture together with
**¼ cup red currant jelly**
Cook over medium heat, stirring constantly, until thickened. Cover and cook 5 minutes longer, stirring occasionally.
Flame with
**3 tablespoons warm cognac or Kirsch**
Serve warm as sauce over ice cream.
Makes 6 servings.

CHERRIES JUBILEE: Cherry sauce heated and flamed in a chafing dish and served over ice cream.

## DANISH RHUBARB

Soften
   **1 envelope gelatine**
in
   **½ cup cold water**
Bring to boil
   **2 cups sweetened cooked rhubarb**
Add softened gelatine and stir until dissolved. Chill until the consistency of unbeaten egg white.
Whip with mixer or rotary beater.
Fold in
   **½ cup heavy cream, whipped**
Turn into a 4-cup mould. Chill until set. Unmould.
Makes 4 to 6 servings.

## BAKED CUSTARD

Preheat oven to 350°F.
Scald together
   **2 cups milk**
   **½ cup granulated sugar**
Cool slightly.
Beat until light
   **4 eggs or 8 egg yolks**
Gradually stir in milk mixture with
   **½ teaspoon vanilla**
Strain and pour into custard cups. Place in pan of hot water.
Bake in preheated 350° oven for 25 to 30 minutes, or until almost set.
Do not overcook. Chill and serve.
Makes 5 to 6 servings.

## SOFT CUSTARD

Scald together
   **2 cups milk**
   **½ cup granulated sugar**
Beat until light
   **3 eggs or 6 egg yolks**
Gradually stir in milk mixture. Return to saucepan or top of double boiler and cook over low heat, stirring constantly, until the custard coats a metal spoon.
Remove from heat and stir in
   **½ teaspoon vanilla**
Chill.
Makes 4 to 6 servings.

## BAKED RICE CUSTARD

Preheat oven to 325°F.
Lightly grease a 1-quart casserole.
Beat together

   **2 eggs**
   **2 cups milk**
Combine with
   **1 cup cooked rice**
   **½ cup lightly packed brown sugar**
   **½ teaspoon salt**
Turn into casserole and set in pan of hot water.
Bake in preheated 325° oven for about 1 hour or until almost set.
Makes 4 to 6 servings.

## VANILLA CREAM PUDDING

Scald
   **2½ cups milk**
In a saucepan, combine
   **3 tablespoons PURITY Flour**
   **½ cup granulated sugar**
   **¼ teaspoon salt**
Gradually add scalded milk. Cook over medium heat, stirring constantly, until thickened. Cover and cook 2 minutes longer, stirring occasionally.
Stir a little of hot mixture into
   **1 egg, slightly beaten**
Then blend into remaining hot mixture. Cook 1 minute longer, stirring constantly.
Remove from heat and blend in
   **1 teaspoon vanilla**
Cool.
Makes 5 to 6 servings.

## PINEAPPLE CREAM PUDDING:

Drain
   **1 (10-ounce) can crushed**
   **pineapple**
Measure juice and add water to make
   **1 cup pineapple juice**
Mix with
   **1 cup undiluted evaporated milk**
Use this liquid instead of milk in above recipe. Cool. Fold in drained, crushed pineapple (1 cup).

## APRICOT CREAM PUDDING:

In a covered saucepan, cook together until tender and thickened (10 minutes)
   **½ cup chopped dried apricots**
   **½ cup granulated sugar**
   **½ cup water**
Stir into hot Vanilla Cream Pudding. Cool.

## APPLE COBBLER

Preheat oven to 375°F.

**Drop Biscuit Dough:**

Sift together
    1¼ cups PURITY Flour
    3 tablespoons granulated sugar
    3 teaspoons baking powder
    ¼ teaspoon salt
With a pastry blender or two knives cut in finely
    ⅓ cup shortening
Mix together and add
    1 egg
    ½ cup milk
Stir with a fork to make a drop batter.

**Apple Filling:**

Peel, core and slice
    3 medium apples
In a saucepan, combine apples and
    ⅓ cup granulated sugar
    1 teaspoon grated lemon rind
    ¾ cup water
    ½ teaspoon cinnamon
Bring to boil, stirring until sugar is dissolved. Reduce heat and cover. Simmer about 8 minutes or until apples begin to soften.
Turn into a 1½-quart casserole.
Drop biscuit dough from a spoon onto hot fruit mixture.
Bake in preheated 375° oven for 25 to 30 minutes or until light golden.
Serve warm with cream.
Makes 5 to 6 servings.

RHUBARB COBBLER: Prepare Apple Cobbler following basic recipe but substituting for apple filling 3 cups cubed fresh or frozen rhubarb, 1 cup granulated sugar and ¾ cup water. Cook as directed.

CANNED FRUIT COBBLER: Prepare Apple Cobbler following basic recipe but substituting for apple filling the following: Put in casserole drained fruit from 1 (19-ounce) can sweetened cherries, sliced peaches or raspberries. Make a fruit sauce by melting 1 tablespoon butter, blending in 2 tablespoons PURITY Flour, and 1 cup fruit syrup; cook until thickened and pour over fruit. Top with Drop Biscuit dough and bake as directed.

## APPLE DUMPLINGS

Preheat oven to 375°F.
Lightly grease a large shallow baking dish
Prepare Purity Pastry (See page 154) and roll ⅛ inch thick into an 18 × 12 inch rectangle. Cut into 6 squares.
Combine
    3 tablespoons butter or margarine
    ¾ teaspoon cinnamon
    ¾ teaspoon allspice
    ¾ teaspoon nutmeg
    ¼ teaspoon cloves
    ⅓ cup lightly packed brown sugar
Peel and core
    6 medium apples
Place one apple on each square of pastry
In centre of each apple place
    1 teaspoon red currant jelly
Spread spice mixture over each apple, bring points of pastry together and seal.
Place in prepared baking dish.
Bake in preheated 375° oven for 30 minutes.
In a saucepan, combine
    1½ cups boiling water
    1½ cups granulated sugar
    3 tablespoons apple juice or water
Cook until sugar is dissolved.
Pour over baked apples and bake for an additional 20 minutes.
Baste frequently. Serve warm.
Makes 6 servings.

MINCEMEAT DUMPLINGS: Prepare Apple Dumplings following basic recipe but substituting 1 tablespoon mincemeat for red currant jelly. Bake as directed.

PEACH DUMPLINGS: Prepare Apple Dumplings following basic recipe but substituting a mixture of ⅓ cup lightly packed brown sugar, ⅓ cup granulated sugar and ½ teaspoon cinnamon for spice mixture, and replace the apples with peeled, whole peaches. Do not bake with sauce but serve with cream.

*For a quick and attractive dessert, fill sherbets with cubes of varied-coloured jelly. Prepare 2 or 3 different jelly powders as directed and chill separately in 8" square pans. Cut the jelly into ¾" squares and lift out with a spatula.*

## STRAWBERRY COMPOTE

In a saucepan, combine
**1 cup granulated sugar**
**¼ cup water**
Bring to boil and boil 5 minutes or until a thick syrup.
Remove from heat and stir in
**¼ cup Grand Marnier**
Pour over
**2 quarts fresh, hulled, strawberries**
Allow to cool.
Bring to a boil then chill completely.
Serve with small cakes or ice cream.
Makes 8 servings.

## CREAM PUFFS

Preheat oven to 375°F.
Grease a baking sheet.
In a saucepan, combine
**½ cup butter**
**1 cup water**
Bring to boil.
All at once, beat in
**1 cup PURITY Flour**
**¼ teaspoon salt**
Continue cooking, beating vigorously until mixture leaves sides of pan. Remove from heat and cool slightly.
Then add, one at a time
**4 eggs**
Beat vigorously until smooth and glossy after adding each egg.
Chill thoroughly.
Drop batter from a spoon, 2-inches apart, onto greased baking sheet, mounding each and swirling top.
Bake in preheated 375° oven for 30 to 40 minutes (45 to 50 for large, 25 to 30 for small puffs), or until light and golden. Slit sides, turn off oven, and let dry in oven. Cool.
Fill with sweetened whipped cream or a cream filling. Dust with icing sugar.
Serve cold.
Makes 12 large, 18 medium, or 3 dozen small puffs.

FROZEN PUFFS: Prepare large Cream Puffs as in basic recipe, fill with ice cream and serve with warm Butterscotch Sauce (See page 119).

CHOCOLATE ECLAIRS: Prepare Cream Puff batter as in basic recipe but shape into 4-inch long, 1-inch wide strips on greased baking sheet. Bake as directed about 40 minutes. When cool fill with Vanilla Cream Pudding (See page 107) and top with Chocolate Glaze (See page 143).

## APPLE CRISP

Preheat oven to 375°F.
Grease a 1½-quart square baking dish.
Cream together
**⅓ cup butter or margarine**
**1¼ cups lightly packed brown sugar**
Stir in until crumbly a mixture of
**⅔ cup PURITY Flour**
**¼ teaspoon cinnamon**
Arrange in prepared casserole
**6 peeled and sliced apples**
Sprinkle with crumbs.
Bake in preheated 375° oven for 40 minutes, or until apples are tender and topping is golden brown.
Makes 6 servings.

CRUNCHY APPLE CRISP: Prepare Apple Crisp following basic recipe but substituting a mixture of ⅓ cup PURITY Flour and ⅔ cup PURITY Rolled Oats for the flour. Bake as directed.

CHERRY CRISP: Prepare Apple Crisp following basic recipe but substituting a mixture of 3 cups pitted fresh sour cherries and ⅓ cup corn syrup for apples. Bake as directed.

RHUBARB CRISP: Prepare Apple Crisp following basic recipe but substituting a mixture of 3 cups diced, fresh or frozen rhubarb and ⅓ cup granulated sugar for apples. Bake as directed.

AMBROSIA CRISP: Prepare Apple Crisp following basic recipe but omitting cinnamon and substituting a mixture of 6 medium oranges, peeled and sectioned; 3 medium bananas, sliced; ¾ cup flaked or desiccated coconut, 2 tablespoons lemon juice and 2 tablespoons PURITY Flour for apples. Bake in preheated 400° oven for 15 to 18 minutes or until topping is golden.

*To blend chocolate smoothly into hot milk, melt chocolate and stir into milk when lukewarm. Beat smooth with rotary beater.*

## PINEAPPLE UPSIDEDOWN CAKE

Preheat oven to 350°F.
Melt in a 9-inch square or deep 9-inch round cake pan
   **3 tablespoons butter or margarine**
Stir in
   **⅓ cup lightly packed brown sugar**
Arrange attractively in pan
   **1 (19-ounce) can sliced pineapple, drained**
Sift together into large mixer bowl
   **1½ cups PURITY Flour**
   **2¾ teaspoons baking powder**
   **½ teaspoon salt**
   **1 cup granulated sugar**
Add
   **⅓ cup shortening**
   **½ cup milk**
Beat for 1 minute at low speed of electric mixer or 150 strokes by hand.
Add
   **¼ cup milk**
   **2 eggs**
Beat for 2 additional minutes at low speed.
Pour batter into prepared pan and bake in preheated 350° oven for 40 to 45 minutes, or until cake springs back when lightly touched.
Immediately invert on serving plate and cool 10 minutes before removing pan.
Place cherry halves in pineapple, if desired.

MAPLE PEAR UPSIDEDOWN CAKE: Prepare Pineapple Upsidedown Cake following basic recipe but substituting 1 (19-ounce) can pear halves for the pineapple and adding ½ teaspoon maple flavouring with shortening.

COCONUT UPSIDEDOWN CAKE: Prepare Pineapple Upsidedown Cake following basic recipe but reduce butter to 2 tablespoons and substitute ¼ cup granulated sugar for ⅓ cup brown sugar; replace pineapple with ½ cup shredded coconut.

PEACH UPSIDEDOWN CAKE: Prepare Pineapple Upsidedown Cake following basic recipe but substituting 1 (19-ounce) can peach halves for pineapple.

PINEAPPLE UPSIDEDOWN CAKE: Pineapple can be arranged attractively in a round or a square pan. When position-ing fruit, keep in mind that cake is inverted. With peach slices, for example, place in pan with thin edge of slice up.

## SAUCY BUTTERSCOTCH PUDDING

Preheat oven to 350°F.
Grease an 8-inch square cake pan.
Sift together
   **1 cup PURITY Flour**
   **1½ teaspoons baking powder**
   **¼ teaspoon salt**
Cream
   **⅓ cup shortening**
Beat in
   **⅔ cup granulated sugar**
Blend in, beating until light and fluffy
   **1 egg**
   **½ teaspoon vanilla**
Add sifted dry ingredients to creamed mixture alternately with
   **⅓ cup milk**
Turn into prepared pan.
In a saucepan, mix together
   **1 cup lightly packed brown sugar**
   **2 tablespoons PURITY Flour**
   **1¾ cups water**
Add
   **2 tablespoons butter or margarine**
Heat just to boiling and pour over batter. Do not stir.
Bake in preheated 350° oven for 45 to 50 minutes.
Makes 6 servings.

## DESSERT MERINGUES

Preheat oven to 250°F.
Beat to form stiff but moist peaks
   **4 egg whites**
   **¼ teaspoon cream of tartar**
Gradually beat in
   **1 cup fruit sugar**
Beat until very stiff and shiny.
Fold in
   **½ teaspoon vanilla**
Cover baking sheets with brown paper. For each shell, drop about ⅓ cup meringue onto paper. Using the back of a spoon, shape into shells. If you prefer, a pastry tube may be used for shaping the shells. Bake in preheated 250° oven for 1 hour. Turn off heat and leave meringues in oven, door ajar, until cooled to room temperature.
Fill with ice cream and sweetened fruit.
Makes 12 meringues.

## CHRISTMAS PUDDING

Grease one 2-quart or two 1-quart moulds.
Sift or blend together
**1⅔ cups PURITY Flour**
**2 teaspoons baking soda**
**½ teaspoon cinnamon**
Combine
**2 cups raisins**
**2 (8-ounce) packages whole glacé**
**cherries**
**2 (8-ounce) packages cut mixed**
**peel**
**1½ cups currants**
Sprinkle with ½ cup flour mixture.
Beat together
**2 cups chopped suet (½ pound)**
**2 cups lightly packed brown sugar**
**2 eggs**
**⅓ cup molasses**
Combine remaining flour mixture with
**2 cups fine, dry bread crumbs**
Add dry ingredients to suet mixture alternately with
**2 cups buttermilk**
Stir in floured fruit together with
**½ cup slivered blanched almonds**
Turn batter into prepared mould. Cover with wax paper and foil and tie tightly. Steam for 3 to 4 hours. Turn out of mould immediately and allow to cool.
To reheat for serving, return to mould, cover as before, and steam 1½ hours.
Makes 10 servings.

STEAMED PUDDINGS: Cover puddings with double thickness of wax paper. Tie tightly, then cover with foil. Place on rack in pan with boiling water or in steamer.

## APRICOT ICE CREAM

Beat together
**2 eggs**
**¼ cup granulated sugar**
**½ teaspoon salt**
Gradually stir in
**1½ cups milk**
Cook over medium heat, stirring constantly until the custard coats a metal spoon.
Cool.
Combine
**1¼ cups heavy cream, whipped**
**¾ cup raisins, chopped and soaked**
**in rum**
**1 cup apricot purée***
Fold into custard mixture.
Pour into a 2-quart bowl and freeze. When firm beat with an electric mixer or rotary beater until smooth, but not melted. Continue freezing until very firm.
*Drain canned apricot halves and purée in colander or blender.
Makes 6 cups.

*Unflavoured gelatine should be softened in cold water before dissolving (use ½ cup water for each envelope) or dry dilute gelatine by mixing with sugar called for in recipe.*

*Metal jelly moulds will chill more quickly than china or glass.*

## PEACH MELBA

Thaw
**1 (15-ounce) package frozen**
**raspberries**
Mash berries and combine in a saucepan with
**½ cup red currant jelly**
Bring to boiling point.
Mix and stir in
**1 tablespoon PURITY Flour**
**3 tablespoons granulated sugar**
Cook over medium heat, stirring constantly, until thickened and clear. Strain and cool.
When ready to serve, top
**6 fresh or canned peach halves**
with
**Ice cream**
Pour sauce over top. Serve immediately.
Makes 6 servings.

## FROZEN LEMON DESSERT

Crush about 26 graham wafers to give
**1 cup graham wafer crumbs**
Lightly grease an 8-inch square cake pan.
Press half of crumbs in pan.
In a saucepan, combine
**½ cup granulated sugar**
**2 egg yolks**
**⅓ cup lemon juice**
**1 tablespoon grated lemon rind**
Cook over medium heat, stirring constantly, until thickened. Cool.
Beat to form stiff but moist peaks
**2 egg whites**
Gradually add
**¼ cup granulated sugar**
Beat until stiff and shiny.
Fold meringue into cooled custard together with
**1¼ cups heavy cream, whipped**
Turn into prepared pan.
Sprinkle with reserved crumbs. Freeze until firm. Cut in squares and serve frozen.
Makes 9 servings.

## MAPLE PARFAIT

Beat until thick
**4 eggs**
Slowly pour in while beating
**1 cup hot maple syrup**
Whip until stiff
**1 pint heavy cream**
Fold into egg mixture.
Freeze until firm (4 hours).
Makes 12 servings.

## ALMOND CHARLOTTE

Line with wax paper and oil a 9 x 5 x 3-inch loaf pan.
Break into small chunks and set aside
**½ pound macaroons**
Arrange attractively in bottom and around sides of prepared pan
**½ pound lady fingers**
Cream
**½ cup unsalted butter**
Blend in, beating until light and fluffy
**1 cup sifted icing sugar**
**3 egg yolks**
Stir in
**½ cup ground almonds**
**1 teaspoon almond flavouring**

Beat to form stiff but moist peaks
**3 egg whites**
Fold into butter mixture.
Cover lady fingers with ½-inch layer of cream filling.
Sprinkle with macaroon crumbs.
Repeat until all is used but finishing with the cream filling.
Freeze for 24 hours or until very hard.
To serve, unmould and fill to top of lady fingers with
**1 pint heavy cream, whipped**
Decorate with maraschino cherries.
Makes 8 to 10 servings.

## LIME SHERBET

Boil together for 10 minutes, stirring frequently
**1¼ cups granulated sugar**
**1 cup water**
Soften
**1 envelope gelatine**
in
**¼ cup cold water**
Add gelatine to boiling syrup and stir until dissolved.
Remove from heat and blend in
**2 cups dry white wine**
**1 tablespoon crème de menthe**
**1 cup fresh lime juice**
Freeze to a mush in ice cream bucket or freezer trays.
Beat together until stiff but not dry
**1 egg white**
**¼ teaspoon salt**
Fold into lime mush and freeze firm.
Makes 8 servings.

## ZABAGLIONE

Beat until very light
**3 egg yolks**
**½ cup sifted icing sugar**
Heat to just below boiling
**½ cup Madeira, Marsala, or sherry wine**
When egg yolks are thick and lemony, transfer to top of double boiler.
Add hot wine, beating constantly, with a rotary beater. Beat until thick and hot.
Serve at once in sherbet glasses, plain or with fresh fruit.
Makes 4 to 6 servings.

## SOUR MILK GINGERBREAD

Preheat oven to 350°F.
Grease a 9-inch square cake pan.
Line bottom with wax paper or dust lightly with flour.
Sift together.
  **2 cups PURITY Flour**
  **½ teaspoon salt**
  **¾ teaspoon baking soda**
  **1½ teaspoons ginger**
Cream
  **⅓ cup shortening**
Beat in
  **⅓ cup lightly packed brown sugar**
Blend in, beating until light and fluffy
  **1 egg**
  **¾ cup table molasses**
Add sifted dry ingredients to creamed mixture alternately with
  **¾ cup sour milk or buttermilk**
Make 3 dry and 2 liquid additions, combining lightly after each.
Turn into prepared pan.
Bake in preheated 350° oven for 40 to 45 minutes, or until cake springs back when lightly touched. Cool 5 minutes, then remove from pan.
Serve warm with whipped cream or Foamy Applesauce. (See page 118).

---

*Small steamed puddings make attractive gifts. Cool thoroughly, wrap in saran and then in gay paper.*

---

## CRÊPES SUZETTES

Prepare and bake French Pancakes (See page 201). Keep warm.
Cream together
  **¼ cup butter or margarine**
  **¼ cup granulated sugar**
  **1 tablespoon grated orange rind**
Spread on pancakes and fold into quarters.
In a chafing dish, combine
  **½ cup shredded orange rind**
  **¾ cup orange juice**
  **2 tablespoons butter or margarine**
  **½ cup granulated sugar**
  **½ cup Grand Marnier or Cognac**
Cook slowly until orange rind is translucent.
Arrange folded pancakes in sauce and reheat. Flame at table with
  **½ cup Grand Marnier or Cognac**
Makes 10 servings.

## APPLE STRUDEL

Blend together
  **1 tablespoon butter**
  **2 tablespoons icing sugar**
  **1 egg yolk**
Stir in
  **2 cups lukewarm water**
With mixer at medium speed beat in
  **2½ cups PURITY Flour**
Blend in by hand
  **2½ cups PURITY Flour**
Knead dough until slightly sticky and bubbles appear. Cut into 6 pieces and shape into round balls. Cover with warm bowl. Let stand 15 minutes. Roll each piece of dough to approximately 9-inches in diameter.

Cream together
  **½ cup butter**
  **½ cup shortening**
Divide in 6 portions and spread on each circle.

Stack the circles of dough on a large table covered with a cloth or sheet dusted with flour. Cover with a warm bowl and let stand 30 minutes. Rewarm the bowl occasionally to keep the dough warm. Pull dough by hand from centre toward the edges. When dough is as transparent as wax paper, cut off thick edges. (This will cover entire table and even hang over edges.)

Let stand for 30 minutes or until dry.

Preheat oven to 375°F.
Peel, core and cut into thin slices sufficient apples to give
  **10 cups sliced apples**
Combine
  **1¼ cups granulated sugar**
  **1 teaspoon cinnamon**
  **½ teaspoon nutmeg**
Cut stretched dough in three equal widths. Mound in a row ⅓ of apples on each portion of dough at table edge. Sprinkle with sugar mixture. Fold over ends of dough to cover apples. Using the table cloth, roll up the three portions of dough like a jelly roll.

Place on rack in jelly roll pan. Bake in 375° oven for 40 to 45 minutes until golden brown and apples are tender. Sprinkle with icing sugar and serve warm. Makes 3 strudels.

## BAKED ALASKA

Prepare Chocolate Brownies (See page 150) or Butterscotch Brownies (See page 151) but bake in a 9-inch round layer cake pan.
Line a bowl or mould 7½ inches in diameter with waxed paper, leaving an overhang.
Press into bowl
**2 pints ice cream (vanilla, coffee or strawberry)**
Cover with wax paper and freeze.
Beat to form stiff but moist peaks.
**5 egg whites (½ cup)**
**½ teaspoon cream of tartar**
Gradually beat in (2 tablespoons at a time)
**⅔ cup granulated sugar**
Beat until very stiff and shiny.

Transfer cake to wooden board. Invert ice cream on cake, removing wax paper. Spread meringue to completely cover cake and ice cream. Return to freezer. (If stored for several days, cover with plastic wrap when hard.)

For serving, preheat oven to 500°F. Bake Alaska for 2 to 3 minutes, or until lightly browned. Then let stand at room temperature for 10 minutes to soften cake layer. Alaska may be baked as soon as it is covered with meringue, but serve immediately.
Makes 12 servings.

## COTTAGE PUDDING

Preheat oven to 350°F.
Grease a 9-inch square cake pan.
Line bottom with wax paper OR dust lightly with flour.
Sift together
**1½ cups PURITY Flour**
**2 teaspoons baking powder**
**½ teaspoon salt**
Cream
**⅓ cup shortening**
Beat in
**1 cup granulated sugar**
Blend in, beating until light and fluffy
**1 egg**
**1 teaspoon vanilla**
Add sifted dry ingredients to creamed mixture alternately with
**1 cup milk**

Make 3 dry and 2 liquid additions, combining lightly after each.
Turn into prepared pan.
Bake in preheated 350° oven for 35 to 40 minutes, or until cake springs back when lightly touched. Cool 5 minutes, then remove from pan.
Serve warm with Brown Sugar Sauce (See page 118).
Makes 9 servings.

---

*Spiced fruit is a welcome change for dessert. Drain a suitable size can of peaches or pears and simmer the juice for 10 minutes with a piece of stick cinnamon and a few whole cloves. Strain, pour over fruit and refrigerate until cold.*

---

## RHUBARB UPSIDEDOWN CAKE

Preheat oven to 350°F.
In a 9-inch square cake pan, melt
**3 tablespoons butter or margarine**
Stir in
**2 cups cut rhubarb (1-inch pieces)**
**½ cup granulated sugar**
**5 drops red food colouring**
Cover with aluminium foil and bake while preparing batter (8 to 10 minutes).
Sift together
**1½ cups PURITY Flour**
**2 teaspoons baking powder**
**½ teaspoon salt**
Cream
**½ cup shortening**
Beat in
**¾ cup granulated sugar**
Blend in, beating until light and fluffy
**2 eggs**
**1 teaspoon vanilla**
Add sifted dry ingredients to creamed mixture alternately with
**¾ cup milk**
Make 3 dry and 2 liquid additions, combining lightly after each.
Turn into prepared pan.
Bake in preheated 350° oven for 40 to 45 minutes, or until cake springs back when lightly touched. Immediately invert on serving plate and cool 10 minutes before removing pan.
Makes 9 servings.

## ALMOND CHIFFON ROLL

**Almond Filling:**
In a saucepan, combine
 ¼ cup PURITY Flour
 ¼ cup granulated sugar
Gradually blend in
 ¾ cup milk
Cook over medium heat, stirring constantly, until mixture comes to boil and starts to thicken.
Stir a little of hot mixture into
 1 egg yolk, slightly beaten
Then blend into remaining hot mixture.
Cook 1 minute longer, stirring constantly.
Remove from heat and blend in
 ¼ cup butter
 ¼ cup slivered, blanched almonds
 1 teaspoon vanilla
Chill thoroughly.

**Chiffon Roll:**
Preheat oven to 325°F.
Grease a 15 x 10-inch jelly roll pan. Line with wax paper.
Beat to form stiff but moist peaks
 ½ cup egg whites
 ¼ teaspoon cream of tartar
Gradually beat in
 ½ cup granulated sugar
Continue beating until very stiff and shiny.
Sift together
 1 cup PURITY Flour
 1½ teaspoons baking powder
 ½ teaspoon salt
 ¼ cup granulated sugar
Add and beat smooth (½ minute with mixer)
 ¼ cup vegetable oil
 2 egg yolks
 2 teaspoons grated orange rind
 ¼ cup orange juice
 2 tablespoons water
 ½ teaspoon vanilla
Fold egg yolk mixture into meringue until blended. Turn into prepared pan.
Bake in preheated 325° oven for 20 to 25 minutes, or until cake springs back when lightly touched. Turn out at once on a towel which has been sprinkled with icing sugar. Remove wax paper and trim off any crisp edges.
Spread with chilled Almond Filling. Roll up starting at narrow side. Make a firm roll wrapping tightly with towel. Chill until ready to serve.
Makes 6 to 8 servings.

## CHEESECAKE

Preheat oven to 325°F.
Mix together
 2½ cups graham wafer crumbs
 ½ cup granulated sugar
 ½ cup melted butter or margarine
Press almost all of mixture evenly on sides and bottom of 9-inch spring form pan, reserving some for the topping.
Beat to form stiff but moist peaks
 5 egg whites
Gradually beat in
 ¼ cup granulated sugar
Beat until stiff and shiny.
Cream until softened
 1 pound cream cheese
Beat in, one at a time
 5 egg yolks
Gradually beat in (in order listed)
 ⅔ cup granulated sugar
 3 tablespoons lemon juice
 ¼ cup PURITY Flour
 1 teaspoon vanilla
 1 cup thick dairy sour cream
Fold in egg white mixture.
Pour into prepared pan. Sprinkle reserved crumbs to form rim on top.
Bake in preheated 325° oven for 1¼ hours, or until almost set. Cool. Top with canned fruit pie filling, if desired.
Makes 12 to 14 servings.

## SACHER TORTE

Make Chocolate Sponge Cake (See page 136) in two 8-inch round layer cake pans.
Cool in pans and then remove.
Fill cooled cake with
 ½ cup strained apricot jam
In a saucepan, combine
 3 ounces, unsweetened chocolate
 1 cup heavy cream (40%)
 1 cup granulated sugar
 1 teaspoon corn syrup
Cook over low heat stirring constantly until chocolate and sugar are melted. Increase heat to medium and cook without stirring for about 5 minutes, or until soft ball stage (236°F. on candy thermometer). Cool to room temperature.
Pour over filled cake. Chill. Remove from refrigerator ½ hour before serving. Traditionally this Austrian specialty is served with sweetened whipped cream.
Makes 12 servings.

## COLD PRALINE SOUFFLÉ

Prepare a 7-inch soufflé dish as in photograph.
Oil a 15 x 10-inch jelly roll pan.
In a small heavy saucepan, combine
**1¼ cups granulated sugar**
**1 cup unblanched almonds**
**¼ teaspoon cream of tartar**
Cook over medium heat, stirring occasionally with a metal spoon, until caramel coloured liquid.
Pour into oiled jelly roll pan and allow to set. Put through nut grinder, or blender to obtain praline powder.
With electric mixer, beat together to form stiff peaks (about 15 minutes at high speed)
**5 whole eggs**
**4 egg yolks**
**1 cup granulated sugar**
**¼ cup Kirsch**
In top of double boiler over boiling water, soften and then dissolve
**2 envelopes gelatine**
**½ cup cold water**
**2 tablespoons lemon juice**
Whip until stiff
**1 cup heavy cream**
**2 tablespoons sifted icing sugar**
**1 teaspoon vanilla**
Fold dissolved gelatine, and whipped cream into egg mixture together with
**¼ cup praline powder**
Turn into prepared 7-inch soufflé dish. Chill until firm. Remove wax paper and garnish sides with praline powder, and top with sweetened whipped cream and red currant jelly.
Makes 10 servings.

PREPARING SOUFFLÉ DISH: Fit a band of waxed paper, foil or brown paper on outside of dish to extend rim. Tie tightly with string. Brush with vegetable oil.

## FRENCH RIVIERA TORTE

Preheat oven to 350°F.
Line bottoms of two 8-inch round layer cake pans with wax paper.
Beat to form stiff but moist peaks
**4 egg whites**
Gradually beat in
**½ cup granulated sugar**
Beat until very stiff and shiny.
Beat until thick and lemon-coloured
**4 egg yolks**
Gradually beat in
**½ cup granulated sugar**
**¼ cup cold water**
**½ teaspoon vanilla**
Mix together and sift over egg yolk mixture (in four portions)
**¾ cup PURITY Flour**
**¾ teaspoon baking powder**
**¼ teaspoon salt**
Fold gently after each addition.
Fold in meringue.
Turn into prepared pans and bake in preheated 350° oven for 25 to 30 minutes, or until cake springs back when lightly touched. Invert and cool in pans. When cool, loosen edges and remove from pans. Peel off wax paper.

**Vanilla Cream Filling:**
In a saucepan combine
**⅓ cup PURITY Flour**
**½ cup granulated sugar**
Gradually blend in
**1½ cups milk**
Cook over medium heat, stirring constantly until thickened. Cool.
Cream
**½ cup butter**
Gradually beat in cooled milk mixture with
**½ teaspoon vanilla**
Chill thoroughly.
Spread Torte layers with filling and allow to set before icing.

**Icing:**
Cream
**¼ cup butter or margarine**
Blend in
**¼ cup cold strong coffee**
**1 tablespoon milk**
**1 teaspoon vanilla**
**1 tablespoon cocoa**
Gradually beat in
**4 cups sifted icing sugar**

Beat until smooth and of good spreading consistency. Ice top and sides of the Torte. Chill until ready to serve.

## FROZEN CHRISTMAS PUDDING

Drain, reserving juices
**1 (10-ounce) can crushed pineapple**
**1 (6-ounce) jar maraschino cherries**
In a saucepan, combine juices with
**½ cup raisins**
Bring to boil.
Remove from heat and stir in
**2½ cups miniature marshmallows**
Stir until dissolved. Cool.
Blend in pineapple and chopped cherries with
**⅓ cup chopped blanched almonds, toasted**
**1 tablespoon grated lemon rind**
**2 tablespoons lemon juice**
**2 tablespoons light rum**
**or**
**2 teaspoons rum flavouring**
Beat to form stiff but moist peaks
**2 egg whites**
Gradually beat in
**⅓ cup granulated sugar**
Beat until stiff and shiny.
Fold into fruit mixture.
Whip until stiff and fold in
**1 cup heavy cream**
Turn into individual jelly moulds, cover with foil and freeze until firm.
Makes 8 servings.

## CHOCOLATE MOUSSE

Melt together over boiling water
**3 squares semi-sweet chocolate**
**¼ cup dry sherry**
Cool.
Beat until thick and lemon-coloured
**4 egg yolks**
Blend in chocolate mixture.
Beat to form stiff but moist peaks
**4 egg whites**
Gradually beat in
**½ cup granulated sugar**
Beat until stiff and shiny.
Fold into chocolate mixture. Turn into serving dish and chill.
Makes 6 servings.

## PINEAPPLE TORTE

Make True Sponge Cake (See page 136) in two ungreased 8-inch round layer cake pans lined with wax paper. Invert and cool in pans and then remove. Peel off wax paper.

**Pineapple Filling:**

In a saucepan, combine
**⅓ cup PURITY Flour**
**¾ cup granulated sugar**
Drain and chop, reserving juice
**1 (19-ounce) can pineapple chunks**
Measure juice and add water to make
**1 cup pineapple juice**
Gradually stir into flour mixture.
Cook over medium heat, stirring constantly, until thickened. Cover and cook 2 minutes longer, stirring occasionally. Remove from heat and stir in chopped pineapple chunks with
**3 tablespoons light rum**
**or**
**1 tablespoon rum flavouring**
Cool. Stirring occasionally.

**Cream Topping:**

Prepare according to package directions
**1 (2-ounce) package whipped dessert topping**
Stir in
**few drops yellow food colouring**
Spread cake layers with filling and spoon cream mixture over top.
Garnish with
**toasted coconut**
Makes 8 to 10 servings.

## HAWAIIAN RICE

In a bowl, combine
**1½ cups cooked rice**
**1 cup miniature or quartered marshmallows***
**¾ cup crushed pineapple, drained**
Chill 2 to 3 hours.
Beat until stiff
**½ pint heavy cream**
Blend in
**3 tablespoons granulated sugar**
Fold into rice mixture. Chill.
Garnish with maraschino cherries, almonds or toasted coconut.
Makes 6 servings.

*Coloured marshmallows may be used.

## COFFEE ANGEL TORTE

Preheat oven to 300°F.
Cut out five 7-inch circles of white or brown paper.
Beat to form stiff but moist peaks
**4 egg whites**
**½ teaspoon cream of tartar**
Gradually beat in
**1 cup lightly packed brown sugar**
Beat until very stiff and shiny.
Spread on paper circles.
Top one meringue with
**½ cup blanched almond halves**
Bake rounds on ungreased baking sheet in preheated 300° oven for 35 minutes, or until lightly browned. Moisten paper and remove. Cool.
Whip to form peaks
**2 pints heavy cream**
Gradually beat in
**½ cup lightly packed brown sugar**
**2 tablespoons instant coffee powder**
Spread plain meringue rounds with cream filling and stack. Top with almond covered round.
Chill 3 to 4 hours.
Makes 10 to 12 servings.

## CHARLOTTE RUSSE

Line a buttered 9-inch springform pan with
**lady or sponge cake fingers**
Scald
**2 cups milk**
In a saucepan, combine
**¼ cup granulated sugar**
**1 envelope gelatine**
**4 egg yolks**
Gradually stir in scalded milk. Cook over medium heat, stirring constantly, until slightly thickened (1 minute).
Remove from heat and blend in
**1 teaspoon vanilla**
or
**1 tablespoon brandy**
Cool.
Beat to form stiff but moist peaks
**4 egg whites**
Gradually beat in
**¼ cup granulated sugar**
Beat until stiff and shiny.
Fold into custard with
**1 cup heavy cream, whipped**
Turn into prepared pan.
Chill until firm.
Makes 10 to 12 servings.

# SWEET SAUCES

## BROWN SUGAR SAUCE

In a saucepan, melt
**2 tablespoons butter or margarine**
Blend in a mixture of
**2 tablespoons PURITY Flour**
**½ cup lightly packed brown sugar**
**¼ teaspoon salt**
Gradually stir in
**1 cup water**
Cook, stirring constantly until thickened.
Remove from heat and stir in
**1 teaspoon vanilla**
Serve hot on steamed or baked puddings.
Makes 1¼ cups.

RAISIN BROWN SUGAR SAUCE: Prepare Brown Sugar Sauce as in basic recipe and blend in ⅓ cup raisins and ¼ teaspoon grated lemon rind.

SPICED BROWN SUGAR SAUCE: Prepare Brown Sugar sauce as in basic recipe and blend in ¼ teaspoon cinnamon and a pinch of nutmeg.

## FOAMY APPLESAUCE

Combine
**1 (15-ounce) can sweetened applesauce**
**¼ teaspoon cinnamon**
Fold in
**2 egg whites, beaten**
**¼ cup heavy cream, whipped**
Serve on hot gingerbread or spice cake.
Makes 2¾ cups.

## APRICOT SAUCE

In a saucepan, combine
**1 cup apricot nectar**
**1 cup honey**
**¼ cup cognac or brandy**
Cook until thoroughly heated. Serve warm on Apple Strudel (See page 113) or ice cream.
Makes 2 cups.

## BRANDY SAUCE

In a saucepan, melt
**¼ cup butter or margarine**
Blend in a mixture of
**¼ cup PURITY Flour**
**⅔ cup lightly packed brown sugar**
Gradually stir in
**1½ cups milk**
Cook over medium heat, stirring constantly, until thickened.
Stir in
**¼ cup brandy**
Serve on steamed or baked puddings.
Makes 2½ cups.

## BUTTERSCOTCH SAUCE

In a saucepan, combine
**1¼ cups lightly packed brown sugar**
**¾ cup corn syrup**
**¼ cup butter or margarine**
Bring to a boil over medium heat, stirring constantly.
Cook, without stirring, until a drop forms a soft ball in cold water (232°F. on candy thermometer). Remove from heat and cool to lukewarm.
Blend in
**½ cup table cream (18%) or undiluted evaporated milk**
**1 teaspoon vanilla**
Cool.
Serve on ice cream.
Makes 2 cups.

## CHOCOLATE SAUCE

In a saucepan, combine
**1 cup lightly packed brown sugar**
**1 cup corn syrup**
**½ cup boiling water**
Bring to a boil, stirring constantly. Reduce heat and cook 2 minutes longer.
Blend in

**3 squares unsweetened chocolate, melted**
**1 teaspoon vanilla**
If necessary, beat smooth with rotary beater.
Cool. Serve at room temperature on ice cream.
Makes 2¼ cups.

## HOT FUDGE SAUCE

Prepare Chocolate Fudge Frosting (See page 142) and cook to 228°F. on candy thermometer. Serve warm on ice cream.
Makes 1 cup.

## HARD SAUCE

Cream
**⅓ cup soft butter or margarine**
Gradually blend in
**1 cup sifted icing sugar or lightly packed brown sugar**
Beat until creamy.
Gradually stir in
**1 teaspoon vanilla or 1 tablespoon brandy, sherry or rum**
Place in serving dish and chill thoroughly. If desired, use a pastry tube to make individual rosettes. Serve chilled on hot steamed or baked puddings.
Makes 1 cup.

## LEMON SAUCE

In a saucepan, combine
**3 tablespoons PURITY Flour**
**½ cup granulated sugar**
**¼ teaspoon salt**
Gradually stir in
**1¼ cups boiling water**
Cook over medium heat, stirring constantly, until thickened. Cover and cook 2 minutes longer, stirring occasionally. Remove from heat and blend in
**2 tablespoons butter or margarine**
**1 tablespoon grated lemon rind**
**¼ cup lemon juice**
Serve hot on steamed or baked puddings.
Makes 1½ cups.

ORANGE SAUCE: Prepare Lemon sauce following basic recipe but substituting orange rind for lemon rind, ¼ cup orange juice for lemon juice and adding 1 tablespoon lemon juice.

# Cakes and Cookies

---

## CAKES

---

### THE "WHY" OF PERFECT CAKES

To turn out perfect cakes every time requires perfectly balanced recipes and an understanding of the principles of cake making. The recipes have all been tolerance tested to ensure perfection and here are a few pointers on cake making itself.

### INGREDIENTS AND MEASURING

**Flour**—Flours are milled from different types of wheat and each type requires the proper proportions of sugar, shortening and other ingredients to give perfect cakes. All these recipes are designed for PURITY All-Purpose Flour.

To measure, simply spoon the flour directly from the bag or canister into a dry measuring cup (these have the cup line at the rim) and fill to overflowing. With a straight-edged spatula or knife, push off the flour that rises above the rim. Cups in the fraction sizes can be filled and levelled in the same way.

**Fat**—These recipes specify either shortening or butter and we recommend that these fats not be interchanged as a liquid adjustment would be required. However, regular margarine may be used instead of butter. (Soft margarine may have too much liquid effect).

The simplest method of measuring fat is to press it firmly into a dry measuring cup making sure there are no hollows underneath.

**Sugar**—Use fine granulated white sugar unless the recipe specifies brown sugar. To measure sugar, follow the same method as for flour. Spoon it into a dry measuring cup to fill to overflowing. Level off with a straight-edged spatula or knife.

**Eggs**—These recipes have been tested using large size eggs but medium or extra large eggs will give good results except in the foam type cakes, where there would need to be an adjustment in the number of eggs. (Approximately 4 extra large eggs = 4½ large eggs = 5 medium eggs.)

**Liquid**—To measure, place liquid measuring cup on table. Pour in liquid until, when you stoop to see the mark at eye level, the liquid is at the required line.

A Raspberry Chiffon Cake seems to shelter an assortment of cookies—Cherry Cheese Brownies, Chinese Chews, Almond Crescents, Marma-Date Square and Glazed Molasses Drops interspersed with chocolate chip, oatmeal, macaroon and shortbread cookies ▶

**Baking Powder**—These recipes are designed for a single acting baking powder. To us double acting baking powder allow ¾ teaspoon for each teaspoon called for in th recipe.

**Temperature of Ingredients**—Before mixing cake be sure all ingredients are at roor temperature for best results.

**Pans**—The size of a cake pan makes a difference and it is advisable to use the siz specified. Grease the bottom of pans with shortening and line bottom with wax pape Or, if you prefer, grease bottom and sides of pan with shortening and dust lightl with flour. Do not grease pans for foam type cakes.

**Beating**—Now that more homes are equipped with a mixer, the step-by-step picture which follow show how to use this time-saver to make perfect cakes. When makin by hand, be sure to cream thoroughly the shortening, sugar and eggs.

## TYPES OF CAKES

For descriptive purposes, we generally divide cakes into three types; the butter o conventional cake; the one-bowl cake; and the foam cake. The first two rely on leavening agent, such as baking powder, to make them light and tender. Foam cake gain at least some and generally most of their lightness from beaten eggs or egg white and include sponge, chiffon and angel cakes.

## CONVENTIONAL CAKES

1. Assemble ingredients and utensils. Set oven control at 350°F. Rub cake pan with shortening and line bottom with wax paper or dust lightly with flour. Measure dry ingredients and sift together.

2. Cream butter or shortening, whichever specified. Gradually blend in sugar. Mixture should remain creamy. If granular, sugar has been added too quickly.

USE PURITY FLOUR, THE JOLLY MILLER FLOUR, FOR HAPPY BAKIN(

3. Beat in eggs and flavouring. Continue beating until light and fluffy. If fat-sugar mixture has become granular, extra beating now will correct.

4. Add dry ingredients to creamed mixture alternately with liquid. Begin and end with dry ingredients. Beat as little as possible after liquid additions at lowest speed. Beat at medium speed after dry additions. Total mixing time for this step should not exceed 6 minutes. Drop pan to allow large air bubbles to escape.

5. Bake in centre of preheated 350° oven. Pans should not touch each other or sides of oven. Cake is fully baked when surface springs back when lightly touched and cake begins to pull away from sides of pan.

6. Cool cake in pan 5 minutes. Then turn out on cloth covered cake rack. Remove pan and wax paper. Turn right side up on rack to cool.

# WHITE CAKE

Preheat oven to 350°F.
Grease two 8-inch round layer cake pans.
Line bottoms with wax paper OR dust lightly with flour.
Sift together
**2⅓ cups PURITY Flour**
**3 teaspoons baking powder**
**1 teaspoon salt**
Cream
**⅔ cup shortening**
Beat in
**1¾ cups granulated sugar**
Blend in, beating until light and fluffy.
**3 eggs**
**1 teaspoon vanilla**
Add sifted dry ingredients to creamed mixture alternately with
**1¼ cups milk**
Make 3 dry and 2 liquid additions, combining lightly after each.
Turn into prepared pans.
Bake in preheated 350° oven for 35 to 40 minutes, or until cake springs back when lightly touched. Cool 5 minutes, then remove from pans.

SPICE CAKE: Prepare White Cake batter following basic recipe but reduce flour to 2¼ cups, and increase milk to 1⅓ cups and add 1½ teaspoons cinnamon, ¾ teaspoon ginger, ¾ teaspoon nutmeg and ¼ teaspoon allspice to the dry ingredients. Bake as directed.

MAPLE NUT CAKE: Prepare White Cake batter following basic recipe but increase milk to 1⅓ cups and substitute 1 teaspoon maple flavouring for the vanilla. Fold ½ cup finely chopped walnuts into the batter. Bake as directed.

MARBLE CAKE: Prepare White Cake batter as in basic recipe. Divide the batter in two portions. To one portion blend in a mixture of 1½ squares unsweetened chocolate melted, 1 tablespoon granulated sugar, ⅛ teaspoon baking soda and 1 tablespoon hot water. Leave second portion of the batter plain. Drop alternate spoonfuls of the two batters into prepared pans. Swirl for a marbled effect. Bake as directed.

# BANANA CAKE

Preheat oven to 350°F.
Grease two 8-inch round layer cake pans.
Line bottoms with wax paper.
Sift together.
**2¼ cups PURITY Flour**
**2 teaspoons baking powder**
**1 teaspoon baking soda**
**½ teaspoon salt**
Cream
**½ cup shortening**
Beat in
**1¼ cups granulated sugar**
Blend in, beating until light and fluffy.
**2 eggs**
**1 teaspoon vanilla**
Add sifted dry ingredients to creamed mixture alternately with
**1 cup mashed ripe bananas**
**¾ cup buttermilk**
Make 3 dry and 2 liquid additions, combining lightly after each.
Turn into prepared pans.
Bake in preheated 350° oven for 30 to 35 minutes, or until cake springs back when lightly touched. Cool 5 minutes, then remove from pans.

# PINK SWIRL CAKE

Preheat oven to 350°F.
Grease a 9-inch square cake pan.
Sprinkle bottom with
**½ cup chopped nuts**
Sift together
**1½ cups PURITY Flour**
**2 teaspoons baking powder**
**½ teaspoon salt**
Cream
**½ cup butter**
Beat in
**1 cup granulated sugar**
Blend in, beating until light and fluffy
**2 eggs**
**1 teaspoon vanilla**
Add sifted dry ingredients to creamed mixture alternately with
**¾ cup milk**
Make 3 dry and 2 liquid additions, combining lightly after each. Turn into pan.
Melt together and swirl on batter.
**⅓ cup red currant jelly**
**1 tablespoon water**
Bake in preheated 350° oven for 45 to 50 minutes, or until cake springs back when lightly touched.
Cool 5 minutes, invert on greased wax paper, remove pan and quickly reinvert on serving plate, nut-side down.

## ALMOND BUTTER CAKE

Preheat oven to 350°F.
Grease a 9-inch square cake pan.
Line bottom with wax paper OR dust lightly with flour.
Sift together
    1½ cups PURITY Flour
    1½ teaspoons baking powder
    ½ teaspoon salt
Cream
    ½ cup butter
Beat in
    1 cup granulated sugar
Blend in, beating until light and fluffy
    2 eggs
    ½ teaspoon almond flavouring
Add sifted dry ingredients to creamed mixture alternately with
    ¾ cup milk
Make 3 dry and 2 liquid additions, combining lightly after each.
Then fold in
    ½ cup chopped almonds
Turn into prepared pan.
Bake in preheated 350° oven for 40 to 45 minutes, or until cake springs back when lightly touched. Cool 5 minutes, then remove from pan.

## ORANGE CAKE

Preheat oven to 350°F.
Grease two 8-inch round layer cake pans.
Line bottoms with wax paper OR dust lightly with flour.
Sift together
    1¾ cups PURITY Flour
    1½ teaspoons baking powder
    1 teaspoon salt
    ½ teaspoon baking soda
Cream
    ½ cup shortening
Beat in
    1¼ cups granulated sugar
Blend in, beating until light and fluffy
    2 egg yolks
    1 egg
Add sifted dry ingredients to creamed mixture alternately with
    1 cup orange juice
Make 3 dry and 2 liquid additions, combining lightly after each.
Turn into prepared pans.
Bake in preheated 350° oven for 30 to

35 minutes, or until cake springs back when lightly touched. Cool 5 minutes, then remove from pans.
Fill and frost with Orange Frosting (See page 141).

*Cake batter may be baked as cup cakes. Fill paper cups or liners (set in muffin cups) about ⅔ full. Bake at 400°F. for 18 to 20 minutes. A batter containing 2 cups flour will yield approximately 1½ dozen medium-sized cup cakes.*

## PINEAPPLE CAKE

Preheat oven to 350°F.
Grease two 8-inch round layer cake pans.
Line bottoms with wax paper OR dust lightly with flour.
Drain, reserving ⅓ cup juice for icing (See page 141) and measure remaining juice
    1 (10-ounce) can crushed
        pineapple
Add to remaining juice
    1 cup (approx.) milk
or sufficient to give 1¼ cups liquid.
Sift together
    2⅓ cups PURITY Flour
    3½ teaspoons baking powder
    1 teaspoon salt
Cream
    ⅔ cup shortening
Beat in
    1⅔ cups granulated sugar
Blend in, beating until light and fluffy.
    3 eggs
    ½ teaspoon vanilla
Add sifted dry ingredients to creamed mixture alternately with liquid.
Make 3 dry and 2 liquid additions, combining lightly after each. Then fold in drained crushed pineapple and turn into prepared pans.
Bake in preheated 350° oven for 35 to 40 minutes or until cake springs back when lightly touched. Cool 5 minutes, then remove from pans.

*Preheat oven to ensure it will be at correct temperature when cake is mixed. An unbaked cake may lose some of its leavening if allowed to stand for any length of time after being mixed.*

## CRANBERRY NUGGET CAKE

Preheat oven to 350°F.
Grease a 9-inch square cake pan.
Line bottom with wax paper OR dust lightly with flour.
Sift together
**1¾ cups PURITY Flour**
**3½ teaspoons baking powder**
**1 teaspoon salt**
Cream
**½ cup shortening**
Beat in
**1¼ cups granulated sugar**
**1 teaspoon vanilla**
Blend in, beating until light and fluffy, (5 minutes)
**3 egg whites**
Add sifted dry ingredients to creamed mixture alternately with
**¾ cup milk**
Make 3 dry and 2 liquid additions, combining lightly after each.
Mix together and fold in
**1 cup diced jellied cranberry sauce**
**¼ cup PURITY Flour**
Turn into prepared pan.
Bake in preheated 350° oven for 35 to 40 minutes, or until cake springs back when lightly touched. Cool 5 minutes, then remove from pan.

## APPLE JUICE CAKE

Preheat oven to 350°F.
Grease two 8-inch round layer cake pans.
Line bottoms with wax paper OR dust lightly with flour.
Sift together
**1¾ cups PURITY Flour**
**2 teaspoons baking powder**
**½ teaspoon salt**
**¼ teaspoon baking soda**
**½ teaspoon cinnamon**
**¼ teaspoon nutmeg**
Cream
**½ cup shortening**
Beat in
**1½ cups lightly packed brown sugar**
Blend in, beating until light and fluffy
**2 eggs**
Add sifted dry ingredients to creamed mixture alternately with
**½ cup milk**
**½ cup apple juice**
Make 3 dry and 2 liquid additions, combining lightly after each.

Then fold in
**½ cup chopped nuts**
Turn into prepared pans.
Bake in preheated 350° oven for 30 t 35 minutes, or until cake springs bac when lightly touched. Cool 5 minute then remove from pans.

## COCOA CAKE

Preheat oven to 350°F.
Grease two 8-inch round layer cake pan
Line bottoms with wax paper.
Sift together
**1¾ cups PURITY Flour**
**½ cup cocoa**
**½ teaspoon salt**
**1 teaspoon baking powder**
**½ teaspoon baking soda**
Cream
**½ cup shortening**
Beat in
**1½ cups granulated sugar**
Blend in, beating until light and fluffy
**2 eggs**
**1 teaspoon vanilla**
Add sifted dry ingredients to creame mixture alternately with
**1¼ cups milk**
Make 3 dry and 2 liquid additions, con bining lightly after each.
Turn into prepared pans.
Bake in preheated 350° oven for 30 t 35 minutes, or until cake springs bac when lightly touched. Cool 5 minute then remove from pans.

## CHOCOLATE CHIPPER CAKE

Preheat oven to 350°F.
Grease a 9-inch square cake pan.
Line bottom with wax paper OR du lightly with flour.
Combine and set aside to cool
**1¼ cups chopped dates**
**1¼ cups boiling water**
Sift together
**2 cups PURITY Flour**
**½ teaspoon salt**
**1 teaspoon baking powder**
**½ teaspoon baking soda**
Cream
**⅔ cup shortening**
Beat in
**1¼ cups granulated sugar**

end in, beating until light and fluffy
**2 eggs**
**2 squares unsweetened**
**chocolate, melted**
**1 teaspoon vanilla**
dd sifted dry ingredients to creamed
mixture alternately with date mixture.
Make 3 dry and 2 liquid additions, combining lightly after each.
urn into prepared pan.
prinkle with
**1 cup (6-ounce package)**
**chocolate chips**
rrange on top of batter
**½ cup pecan halves**
ake in preheated 350° oven for 45 to
0 minutes, or until cake begins to pull
way from sides of pan. Cool 5 minutes,
hen remove from pan.

## DEVIL'S FOOD CAKE

eheat oven to 350°F.
rease two 8-inch or 9-inch round layer
ke pans.
ne bottoms with wax paper OR dust
ghtly with flour.
ft together
**1½ cups PURITY Flour**
**1½ teaspoons baking powder**
**½ teaspoon baking soda**
**¾ teaspoon salt**
**½ cup cocoa**
ream
**½ cup shortening**
eat in
**1⅓ cups granulated sugar**
end in, beating until light and fluffy
**3 eggs**
**½ teaspoon vanilla**
dd sifted dry ingredients to creamed
ixture alternately with
**1¼ cups milk**
ake 3 dry and 2 liquid additions, com-
ning lightly after each.
rn into prepared pans.
ke in preheated 350° oven for 30 to
minutes, or until cake springs back
hen lightly touched. Cool 5 minutes,
en remove from pans.

## APRICOT CAKE

eheat oven to 350°F.
rease two 8-inch round layer cake pans.
ne bottoms with wax paper OR dust
ghtly with flour.

Sift together
**2⅓ cups PURITY Flour**
**3 teaspoons baking powder**
**1 teaspoon salt**
Cream
**⅔ cup shortening**
Beat in
**1¾ cups granulated sugar**
Blend in, beating until light and fluffy
**3 eggs**
**½ teaspoon lemon flavouring**
Mix together
**¼ cup milk**
**1 cup apricot nectar**
Add sifted dry ingredients to creamed
mixture alternately with liquid.
Make 3 dry and 2 liquid additions, combining lightly after each.
Turn into prepared pans.
Bake in preheated 350° oven for 35 to
40 minutes, or until cake springs back
when lightly touched. Cool 5 minutes,
then remove from pans.

## APPLE SPICE CAKE

Preheat oven to 350°F.
Grease an 8-inch or 9-inch square cake
pan.
Line bottom with wax paper OR dust
lightly with flour.
Sift together.
**1¾ cups PURITY Flour**
**2½ teaspoons baking powder**
**½ teaspoon salt**
**1 teaspoon cinnamon**
**½ teaspoon nutmeg**
Cream
**½ cup shortening**
Beat in
**1¼ cups lightly packed**
**brown sugar**
Blend in, beating until light and fluffy
**2 eggs**
Add sifted dry ingredients to creamed
mixture alternately with a mixture of
**½ cup sweetened applesauce**
**⅔ cup milk**
Make 3 dry and 2 liquid additions, combining lightly after each.
Turn into prepared pan.
Bake in preheated 350° oven for 45 to
50 minutes, or until cake springs back
when lightly touched. Cool 5 minutes,
then remove from pan.

## BOILED RAISIN CAKE

Preheat oven to 350°F.
Grease an 8-inch square cake pan.
Line bottom with wax paper OR dust lightly with flour.
In a saucepan, combine
 **1 cup raisins**
 **1½ cups water**
Bring to a boil and boil for 5 minutes.
Then drain, reserving liquid.
Sift together
 **1¾ cups PURITY Flour**
 **1½ teaspoons baking powder**
 **½ teaspoon baking soda**
 **½ teaspoon salt**
 **1 teaspoon cinnamon**
 **½ teaspoon nutmeg**
Cream
 **½ cup butter**
Beat in
 **1 cup lightly packed brown sugar**
Blend in, beating until light and fluffy
 **1 egg**
Add sifted dry ingredients to creamed mixture alternately with
 **⅔ cup raisin liquid**
Make 3 dry and 2 liquid additions, combining lightly after each.
Fold in drained raisins.
Turn into prepared pan.
Bake in preheated 350° oven for 50 to 55 minutes, or until cake springs back when lightly touched. Cool 5 minutes, then remove from pan.
Fill and frost with Brown Sugar Icing (See page 142).

## MINCEMEAT FRUIT CAKE

Preheat oven to 275°F.
Grease an 8 × 8 × 3-inch fruit cake pan, line with brown paper and grease again.
Sift together
 **1¾ cups PURITY Flour**
 **½ teaspoon baking soda**
 **1 tablespoon instant coffee powder**
 **1 teaspoon cinnamon**
 **½ teaspoon allspice**
Cream
 **⅔ cup butter**
Beat in
 **1¼ cups lightly packed brown sugar**
One at a time, blend in and beat until light and fluffy
 **4 eggs**

Add sifted dry ingredients to creamed mixture alternately with
 **1 tablespoon molasses**
 **1 tablespoon brandy**
 **1 teaspoon vanilla**
Mix together and stir in
 **2½ cups canned mincemeat**
 **1 (8-ounce) package red glacé cherries**
 **1 (8-ounce) package glacé pineapple, chopped**
 **1 cup blanched slivered almonds**
 **½ cup PURITY Flour**
Turn into prepared pan.
Bake in preheated 275° oven for 3½ to 4 hours or until cake tests done with a toothpick.
Remove from pan and lift off brown paper.
Cool and store.

## CHRISTMAS CAKE

Preheat oven to 275°F.
Grease an 8 × 8 × 3-inch fruit cake pan, line with brown paper and grease again
Combine and let stand overnight
 **2 cups raisins**
 **1 cup currants**
 **1 cup chopped dates**
 **2 (8-ounce) packages glacé cherries**
 **1 (8-ounce) package chopped mixed peel**
 **1 (4-ounce) package chopped walnuts**
 **½ cup brandy**
The next day, dredge fruit mixture in
 **½ cup PURITY Flour**
Sift together
 **2 cups PURITY Flour**
 **½ teaspoon salt**
 **½ teaspoon baking soda**
 **1 teaspoon cloves**
 **1 teaspoon allspice**
 **1 teaspoon cinnamon**
Cream
 **1 cup butter**
Gradually, beat in
 **2 cups lightly packed brown sugar**
 **6 eggs**
Mix together
 **¾ cup molasses**
 **¾ cup apple juice**
Add sifted dry ingredients to creamed mixture alternately with liquid.

...ake 3 dry and 2 liquid additions, com-
...ning lightly after each. Fold in floured
...uit.
...urn into prepared pan.
...ake in preheated 275° oven for 3 to 3½
...ours or until cake tests done with a
...othpick.
...emove from pan and lift off brown
...aper. Cool and store.

## LIGHT FRUIT CAKE

...eheat oven to 275°F.
...ace pan of water in oven.
...rease an 8 × 8 × 3-inch fruit cake pan,
...ne with brown paper and grease again.
...ombine
    **1 pound raisins, plumped***
    **1 cup ground almonds**
    **1 (8-ounce) package glacé
      red cherries**
    **1 (4-ounce) package glacé
      green cherries**
    **1 (4-ounce) package glacé
      pineapple, chopped**
    **1 (4-ounce) package chopped
      citron peel**
...redge fruit mixture in
    **½ cup PURITY Flour**

Cream together
    **½ cup butter**
    **½ cup shortening**
Gradually, beat in
    **1⅓ cups granulated sugar**
    **4 egg yolks**
    **2 teaspoons almond flavouring**
Mix together
    **⅓ cup brandy**
    **⅓ cup milk**
Add to creamed mixture alternately with liquid
    **2¼ cups PURITY Flour**
Make 3 dry and 2 liquid additions, combining lightly after each.
Beat together to form stiff but moist peaks
    **4 egg whites**
    **¾ teaspoon cream of tartar**
Fold in batter. Then fold in floured fruit. Turn into prepared pan.
Bake in preheated 275° oven for 3 to 3½ hours or until cake tests done with a toothpick.
Remove from pan and lift off brown paper. Cool and store.

*To plump raisins—cover with boiling water. Let stand 5 minutes and drain.

## ONE-BOWL CAKES

1. Assemble ingredients and utensils. Set oven control at 350°F. Grease and line bottom of cake pans with wax paper or dust lightly with flour.

2. Measure dry ingredients and sift into large mixer bowl.

3. Add shortening (not butter), first por
tion of liquid and flavouring.

4. Beat for 1 minute at low (No. 3) speed
of electric mixer. Scrape sides of bowl
Batter should be very stiff.

5. Add remaining liquid and eggs. Bea
for 2 additional minutes at low speed
scraping sides of bowl.

6. Turn into prepared pans. Batter shoulc
½ fill pan. Drop pan to allow large ai
bubbles to escape. Bake in preheatec
350° oven until cake springs back wher
lightly touched. Remove from pans anc
cool as for conventional cake.

## WHITE CAKE

Preheat oven to 350°F.
Grease two 8-inch round layer cake pans.
Line bottoms with wax paper OR dust lightly with flour.
Sift together into large mixer bowl
**2¼ cups PURITY Flour**
**4 teaspoons baking powder**
**¾ teaspoon salt**
**1½ cups granulated sugar**
Add
**½ cup shortening**
**¾ cup milk**
**1 teaspoon vanilla**
Beat for 1 minute at low speed of electric mixer or 150 strokes by hand.
Add
**¼ cup milk**
**3 eggs**
Beat for 2 additional minutes at low speed.
Pour batter into prepared pans and bake in preheated 350° oven for 35 to 40 minutes, or until cake springs back when lightly touched. Cool 5 minutes, then remove from pans.

CHOCOLATE MARBLE—Prepare White Cake following basic recipe and to ⅓ of finished batter add 1 square semi-sweet chocolate, melted. Evenly divide the white batter between 2 layer pans. Drop equal amounts of chocolate batter on each and swirl in.

COCONUT-MINT—Prepare White Cake following basic recipe but omit vanilla and add ½ teaspoon mint flavouring and 4 to 5 drops of green food colouring instead. Fold in ½ cup shredded coconut.

COFFEE—Prepare White Cake following basic recipe and add 2 tablespoons instant coffee powder with dry ingredients. Omit granulated sugar and add 1½ cups brown sugar with shortening. Use buttermilk and adjust leavening to 1¾ teaspoons baking powder and 1 teaspoon baking soda. Use only ½ teaspoon vanilla.

SPICE—Prepare White Cake following basic recipe and add 1 teaspoon cinnamon, ½ teaspoon nutmeg and ¼ teaspoon ground cloves with dry ingredients.

## CHOCOLATE CAKE

Preheat oven to 350°F.
Grease two 9-inch round layer cake pans.
Line bottoms with wax paper.
Sift together into large mixer bowl
**2 cups PURITY Flour**
**⅔ cup cocoa**
**1½ teaspoons baking powder**
**¾ teaspoon baking soda**
**1 teaspoon salt**
**1 cup granulated sugar**
Add
**⅔ cup shortening**
**1 cup lightly packed brown sugar**
**1 cup milk**
**1 teaspoon vanilla**
Beat for 1 minute at low speed of electric mixer or 150 strokes by hand.
Add
**¼ cup milk**
**3 eggs**
Beat for 2 minutes at low speed.
Pour batter into prepared pans and bake in preheated 350° oven for 35 to 40 minutes, or until cake springs back when lightly touched. Cool 5 minutes, then remove from pans.

## CONFETTI CAKE

Preheat oven to 350°F.
Grease two 8-inch round layer cake pans.
Line bottoms with wax paper OR dust lightly with flour.
Sift together into large mixer bowl
**2¼ cups PURITY Flour**
**4 teaspoons baking powder**
**¾ teaspoon salt**
**1⅓ cups granulated sugar**
Add
**½ cup shortening**
**¾ cup milk**
**1 teaspoon vanilla**
Beat for 1 minute at low speed of electric mixer or 150 strokes by hand.
Add
**¼ cup milk**
**3 eggs**
Beat for 2 minutes at low speed.
Fold in
**¼ cup decorator beads**
**(non pariels)**
Pour batter into prepared pans and bake in preheated 350° oven for 35 to 40 minutes, or until cake springs back when lightly touched. Cool 5 minutes, then remove from pans.

## PUMPKIN CAKE

Preheat oven to 350°F.
Grease two 8-inch round layer cake pans.
Line bottoms with wax paper OR dust lightly with flour.
Sift together into large mixer bowl
    1⅔ cups PURITY Flour
    3 teaspoons baking powder
    1 teaspoon baking soda
    ½ teaspoon salt
    ½ teaspoon allspice
    1 teaspoon cinnamon
    1½ cups granulated sugar
Add
    ½ cup shortening
    ¾ cup buttermilk
    1 teaspoon vanilla
Beat for 1 minute at low speed of electric mixer or 150 strokes by hand.
Add
    ⅓ cup canned pumpkin
    ¼ cup buttermilk
    3 eggs
Beat for 2 additional minutes at low speed.
Pour batter into prepared pans and bake in preheated 350° oven for 35 to 40 minutes, or until cake springs back when lightly touched.
Cool 5 minutes, then remove from pans.

## ORANGE CAKE

Preheat oven to 350°F.
Grease an 8-inch square cake pan.
Line bottom with wax paper OR dust lightly with flour.
Sift together into small mixer bowl
    1½ cups PURITY Flour
    3 teaspoons baking powder
    ½ teaspoon salt
    1 cup granulated sugar
Add
    ½ cup shortening
    ⅔ cup milk
Beat for 1 minute at low speed of electric mixer or 150 strokes by hand.
Add
    3 tablespoons frozen orange
        concentrate, thawed
    2 eggs
Beat for 2 additional minutes at low speed.
Pour batter into prepared pan and bake in preheated 350° oven for 40 to 45 min-

utes or until cake springs back when lightly touched.
Combine and spread on hot cake
    ½ cup lightly packed brown sugar
    2 tablespoons PURITY Flour
    ¼ cup butter or margarine, melted
    1 tablespoon frozen orange
        concentrate, thawed
    ½ cup chopped nuts
Broil 2 to 3 minutes or until golden brown. Cool 15 minutes, then invert on wax paper to remove pan. Turn topping side up on serving plate.

---

*If the recipe calls for a covered casserole or frypan, a piece of aluminum foil may be used.*

---

## CRUMB CAKE

Preheat oven to 350°F.
Grease a 9-inch square cake pan.
Line bottom with wax paper OR dust lightly with flour.
Sift together
    1¾ cups PURITY Flour
    ¼ teaspoon salt
    1 teaspoon cinnamon
    ¼ teaspoon nutmeg
    ¼ teaspoon cloves
In small bowl of electric mixer cream
    ¾ cup butter
Beat in
    1 cup granulated sugar
Add sifted dry ingredients to creamed mixture and blend until mixture resembles cornmeal.
Reserve 1 cup of this mixture and set aside.
Add to remainder
    1 teaspoon baking soda
    2 eggs
    ¼ cup buttermilk or sour
        milk
Beat for 1 minute at low speed of electric mixer.
Add
    ½ cup buttermilk or sour
        milk
Beat for an additional 2 minutes at low speed.
Pour batter into prepared pan. Sprinkle with reserved crumb mixture.
Bake in preheated 350° oven for 40 to 50 minutes or until cake begins to pull away from sides of pan. Cool 5 minutes, then remove from pan.

## MARASCHINO CHERRY CAKE

Preheat oven to 350°F.
Grease two 8-inch round layer cake pans. Line bottoms with wax paper OR dust lightly with flour.
Sift together into large mixer bowl
**2¼ cups PURITY Flour**
**3½ teaspoons baking powder**
**¾ teaspoon salt**
**1½ cups granulated sugar**
Add
**½ cup shortening**
**⅔ cup milk**
**1 teaspoon vanilla**
Beat for 1 minute at low speed of electric mixer of 150 strokes by hand.
Add
**⅓ cup maraschino cherry juice**
**3 eggs**
Beat for 2 additional minutes at low speed.
Fold in
**½ cup finely chopped maraschino cherries**
Pour batter into prepared pans and bake in preheated 350° oven for 35 to 40 minutes, or until cake springs back when lightly touched. Cool 5 minutes, then remove from pans.

---

*When creaming butter (or shortening) and sugar together, remember it is impossible to beat too much at this stage— air is being whipped into the batter and the more the better.*

---

## PEACHY-ORANGE CAKE

Preheat oven to 350°F.
Grease two 8-inch round layer cake pans. Line bottoms with wax paper OR dust lightly with flour.
Sift together into large mixer bowl
**2⅓ cups PURITY Flour**
**2 teaspoons baking powder**
**1 teaspoon baking soda**
**¾ teaspoon salt**
**1 cup granulated sugar**
Add
**½ cup shortening**
**⅔ cup peach jam**
**⅔ cup orange juice**
**½ teaspoon vanilla**
Beat for 1 minute at low speed of electric mixer or 150 strokes by hand.
Add
**⅓ cup buttermilk**
**3 eggs**
Beat for 2 additional minutes at low speed.
If desired, fold in
**½ cup chopped walnuts**
Pour batter into prepared pans and bake in preheated 350° oven for 35 to 40 minutes, or until cake springs back when lightly touched. Cool 5 minutes, then remove from pans.

---

*Before baking butter or one-bowl cakes, drop pans on table top to allow any large air bubbles to escape or run a table knife through batter.*

---

## LEMON FEATHER CAKE

Preheat oven to 350°F.
Grease two 8-inch round layer cake pans. Line bottoms with wax paper OR dust lightly with flour.
Sift together into large mixer bowl
**2¼ cups PURITY Flour**
**1¾ teaspoons baking powder**
**1 teaspoon baking soda**
**½ teaspoon salt**
**1½ cups granulated sugar**
Add
**½ cup shortening**
**⅔ cup milk**
**3 tablespoons lemon juice**
**2½ tablespoons grated lemon rind**
Beat for 1 minute at medium speed of electric mixer or 150 strokes by hand.
Add
**⅓ cup milk**
**2 eggs**
**5 drops yellow food colouring**
Beat for 2 additional minutes at low speed.
Pour batter into prepared pans and bake in preheated 350° oven for 30 to 35 minutes, or until cake springs back when lightly touched. Cool 5 minutes, then remove from pans.

## SPONGE CAKES

1. Assemble ingredients and utensils. Separate eggs and allow to come to room temperature. Set oven control at 350°F. Beat egg whites and cream of tartar to form stiff but moist peaks at highest speed of mixer.

2. Very gradually beat in sugar. Beat until very stiff and shiny. If egg whites were underbeaten in (1), extra beating now will correct. Overbeating in (1) cannot be corrected.

3. Beat egg yolks until very thick and lemon-coloured at highest speed of mixer. Beat in sugar, liquid and flavouring.

4. Sift flour over egg yolk mixture in four portions.

5. Fold in flour gently after each addition, with rubber spatula or wooden spoon. Press spatula down one side of bowl, across bottom and up the opposite, lifting batter over flour. Turn bowl and repeat until smoothly blended.

6. Add egg yolk mixture to meringue and fold in until evenly blended. No blobs of white meringue should be visible.

7. Turn batter into an ungreased tube pan and cut gently through batter with a knife to remove large air bubbles.

8. Bake in preheated 350° oven for prescribed time or until cake springs back when lightly touched. Invert on custard cup, or ears of pan and allow to cool completely in pan. Loosen edges and remove.

## TRUE SPONGE

Preheat oven to 350°F.
Beat to form stiff but moist peaks
**4 egg whites**
**¾ teaspoon cream of tartar**
Gradually beat in
**¼ cup fruit sugar**
Beat until very stiff and shiny.
Beat until thick and lemon-coloured
**4 egg yolks**
Gradually beat in
**⅔ cup fruit sugar**
**¼ cup cold water**
**1 teaspoon lemon juice**
**1 teaspoon vanilla**
Sift over egg yolk mixture (in four portions)
**¾ cup PURITY Flour**
Fold gently after each addition.
Fold in meringue.
Turn into an ungreased 8-inch tube pan.
Cut gently through batter with a knife to remove air bubbles.
Bake in preheated 350° oven for 55 to 65 minutes. Invert and cool in pan. When cool, loosen edges and remove from pan.

## COFFEE SPONGE CAKE

Preheat oven to 350°F.
Beat to form stiff but moist peaks
**5 egg whites**
**½ teaspoon cream of tartar**
Gradually beat in
**½ cup granulated sugar**
Beat until very stiff and shiny.
Beat until thick and lemon-coloured
**5 egg yolks**
Gradually beat in
**⅔ cup granulated sugar**
**½ cup cold strong coffee**
Sift over egg mixture (in four portions)
**1 cup PURITY Flour**
**½ teaspoon salt**
Fold gently after each addition.
Fold in meringue together with
**½ cup finely chopped pecans**
Turn into an ungreased 10-inch tube pan.
Cut gently through batter with a knife to remove air bubbles.
Bake in preheated 350° oven for 55 to 65 minutes. Invert and cool in pan. When cool, loosen edges and remove from pan.

## CHOCOLATE SPONGE CAKE

Preheat oven to 325°F.
Beat to form stiff but moist peaks
**5 egg whites**
**½ teaspoon cream of tartar**
Gradually beat in
**⅓ cup granulated sugar**
Beat until very stiff and shiny.
Beat until thick and lemon-coloured
**5 egg yolks**
Gradually beat in
**½ cup granulated sugar**
**½ cup cold water**
**½ teaspoon vanilla**
Sift together and then sift over egg mixture
**½ cup PURITY Flour**
**½ cup cocoa**
Fold gently after each addition.
Fold in meringue.
Turn into an ungreased 8-inch tube pan.
Cut gently through batter with a knife to remove air bubbles.
Bake in preheated 325° oven for 55 to 60 minutes. Invert and cool in pan. When cool, loosen edges and remove from pan.

---

*When adding dry ingredients alternately with liquid, it is possible to overbeat, especially after each liquid addition, so beat quickly and lightly.*

---

## ANGEL CAKE

Preheat oven to 350°F.
Blend together
**1 cup PURITY flour**
**¼ cup sugar**
Beat to form stiff but moist peaks
**1¼ cups egg whites**
**1¼ teaspoons cream of tartar**
**¼ teaspoon salt**
**¾ teaspoon vanilla**
**¼ teaspoon almond flavouring**
Gradually beat in, beating until stiff and shiny
**1 cup fruit sugar**
Sift dry ingredients over egg white mixture in four portions, folding gently after each addition.
Turn into an ungreased 9-inch tube pan.
Bake in preheated 350° oven for 40 to 45 minutes, or until cake springs back when lightly touched. Invert and cool in pan. When cool, loosen edges and remove from pan.

## JELLY ROLL

Preheat oven to 400°F.
Grease a 15 x 10 x 1-inch jelly roll pan and line with wax paper.
Sift together
  **1 cup PURITY Flour**
  **1 teaspoon baking powder**
  **¼ teaspoon salt**
Beat until thick and lemon-coloured
  **4 eggs**
  **1 cup granulated sugar**
  **1 teaspoon lemon juice**
Gradually beat in
  **¼ cup hot milk**

Beat until very thick.
Sift dry ingredients over egg mixture in four portions, folding gently after each addition.
Turn into prepared pan.
Bake in preheated 400° oven for 10 to 12 minutes, or until cake springs back when lightly touched.
Turn out immediately on a towel sprinkled with icing sugar.
Remove wax paper and roll, rolling towel up in cake.
Cool.
Unroll, fill with jam, jelly or filling and re-roll.

## CHIFFON CAKES

1. Assemble ingredients and utensils. Separate eggs and allow to come to room temperature. Set oven control at 350°F. Sift together flour, baking powder, salt and specified portion of sugar into small bowl of mixer. Add vegetable oil, egg yolks, liquid and flavourings. Beat smooth, about ½ minute.

2. Beat egg whites and cream of tartar to form stiff but moist peaks. Very gradually beat in specified amount of sugar. Beat until very stiff and shiny, as picture shows.

3. Fold egg yolk mixture into meringue until no meringue is visible. Turn into ungreased tube pan. Bake in preheated 350° oven for specified time. Invert and cool in pan. Loosen edges and remove.

## CHIFFON CAKE

Preheat oven to 350°F.
Sift together
**1½ cups PURITY Flour**
**2½ teaspoons baking powder**
**1 teaspoon salt**
**¾ cup granulated sugar**
Add and beat smooth (½ minute with mixer)
**½ cup vegetable oil**
**6 egg yolks**
**¾ cup water**
**1 teaspoon vanilla**
Beat together to form soft peaks
**6 egg whites**
**½ teaspoon cream of tartar**
Gradually beat in
**¾ cup granulated sugar**
Continue beating until very stiff and shiny.
Fold egg yolk mixture into meringue until blended.
Turn into an ungreased 10-inch tube pan. Bake in preheated 350° oven for 55 to 65 minutes, or until cake springs back when lightly touched. Invert and cool in pan. When cool, loosen edges and remove from pan.

**ORANGE CHIFFON CAKE:** Prepare Chiffon Cake following basic recipe but substituting ½ cup orange juice and ¼ cup water for the water, and blend in 2 tablespoons finely grated orange rind.

**LEMON CHIFFON CAKE:** Prepare Chiffon Cake following basic recipe but substituting 1 tablespoon lemon juice for 1 tablespoon water, and 1 tablespoon finely chopped grated lemon rind for the vanilla.

**SPICE CHIFFON CAKE:** Prepare Chiffon Cake as in basic recipe and blend in 2 teaspoons cinnamon, 1 teaspoon ginger, ½ teaspoon nutmeg, and ½ teaspoon cloves with the dry ingredients.

## CHOCOLATE CHIFFON CAKE

Preheat oven to 350°F.
Stir until smooth
**½ cup cocoa**
**¾ cup boiling water**
Cool.
Sift together
**1 cup PURITY Flour**
**3 teaspoons baking powder**
**1 teaspoon salt**
**⅔ cup granulated sugar**
Add chocolate mixture with
**½ cup vegetable oil**
**6 egg yolks**
**1 teaspoon vanilla**
Beat smooth (½ minute with mixer).
Beat together to form soft peaks
**6 egg whites**
**½ teaspoon cream of tartar**
Gradually beat in
**⅔ cup granulated sugar**
Continue beating until very stiff and shiny.
Fold egg yolk mixture into meringue until blended.
Turn into an ungreased 10-inch tube pan. Bake in preheated 350° oven for 55 to 65 minutes, or until cake springs back when lightly touched. Invert and cool in pan. When cool, loosen edges and remove from pan.

## RASPBERRY CHIFFON CAKE

Preheat oven to 350°F.
Thaw and drain, reserving juice
**1 (15-ounce) package frozen raspberries (40%sugar)**
Sift together
**1½ cups PURITY Flour**
**3 teaspoons baking powder**
**1 teaspoon salt**
**⅓ cup granulated sugar**
Add and beat smooth (½ minute with mixer)
**½ cup vegetable oil**
**6 egg yolks**
**½ cup raspberry juice**
**⅔ cup drained mashed raspberries**
**2 tablespoons lemon juice**
Beat together to form soft peaks
**6 egg whites**
**½ teaspoon cream of tartar**
Gradually beat in
**½ cup granulated sugar**
Continue beating until very stiff and shiny.
Fold egg yolk mixture into meringue until blended.
Turn into an ungreased 10-inch tube pan. Bake in preheated 350° oven for 55 to 65 minutes, or until cake springs back when lightly touched. Invert and cool in pan. When cool, loosen edges and remove from pan.

## ORANGE PINEAPPLE CHIFFON CAKE

Preheat oven to 350°F.
Sift together
  **1½ cups PURITY Flour**
  **3 teaspoons baking powder**
  **1 teaspoon salt**
  **⅓ cup granulated sugar**
Add and beat smooth (½ minute with mixer)
  **½ cup vegetable oil**
  **6 egg yolks**
  **½ cup drained canned crushed pineapple**
  **¼ cup pineapple juice**
  **¼ cup frozen orange concentrate, thawed**
  **2 tablespoons lemon juice**
Beat together to form soft peaks
  **6 egg whites**
  **½ teaspoon cream of tartar**
Gradually beat in
  **½ cup granulated sugar**
Continue beating until very stiff and shiny.

Fold egg yolk mixture into meringue until blended.

Turn into an ungreased 10-inch tube pan. Bake in preheated 350° oven for 55 to 65 minutes, or until cake springs back when lightly touched. Invert and cool in pan. When cool, loosen edges and remove from pan.

# FILLINGS

## VANILLA CREAM FILLING

Scald
  **1 cup milk**
In a saucepan, combine
  **3 tablespoons PURITY Flour**
  **¼ cup granulated sugar**
  **Pinch of salt**
Gradually add scalded milk. Cook over medium heat, stirring constantly, until thickened. Cover and cook 2 minutes longer, stirring occasionally.
Stir a small amount of hot mixture into
  **1 egg, slightly beaten**
Then blend into remaining hot mixture. Cook 1 minute longer, stirring constantly. Remove from heat and blend in
  **1 tablespoon butter or margarine**
  **½ teaspoon vanilla**
Cool.
Makes 1 cup or sufficient to fill an 8 or 9-inch layer cake.

ALMOND CREAM FILLING: Prepare Vanilla Cream Filling following basic recipe but substituting ¼ teaspoon almond flavouring for vanilla, and stir in ½ cup slivered blanched almonds.

BANANA CREAM FILLING: Prepare Vanilla Cream Filling following basic recipe and just before using stir in 1 banana, sliced.

COCONUT CREAM FILLING: Prepare Vanilla Cream Filling following basic recipe and stir in ½ cup desiccated coconut.

COFFEE CREAM FILLING: Prepare Vanilla Cream Filling following basic recipe and add 2 teaspoons instant coffee powder to the scalded milk.

## BUTTERSCOTCH CREAM FILLING

Scald
  **1 cup milk**
In a saucepan, combine
  **3 tablespoons PURITY Flour**
  **½ cup lightly packed dark brown sugar**
Gradually add scalded milk. Cook over medium heat, stirring constantly, until thickened. Cover and cook 2 minutes longer, stirring occasionally.
Stir a small amount of hot mixture into
  **1 egg, slightly beaten**
Then blend into remaining hot mixture. Cook 1 minute longer, stirring constantly. Remove from heat and blend in
  **1 tablespoon butter or margarine**
  **½ teaspoon vanilla**
Cool.
Makes sufficient to fill an 8 or 9-inch layer cake.

## CHOCOLATE CREAM FILLING

Scald
**1 cup milk**
In a saucepan, combine
**3 tablespoons PURITY Flour**
**½ cup granulated sugar**
**¼ cup cocoa**
Gradually add scalded milk. Cook over medium heat, stirring constantly, until thickened. Cover and cook 2 minutes longer, stirring occasionally.
Stir a small amount of hot mixture into
**1 egg, slightly beaten**
Then blend into remaining hot mixture. Cook 1 minute longer, stirring constantly. Remove from heat and blend in
**1 tablespoon butter or margarine**
**½ teaspoon vanilla**
Cool.
Makes sufficient to fill an 8 or 9-inch layer cake.

## LEMON FILLING

In a saucepan, combine
**¼ cup PURITY Flour**
**½ cup granulated sugar**
**Pinch of salt**
Gradually stir in
**1 cup boiling water**
Cook over medium heat, stirring constantly, until thickened. Cover and cook 2 minutes longer, stirring occasionally.
Stir a small amount of hot mixture into
**1 egg, slightly beaten**
Then blend into remaining hot mixture. Cook 1 minute longer, stirring constantly. Remove from heat and blend in
**1 tablespoon butter or margarine**
**1 teaspoon grated lemon rind**
**3 tablespoons lemon juice**
Cool.
Makes sufficient to fill an 8 or 9-inch layer cake.

# FROSTINGS

## BUTTER FROSTING

Cream
**3 tablespoons soft butter**
Beat in
**½ teaspoon vanilla**
**Few grains salt.**
Blend in
**2 cups sifted icing sugar**
alternately with
**2 to 2½ tablespoons warm cream or milk**
Beat until smooth and of good spreading consistency.
Add more sifted icing sugar or milk, if necessary
Makes sufficient for top and sides of a 8 or 9-inch square cake or about 1½ dozen medium-size cup cakes. Double recipe to fill and frost two 8 or 9-inch layers.

CHOCOLATE BUTTER FROSTING: Prepare Butter Frosting following basic recipe and add 1 square unsweetened chocolate, melted, to the creamed butter.

COCOA BUTTER FROSTING: Prepare Butter Frosting following basic recipe but sift 3 tablespoons cocoa with icing sugar.

COFFEE BUTTER FROSTING: Prepare Butter Frosting following basic recipe but omit the vanilla. Dissolve ½ teaspoon instant coffee powder in 2 tablespoons boiling water and use it in place of the warm cream.

MOCHA BUTTER FROSTING: Prepare Butter Frosting following basic recipe but add 1 square unsweetened chocolate, melted, or 3 tablespoons cocoa, to the creamed butter. Substitute 2 to 2½ tablespoons hot coffee for the cream.

ORANGE BUTTER FROSTING: Prepare as for Butter Frosting following basic recipe omitting the vanilla and substituting 2 to 2½ tablespoons orange juice for the cream. Finally, blend in 1 teaspoon finely grated orange rind.

## ICING A CAKE

1. Brush crumbs from cooled cake. Place bottom layer, top side down, on serving plate. Cover with filling or frosting. Place second layer top side up.

2. Protect plate edge with 4 strips of wax paper. Frost sides and top of cake.

3. Carefully remove wax paper strips. Swirl frosting attractively.

## PINEAPPLE BUTTER FROSTING

In a saucepan, combine
**⅓ cup butter**
**⅓ cup pineapple juice**
**⅔ cup granulated sugar**
Heat until sugar is dissolved.
Remove from heat and gradually beat in
**3 to 4 cups sifted icing sugar**
Add sufficient icing sugar to give a good spreading consistency.
Makes sufficient to fill and frost two 8 or 9-inch layers.

## ORANGE FROSTING

In a saucepan, combine
**¾ cup granulated sugar**
**¼ cup corn syrup**
**1 tablespoon frozen orange concentrate, thawed**
**¼ teaspoon salt**
Bring just to boiling point.
Beat to form stiff but moist peaks
**2 egg whites**
**¼ teaspoon cream of tartar**
Gradually add hot syrup, beating until very stiff and shiny. Spread between layers, on top and sides of cooled cake.

## BANANA ICING

Cream together
  **½ cup butter**
  **½ cup mashed bananas**
Gradually blend in
  **3½ cups sifted icing sugar**
  **1 tablespoon lemon juice**
  **1 teaspoon vanilla**
Chill until of spreading consistency.
Makes sufficient to fill and frost two 8
or 9-inch layers.

## BROWN SUGAR ICING

In a saucepan, combine
  **½ cup butter**
  **⅔ cup light cream**
  **2½ cups lightly packed brown sugar**
Bring to a boil and cook 2 minutes, stirring constantly.
Remove from heat and gradually beat in
  **3 to 4 cups sifted icing sugar**
Add sufficient icing sugar to give good
spreading consistency.
Makes sufficient to fill and frost two 8
or 9-inch layers.

## LEMON BUTTER ICING

Cream
  **½ cup butter**
Gradually blend in
  **1¾ cups sifted icing sugar**
  **1 tablespoon lemon juice**
  **1 tablespoon grated lemon rind**
Makes sufficient icing for top and sides
of an 8 or 9-inch square cake.
Double recipe to fill and frost two 8 or
9-inch layers.

ORANGE BUTTER ICING: Prepare
Lemon Butter Icing following basic recipe
but substituting orange juice and rind for
lemon juice and rind.

*To colour coconut: Add food colouring
to 1 teaspoon water and toss the coconut
until evenly coloured.*

## CHOCOLATE FUDGE FROSTING

In a saucepan, combine
  **¾ cup granulated sugar**
  **½ cup cold water**
  **1 tablespoon corn syrup**
Cover and bring to boil.

Remove cover and continue cooking
until a drop will form a soft ball in cold
water (236°F. on candy thermometer).
Cool to lukewarm (110°F.) without stirring.
Stir in
  **2 squares unsweetened chocolate,
  melted**
  **2 tablespoons butter**
  **½ teaspoon vanilla**
Stir until a good spreading consistency.
Makes sufficient for top and sides of an
8 or 9-inch square cake.
Double recipe to fill and frost two 8 or
9-inch layers.

## GOLDEN SNOWY FROSTING

In covered saucepan, combine
  **1½ cups lightly packed brown sugar**
  **½ cup water**
  **2 tablespoons corn syrup**
  **¼ teaspoon cream of tartar**
  **1 tablespoon molasses**
Bring to boil. Uncover and continue
cooking, without stirring, until a drop
forms a soft ball in cold water (236°F. on
candy thermometer).
Beat to form stiff but moist peaks
  **2 egg whites**
Very gradually, beat in hot syrup. Continue beating until very stiff and shiny.
Beat in
  **½ teaspoon vanilla or maple
  flavouring**
Makes sufficient to fill and frost two 8
or 9-inch layers.

## JIFFY SNOWY FROSTING

Bring to boil
  **1¼ cups corn syrup**
Beat to form stiff but moist peaks
  **2 egg whites**
Very gradually, beat in hot syrup. Continue beating until very stiff and shiny.
Beat in
  **1 teaspoon vanilla**
  **¼ teaspoon food colouring (if
  desired)**
Makes sufficient to fill and frost two 8
or 9-inch layers.

MAPLE FROSTING: Prepare Jiffy Snowy
Frosting following basic recipe but substituting 1¼ cups maple syrup for corn
syrup.

## SEVEN-MINUTE FROSTING

In top of double boiler, combine
 **¾ cup granulated sugar**
 **Pinch of cream of tartar**
 **Pinch of salt**
 **3 tablespoons cold water**
 **1 egg white**
Cook over boiling water, beating constantly with an electric mixer or rotary beater until the frosting forms stiff but moist peaks (about 4 to 7 minutes). Scrape sides and bottom of pan occasionally. Remove from heat and fold in
 **½ teaspoon vanilla**
Makes sufficient to frost an 8 or 9-inch square cake. Double recipe to fill and frost two 8 or 9-inch layers. This will take a slightly longer beating time.

CHOCOLATE SEVEN MINUTE FROSTING: Prepare Seven Minute Frosting following basic recipe and gently fold in 1 square unsweetened chocolate, which has been melted and cooled.

PEPPERMINT SEVEN MINUTE FROSTING: Prepare Seven Minute Frosting following basic recipe but substituting 3 or 4 drops peppermint extract for vanilla. Tint a pale green, if desired.

SPICED SEVEN MINUTE FROSTING: Prepare Seven Minute Frosting following basic recipe and blend in ¼ teaspoon cinnamon and a pinch of ginger or nutmeg with the sugar.

## BROILED TOPPING

Combine
 **¼ cup soft butter**
 **½ cup lightly packed brown sugar**
 **3 tablespoons undiluted evaporated milk**
 **½ cup desiccated coconut or chopped nuts**
 **1 tablespoon grated orange rind (optional)**
Spread over top of warm cake and place cake under broiler for 2 to 3 minutes or until topping is bubbly and golden. Flavour is excellent with chocolate, orange or butter cake.

## CHOCOLATE GLAZE

In a small saucepan, combine
 **1 (6-ounce) package chocolate chips**
 **1 (6-ounce) can undiluted evaporated milk**
Cook over low heat, stirring constantly, until mixture comes to boil. Cook gently, stirring constantly until thickened (about 3 to 5 minutes).
Cool, stirring occasionally.
Makes about 1 cup.

# COOKIES

## MERINGUE DAINTIES

Preheat oven to 275°F.
Lightly grease a baking sheet.
Combine
 **1½ cups coarsely chopped dates**
 **1 cup mixed glacé fruit**
 **½ cup sifted icing sugar**
Beat to form stiff but moist peaks
 **2 egg whites**
Gradually beat in
 **½ cup sifted icing sugar**
Fold in date mixture with
 **1 cup chopped almonds**
Drop batter from a teaspoon about 2 inches apart onto greased baking sheet. Bake in preheated 275° oven for 12 to 15 minutes or until delicately browned. Makes 4 dozen cookies.

SOUTHERN DAINTIES: Prepare Dainties following basic recipe but substituting 1 cup coconut for almonds, and stir in ½ cup apricot jam or orange marmalade.

CHIP DAINTIES: Prepare Dainties following basic recipe but substituting 1 cup chocolate or butterscotch chips for almonds.

MINT-TOPPED DAINTIES: Prepare Dainties as in basic recipe and make a slight depression in the centre of the cookie. Fill with mint chocolate topping.

## CHOCOLATE CHIP COOKIES

Preheat oven to 350°F.
Lightly grease a baking sheet.
Sift together
    **1 cup PURITY Flour**
    **½ teaspoon baking soda**
    **½ teaspoon salt**
Cream together
    **½ cup butter**
    **½ cup granulated sugar**
    **¼ cup lightly packed brown sugar**
Beat in
    **1 egg**
    **1 teaspoon vanilla**
Beat until light and fluffy. Stir in dry ingredients.
Fold in
    **1 cup (6-ounce package) chocolate chips**
    **½ cup chopped walnuts**
Drop batter from a teaspoon about 2 inches apart onto greased baking sheet. Bake in preheated 350° oven for 10 to 12 minutes or until golden brown.
Makes 3 dozen cookies.

Drop batter from a teaspoon about 2 inches apart on greased baking sheet. Bake as directed, being careful not to overbake. Generally cookies crispen on cooling.

## CHOCOLATE DROPS

Preheat oven to 350°F.
Lightly grease a baking sheet.
Sift together
    **1 cup PURITY Flour**
    **½ teaspoon baking powder**
    **½ teaspoon salt**
    **½ cup cocoa**

Cream together
    **⅔ cup shortening**
    **1½ cups lightly packed brown sugar**
    **1 teaspoon vanilla**
Beat in
    **1 egg**
Beat until light and fluffy.
Stir in dry ingredients alternately with
    **¼ cup buttermilk or sour milk**
Drop batter from a teaspoon about 2 inches apart onto greased baking sheet. Bake in preheated 350° oven for 10 to 12 minutes or until edges are crisp.
Makes 4 dozen cookies.

*To re-crisp cookies, bake on ungreased baking sheet in preheated 300° oven for 3 to 5 minutes. Freshen soft drop cookies by reheating in a covered pan in preheated 300° oven for 8 to 10 minutes.*

## GLAZED MOLASSES DROPS

Preheat oven to 350°F.
Lightly grease a baking sheet.
Sift together
    **1½ cups PURITY Flour**
    **½ teaspoon baking soda**
    **½ teaspoon salt**
    **½ teaspoon ginger**
    **½ teaspoon cinnamon**
Cream together
    **½ cup shortening**
    **½ cup lightly packed brown sugar**
Beat in
    **1 egg**
    **¼ cup molasses**
Beat until light and fluffy. Stir in dry ingredients.
Fold in
    **½ cup raisins**
    **½ cup chopped walnuts**
Drop batter from a teaspoon about 2 inches apart onto greased baking sheet. Bake in preheated 350° oven for 10 to 12 minutes or until golden brown.
While cookies are still warm, glaze with a mixture of
    **1 cup sifted icing sugar**
    **1 tablespoon soft butter or margarine**
    **1½ tablespoons milk**
    **½ teaspoon vanilla**
    **Pinch of salt**
Makes 4 dozen cookies.

## DATE AND NUT DROPS

Preheat oven to 350°F.
Lightly grease a baking sheet.
Sift together
**2 cups PURITY Flour**
**1 teaspoon baking soda**
**1 teaspoon salt**
**1 teaspoon cinnamon**
Cream together
**1 cup shortening**
**1 cup lightly packed brown sugar**
**¾ cup granulated sugar**
Beat in
**2 eggs**
**1 teaspoon vanilla**
Beat until light and fluffy. Stir in dry ingredients.
Fold in
**2 cups chopped dates**
**1 cup chopped walnuts**
Drop batter from a teaspoon about 2 inches apart onto greased baking sheet.
Bake in preheated 350° oven for 10 to 12 minutes or until golden brown.
Makes 5 dozen cookies.

## COCONUT COOKIES

Preheat oven to 350°F.
Lightly grease a baking sheet.
Sift together
**2 cups PURITY Flour**
**1 teaspoon baking soda**
**½ teaspoon salt**
Cream together
**½ cup butter**
**1¼ cups granulated sugar**
Beat in
**2 eggs**
Beat until light and fluffy. Stir in dry ingredients.
Fold in
**1 cup coconut**
Drop batter from a teaspoon about 2 inches apart onto greased baking sheet.
Bake in preheated 350° oven for 10 to 12 minutes or until golden brown.
Makes 4 dozen cookies.

AMBROSIA COOKIES: Prepare Coconut Cookie dough following basic recipe but stir in 1 tablespoon grated orange rind, and mix coconut with ½ cup orange juice.

NUT CHERRY: Prepare Coconut Cookie dough following the basic recipe but combine coconut with ¼ cup maraschino cherry juice and ½ cup chopped maraschino cherries, and stir in 1 teaspoon almond flavouring, and ½ cup chopped pecans.

## SPICED GINGER MOUNDS

Preheat oven to 325°F.
Lightly grease a baking sheet.
Sift together
**2 cups PURITY Flour**
**1 teaspoon baking soda**
**1 teaspoon cinnamon**
**1 teaspoon cloves**
**1 teaspoon ginger**
**¼ teaspoon salt**
Cream together
**¾ cup shortening**
**1 cup granulated sugar**
Beat in
**1 egg**
**¼ cup molasses**
Beat until light and fluffy.
Stir in dry ingredients. Shape into small balls and roll each in granulated sugar.
Place on greased baking sheet about 2 inches apart.
Bake in preheated 325° oven for 12 to 15 minutes or until golden brown.
Makes 4 dozen cookies.

## MACAROONS

Preheat oven to 350°F.
Lightly grease a baking sheet.
Beat to form stiff but moist peaks
**4 egg whites**
Gradually beat in until stiff and shiny
**1¼ cups granulated sugar**
Stir in
**¾ cup PURITY Flour**
**½ teaspoon salt**
**½ teaspoon vanilla**
Fold in
**2½ cups coconut**
Drop batter from a teaspoon about 2 inches apart onto greased baking sheet.
Bake in preheated 350° oven for 10 to 12 minutes or until delicately golden.
Makes 4 dozen cookies.

CHOCOLATE MACAROONS: Prepare Macaroons following basic recipe and stir in 2 squares melted semi-sweet chocolate, before adding coconut.

## PEANUT BUTTER COOKIES

Preheat oven to 350°F.
Lightly grease a baking sheet.
Sift together
  **1¼ cups PURITY Flour**
  **½ teaspoon baking soda**
  **¼ teaspoon salt**
Cream together
  **⅔ cup peanut butter**
  **½ cup shortening**
  **⅔ cup lightly packed brown sugar**
  **½ cup granulated sugar**
Blend in
  **1 egg**
Stir in dry ingredients. Shape into small balls and place on a greased baking sheet about 3 inches apart. Press ½ inch thick with floured fork.
Bake in preheated 350° oven for 12 to 15 minutes or until nicely browned.
Makes 4 dozen cookies.

Cookies may be shaped by hand into small balls. Place on greased baking sheet and flatten with floured fork or glass tumbler.

## OATMEAL COOKIES

Preheat oven to 375°F.
Lightly grease a baking sheet.
Sift together
  **1¼ cups PURITY Flour**
  **½ teaspoon salt**
  **½ teaspoon baking soda**
  **½ teaspoon cinnamon**
Stir in
  **1¼ cups PURITY Rolled Oats**
Cream together
  **½ cup butter**
  **½ cup lightly packed brown sugar**

Blend in
  **¼ cup water**
Stir in dry ingredients. Shape into small balls and place on a greased baking sheet about 3-inches apart. Press ¼ inch thick with fork dipped in sugar.
Bake in preheated 375° oven for 8 to 10 minutes.
Makes 5 dozen cookies.
This traditional favourite may be varied with the addition of ½ cup chopped dried apricots, gum drops, dates, or 1 teaspoon cinnamon.

## APRICOT-CHOCOLATES

Combine in a saucepan
  **1 (6-ounce) can undiluted evaporated milk**
  **4 squares semi-sweet chocolate**
Cook, stirring constantly, until smooth.
Remove from heat and stir in
  **½ teaspoon vanilla**
Blend in
  **2½ cups crushed vanilla wafers**
  **½ cup sifted icing sugar**
  **½ cup chopped dried apricots**
Allow to cool until firm enough to shape (one hour at room temperature).
Form into 1-inch balls and roll in
  **chopped pecans**
Makes 4 dozen cookies.
RAISIN SMOOTHIES: Prepare Apricot-Chocolates following basic recipe but substituting ½ cup chopped raisins and ¼ cup chopped pecans for chopped dried apricots.

## ALMOND CRESCENTS

Preheat oven to 300°F.
Cream until very light
  **1¼ cups butter**
Blend in
  **½ cup lightly packed brown sugar**
  **1 egg yolk**
  **1 teaspoon almond flavouring**
Beat until light and fluffy.
Gradually stir in
  **1 cup chopped almonds**
  **2½ cups PURITY Flour**
Knead well to blend in last of flour.
Turn onto lightly floured surface and roll ¼ inch thick. Cut into crescents with floured cookie cutter.
Bake on ungreased baking sheet in preheated 300° oven for 18 to 20 minutes.
Makes 3 dozen cookies.

## ORANGE-HONEY COOKIES

Preheat oven to 350°F.
Lightly grease a baking sheet.
Sift together
**2 cups PURITY Flour**
**½ teaspoon baking powder**
**¼ teaspoon baking soda**
**¼ teaspoon salt**
Cream together
**¾ cup butter**
**⅓ cup granulated sugar**
**½ cup honey**
Blend in
**1 egg**
**1 tablespoon grated orange rind**
Stir in dry ingredients. Cover and chill for 1½ hours.
Turn onto lightly floured surface and roll ¼ inch thick. Cut into desired shapes with floured cookie cutters.
Bake on greased baking sheet in preheated 350° oven for 10 to 12 minutes. When cool, frost or fill with Orange Butter Cream.
Makes 3 dozen single cookies.

## ORANGE BUTTER CREAM

Cream
**¼ cup butter**
Gradually blend in
**2 cups sifted icing sugar**
alternately with
**1½ tablespoons orange juice**
**1 teaspoon grated orange rind**
Spread on cooled cookies.

## GLAZED LEMON WAFERS

Preheat oven to 325°F.
Lightly grease a baking sheet.
With a fork blend together
**2 cups PURITY Flour**
**1¾ cups granulated sugar**
**1 cup soft butter**
**½ teaspoon salt**
Sprinkle over top and stir in
**1 tablespoon grated lemon rind**
**1 tablespoon lemon juice**
Chill if necessary. Turn onto lightly floured surface and roll ¼ inch thick. Cut into desired shapes with floured cookie cutters.
Bake on greased baking sheet in preheated 325° oven for 10 to 12 minutes. While still warm glaze with a mixture of

**1 cup sifted icing sugar**
**1½ tablespoons milk**
**1 tablespoon soft butter**
**½ teaspoon vanilla**
Makes 3 dozen cookies.

TANGY MINCEMEAT CHEWS: Prepare Lemon Wafer dough following basic recipe and blend in ¾ cup mincemeat. Shape into small balls and place on a greased baking sheet about 3 inches apart. Press with floured glass to flatten.

---

*To prevent sticking, use a pastry cloth and covered rolling pin when making rolled rookies.*

---

## SHORTBREAD

Preheat oven to 300°F.
Cream until very light
**1 cup butter**
Blend in
**⅔ cup lightly packed brown sugar**
Beat until light and fluffy.
Gradually stir in
**2 cups PURITY Flour**
Knead well to blend in last of flour.
Chill for one hour. Turn onto lightly floured surface and roll ¼ inch thick and cut into desired shapes with floured cookie cutters, or roll dough into two circles ½ inch thick and prick with fork.
Bake on ungreased baking sheet in preheated 300° oven for 18 to 20 minutes or until set. Allow 40 to 45 minutes baking time for circles.
Makes 2 dozen cookies.

Rolled cookies are rolled out to desired thickness on lightly floured surface. Cut with floured cookie cutter and place on baking sheet.

## ALMOND CRISPS

Preheat oven to 400°F.
Lightly grease a baking sheet.
Sift together
  **2¼ cups PURITY Flour**
  **½ teaspoon baking soda**
  **½ teaspoon salt**
Cream together
  **1 cup butter**
  **1 cup granulated sugar**
  **1 cup lightly packed brown sugar**
  **1 teaspoon almond flavouring**
Beat in
  **1 egg**
  **2 tablespoons water**
Beat until light and fluffy.
Stir in dry ingredients with
  **1 cup chopped blanched almonds**
Shape dough into a roll 2 inches in diameter. Wrap and chill for 4 hours. Cut into ⅛-inch thick slices.
Bake on greased baking sheet in preheated 400° oven for 5 to 7 minutes or until golden brown.
Makes 5 dozen cookies.

**CINNAMON CRISPS:** Prepare Almond Crisp dough following basic recipe and blend in 1 teaspoon cinnamon.

**HONEY-LEMON CRISPS:** Prepare Almond Crisp dough following basic recipe but substituting 1 tablespoon lemon rind, 2 tablespoons lemon juice, and ¼ cup honey for the almond flavouring and water. Cut in ¼-inch thick slices.

**RUM & BUTTER CRISPS:** Prepare Almond Crisp dough following basic recipe but substituting 1½ teaspoons rum flavouring and 1 cup chopped pecans for the almond flavouring and almonds.

**RAISIN MOUNDS:** Prepare Almond Crisp dough following basic recipe and stir in 1 cup plumped raisins.

## BUTTERSCOTCH SLICES

Preheat oven to 375°F.
Lightly grease a baking sheet.
Sift together
  **3 cups PURITY Flour**
  **1 teaspoon baking soda**
  **¼ teaspoon salt**
Cream together
  **½ cup butter**
  **2 cups lightly packed brown sugar**
  **½ teaspoon vanilla**

Beat in
  **2 eggs**
Beat until light and fluffy.
Stir in dry ingredients with
  **½ cup chopped nuts**
Shape dough into a roll 2 inches in diameter. Wrap in wax paper and chill for 4 hours. Cut into ¼-inch thick slices.
Bake on greased baking sheet in preheated 375° oven for 5 to 7 minutes or until golden brown.
Makes 6 dozen cookies.

**CHERRY SLICE:** Prepare Butterscotch Slices following basic recipe but stir in ½ cup chopped maraschino cherries. Red and green cherries produce a festive cookie.

**BUTTERSCOTCH CHEWS:** Prepare Butterscotch Slices following basic recipe but stir in ¾ cup crushed corn flakes to produce a soft, chewy, cookie.

Refrigerator cookie dough is shaped into rolls by rolling back and forth with the hands. Wrap and chill until firm. Slice with a very sharp knife and bake slices on baking sheet.

## SNOWBALLS

Beat with a wooden spoon until smooth
  **1 (4-ounce) package soft cream cheese**
Gradually blend in
  **1½ cups sifted icing sugar**
  **1 cup vanilla wafer crumbs**
  **¼ teaspoon salt**
  **½ cup chopped maraschino cherries**
Cover and refrigerate for one hour.
Shape into 1-inch balls.

Roll in
**vanilla wafer crumbs**
Chill.
Makes 3 dozen cookies.

PINEAPPLE SNOWBALLS: Prepare Snowballs following basic recipe but increasing icing sugar to 2½ cups. Replace chopped cherries with a mixture of ½ cup drained crushed pineapple and ½ cup quartered miniature marshmallows. Roll in coconut.

## CHOCOLATE WAFERS

Preheat oven to 350°F.
Lightly grease a baking sheet.
Sift together
 **1¾ cups PURITY Flour**
 **½ teaspoon baking powder**
 **½ teaspoon salt**
Cream together
 **½ cup shortening**
 **1¼ cups lightly packed brown sugar**
Stir in
 **1½ squares unsweetened chocolate, melted**
 **2 tablespoons milk**
 **½ teaspoon vanilla**
 **1 egg, beaten**
Beat until light and fluffy. Stir in dry ingredients. Shape dough into a roll 2 inches in diameter. Wrap in wax paper and chill for 4 hours. Cut into ⅛-inch thick slices.
Bake on greased baking sheet in preheated 350° oven for 8 to 10 minutes or until edges are crisp.
Makes 4 dozen cookies.

HALLOWE'EN POLKA DOTS: Prepare Chocolate Wafer dough following basic recipe and stir in 1 cup (6-ounce package) butterscotch chips.

CHOCO-NUT WAFERS: Prepare Chocolate Wafer dough following basic recipe and stir in 1 cup coconut and 1 cup chopped nuts.

## SPRITZ COOKIES

Preheat oven to 400°F.
Blend or sift together
 **2¼ cups PURITY Flour**
 **¼ teaspoon salt**
Cream together
 **1 cup butter**

 **1 cup granulated sugar**
 **2 teaspoons vanilla**
Beat in
 **1 egg**
Beat until light and fluffy.
Stir in dry ingredients. Press through cookie press onto an ungreased baking sheet about 1 inch apart.
Bake in preheated 400° oven for 6 to 8 minutes or until golden.
Allow to cool 5 minutes on cookie sheet before removing.
Makes 7 dozen cookies.

CHOCOLATE SPRITZ: Prepare Spritz dough following basic recipe and blend in 2 squares melted unsweetened chocolate.

BUTTERSCOTCH SPRITZ: Prepare Spritz dough following basic recipe but substituting 1⅓ cups lightly packed brown sugar for granulated sugar.

CINNAMON SPRITZ: Prepare Butterscotch Spritz dough and blend in 1 teaspoon cinnamon.

ORANGE SPRITZ: Prepare Spritz dough following basic recipe but substituting ⅓ cup orange concentrate for the egg and vanilla.

LEMON SPRITZ: Prepare Spritz dough following basic recipe but substituting ¼ cup lemon concentrate for the egg and vanilla.

For Spritz Cookies, use a cookie press. With press in upright position, force out dough onto ungreased baking sheet, release pressure or unscrew, then lift press. Shaped dough should remain on cookie sheet.

## CHOCOLATE BROWNIES

Preheat oven to 325°F.
Grease an 8-inch square cake pan.
Sift together
 ¾ cup PURITY Flour
 ⅓ cup cocoa
 ¼ teaspoon salt
 1 cup granulated sugar
Stir in
 ½ cup shortening
 2 eggs
 3 tablespoons water
 1 teaspoon vanilla
Beat until smooth.
Stir in
 ½ cup chopped nuts
Turn into prepared pan.
Bake in preheated 325° oven for 25 to 30 minutes, or until brownies begin to pull away from sides of pan.
Makes 24 squares.

CHERRY CHEESE BROWNIE: Prepare brownie batter as in basic recipe and spread ⅔ in prepared pan. Beat together until light and fluffy, 1 (4-ounce) package cream cheese and 1 egg. Gradually blend in a mixture of ½ cup granulated sugar and 2 tablespoons PURITY Flour. Stir in ½ cup chopped maraschino cherries, drained. Pour over brownie base and gently spoon remaining batter on top completely covering cheese mixture. Bake in preheated 325° oven for 30 to 35 minutes, or until brownies begin to pull away from sides of pan.

CHOCOLATE-BUTTER BROWNIE: Prepare Chocolate Brownie batter as in basic recipe and turn into a greased 13 x 9 x 2-inch pan. Prepare Butterscotch Brownie batter (See page 151) and spread on top of chocolate batter. Bake in preheated 350° oven for 28 to 30 minutes, or until brownies begin to pull away from sides of pan.

COCONUT-CREAM BROWNIES: Prepare Brownie batter as in basic recipe and spread ⅔ in prepared pan. In a small saucepan, combine ⅓ cup undiluted evaporated milk and ⅓ cup granulated sugar. Cook over medium heat, stirring occasionally, for 5 minutes. Remove from heat and stir in 1 teaspoon almond flavouring and 1½ cups flaked coconut. Spread over brownie base and gently

spoon remaining batter on top completely covering cream mixture. Bake in preheated 350° oven for 30 to 35 minutes or until brownies begin to pull away from sides of pan.

PEANUT BUTTER-CREAM BROWNIES: Prepare Coconut-Cream Brownie variation and blend ⅓ cup peanut butter into creamy mixture before adding coconut.

## CHINESE CHEWS

Preheat oven to 350°F.
Grease an 8-inch square cake pan.
Blend or sift together
 ¾ cup PURITY Flour
 ½ teaspoon baking powder
 ¼ teaspoon salt
 1 cup granulated sugar
Stir in
 1 cup chopped dates
 ¾ cup chopped walnuts
Beat until foamy
 2 eggs
Blend with dry ingredients.
Turn into prepared pan.
Bake in preheated 350° oven for 25 to 30 minutes. Cool and cut into bars.
Makes 24 bars.

## MARMA-DATE SQUARES

Preheat oven to 350°F.
Grease two 8-inch square cake pans.
Blend together
 2 cups PURITY Flour
 ½ teaspoon salt
Cream together
 ½ cup soft butter
 ¾ cup granulated sugar
Beat in
 1 egg
 ¼ cup milk
Blend in dry ingredients.
Press dough into prepared pans. Bake in preheated 350° oven for 15 minutes.
Mix together
 ½ cup orange marmalade
 ¼ cup milk
 2 eggs, beaten
Combine and stir in
 ½ cup granulated sugar
 1½ cups chopped dates
 1½ cups raisins
 1 cup chopped nuts

Spread over baked pastry (about 2 cups of mixture on each). Return to oven and continue baking for 25 minutes or until set. Decorate with bits of red and green glacé cherries and nuts.
Makes 48 squares.

## CHOCO-TOFFEE DREAM BARS

Preheat oven to 350°F.
Grease a 13 x 9 x 2-inch cake pan.

**PASTRY:**

Combine
**2 cups PURITY Flour**
**½ cup lightly packed brown sugar**
**¼ teaspoon salt**
With a fork blend in until crumbly
**¾ cup soft butter**
Press into bottom of prepared pan.
Bake in preheated 350° oven for 10 minutes.

**TOPPING:**

Blend together
**¼ cup PURITY Flour**
**½ teaspoon baking powder**
**½ teaspoon salt**
Beat until foamy
**2 eggs**
Stir in
**1 teaspoon vanilla**
**1½ cups lightly packed brown sugar**
Blend in dry ingredients and then stir in
**1 cup coconut**
**1 cup raisins, plumped***
**¾ cup chopped walnuts**
**1½ cups chocolate chips**
Spread over baked pastry. Return to oven and bake for an additional 25 to 30 minutes. Cool and cut into bars.
Makes 4 dozen bars.
* To plump raisins—cover with boiling water. Let stand 5 minutes and then drain.

## DATE-FILLED CAKE SQUARES

Preheat oven to 350°F.
Grease a 9-inch square cake pan.
In a saucepan, bring to boil
**2 cups chopped dates**
**1 cup water**
Blend in

**½ cup granulated sugar**
**½ cup chopped nuts**
Continue cooking until thickened, stirring constantly. Cool.
Sift together
**1¾ cups PURITY Flour**
**½ teaspoon baking soda**
**¼ teaspoon salt**
Stir in
**2 cups PURITY Rolled Oats**
Cream together
**1 cup shortening**
**1 cup lightly packed**
**brown sugar**
Blend in dry ingredients alternately with
**½ cup buttermilk or sour milk**
Press half into prepared pan. Cover with cooled date filling.
Top with remaining dough and pat smooth.
Bake in preheated 350° oven for 35 to 40 minutes.
Cool and cut into squares.
Makes 20 squares.

## BUTTERSCOTCH BROWNIES

Preheat oven to 350°F.
Grease an 8-inch square cake pan.
Blend together
**1¼ cups PURITY Flour**
**¼ teaspoon salt**
Combine
**½ cup soft butter**
**1½ cups lightly packed**
**brown sugar**
Stir in
**2 eggs**
**2 teaspoons vanilla**
Beat until light and fluffy.
Blend in dry ingredients with
**½ cup chopped pecans**
Turn into prepared pan.
Bake in preheated 350° oven for 25 to 30 minutes.
Cool and cut into bars.
Makes 24 bars.

SUNDAE CENTRE BROWNIE: Prepare Butterscotch Brownie batter as in basic recipe. Spread ⅔ batter in prepared pan and top with ¼ cup chocolate or butterscotch sundae topping. Spoon remaining batter over sauce. Bake in preheated 350° oven for 30 to 35 minutes.

## MARDI GRAS BARS

Preheat oven to 350°F.
Grease a 9-inch square cake pan.

**PASTRY:**

Blend together
   1¼ cups PURITY Flour
   ¼ teaspoon salt
Cream together
   ⅔ cup lightly packed
      brown sugar
   ½ cup butter
   2 egg yolks
   ½ teaspoon vanilla
Blend in dry ingredients.
Press into bottom of prepared pan.
Bake in preheated 350° oven for 15 minutes.

**TOPPING:**

Beat to form stiff peaks
   2 egg whites
Blend in
   2 tablespoons PURITY Flour
   ½ cup chocolate sundae
      topping
Stir in
   ½ cup coconut
   ½ cup chopped maraschino
      cherries
   ½ cup chopped nuts
Spread over baked crust.
Return to oven and bake for an additional 18 to 20 minutes.
Cool and cut into bars.
Makes 24 bars.

## FRUIT FIESTA BARS

Preheat oven to 350°F.
Grease a 13 × 9 × 2-inch cake pan.
Sift together
   1¾ cups PURITY Flour
   ½ teaspoon baking powder
   ½ teaspoon salt
   ¼ teaspoon baking soda
      Pinch of nutmeg
Cream together
   ½ cup butter
   ¾ cup lightly packed brown
      sugar
Beat in until light and fluffy
   2 eggs
   ½ teaspoon vanilla
Stir in
   1 cup mashed ripe bananas

   ⅔ cup apricot jam
Blend in dry ingredients with
   ½ cup chopped nuts
Turn into prepared pan.
Bake in preheated 350° oven for 25 to 30 minutes.
Remove from oven and immediately spread with
   ⅓ cup apricot jam
Sprinkle with
   ⅓ cup chopped nuts
Cool and cut into bars.
Makes 4 dozen bars.

## PEANUT CRUNCH SQUARES

Grease an 8-inch square cake pan.
In a saucepan, combine
   ¾ cup lightly packed brown
      sugar
   ¾ cup corn syrup
Bring to a boil, stirring constantly. Cover and cook over medium heat until sugar is dissolved (about 2 minutes).
Remove from heat and stir in
   ⅔ cup peanut butter
   2 cups crisp sugar-coated
      cereal
   1½ cups corn flakes
Press into prepared pan.
If desired, sprinkle over top and press in
   ½ cup sugar-coated
      cereal crumbs
Makes 16 squares.

## ANGEL BITES

In a saucepan, combine
   1 cup chopped dates
   ½ cup chopped walnuts
   ¾ cup granulated sugar
   ½ cup butter
   2 eggs, beaten
   ½ teaspoon salt
Cook over low heat until dates are softened (about 10 minutes).
Cool for about 5 minutes and blend in
   2 cups corn flakes
   1 cup coconut
   1 teaspoon vanilla or
      rum flavouring
Shape into 1-inch balls and roll in
   ½ cup coconut
Makes 3 dozen cookies.

**CHERRY BITES:** Prepare Angel Bites following basic recipe and stir in 1 cup finely chopped maraschino cherries.

## PEANUT CHUBBIES

In a saucepan, combine,
**2 cups lightly packed brown
  sugar
½ cup undiluted evaporated milk
2 tablespoons butter or margarine**
Bring to a boil and cook, stirring constantly, until thickened and smooth (about 5 minutes).
Remove from heat and stir in
**¾ cup peanut butter
½ teaspoon vanilla**
Blend in
**1 cup PURITY Rolled Oats
½ cup chopped pretzels
½ cup salted peanuts
½ cup chocolate chips**
Drop from a teaspoon onto wax paper.
Chill until set.
Makes 4 dozen cookies.

## CHUNKY CHOCOLATE MORSELS

In a saucepan, bring to a boil
**1½ cups granulated sugar
½ cup butter
⅓ cup cocoa
1 teaspoon salt
½ cup milk**
Cook over medium heat until mixture is thickened (about 5 minutes).
Remove from heat and blend in
**1½ teaspoons rum flavouring**
Then stir in
**2 cups PURITY Rolled Oats
2 cups coconut
1 cup halved miniature
  marshmallows
1 cup chopped walnuts
½ cup chopped maraschino
  cherries**
Shape into 1-inch balls.
Roll in
**coconut**
Makes 5 dozen cookies.

*Many baked squares keep better when left in the pans in which they were baked. Be sure to keep them closely covered with foil or plastic wrap.*

## SOUTHERN BARS

Preheat oven to 350°F.
Melt in an 8-inch square cake pan
**¼ cup butter or margarine**
Spread in even layers over the butter
**1 cup graham wafer crumbs
1 cup desiccated coconut
1 cup chocolate chips
1 cup chopped nuts**
Drizzle over surface
**1 (15-ounce) can sweetened
  condensed milk**
Bake in preheated 350° oven for 25 to 30 minutes.
Cool in pan and cut into bars.
Makes 24 bars.

*To freeze baked cookies, pack in container with rigid sides, dividing each layer with transparent plastic wrap. To serve, arrange on cookie plate, cover with plastic wrap and allow to thaw for 5 to 10 minutes.*

## CHEESE DREAM SQUARES

Preheat oven to 350°F.
Cream together
**¼ cup butter or margarine
¼ cup processed cheese spread
½ cup lightly packed brown sugar
½ teaspoon vanilla**
Blend in
**1 cup PURITY Flour**
Press dough into an ungreased 8-inch square cake pan. Bake in preheated 350° oven for 12 minutes.
Cool and spread with
**¼ cup grape jelly or
  blueberry jam**
Beat with a fork
**2 eggs**
Stir in
**1 cup lightly packed brown sugar**
Blend together and stir in
**¼ cup PURITY Flour
½ teaspoon baking powder
¾ cup chopped walnuts
¾ cup desiccated coconut**
Gently spoon over jelly.
Return to oven and bake for an additional 30 to 35 minutes.
Cool and cut into squares.
Makes 16 squares.

# Pastry and Pies

## PASTRY

Undoubtedly, the most popular dessert in Canada for many, many years, pies continue as favourites. The secret of tender, flaky pastry has been treasured by homemakers and passed on from mother to daughter, friend to friend. Lard or butter pastry has a different flavour to shortening pastry but the principles are the same. Cut the fat into the flour, leaving some pieces as large as peas and the rest so fine that it coats the flour preventing it from dusting. Add one tablespoon cold water in one spot and mash with a fork, as if mashing potatoes. Repeat, adding the water to a dry place each time, until all is moistened. Butter pastry should feel crumbly but if tightly wrapped and stored in the refrigerator it will become more uniform. Lard and shortening pastry should be moistened until the mixture holds together readily. Before rolling out, chill lard pastry first, but shortening pastry may be rolled out as soon as mixed.

### PURITY PASTRY

Measure
   1¾ cups PURITY Flour
Mix in
   ¾ teaspoon salt
With a pastry blender or two knives, cut in until the consistency of coarse meal with a few larger pieces

¾ cup lard or shortening
   (or half and half)
One at a time, sprinkle with
   4-5 tablespoons cold water
Mix lightly with a fork until dough clings together and cleans easily from the bowl. Chill until ready to use.
Makes one two-crust 9-inch pie or two 9-inch pie shells.

### TO ROLL PASTRY:

Use a lightly floured surface, preferably a pastry cloth and a covered rolling pin. Divide pastry in two and form each half into a flattened ball. (If making a double crust pie, make one portion slightly larger and use it for the bottom crust.)

Roll lightly, from the centre to the edge each time, until the pastry is about 1" larger than inverted pie plate. (When making tarts, roll to 1/8" thickness.)

### TO LINE A PIE PLATE:

Roll pastry over rolling pin and transfer it to the pie plate. Unroll and ease into place, being careful not to stretch the pastry. Trim off any extra pastry.

### BAKED PIE SHELLS:

Flute edge of the pastry in your favourite way. Prick with a fork at 1" intervals. Bake in a preheated 450° oven for 10 to 12 minutes or until golden brown. Cool before adding the cooked filling.

**An ice cream pie in graham wafer crust topped with butterscotch sauce snuggles up to an Accordian Pink Apple Pie, an Apricot Pie and a lattice-topped raspberry pie ▶**

**UNBAKED PIE SHELLS:**

Prepare as above but do not prick the pastry. Add uncooked filling and bake as directed in the filling recipe.

**DOUBLE CRUST PIES:**

Add filling to the pastry lined pie plate and moisten the edge. Roll out top crust, roll over rolling pin and unroll on filled pie. Trim off excess pastry; seal the edge and flute. Make slits in centre to allow steam to escape. Bake as directed in the filling recipe.

## PURITY PASTRY MIX

Blend together
**1 (2-pound) bag PURITY Flour
1 tablespoon salt**
With a pastry blender or two knives, cut in until the consistency of coarse meal with a few larger pieces
**2⅔ cups shortening**
Store mix at room temperature in a covered canister until ready to use.

**For two crust pie:**

Measure
**2 cups PURITY Pastry Mix**
One at a time, sprinkle with
**3-4 tablespoons cold water**
Mix lightly with a fork until dough clings together and cleans easily from the bowl. Makes one two-crust 9-inch pie or two 9-inch pie shells.

## NEVER-FAIL PASTRY

Mix together
**5½ cups PURITY FLour
1½ teaspoons salt
1 teaspoon baking powder
3 tablespoons brown sugar**
With a pastry blender or two knives cut in until the consistency of coarse meal with a few larger pieces
**1 pound lard or shortening**
Break into a measuring cup and beat slightly
**1 egg**
Add
**1 tablespoon vinegar**
Fill cup to ¾ mark with
**cold water**
and blend together.
With a fork, gradually stir liquid mixture into flour mixture. Add only enough liquid to make dough cling together and clean easily from the bowl.

Wrap tightly in wax paper and chill until ready to use.
Makes three 9-inch double-crust pies or six 9-inch pie shells.

## CHEEZY PIE CRUST

Blend together
**2 cups PURITY FLour
3 tablespoons granulated sugar
1 teaspoon salt**
With a pastry blender or 2 knives, cut in until the consistency of coarse meal with a few larger pieces
**½ cup shortening
1 (4-ounce) package cream cheese**
One at a time, sprinkle with
**3 tablespoons cold water**
Mix with a fork using just enough water to make a dough which will cling together and clean easily from the bowl. Roll out as in PURITY Pastry (See page 154).
Makes one 9-inch two crust pie.

*To ensure pastry rolls out to a well-shaped circle, shape pastry into a round disk, flat on top and bottom. Shape edges of disk smoothly. Then roll pastry, always starting at centre of dough and rolling to outside edges. Vary starting position of rolling pin and direction of roll to cover complete circle.*

## COOKIE PRESS PASTRY

Preheat oven to 350°F.
Cream
**1 cup butter**
Beat in
**½ cup sifted icing sugar
½ teaspoon vanilla**
Blend in yolks.
**2 egg yolks**

stir in
**2 cups PURITY Flour**
Press dough through cookie press on an
ungreased 9-inch pie plate or use a pastry
tube and swirl attractively on bottom and
side of pie plate.
Bake in preheated 350° oven for 20 to
25 minutes or until light golden.
Makes one 9-inch pie shell.

---

*Perfect pastry has flakes layered through
the crust and cuts readily with a fork. Too
much water, underbaking, or excessive
handling, causes pastry to lose its tenderness. Dry mealy pastry results from
cutting the fat in too finely and using too
little liquid.*

---

## POLISH CHRUST

Preheat deep fat to 375°F.
Beat together until light and fluffy
**6 egg yolks**
**¼ teaspoon salt**
**⅓ cup granulated sugar**
Stir in
**¼ cup heavy cream**
**Pinch of mace**
Gradually add
**2 cups PURITY Flour**
This should make a soft dough. (A little
additional flour may be necessary.) Chill.
Roll out dough as thin as possible, half
at a time, on floured surface.
Cut into 1 × 3-inch strips. Make a slit
down centre of each strip. Turn one end of
strip in through slit.
Deep fry in shortening which has been
preheated to 375°. Turn once. Drain on
absorbent paper.
Sprinkle with icing sugar.
Makes 4 dozen.

## CRUMB CRUSTS

### GRAHAM WAFER

Preheat oven to 350°F.
Combine
**1½ cups graham wafer crumbs**
**⅓ cup granulated sugar**
**½ teaspoon cinnamon**
With a fork, stir in
**½ cup melted butter or margarine**
Reserve ¼ cup of mixture for topping.

Press remaining crumbs into 9-inch pie
plate, covering bottom, sides and rim,
evenly.
Bake in preheated 350° oven for 10 minutes.

### CHOCOLATE WAFER

Combine
**1½ cups chocolate wafer crumbs**
**¼ cup granulated sugar**
With a fork, stir in
**⅓ cup melted butter or margarine**
Reserve ¼ cup of mixture for topping.
Press remaining crumbs into 9-inch pie
plate. Do not bake.

### GINGER WAFER

Combine
**1½ cups ginger wafer crumbs**
**¼ cup granulated sugar**
With a fork, stir in
**⅓ cup melted butter or margarine**
Reserve ¼ cup of mixture for topping.
Press remaining crumbs into 9-inch pie
plate. Do not bake.

### VANILLA WAFER

Combine
**1½ cups vanilla wafer crumbs**
**¼ cup granulated sugar**
With a fork, stir in
**⅓ cup melted butter or margarine**
Reserve ¼ cup of mixture for topping.
Press remaining crumbs into 9-inch pie
plate. Do not bake.

### ZWIEBACK

Combine
**1½ cups zwieback crumbs**
**¾ cup granulated sugar**
**½ teaspoon cinnamon**
With a fork, stir in
**⅓ cup melted butter or margarine**
Reserve ¼ cup of mixture for topping.
Press remaining crumbs into 9-inch pie
plate. Do not bake.

---

*For best results, roll out pastry dough on
canvas cloth with rolling pin covered in
a stockingette. The strands of cloth hold
flour to prevent dough from sticking and
at the same time extra flour is not worked
into dough.*

---

## ONE CRUST PIES

Measure and blend together flour and salt. Cut in shortening until the consistency of coarse meal with a few large pieces and the flour no longer dusts.

Add the water, a tablespoon at a time, mashing with a fork. Add only enough water to make dough hold together.

Divide dough in half and roll out each on lightly floured surface. Roll from centre to outside edge to keep dough circular in shape.

Fit into pie plate, being careful not to stretch pastry. For pie shell: trim, leaving a ½-inch overhang. Tuck under and flute pressing curved portions over outside edge of pie plate.

# PIES

## PASTRY TRICKS

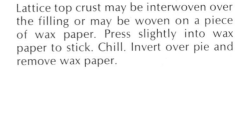

Lattice top crust may be interwoven over the filling or may be woven on a piece of wax paper. Press slightly into wax paper to stick. Chill. Invert over pie and remove wax paper.

Many attractive edgings may be made. A combination of fluting and fork trim is shown.

Pastry cut-outs may be used to trim edge of pie. Pointed fluting is also shown.

---

### RHUBARB PIE

Preheat oven to 450°F.
Prepare pastry; roll out half of dough and line a 9-inch pie plate. Trim. Roll out top crust.
Mix together
   **1 to 1½ cups granulated sugar**
   **⅓ cup PURITY Flour**
Combine with
   **4 cups cut rhubarb**
      **(1-inch pieces)**

Turn into pastry-lined pie plate.
Dot with
   **1 tablespoon butter or margarine**
Cover with top crust. Seal and flute edges and slit or prick top.
Bake in preheated 450° oven for 15 minutes, or until pastry is golden. Reduce heat to 350° and continue baking 40 to 45 minutes longer, or until fruit is tender and bubbly at centre.
Makes one 9-inch pie.

## FRESH APPLE PIE

Preheat oven to 450°F.
Prepare pastry; roll out half of dough and line a 9-inch pie plate. Trim. Roll out top crust. Peel, core and cut into thick slices sufficient apples to give
    **6 cups peeled, sliced apples**
Combine
    **⅔–1 cup granulated sugar
    (depending upon tartness
    of apples)
    ½ teaspoon cinnamon or nutmeg
    Pinch of salt**
Place one half of apple slices in pastry-lined pie plate. Sprinkle with half of sugar mixture. Add remaining apples, heaping them in centre.
Sprinkle remaining sugar mixture over top.
Dot with
    **1 tablespoon butter or margarine**
Cover with top crust. Seal edges, flute, and slash top.
Bake in preheated 450° oven for 15 minutes or until pastry is golden.
Reduce heat to 350° and continue baking 40 to 45 minutes longer or until apples are tender.
Makes one 9-inch pie.
NOTE:-If apples are especially juicy, combine 1 tablespoon PURITY Flour with the sugar mixture. If apples are dry, sprinkle them with about 2 tablespoons water.

## APPLE PIE

Preheat oven to 450°F.
Prepare pastry; roll out half of dough and line a 9-inch pie plate.
Trim. Roll out top crust.
Peel, core and cut into thick slices sufficient apples to make
    **7 cups sliced cooking apples**
Mix together and combine with apples
    **½ cup granulated sugar
    ¼ cup lightly packed brown
    sugar
    2 tablespoons PURITY Flour
    1 teaspoon grated lemon rind
    ½ teaspoon cinnamon
    Pinch of salt**
Turn into pastry lined pie plate.
Sprinkle with
    **juice of 1 lemon**

Cover with top crust. Seal and flute edges. Slit or prick top.
Bake in preheated 450° oven for 15 minutes or until pastry is golden.
Reduce heat to 350° and continue baking 40 to 45 minutes longer or until apples are tender.
Makes one 9-inch pie.

## ACCORDIAN PINK APPLE PIE

Preheat oven to 450°F.
Prepare pastry; roll out half of dough and line a 1½-quart rectangular baking dish.
Roll out remaining pastry and cut into 9 strips, ¾-inch wide.
Combine
    **½ cup granulated sugar
    ¼ cup red crushed cinnamon
    candies
    1 tablespoon PURITY Flour**
Stir in
    **7 cups peeled apple wedges**
Turn into pastry-lined dish. Arrange strips perpendicular to the long sides of the dish to produce an accordian effect. Seal and flute edges.
Bake in preheated 450° oven for 15 minutes or until pastry is golden.
Reduce heat to 350° and continue baking 35 to 40 minutes longer.
Cool. Serve with cheese.
Makes 6 servings.

## DOUBLE DECKER
## APPLE PIE

Preheat oven to 450°F.
Line one 9-inch pie plate with a circle of aluminium foil so there is a 1-inch overhang at the edge.
Melt together and pour in prepared pie plate
    **3 tablespoons soft butter
    ½ cup lightly packed brown
    sugar**
Arrange attractively on top
    **red and green glacé cherries**
Prepare 1½ recipes of PURITY Pastry (See page 154). Roll out one third of dough and line a second 9-inch pie plate. Trim. Roll out two top crusts.
Peel, core and cut into thick slices sufficient apples to make
    **12 cups sliced apples**

Mix together and combine with apples
**1 cup granulated sugar**
**¼ cup PURITY Flour**
**1 teaspoon cinnamon**
**½ teaspoon nutmeg**
Place one half of apple mixture in each pie plate. Arrange apples in attractive pattern in foil-lined pie plate.
Cover with top crusts. Seal and flute edges. Slit or prick tops.
Bake both pies in preheated 450° oven for 15 minutes or until pastry is golden. Reduce heat to 350° and continue baking 30 to 35 minutes longer, or until apples are tender. Cool to lukewarm.
Invert foil-lined pie over two crust pie. Remove plate and foil.
If desired, flame with
**¼ cup warm brandy**
Makes 12 servings.

## FRESH BERRY PIE

Preheat oven to 450°F.
Prepare pastry; roll out half of dough and line a 9-inch pie plate. Trim. Roll out top crust.
Mix together
**¾ cup granulated sugar***
**¼ cup PURITY Flour**
**Pinch of salt**
Combine with
**4¼ cups berries**
Turn into pastry-lined pie plate.
Dot with
**1 tablespoon butter or margarine**
Cover with top crust. Seal and flute edges. Slit or prick top.
Bake in preheated 450° oven for 15 minutes, or until pastry is golden. Reduce heat to 350° and continue baking 50 to 55 minutes longer or until filling is thickened and fruit is tender.
Makes one 9-inch pie.
If using strawberries, increase sugar to 1 cup.

## FRESH CHERRY PIE

Preheat oven to 450°F.
Prepare pastry; roll out half of dough and line a 9-inch pie plate. Trim. Roll out top crust.
Mix together
**1½ cups granulated sugar**
**¼ cup PURITY Flour**
Combine with

**4¼ cups pitted sour cherries**
Turn into pastry-lined pie plate.
Dot with
**2 tablespoons butter or margarine**
Sprinkle with
**½ teaspoon almond flavouring**
Cover with top crust. Seal and flute edges.
Slit or prick top.
Bake in preheated 450° oven for 15 minutes, or until pastry is golden. Reduce heat to 350° and continue baking 50 to 55 minutes longer or until filling has thickened.
Makes one 9-inch pie.

## SLICED LEMON PIE

Preheat oven to 425°F.
Prepare pastry; roll out half of dough and line a 9-inch pie plate. Trim. Roll out top crust.
Slice into paper thin slices
**1 large lemon**
Combine in a saucepan with
**½ cup water**
Bring to a boil; cover and simmer until rind is tender and transparent (about 10 minutes).
Mix together
**1¼ cups granulated sugar**
**2 tablespoons PURITY Flour**
**¼ teaspoon salt**
Beat together and blend into flour mixture
**¼ cup butter or margarine**
**3 egg yolks**
Stir in lemon and water mixture.
Beat to form stiff but moist peaks
**3 egg whites**
Fold into lemon mixture.
Turn into pastry lined pie plate. Cover with top crust. Seal and flute edges. Slit or prick top.
Bake in preheated 425° oven for 15 minutes, or until pastry is golden. Reduce heat to 350° and continue baking until filling is set, about 20 minutes longer.
Makes one 9-inch pie.

*To help prevent fruit pies from boiling over, a foil or glass cone may be set in the centre. This allows the steam to escape, but should be removed before serving, of course.*

## ORANGE-MINCEMEAT PIE

Preheat oven to 450°F.
Prepare pastry; roll out half of dough and line a 9-inch pie plate. Trim. Roll out top crust.
Mix together
  **2 cups mincemeat**
  **2 cups fresh orange sections**
Turn into pastry-lined pie plate. Cover with top crust. Seal and flute edges. Slit or prick top.
Bake in preheated 450° oven for 15 minutes or until pastry is golden. Reduce heat to 350° and continue baking 30 to 35 minutes longer.
Serve with an orange sauce made by heating together
  **½ cup honey**
  **¼ cup frozen orange concentrate, thawed**
  **¼ cup brandy**
Makes one 9-inch pie.

---

*To protect the oven from spillovers when baking fruit pies, place a piece of foil on rack beneath pie. Do not lay foil on element or cover racks completely.*

---

## PEACH PIE

Preheat oven to 450°F.
Prepare pastry; roll out half of dough and line a 9-inch pie plate. Trim. Roll out top crust.
Blanch peaches in boiling water for 1 minute, place in cold water.
Remove skins and stones. Slice sufficient to make
  **4 cups sliced peaches**
Combine
  **¾ cup granulated sugar**
  **3 tablespoons PURITY Flour**
  **½ teaspoon cinnamon**
Place half of peach slices in the pastry-lined pie plate. Sprinkle with half sugar mixture. Add remaining peaches and sugar.
Dot with
  **1 tablespoon butter or margarine**
Cover with top crust. Seal and flute edges. Slit or prick top.
Bake in preheated 450° oven for 15 minutes or until pastry is golden.
Reduce heat to 350° and continue baking 30 to 35 minutes longer.
Makes one 9-inch pie.

## RAISIN PIE

Preheat oven to 450°F.
Prepare pastry; roll out half of dough an line a 9-inch pie plate. Trim. Roll out to crust.
Simmer together for 10 minutes
  **2 cups raisins**
  **2 cups water**
Mix together and gradually stir in
  **½ cup granulated sugar**
  **2 tablespoons PURITY Flour**
  **Pinch of salt**
Blend in
  **½ teaspoon vanilla**
  **1 tablespoon butter or margarine**
  **1 tablespoon lemon juice**
  **(optional)**
Cool. Turn into pastry-lined pie plat Cover with top crust. Seal and flute edg and slit or prick top.
Bake in preheated 450° oven for 15 mi utes, or until pastry is golden. Reduc heat to 350° and continue baking 25 30 minutes longer.
Makes one 9-inch pie.

## RASPBERRY LATTICE PIE

Preheat oven to 350°F.
Lightly grease a 9-inch pie plate.
Combine
  **2 cups PURITY Flour**
  **½ cup granulated sugar**
Cream together
  **1 cup butter**
  **2 egg yolks**
  **½ teaspoon almond flavouring**
Stir in flour mixture. Form into a ball an chill, if necessary. Press ¾ of dough o bottom and sides of pie plate.
Sprinkle with
  **½ cup chopped almonds**
Spread over top
  **1½ cups raspberry pie filling**
Press remaining dough through past tube onto ungreased baking sheet to gi lattice top. Trim to give a circle 8 inch in diameter. Freeze firm (about 5 mi utes) and then slide onto top of pie.
Bake in preheated 350° oven for 25 30 minutes or until golden.
Cool.
Makes one 9-inch pie.

## FRESH RASPBERRY PIE

Preheat oven to 450°F.
Prepare pastry; roll out half of dough and line a 9-inch pie plate. Trim. Roll out top crust.
Mix together
  **¾ cup granulated sugar**
  **¼ cup PURITY Flour**
  **Pinch of salt**
Combine with
  **4 cups fresh raspberries**
Turn into pastry-lined pie plate.
Dot with
  **1 tablespoon butter or margarine**
Cover with top crust. Seal and flute edges. Slit or prick top crust.
Bake in preheated 450° oven for 15 minutes or until pastry is golden. Reduce heat to 350° and continue baking 30 to 35 minutes longer, or until filling bubbles.
Makes one 9-inch pie.

## RASPBERRY-PEAR PIE

Preheat oven to 450°F.
Prepare pastry, roll out half of dough and line a 9-inch pie plate. Trim. Roll out top crust.
Mix together
  **½ cup granulated sugar**
  **2 tablespoons PURITY Flour**
Combine with
  **1 (19-ounce) can sliced pears, drained**
  **1 (15-ounce) package frozen raspberries, thawed**
Turn into pastry-lined pie plate. Cover with top crust. Seal and flute edges. Slit or prick top.
Bake in preheated 450° oven for 15 minutes or until pastry is golden. Reduce heat to 350° and continue baking 30 to 35 minutes longer.
Makes one 9-inch pie.

## TARTE AUX FRAISES

Preheat oven to 425°F.
Prepare pastry; roll out half of dough and line a 9-inch pie plate or 10-inch flan ring. Trim. Flute edge and prick. Bake in preheated 425° oven for 10 to 12 minutes, or until golden. Cool.
In a saucepan, combine
  **1 envelope gelatine**
  **⅓ cup granulated sugar**
Stir in
  **⅔ cup milk**
Heat to just below boiling point or until gelatine and sugar are dissolved.
Chill until the consistency of unbeaten egg white.
Whip together until stiff
  **1½ cups heavy cream**
  **2 teaspoons vanilla**
Whip gelatine mixture until frothy and fold in whipped cream. Turn into baked pie shell and chill until firm.
Arrange attractively on top of pie
  **1 quart fresh strawberries, hulled**
Melt together
  **⅓ cup red currant jelly**
  **2 tablespoons sherry or water**
Spoon over strawberries to glaze. Chill. Just before serving, dust with icing sugar to form a 2-inch ring around outside edge.
Makes one 9-inch pie.

## ORANGE PUMPKIN PIE

Preheat oven to 450°F.
Prepare pastry; roll out half of dough and line a 9-inch pie plate. Trim. Flute edge but do not prick.
Mix together
  **⅔ cup lightly packed brown sugar**
  **1 teaspoon cinnamon**
  **½ teaspoon salt**
  **½ teaspoon ginger**
  **¼ teaspoon nutmeg**
  **½ teaspoon grated orange rind**
Blend in
  **2 eggs, slightly beaten**
Stir in
  **1¼ cups canned or sieved cooked pumpkin**
  **1 cup milk**
  **⅓ cup strained orange juice**
  **¼ cup water**
  **¼ teaspoon vanilla**
Turn into prepared pie shell.
If desired, sprinkle with
  **3 tablespoons slivered unblanched almonds**
Bake in preheated 450° oven for 10 minutes, then reduce heat to 325° and continue baking about 40 minutes longer, or until pumpkin custard is almost set.
Makes one 9-inch pie.

## MERINGUE FOR PIES

Preheat oven to 375°F.
Beat together to form stiff but moist peaks
**3 egg whites**
**½ teaspoon cream of tartar**
Very gradually beat in

**⅓ cup granulated sugar**
Beat until very stiff and shiny.
Spread on lukewarm pie, touching pastry rim all the way around. Swirl points.
Bake in preheated 375° oven until tips become golden (about 12 minutes).
Cool at room temperature.

## MERINGUE FOR PIES

Beat egg whites and cream of tartar to form stiff but moist peaks or sufficiently beaten that if bowl were inverted, egg whites would not slip out.

Very gradually add sugar. Beat until very stiff and shiny. Use very fine granulated sugar or fruit sugar for best results.

Spread on lukewarm pie, touching pastry rim all the way around. Swirl points. Bake in preheated 375° oven until tips become golden. Cool at room temperature.

## VANILLA CREAM PIE

Preheat oven to 425°F.
Prepare pastry; roll out half of dough and line a 9-inch pie plate. Trim. Flute edge and prick. Bake in preheated 425° oven for 10 to 12 minutes, or until golden. Cool.
Scald
**3 cups milk**
In a saucepan, combine
**¾ cup granulated sugar**
**⅓ cup PURITY Flour**
**¼ teaspoon salt**
Gradually add scalded milk. Cook over medium heat, stirring constantly, until thickened. Cover and cook 2 minutes longer, stirring occasionally.
Stir a small amount of hot mixture into
**3 egg yolks, slightly beaten**
Then blend into remaining hot mixture. Cook 1 minute longer, stirring constantly. Remove from heat and blend in
**2 tablespoons butter or margarine**
**1 teaspoon vanilla**
Cool to lukewarm and turn into baked 9-inch pie shell.
If desired, top with a meringue (See page 164).
Makes one 9-inch pie.

**BANANA CREAM PIE:** Prepare Vanilla Cream Pie as in basic recipe but slice 3 bananas in baked pie shell before pouring in filling.

**CHOCOLATE CREAM PIE:** Prepare Vanilla Cream Pie following basic recipe but increase sugar to 1 cup and melt 2 squares unsweetened chocolate in milk as it is being heated.

**COCONUT CREAM PIE:** Prepare Vanilla Cream Pie following basic recipe but add 1 cup shredded coconut to milk as it is being heated and substitute ½ teaspoon almond flavouring for half the vanilla.

**COFFEE CREAM PIE:** Prepare Vanilla Cream Pie following basic recipe but add 1½ tablespoons instant coffee powder to milk as it is being heated. If desired, sprinkle meringue with slivered blanched almonds before baking.

**PINEAPPLE CREAM PIE:** Prepare Vanilla Cream Pie as in basic recipe but stir in ½ cup drained crushed pineapple before turning into baked pie shell.

## MODERN SUGAR PIE

Preheat oven to 425°F.
Prepare pastry; roll out half of dough and line a 9-inch pie plate. Trim. Flute edge, but do not prick.
In the top of a double boiler combine
**1½ cups corn syrup**
**1 cup sweetened condensed milk**
Heat over boiling water for 5 minutes or until blended.
Pour into prepared pie shell.
Sprinkle with
**½ cup pecan halves.**
Bake in 425° oven for 10 minutes. Reduce heat to 350° and continue baking 20 to 25 minutes longer, or until filling bubbles in the centre.
Makes one 9-inch pie.

## PINEAPPLE PECAN PIE

Preheat oven to 450°F.
Prepare pastry; roll out half of dough and line a 9-inch pie plate. Trim. Flute edge but do not prick.
Mix together
**½ cup lightly packed brown sugar**
**2 tablespoons PURITY Flour**
**½ teaspoon salt**
Cream
**¼ cup butter or margarine**
Gradually add brown sugar mixture.
Blend in
**3 eggs, slightly beaten**
**1 cup corn syrup**
**1 teaspoon vanilla**
Drain and fold in
**1 cup pineapple tidbits**
along with
**1 cup pecan halves**
Turn into prepared pie shell.
Bake in preheated 450° oven for 10 minutes, or until pastry is golden. Reduce heat to 325° and continue baking for 30 to 35 minutes longer, or until filling is set. Cool before serving.
Makes one 9-inch pie.

## MARZIPAN PIE

Preheat oven to 350°F.
Prepare pastry; roll out half of dough and line a 9-inch pie plate. Trim and flute edge. Do not prick.
Spread on bottom and sides of pastry-lined pie plate
**½ cup raspberry jam**
Cream
**½ cup butter**
Beat in
**⅔ cup granulated sugar**
Blend in, beating until light and fluffy
**2 eggs**
Gradually stir in a mixture of
**½ cup PURITY Flour**
**¼ teaspoon salt**
Divide into two equal portions and to one add
**2-3 drops green food colouring**
Turn into pie plate.
To remaining portion add
**2-3 drops red food colouring**
Spoon over top of green layer.
Bake in preheated 350° oven for 35 minutes or until top springs back when lightly touched. Cool.
Cream together
**2 tablespoons butter**
**2 tablespoons milk**
**1½ cups sifted icing sugar**
**1 teaspoon almond flavouring**
Spread on top of cooled pie.
Makes one 9-inch pie.

## BUTTERSCOTCH PIE

Preheat oven to 425°F.
Prepare pastry; roll out half of dough and line a 9-inch pie plate. Trim. Flute edge and prick. Bake in 425° oven for 10 to 12 minutes, or until golden. Cool.
Scald
**2¾ cups milk**
In a saucepan, combine
**1¼ cups lightly packed dark brown sugar**
**¼ cup cornstarch**
**½ teaspoon salt**
Gradually add scalded milk. Cook over medium heat, stirring constantly, until thickened and boiling gently. Reduce heat, cover and cook for 2 minutes longer, stirring occasionally.
Stir a small amount of hot mixture into
**3 egg yolks, beaten**

then blend into remaining hot mixture Cook for 2 minutes longer, stirring constantly.
Remove from heat and blend in
**2 tablespoons butter or margarine**
**1 teaspoon vanilla**
Cool to lukewarm and pour into prepared pie shell.
If desired, top with meringue (See page 164) of
**3 egg whites**
**¼ teaspoon cream of tartar**
**⅓ cup granulated sugar**
Return to preheated 375° oven for 12 minutes, or until meringue is golden.
Cool at room temperature.
Makes one 9-inch pie.

## LEMON MERINGUE PIE

Preheat oven to 425°F.
Prepare pastry; roll out half of dough and line a 9-inch pie plate. Trim. Flute edge and prick. Bake in preheated 425° oven for 10 to 12 minutes, or until golden. Cool.
In a saucepan, combine
**1¼ cups granulated sugar**
**¼ cup PURITY Flour**
**3 tablespoons cornstarch**
**¼ teaspoon salt**
Gradually stir in
**3 cups boiling water**
Cook over medium heat, stirring constantly, until thickened. Cover and cook 2 minutes longer, stirring occasionally.
Stir a small amount of hot mixture into
**3 egg yolks, slightly beaten**
Then blend into remaining hot mixture. Cook 1 minute longer, stirring constantly.
Remove from heat and blend in
**1 tablespoon butter or margarine**
**1 tablespoon grated lemon rind**
**½ cup strained lemon juice**
Cool to lukewarm and turn into baked 9-inch pie shell.
Top with a meringue (See page 164) of
**3 egg whites**
**¼ teaspoon cream of tartar**
**6 tablespoons granulated sugar**
Makes one 9-inch pie.

## DUTCH APPLE PIE

Preheat oven to 450°F.
Prepare pastry; roll out half of dough and line a 9-inch pie plate. Trim and flute edge. Do not prick.
Combine
  **¾ cup granulated sugar**
  **3 tablespoons PURITY Flour**
Stir in and beat smooth with rotary beater
  **1 cup thick dairy sour cream**
Arrange in unbaked 9-inch pie shell
  **5 cups peeled apple quarters**
Pour sour cream mixture over top.
Bake in preheated 450° oven for 15 minutes, then reduce heat to 350° and continue baking 35 to 40 minutes longer, or until fruit is tender and filling set.
Sprinkle over hot pie
  **¼ cup lightly packed brown sugar**
Broil for 2 to 3 minutes, or until sugar is melted. Serve warm.
Makes one 9-inch pie.

## SNOW-TOPPED APPLE PIE

Preheat oven to 425°F.
Prepare pastry; roll out half of dough and line a 9-inch pie plate. Trim. Flute edge and prick. Bake in preheated 425° oven for 10 to 12 minutes, or until golden. Cool.
In a large saucepan, combine
  **¾ cup maple syrup**
  **¼ cup water**
  **7 cups peeled sliced apples**
Bring to boil, cover and simmer until apples are just tender (about 10 minutes). Stir occasionally.
Drain, reserving syrup.
Meanwhile, in a saucepan, melt
  **2 tablespoons butter or margarine**
Stir in
  **¼ cup PURITY Flour**
Add reserved syrup and cook, stirring constantly, until thickened.
Pour over drained apples and turn into prepared pie shell.
Beat together until fluffy
  **2 (4-ounce) packages cream cheese**
  **1½ cups sifted icing sugar**
  **2-3 tablespoons milk**
  **1 teaspoon vanilla**
Swirl on cooled pie and garnish with unpeeled apple wedges dipped in lemon juice.
Makes one 9-inch pie.

## FRESH CHERRY CUSTARD PIE

Preheat oven to 425°F.
Prepare pastry; roll out half of dough and line a 9-inch pie plate. Trim and flute edge. Do not prick.
Mix together
  **1⅓ cups granulated sugar**
  **5 tablespoons PURITY Flour**
Combine and blend in
  **3 eggs**
  **¼ cup milk**
  **2 tablespoons melted butter**
Beat smooth with rotary beater.
Stir in
  **4 cups pitted sweet cherries, drained**
Pour into pastry-lined pie plate.
Immediately bake in preheated 425° oven for 15 minutes or until pastry is golden. Reduce heat to 350° and continue baking 35 to 40 minutes longer or until filling is set around edges and slightly soft in the centre. Cool.
Makes one 9-inch pie.

## APRICOT PIE

Preheat oven to 425°F.
Prepare pastry; roll out half of dough and line a 9-inch pie plate. Trim. Flute edge and prick. Bake in preheated 425° oven for 10 to 12 minutes, or until golden. Cool.
Prepare according to package directions
  **1 (4-ounce) package coconut cream pudding mix**
Cool. Then fold in
  **1 cup heavy cream, whipped**
Spread bottom of baked pie shell with
  **½ cup apricot jam**
Sprinkle with
  **¼ cup ground almonds**
Gently spoon coconut cream over top and chill.
Arrange attractively on top
  **1 (14-ounce) can apricot halves, drained**
In a saucepan, combine
  **¼ cup strained apricot jam**
  **2 tablespoons water**
Heat until liquid and spoon over top to glaze.
Chill.
Serve garnished with toasted coconut.
Makes one 9-inch pie.

## FRESH STRAWBERRY BAVARIAN PIE

Preheat oven to 425°F.
Prepare pastry; roll out half of dough and line a 9-inch pie plate. Trim. Flute edge and prick. Bake in preheated 425° oven for 10 to 12 minutes, or until golden. Cool.
Slice
  **¾ cup fresh strawberries**
Sprinkle with
  **¼ cup granulated sugar**
Allow to stand until juicy, then mash with fork.
In a saucepan, combine
  **¼ cup granulated sugar**
  **2 tablespoons PURITY Flour**
  **1 envelope gelatine**
  **½ teaspoon salt**
Beat together
  **2 egg yolks**
  **½ cup cold water**
Stir egg yolk mixture into gelatine mixture and cook over medium heat, stirring constantly, until thickened. Blend in sweetened mashed strawberries. Chill until the consistency of unbeaten egg white.
Beat to form stiff but moist peaks
  **2 egg whites**
Gradually beat in
  **¼ cup granulated sugar**
Beat until stiff and shiny.
Whip until stiff
  **½ cup heavy cream**
Fold into gelatine mixture with meringue. Turn into baked pie shell. Chill until firm. Makes one 9-inch pie.

## CREAM PUFF PIE

Preheat oven to 375°F.
Lightly grease a baking sheet.
Make half recipe Cream Puffs (See page 107).
Using a pastry tube form a 9-inch round base on baking sheet. Completely surround circumference with rosettes of dough to form the edge of the pie. Bake in preheated 375° oven for 30 to 35 minutes or until puffed and golden.
Prepare according to package directions
  **1 (4-ounce) package instant lemon pudding mix**
Fold in
  **½ pint sour cream**
  **¼ cup lemon juice**

Turn into baked cream puff shell.
  **1 tablespoon grated lemon rind**
Chill until firm (at least 1 hour).
Gently spoon over top
  **1 (19-ounce) can blueberry pie filling**
Garnish with whipped cream.
Makes one 9-inch pie.

## MOCHA MERINGUE PIE

Preheat oven to 275°F.
Grease a 9-inch pie plate.
Beat to form stiff but moist peaks
  **2 egg whites**
  **¼ teaspoon cream of tartar**
Gradually, beat in
  **¼ cup granulated sugar**
  **½ teaspoon instant coffee powder**
Spread meringue in prepared pie plate mounding edge higher than centre. Bake in preheated 275° oven for 60 minutes. Cool.
In a saucepan, combine
  **⅔ cup granulated sugar**
  **¼ cup cocoa**
  **1 envelope gelatine**
  **¼ teaspoon salt**
Gradually stir in
  **1½ cups boiling water**
  **2 tablespoons butter or margarine**
Cook over medium heat, stirring constantly, until slightly thickened and gelatine is dissolved. Beat smooth.
Stir a little of hot mixture into
  **3 egg yolks, beaten**
Then blend into remaining hot mixture. Cook 1 minute longer stirring constantly.
Stir in
  **1½ teaspoons vanilla**
Chill until the consistency of unbeaten egg white. Beat until smooth and fluffy.
Beat to form stiff but moist peaks
  **1 egg white**
Gradually, beat in
  **2 tablespoons granulated sugar**
Beat until very stiff and shiny. Fold into chocolate mixture.
Turn into meringue shell and chill until firm.
If desired, top with whipped coffee cream made by whipping until stiff.
  **½ pint heavy cream**
  **¼ cup granulated sugar**
  **1 tablespoon instant coffee powder**
Makes one 9-inch pie.

# FRUIT TOPPED PIE

## BUTTER CRUMB CRUST:

Preheat oven to 300°F.
Lightly grease a 9-inch pie plate.
Mix together
    **1⅓ cups PURITY Flour**
    **2 tablespoons icing sugar**
With a fork, stir in
    **½ cup butter, melted**
Mix until crumbly. Press into prepared pie plate; pat evenly. Prick. Bake in preheated 300° oven for 30 to 35 minutes, or until lightly browned. Cool.

## FILLING:

Beat together until smooth
    **1 (4-ounce) package cream cheese**
    **½ cup sifted icing sugar**
    **½ teaspoon vanilla**
Whip until stiff
    **1 cup heavy cream**
Carefully fold into cream cheese mixture. Spread evenly in prepared pie shell.
Spoon over top
    **1 (19-ounce) can prepared fruit pie filling**
Chill.
Serve topped with whipped cream, if desired.
Makes one 9-inch pie.

# LEMON CHIFFON PIE

Preheat oven to 425°F.
Prepare pastry; roll out half of dough and line a 9-inch pie plate. Trim. Flute edge and prick. Bake in preheated 425° oven for 10 to 12 minutes, or until golden. Cool.
In a saucepan, combine
    **1 envelope gelatine**
    **½ cup granulated sugar**
    **½ teaspoon salt**
Beat together
    **3 egg yolks**
    **1 cup cold water**
    **⅓ cup lemon juice**
    **2 teaspoons finely grated lemon rind**
Stir egg yolk mixture into gelatine mixture and cook over medium heat, stirring constantly, until gelatine dissolves. Chill until the consistency of unbeaten egg white.

Beat to form stiff but moist peaks
    **3 egg whites**
Gradually beat in
    **¼ cup granulated sugar**
Beat until stiff and shiny.
Fold the meringue into cooled gelatine mixture. Turn into prepared pie shell.
Chill for 2 to 3 hours or until firm.
Makes one 9-inch pie.

# LIME CHIFFON PIE

Preheat oven to 425°F.
Prepare pastry; roll out half of dough and line a 9-inch pie plate. Trim. Flute edge and prick. Bake in preheated 425° oven for 10 to 12 minutes, or until golden. Cool.
In a saucepan, combine
    **1 envelope gelatine**
    **¾ cup granulated sugar**
Beat together
    **4 egg yolks**
    **½ cup water**
    **1 (6-ounce) can frozen limeade, thawed**
Stir egg yolk mixture into gelatine and cook over medium heat, stirring constantly, until gelatine dissolves. Chill until the consistency of unbeaten egg white.
Beat to form stiff but moist peaks
    **4 egg whites**
    **¼ teaspoon cream of tartar**
Gradually beat in
    **½ cup granulated sugar**
Beat until stiff and shiny.
Fold into gelatine mixture with
    **3 drops green food colouring**
Turn into baked pie shell and chill until firm (at least 1 hour). If desired, garnish with whipped cream and maraschino cherries.
Makes one 9-inch pie.

---

*Cream and custard type pies must always be refrigerated if they are to be kept for more than an hour before serving. This is necessary to prevent food poisoning. Keep any leftovers refrigerated as well, and serve them within 24 hours. Refrigerate chiffon pies to keep them firm and fresh for serving.*

---

## CRÊPES SUZETTE PIE

Preheat oven to 425°F.
Prepare pastry; roll out half of dough and line a 9-inch pie plate. Trim. Flute edge and prick. Bake in preheated 425° oven for 10 to 12 minutes or until golden. Cool.

### FILLING

In a saucepan, combine
**½ cup granulated sugar**
**¼ cup PURITY Flour**
**Pinch of salt**
Stir in
**2 cups orange juice**
**¼ cup Grand Marnier**
Cook over medium heat, stirring constantly, until thickened. Do not boil.
Stir a small amount of hot mixture into
**2 egg yolks, beaten**
Then blend into remaining hot mixture. Cook 1 minute longer, stirring constantly. Remove from heat.
Blend in
**2 tablespoons butter or margarine**
**2 teaspoons grated orange rind**
Prepare French Pancakes (See page 205), making 7-inch pancakes to fit into pie shell. Spread ¼-inch of orange filling in baked pie shell and cover with one pancake. Fill pie shell, alternating layers and top with a pancake.
Before serving soak
**5 sugar cubes**
in
**¼ cup warmed Grand Marnier**
Arrange cubes on a flower shaped orange peel in centre of pie. Flame.
Makes one 9-inch pie.

## CRANBERRY-ALASKA PIE

Preheat oven to 425°F.
Prepare pastry; roll out half of dough and line a 9-inch pie plate. Trim. Flute edge and prick. Bake in preheated 425° oven for 10 to 12 minutes or until golden. Cool.
Beat until very smooth and fluffy
**1 (4-ounce) package cream cheese**
**¼ cup granulated sugar**
**½ teaspoon vanilla**
Blend in
**1 (14-ounce) can whole cranberry**
**sauce**
Fold in
**1 pint vanilla ice cream**

Spread in baked pie shell. Wrap and freeze. This can be stored in the freezer up to 2 months.
Just before serving:
Preheat oven to 425°F.
Top with a meringue (See page 164) of
**3 egg whites**
**¼ teaspoon cream of tartar**
**⅓ cup granulated sugar**
Cover frozen pie with meringue, being careful to have it touch pastry edge, all the way around. Bake in preheated 425° oven until lightly browned. Serve immediately.
Makes one 9-inch pie.

## ICE CREAM PIE

Preheat oven to 425°F.
Prepare pastry; roll out half of dough and line a 9-inch pie plate. Trim. Flute edge and prick. Bake in preheated 425° oven for 10 to 12 minutes, or until golden. Cool.
Mix together
**¾ cup crushed peppermint**
**candy sticks**
**3 pints vanilla ice cream**
Scoop into baked pie shell. Wrap and freeze. This can be stored in freezer up to 2 months. Just before serving spoon over ice cream
**chocolate fudge sundae**
**topping**
If desired, garnish with whipped cream and walnuts.
Makes one 9-inch pie.

## ALMOND TARTS

Preheat oven to 425°F.
Prepare sufficient pastry and roll out on floured surface. Cut with floured cookie cutter and line 3½ dozen tiny (1½-inch) tart pans.
Arrange in each tart pan
**1 whole blanched almond**
Stir together
**1 egg**
**1 tablespoon butter or margarine**
**1¼ cups lightly packed brown**
**sugar**
**1 teaspoon vanilla**
Spoon into tart pans.
Bake in preheated 425° oven for 15 to 20 minutes, or until pastry is golden.
Makes 3½ dozen tarts.

## BUTTER TARTS

Preheat oven to 375°F.
Prepare sufficient pastry and roll out on
floured surface. Cut with floured cookie
cutter and line 12 medium sized muffin
cups. Do not prick.
Pour sufficient boiling water to cover
over
**½ cup raisins**
Let stand until plumped and then drain.
Arrange in tart shells.
Mix together
**¼ cup butter or margarine**
**½ cup lightly packed brown sugar**
Stir in
**1 cup corn syrup**
**2 eggs, slightly beaten**
**¼ teaspoon salt**
**1 teaspoon vanilla**
Combine just until blended. Spoon into
unbaked tart shells, filling each about ⅔
full.
Bake in preheated 375° oven for 15 to
18 minutes. Do not allow filling to bubble over.
Makes 12 tarts.

## LADY FINGER PIE

Line bottom and side of a 9-inch pie plate
with
**16 lady fingers**
In top of double boiler, melt over direct
heat
**½ cup milk**
**2 (4-ounce) almond chocolate
bars**
Place over boiling water and fold in
**20 large marshmallows**
Remove from heat when half melted and
continue folding until smooth. Cool.
Fold in
**½ pint heavy cream, whipped**
Turn half of mixture into prepared pie
shell.
Arrange on top
**10 rum soaked lady fingers**
Spoon remaining chocolate mixture over
top. Chill.
Serve topped with lady fingers or
whipped cream.
Makes one 9-inch pie.

## CHOCOLATE FUDGE TARTS

Preheat oven to 375°F.
Prepare sufficient pastry and roll out on
floured surface. Cut with floured cookie
cutter and line 24 medium-sized muffin
cups. Do not prick.
Melt over hot water
**2 squares unsweetened chocolate**
**2 tablespoons butter or margarine**
Mix together
**3 eggs**
**1 cup lightly packed brown sugar**
**¾ cup corn syrup**
Combine with chocolate mixture and
beat with electric mixer or rotary beater
until smooth.
Fill pastry-lined tart shells ⅔ full.
Bake in preheated 375° oven for 20 to
25 minutes or until puffed.
Makes 24 tarts.

## RASPBERRY TARTS

Preheat oven to 350°F.
**Pastry:**
Cream together
**⅔ cup butter**
**½ cup lightly packed brown sugar**
Beat in
**1 egg**
**1 teaspoon vanilla**
Blend in
**1½ cups PURITY Flour**
Press into 12 ungreased medium sized
muffin cups.
**Filling:**
Cream together
**⅓ cup butter or margarine**
**¼ cup granulated sugar**
Beat in
**1 egg**
**2 teaspoons lemon juice**
**½ tablespoon grated lemon rind**
Blend together and stir in
**½ cup PURITY Flour**
**½ teaspoon baking powder**
Spoon into each tart shell
**1 teaspoon raspberry jam**
Top with batter, filling about ⅔ full.
Bake in preheated 350° oven for 15 to
20 minutes or until golden.
Makes 12 tarts.

# Breads

---

## YEAST BREADS

---

### THE "WHY" OF PERFECT BREAD

The modern day revival of making bread in the home can be attributed to simpler recipes and to the tremendous satisfaction this pleasant task gives to the whole family. What a joy to take the fragrant, golden loaves from the oven and how the family appreciate their crusty tender goodness.

A short explanation of the role of the various ingredients and how they affect the resulting bread, provides the key to successful bread making. This, combined with the mastering of a few simple skills pictured on the following pages, will open the door to successful bread making until even the most complicated of recipes may be readily produced.

### INGREDIENTS

**Hard Wheat Flour**—is the most important basic ingredient because it contains the necessary proteins to make gluten, which gives bread its "elastic" quality. This enables the dough to hold the gas produced by the yeast and thus expand or "rise". It is essential that the flour be uniform in protein content—and this is why at PURITY we employ protein-testing and quality-controls to assure you a reliable uniform flour.

**Yeast**—is a tiny living plant which grows very quickly under proper conditions, producing carbon-dioxide gas which makes the dough rise. It may be purchased in two forms—active dry yeast which is in tiny brown pellets, and compressed fresh yeast in cake form. Since the active dry yeast keeps longer and does not require refrigeration it is the more widely used and recipes in this book call for it.

**Note:** To substitute fresh yeast for active dry yeast, use one yeast cake for each envelope of dry yeast. Do not sweeten the lukewarm water which should be at 80°F. instead of 100°F. as specified in the recipe. Then just crumble yeast cake into the specified amount of water, to let stand 10 minutes and stir.

**Sugar**—is food for the yeast, helping it to produce carbon dioxide gas. It also improves the flavour of bread and helps give a golden brown crust. Some recipes call for molasses, honey, or other sugars to give a different colour as well as flavour to the breads.

**Salt**—acts as a control for the yeast action and brings out the flavour.

**Shortening**—makes the dough easier to handle, gives that all-important tenderness and helps to improve the flavour and keeping qualities of the bread or rolls. Sometimes butter is used instead of shortening.

**Liquid**—binds together the other ingre-

dients and is usually milk or water. Bread and rolls made with milk have a soft grain and white crumb, while water gives a crisper crust and less fine grain. Milk must be scalded and then cooled to

lukewarm so that it will not interfere with the yeast action. Sometimes, the water is boiled first primarily for mixing with cereal or other grains which might be included in the recipes.

## METHODS OF BREAD MAKING

**1. Batter Method:** The ingredients are beaten together to form a batter which is not subsequently kneaded. Usually one rising is required. The resulting light open texture, characteristic of this type of bread, is particularly suited to coffee cakes, casserole breads, English muffins, pancakes, and crumpets.

**2. Sponge Method:** This is an old-fashioned way to make yeast doughs. The yeast is combined with lukewarm water, sugar and flour to make a batter. This is allowed to rise until it is bubbly and resembles a sponge. The remaining flour and other ingredients are then added and the dough is kneaded and finished in the same way as for the Straight Dough Method. In general, two risings follow the sponge rising. For the most part, this method has given way to the Straight Dough Method which saves time without any resulting loss in quality.

**3. Straight Dough Method:** This is the most common way to combine yeast doughs. The ingredients are blended to form a stiff dough which is subsequently kneaded for about 8 minutes. The dough is allowed to rise and then punched down and shaped into loaves or rolls. A second rising takes place in the pans. This

technique has been fully illustrated on pages 175 to 177.

**4. Refrigerator Doughs:** These are mixed by the Straight Dough Method, but are generally richer with more shortening and some egg. This slows the rising of the dough when stored at refrigerator temperatures. These doughs will keep approximately two weeks in the refrigerator but the time will vary with the recipes. Almost any dough may be stored in the refrigerator and it will continue to rise while cooling to the temperature of the refrigerator. For example: the PURITY White Bread recipe which makes four loaves, may be refrigerated overnight instead of setting it to rise in a warm place. In the morning the dough will have risen sufficiently for punching down and shaping into loaves. However this dough will take longer to rise in the pans.

**5. Easy-Loaf Method:** This does not call for two complete risings. For this reason the recipe has a higher proportion of yeast, and acid ingredients such as cream of tartar may be added. This time saving method produces a fragrant, open-textured loaf that is especially nice when served warm.

## SCORING BREAD

| Shape | |
|---|---|
| Well proportioned loaf | 10 |
| Nicely rounded top | 5 |
| No cracks, bulges or bumps | 5 |

| Crust | |
|---|---|
| Even, golden brown | 10 |
| Smooth surface | 5 |
| Tender crust | 5 |

| Volume | |
|---|---|
| Light in proportion to its size | 10 |

| Texture | |
|---|---|
| Tender, moist crumb | 10 |
| No doughiness | 5 |
| Fine even grain with no air bubbles | 10 |
| Nice crumb colour—no streaks | 5 |

| Flavour | |
|---|---|
| Sweet, natural flavour and aroma | 20 |
| Total: | 100 points |

## THE "HOW" OF PERFECT BREAD

**Step 1:** Assemble all the ingredients and utensils necessary. Measure the PURITY Flour by spooning it into a cup and levelling off.

**Step 2:** Set the milk to heat and begin softening the yeast. Active dry yeast works best at a temperature of 100°F. which we refer to as lukewarm. To test, drop a little liquid on the inside of the wrist. If it feels very slightly warm, the liquid is at the proper temperature.

**Step 3:** When the milk has reached the scalding point, pour it into a large mixing bowl and add sugar, salt, shortening and other liquid. Stir until shortening melts. Cool to lukewarm. Blend in yeast. If eggs are used, they may be beaten together slightly and blended in now. Beat in the first portion of flour mentioned in the recipe. This may be done with mixer at medium speed. It is important to fully beat at this stage in order to develop the gluten.

**Step 4:** With a wooden spoon, beat in the remaining half of the flour gradually, until too stiff to beat with a spoon. Work in the last of the flour with a rotating motion of the hand.

**Step 5: Knead the Dough:** Kneading develops the gluten (elastic quality). Turn dough out on a floured surface. Press into a smooth, slightly flat ball. Then, as shown, fold the dough over towards yourself. Now, with the heels of your hands, push the dough away from yourself. Give it a quarter turn and repeat this action with a rhythmic motion until the dough is sufficiently kneaded (about 8 to 10 minutes). Dough is kneaded enough when the surface is smooth and satiny, and looks to be stretched; and when the dough feels springy and elastic to the touch.

**Step 6: First Rising:** Place dough smooth side down, in a heavily greased large bowl. Then, turn dough over, smooth side up, thus greasing the surface. Cover the bowl with greased wax paper and a damp cloth and set in a warm place to rise. Allow the dough to rise until twice its original size, about 1¼ to 1½ hours. To test, press two fingers into the dough and withdraw them quickly. If they leave a deep impression, the dough has risen enough and is ready for punching down.

**Step 7: Punch Down:** Punch down after the first rising by thursting your fist into the dough. As the dough collapses, pull in the edges and fold them into the centre.

**Step 8:** Turn dough out of bowl and divide into equal pieces. It is important to have the pieces of the same size for uniformity in the finished loaves.

**Step 9: Shape the Loaves:** (a) Press or roll one ball of dough into a rectangle, measuring about 8 inches wide by 10 inches long. Press out all large air bubbles. This will give your bread a smooth, even texture so important in good bread making.

(b) **Fold:** Folding is a most important step in the appearance of your finished loaves. Be sure to fold and seal all ends very carefully. First, fold far side of the dough into the centre; then the near side to the centre; press out any trapped air bubbles. Seal well by pressing "seam" firmly with fingers.

(c) **Stretch:** Stretch the dough slightly to make it uniform in size, then fold the ends in to meet the centre. Press out any entrapped air bubbles. Seal, as before, by pressing "seams" firmly with fingers. Again, we remind you that appearance counts for a good "score".

(d) **Final Shaping:** The final shaping of the loaf is next. Fold the dough again and seal the edges carefully by pinching together with the fingers. Repeat the folding, stretching and shaping steps with remaining balls of dough. You are now ready for the 8½ × 4½-inch bread pans, which have been lightly greased.

**Step 10: Second Rising:** Place shaped loaves in greased bread pans with folded side down. Cover with greased wax paper and a damp cloth. Let rise until doubled in bulk (about one hour). A gentle touch of the fingers leaves a slight impression when the loaves are oven ready.

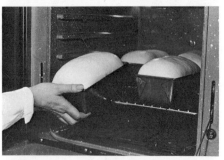

**Step 11: Baking the Bread:** (a) If desired, the loaves may be brushed with milk or egg and water mixture. Bake the bread in a hot oven—400°F. until nicely browned. This takes about 30 to 35 minutes. Now you will be able to sniff the wonderful aroma that only home-baked bread can give.

(b) Bread is done when the crust is an even golden brown and the loaves lift free from the pan and sound hollow when tapped on the bottom. Remove bread from the pan at once and place on a rack to cool.

(c) If a softer crust is preferred, brush the top of each loaf with soft butter while still hot.

**Step 12: Storing Bread:** (a) When thoroughly cool, wrap loaves and store in a well ventilated bread box at room temperature. OR

(b) Wrap tightly in freezer wrap and keep in home freezer or the freezing compartment of the refrigerator. For convenience, bread to be stored in the freezer may be sliced first and then when ready to use, simply remove the number of slices required.

## WHITE BREAD

Scald
   **2 cups milk**
Pour into a large bowl and add
   **¼ cup granulated sugar**
   **4 teaspoons salt**
   **¼ cup shortening**
   **1 cup water**
Stir until shortening melts. Cool to luke-warm.
Meanwhile dissolve
   **2 teaspoons sugar**
in
   **1 cup lukewarm water (100°F.)**
Over this, sprinkle
   **2 envelopes active dry yeast**
Let stand for 10 minutes. Then stir briskly with a fork. Add softened yeast to luke-warm milk mixture. Stir.
Beat in
   **5 cups PURITY Flour**
Beat vigorously by hand or with electric mixer.
Then gradually beat in with a spoon an additional
   **4½ to 5 cups PURITY Flour**
Work in last of flour with a rotating mo-tion of the hand. Turn dough onto a floured surface and knead 8 to 10 min-utes. Shape into a smooth ball and place in a greased bowl, rotating dough to grease surface. Cover with a damp cloth and let rise until doubled (about 1½ hours). Keep in a warm place. Punch down and shape into 4 loaves. Place in greased 8½ × 4½-inch loaf pans, grease tops, cover and let rise again until dou-bled (about 1 hour).
Bake in preheated 400° oven for 30 to 35 minutes.
Makes 4 loaves.

## PURITY EASY LOAF

Scald
   **2¾ cups milk**
Pour into a large bowl and add
   **¼ cup granulated sugar**
   **2 tablespoons salt**
   **⅓ cup shortening**
Stir until shortening melts. Cool to luke-warm.
Meanwhile, dissolve
   **1 tablespoon sugar**
in
   **1½ cups lukewarm water (100°F.)**

Over this, sprinkle
   **3 envelopes active dry yeast**
Let stand for 10 minutes. Then stir briskly with a fork. Add softened yeast to luke-warm milk mixture. Stir.
Beat in
   **5 cups PURITY Flour**
Beat vigorously by hand or with electric mixer.
Then gradually beat in with a spoon an additional
   **5½ to 6 cups PURITY Flour**
Work in last of flour with a rotating mo-tion of the hand. Turn dough onto a lightly floured surface and knead 8 to 10 minutes. Shape into a smooth ball, cover with wax paper and a cloth dampened with hot water and let rest for 20 min-utes. Divide in four. Roll out each por-tion, pressing out any large bubbles. Fold over and roll up tightly, shaping into loaves. Place in greased 8½ × 4½-inch loaf pans. Cover with oiled wax paper and a damp cloth and let rise in a warm place until doubled (about 1¼ hours) OR place in refrigerator for 2 to 24 hours. (Let refrigerated loaves stand 20 minutes at room temperature before baking.)
Bake in preheated 400° oven for 30 to 35 minutes.
Makes 4 loaves.

## WHOLE WHEAT BREAD

Scald
   **1½ cups milk**
Pour into a large bowl and add
   **½ cup lightly packed brown sugar**
   **2 tablespoons salt**
   **½ cup shortening**
Stir until shortening melts.
Add
   **2¼ cups water**
Cool to lukewarm.
Meanwhile, dissolve
   **2 teaspoons sugar**
in
   **1 cup lukewarm water (100°F.)**
Over this, sprinkle
   **2 envelopes active dry yeast**
Let stand for 10 minutes. Then stir briskly with a fork. Add softened yeast to luke-warm milk mixture. Stir.
Beat in
   **6 cups whole wheat flour**
Beat vigorously by hand or with electric mixer.

Then gradually beat in with a spoon
**6 to 6½ cups PURITY Flour**
Work in last of flour with a rotating motion of the hand. Turn dough onto a floured surface and knead 8 to 10 minutes. Shape into a smooth ball and place in a greased bowl, rotating dough to grease surface. Cover with a damp cloth and let rise until doubled (about 1¼ hours.) Keep in a warm place. Punch down and shape into 4 loaves. Place in greased 8½ × 4½-inch loaf pans, grease tops slightly, cover and let rise again until doubled (about 1 hour).
Bake in preheated 400° oven for 30 to 35 minutes.
Makes 4 loaves.

MOLASSES WHOLE WHEAT BREAD:
Replace brown sugar with ½ cup molasses in above recipe and proceed as directed.

## RYE BREAD

Scald
**2⅔ cups milk**
Pour into a large bowl and add
**½ cup lightly packed brown sugar**
**4 teaspoons salt**
**¼ cup shortening**
Stir until shortening melts. Cool to lukewarm.
Meanwhile, dissolve
**2 teaspoons sugar**
in
**1 cup lukewarm water (100°F.)**
Over this, sprinkle
**2 envelopes active dry yeast**
Let stand for 10 minutes. Then stir briskly with a fork. Add softened yeast to lukewarm milk mixture. Stir.
Beat in
**4½ cups dark rye flour**
Beat vigorously by hand or with electric mixer.
Then gradually beat in with a spoon
**4 to 4½ cups PURITY Flour**
Work in last of flour with a rotating motion of the hand. Turn dough onto a floured surface and knead 8 to 10 minutes. Shape into a smooth ball and place in a greased bowl, rotating dough to grease surface. Cover with a damp cloth and let rise until 1½ times original volume (about 1½ hours). Keep in a warm place. Punch down and shape into 4

loaves. Place in greased 8½ × 4½-inch loaf pans, grease tops slightly and let rise again until 1½ times volume (about 1 hour).
Bake in preheated 400° oven for 30 to 35 minutes.
Makes 4 loaves.

*To make Melba Toast: cut day-old bread into ⅛-inch slices. Remove crusts if you like. Cut into desired shapes and place on a baking sheet. Dry slowly in a 300°F. oven until crisp and golden brown—about 20 minutes.*

## RAISIN BREAD

Scald
**2 cups milk**
Mix together
**¼ cup granulated sugar**
**1 tablespoon salt**
**1 teaspoon cinnamon**
Pour hot milk into a large bowl with sugar mixture and
**¼ cup shortening**
Stir until shortening melts. Cool to lukewarm.
Mix in
**1½ cups raisins**
Meanwhile, dissolve
**1 teaspoon sugar**
in
**½ cup lukewarm water (100°F.)**
Over this, sprinkle
**1 envelope active dry yeast**
Let stand for 10 minutes. Then stir briskly with a fork. Add softened yeast to lukewarm milk mixture. Stir.
Beat in
**2½ cups PURITY Flour**
Beat vigorously by hand or with electric mixer.
Then gradually beat in with a spoon an additional
**2½ to 3 cups PURITY Flour**
Work in last of four with a rotating motion of the hand. Turn dough onto a floured surface and knead 8 to 10 minutes. Shape into a smooth ball. Try to prevent the raisins from protruding through the top of the dough as this will cause loss of the gases and poor rising. Place in a greased bowl, rotating dough to grease surface. Cover with a damp cloth and let rise until doubled (about

2 hours). Keep in a warm place. Punch down and shape into 2 loaves. Place in greased 8½ × 4½-inch loaf pans, grease tops slightly, cover and let rise again until doubled (about 1½ hours).
Bake in preheated 400° oven for 30 to 35 minutes.
Makes 2 loaves.

## OLD FASHIONED PORRIDGE BREAD

Pour
   **3 cups boiling water**
Over
   **2 cups PURITY Rolled Oats**
   **¼ cup shortening**
Stir until shortening melts and let stand for about 20 minutes, stirring occasionally.
Meanwhile, dissolve
   **2 teaspoons sugar**
in
   **1 cup lukewarm water (100°F.)**
Over this, sprinkle
   **2 envelopes active dry yeast**
Let stand for 10 minutes. Then stir briskly with a fork.
Stir into partially cooled rolled oat mixture
   **⅔ cup table molasses**
   **4 teaspoons salt**
Cool to lukewarm.
Add softened yeast to the lukewarm rolled oat mixture. Stir.
Beat in
   **2½ cups PURITY Flour**
Beat vigorously by hand or with electric mixer.
Then gradually beat in with a spoon an additional
   **5½ to 6 cups PURITY Flour**
Work in last of flour with a rotating motion of the hand. Turn dough onto a floured surface and knead 8 to 10 minutes. Shape into a smooth ball and place in a greased bowl, rotating dough to grease surface. Cover and let rise until doubled (about 1½ hours). Keep in a warm place. Punch down and shape into 4 loaves. Place in greased 8½ × 4½-inch loaf pans, grease tops, cover and let rise again until doubled (about 1 hour).
Bake in preheated 400° oven for 30 to 35 minutes.
Makes 4 loaves.

## SOURDOUGH BREAD

In a large bowl, dissolve
   **1 teaspoon sugar**
in
   **½ cup lukewarm water (100°F.)**
Over this sprinkle
   **1 envelope active dry yeast**
Let stand for 10 minutes. Then stir briskly with a fork.
Stir in
   **4 cups lukewarm water**
   **1 tablespoon salt**
   **1 tablespoon sugar**
   **4 cups PURITY Flour**
Cover. Let stand at room temperature for 3 days, stirring batter down daily.
On third day, scald
   **1 cup milk**
Stir in
   **¼ cup granulated sugar**
   **2 tablespoons shortening**
   **2 teaspoons salt**
Cool to lukewarm. Blend in 3½ cups yeast mixture. (To remainder add 3 cups lukewarm water and 3 cups PURITY Flour Let stand at room temperature 1 day then pour into sealer and refrigerate. Use next time for bread.)
Beat in
   **3 cups PURITY Flour**
Beat vigorously by hand or with electric mixer.
Then gradually beat in with a wooden spoon an additional
   **4 to 4½ cups PURITY Flour**
Work in last of flour with a rotating motion of the hand. Turn dough onto a floured surface and knead 8 to 10 minutes. Shape into a smooth ball and place in a greased bowl, rotating dough to grease surface. Cover and let rise until doubled (about 1½ hours). Punch down and divide into four. Roll out each portion and shape into loaves. Place in greased 8½ × 4½-inch loaf pans. Grease tops and let rise again until doubled (about 45 minutes). Bake in preheated 400° oven for 30 to 35 minutes.
Makes 4 loaves.

*Most sweet yeast breads are best when served warm, right from the oven. To reheat, wrap in aluminum foil and place in a preheated 350°F. oven for 10 to 15 minutes.*

# FRENCH BREAD

Pour into a large bowl
**1¼ cups boiling water**
Add
**1 tablespoon sugar**
**2 teaspoons salt**
**¼ teaspoon ginger**
**1 tablespoon shortening**
Stir until shortening melts. Cool to lukewarm.
Meanwhile, dissolve
**1 teaspoon sugar**
in
**½ cup lukewarm water (100°F.)**
Over this, sprinkle
**1 envelope active dry yeast**
Let stand for 10 minutes. Then stir briskly with a fork. Add softened yeast to lukewarm mixture. Stir.
Beat in
**2 cups PURITY Flour**
Beat vigorously by hand or with electric mixer.
Then gradually beat in with a spoon an additional
**2 to 2½ cups PURITY Flour**
Work in last of flour with a rotating motion of the hand. Turn dough onto a floured surface and knead 8 to 10 minutes. Shape into a smooth ball and place in a greased bowl, rotating dough to grease surface. Cover with a damp cloth and let rise until doubled (about 1½ hours). Keep in a warm place. Punch down and shape into 3 narrow loaves, 12 inches long. Place well apart on a greased baking sheet. Slash top diagonally with scissors. Cover with greased wax paper and a damp cloth and let rise until doubled in unheated oven with a pan of boiling water. Brush lightly with water. (To improve crustiness, if possible bathe loaves after second rising with steam. An electric kettle is ideal.)
With a pan of boiling water in the oven, bake in preheated 425° oven for 25 minutes.
Makes 3 loaves.

# CASSEROLE BREAD

Scald
**1¼ cups milk**
Pour into a large bowl and add
**¼ cup granulated sugar**
**2 teaspoons salt**
**⅓ cup shortening**
Stir until shortening melts. Cool to lukewarm and beat in
**1 egg**
Meanwhile, dissolve
**1 teaspoon sugar**
in
**½ cup lukewarm water (100°F.)**
Over this, sprinkle
**1 envelope active dry yeast**
Let stand for 10 minutes. Then stir briskly with a fork. Add softened yeast to lukewarm milk mixture. Stir.
Beat in
**2½ cups PURITY Flour**
Beat vigorously by hand or with electric mixer for 3 minutes or until smooth. With a spoon beat in an additional
**½ cup PURITY Flour**
Cover with greased wax paper and a damp cloth and let rise until doubled (about 1½ hours). Keep in a warm place. Stir down risen dough and turn into a greased 1½ quart casserole.
Bake uncovered in preheated 400° oven for 40 to 45 minutes.
Makes one loaf.

# WHEAT GERM BREAD

Pour
**3 cups boiling water**
over
**2 cups wheat germ**
**¼ cup shortening**
Stir until shortening melts and let stand for about 20 minutes, stirring occasionally.
Meanwhile, dissolve
**2 teaspoons sugar**
in
**1 cup lukewarm water (100°F.)**
Over this, sprinkle
**2 envelopes active dry yeast**
Let stand for 10 minutes. Then stir briskly with a fork.
Add to partially cooled wheat germ mixture
**⅔ cup table molasses**
**4 teaspoons salt**
Cool to lukewarm.
Add softened yeast to the lukewarm wheat germ mixture. Stir.
Beat in
**3½ cups PURITY Flour**

Beat vigorously by hand or with electric mixer.
Then gradually beat in with a spoon an additional
**5 to 5½ cups PURITY Flour**
Work in last of flour with a rotating motion of the hand. Turn dough onto a floured surface and knead 8 to 10 minutes. Shape into a smooth ball and place in a greased bowl, rotating dough to grease surface. Cover with a damp cloth and let rise until doubled (about 1¼ hours). Keep in a warm place. Punch down and shape into 4 loaves. Place in greased 8½ × 4½-inch loaf pans, grease tops slightly, cover and let rise again until doubled (about 1 hour).
Bake in preheated 400° oven for 30 to 35 minutes.
Makes 4 loaves.

## GERMAN DARK RYE BREAD

Pour into a large bowl
**2 cups hot strong coffee**
Add
**¼ cup shortening**
**⅔ cup table molasses**
**5 teaspoons salt**
Stir until shortening melts. Cool to lukewarm.
Meanwhile, dissolve
**2 teaspoons sugar**
in
**1 cup lukewarm water (100°F.)**
Over this, sprinkle
**2 envelopes active dry yeast**
Let stand for 10 minutes. Then stir briskly with a fork. Add to cooled coffee mixture.
Beat in
**3 cups PURITY FLour**
**2 cups dark rye flour**
Beat vigorously by hand or with electric mixer.
Then gradually beat in with a spoon
**2 cups dark rye flour**
**2 to 2½ cups PURITY Flour**
Work in last of flour with a rotating motion of the hand. Turn dough onto a floured surface and knead 8 to 10 minutes. Shape into a smooth ball and place in a greased bowl, rotating dough to grease surface. Cover with a damp cloth and let rise until 1½ times original volume (about 1½ hours). Keep in a warm

place. Punch down and shape into 3 loaves. Place in greased 8½ × 4½-inch loaf pans, grease tops slightly and let rise again until 1½ times original volume (about 1 hour).
Bake in preheated 400° oven for 30 to 35 minutes.
Makes 3 loaves.

## ONION BREAD

In a saucepan, combine and simmer covered for 10 minutes
**3½ cups water**
**2 envelopes dried onion**
**soup mix**
Pour into a large bowl and add
**¼ cup granulated sugar**
**¼ cup grated Parmesan cheese**
**1 tablespoon salt**
**2 tablespoons shortening**
Stir until shortening melts. Cool to lukewarm.
Meanwhile, dissolve
**1 teaspoon sugar**
in
**½ cup lukewarm water (100°F.)**
Over this, sprinkle
**1 envelope active dry yeast**
Let stand for 10 minutes. Then stir briskly with a fork. Add softened yeast to lukewarm milk mixture. Stir.
Beat in
**4 cups PURITY Flour**
Beat vigorously by hand or with electric mixer.
Then gradually beat in with a spoon an additional

**4 to 5 cups PURITY Flour**
Work in last of flour with a rotating motion of the hand. Turn dough onto a floured surface and knead 8 to 10 minutes. Shape into a smooth ball and place in a greased bowl, rotating dough to grease surface. Cover with a damp cloth and let rise until doubled (about 1¼ hours). Keep in a warm place. Punch down and shape into 3 narrow loaves, 12 inches long. Place well apart on greased baking sheet. Slash top diagonally with scissors. Cover with greased wax paper and a damp cloth and let rise until doubled (about ¾ hour) in unheated oven with a pan of boiling water. Brush lightly with water. (To improve crustiness, if possible bathe loaves after second

rising with steam. An electric kettle is ideal.)
With a pan of boiling water in the oven bake in preheated 425° oven for 25 minutes.
Makes 3 French sticks.

---

*To make Toast Cups remove crusts from thinly sliced bread and brush with melted butter or margarine. Press each slice into a large muffin cup. Bake in preheated 375°F. oven for 12 to 15 minutes or until golden. Use as you would patty shells.*

---

### FINNISH COFFEE BREAD

Scald
  **¾ cup milk**
Pour into a large bowl and add
  **½ cup granulated sugar**
  **1 teaspoon salt**
  **⅓ cup butter**
  **½ teaspoon ground cardamon**
Stir until butter melts. Cool to lukewarm.
Stir in
  **3 eggs, slightly beaten**
Meanwhile, dissolve
  **1 teaspoon sugar**
in
  **½ cup lukewarm water (100°F.)**
Over this, sprinkle
  **1 envelope active dry yeast**
Let stand for 10 minutes. Then stir briskly with a fork. Add softened yeast to lukewarm milk mixture. Stir.

Beat in
  **3 cups PURITY Flour**
Beat vigorously by hand or with electric mixer.
Then gradually beat in with a spoon an additional
  **2½ to 3 cups PURITY Flour**
Work in last of flour with a rotating motion of the hand. Turn dough onto a floured surface and knead 8 to 10 minutes. Shape into a smooth ball and place in a greased bowl, rotating dough to grease surface. Cover with a damp cloth and let rise until doubled (about 2 hours). Punch down and divide into 4 parts. Shape each portion into a round flat loaf and place on greased cookie sheet. Cover, and let rise again until doubled (about 1¼ hours).
Bake in preheated 375° oven for 30 to 35 minutes.
As soon as bread is removed from oven, brush with a mixture of
  **2 tablespoons sugar**
  **1 tablespoon hot coffee**
Sprinkle with
  **granulated sugar**
Cut in wedges and serve warm.
Makes 4 loaves.

---

*If you store bread in a breadbox at room temperature it will stay soft but may not keep too long in warm weather. If you store it in the refrigerator it will be safe from mould but will not stay soft.*

---

# FANCY ROLLS

## PAN ROLLS

After dough has been punched down and rolled, shape each piece into a cylinder about 1½ inches in diameter. Cut each into 8 equal pieces. Shape each piece of dough into a ball. Place 16 balls, almost touching in a greased 8 or 9-inch square pan. Brush with melted butter or margarine. Cover with greased wax paper and a damp cloth and let rise until doubled (about ¾ hour). Bake at 375°F. for 25 to 30 minutes.

### CLOVERLEAF ROLLS

**Step 1:** After dough has been punched and rolled out, shape each piece of dough into a cylinder about 1½ inches in diameter and cut each into 8 equal pieces.
**Step 2:** Cut each piece of dough in three and form into balls. Brush with melted butter or margarine. Place three in each section of greased muffin cups. Cover with greased wax paper and a damp cloth and let rise until doubled (about ¾ hour). Bake at 375°F. for 18 to 20 minutes.

### PARKERHOUSE ROLLS

After dough has been punched down, roll each piece of dough to ¼-inch thickness. Cut into rounds with a 2½ or 3-inch cutter. Crease each round with back of a knife, just off-centre; brush with melted butter. Fold over with wider half on top, pressing edges together. Place on a greased baking sheet, brush with melted butter or margarine. Cover with greased wax paper and a damp cloth and let rise until doubled (about ¾ hour). Bake at 375°F. for 18 to 20 minutes.

### CRESCENTS

After dough has been punched down, roll each piece into a round about 8-inches in diameter. Brush with melted butter or margarine. Cut each round into 8 pie-shaped wedges. Starting from wide end, roll up each wedge and place on a greased baking sheet. Round slightly to form a crescent, tucking ends under. Brush with melted butter or margarine. Cover with greased wax paper and a damp cloth and let rise until doubled (about ¾ hour). Bake at 375°F. for 18 to 20 minutes.

## FAN TANS

After dough has been punched down, roll each piece into a rectangle measuring 9 inches by 5 inches. Brush with melted butter or margarine. Cut each rectangle into five 1-inch strips.
Place strips in piles of 5, butter side up. Cut the pile into six 1½-inch pieces. Place, cut side down in greased muffin cups. Cover with greased wax paper and a damp cloth and let rise until doubled (about ¾ hour). Bake in preheated 375° oven for 18 to 20 minutes.

## BOWKNOTS

After the dough has been punched down, roll each piece into rectangles which are ¾-inch thick and 6 inches wide. Cut each rectangle into strips, 6 inches long and ¾-inch wide. Roll each strip slightly before tying. Tie each strip into a knot, as indicated.
Place on a greased baking sheet. Brush with melted butter or margarine. Cover with greased wax paper and a damp cloth and let rise until doubled (about ¾ hour). Bake in preheated 375° oven for 18 to 20 minutes.

*Reheat rolls by one of these methods:*
*(a) Place rolls in a moistened paper bag and heat in a 350°F. oven for about 10 minutes.*
*(b) Sprinkle rolls very lightly with water and then wrap in aluminum foil. Heat for about 10 minutes in a 350°F. oven or on a rack in an electric frying pan heated to this temperature.*
*(c) Heat rolls in a bun warmer or in the top of a double boiler over hot water.*

DISCOVER HOW GOOD A COOK YOU REALLY ARE—USE PURITY FLOUR

## BASIC ROLLS

Scald
**1½ cup milk**
Pour into a large bowl and add
**¼ cup granulated sugar**
**2 teaspoons salt**
**¼ cup shortening**
Stir until shortening melts. Cool to lukewarm.
Meanwhile, dissolve
**1 teaspoon sugar**
in
**½ cup lukewarm water (100°F.)**
Over this sprinkle
**1 envelope active dry yeast**
Let stand for 10 minutes. Then stir briskly with a fork. Add softened yeast to lukewarm milk mixture together with
**1 egg, beaten**
Stir.
Beat in
**3 cups PURITY Flour**
Beat vigorously by hand or with electric mixer.
Then gradually beat in with a spoon an additional
**2 to 2½ cups PURITY Flour**
Work in last of flour with a rotating motion of the hand. Turn dough onto a floured surface and knead 8 to 10 minutes. Shape into a smooth ball and place in a greased bowl, rotating dough to grease surface. Cover with a damp cloth and let rise until doubled (about 1½ hours). Keep in a warm place. Punch down, divide in 4, and shape into rolls, (See page 184). Cover with a damp cloth and let rise in a warm place until doubled (about 45 minutes).
Bake in preheated 400° oven for 15 to 20 minutes.
Makes about 4 dozen rolls.

## REFRIGERATOR ROLLS

Scald.
**1½ cups milk**
Pour into a large bowl and add
**½ cup granulated sugar**
**2 teaspoons salt**
**½ cup shortening**
Stir until shortening melts. Cool to lukewarm.
Meanwhile, dissolve
**2 teaspoons sugar**

in
**1 cup lukewarm water (100°F.)**
Over this, sprinkle
**2 envelopes active dry yeast**
Let stand for 10 minutes. Then stir briskly with a fork.
Add softened yeast to lukewarm milk mixture together with
**2 eggs, beaten**
Stir.
Beat in
**4 cups PURITY Flour**
Beat vigorously by hand or with electric mixer.
Then gradually beat in with a spoon an additional
**3 to 4 cups PURITY Flour**
Work in last of flour with a rotating motion of the hand. Turn dough onto a floured surface and knead 8 to 10 minutes. Shape into a smooth ball and place in an oiled bowl, rotating to grease surface. Cover tightly with two layers of wax paper or aluminium foil and tie securely. Place in refrigerator. Allow to rise at least 4 hours. About 2 hours before using, punch down, divide in 4, and shape into rolls, (See page 184). Cover with damp cloth and let rise in a warm place until doubled (about 1½ hours).
Bake in preheated 400° oven for 15 to 20 minutes or until golden.
Makes 4 dozen rolls.

## BATTER ROLLS

Scald
**1½ cups milk**
Pour into a large bowl and add
**¼ cup granulated sugar**
**2 teaspoons salt**
**¼ cup shortening**
Stir until shortening melts. Cool to lukewarm.
Meanwhile, dissolve
**1 teaspoon sugar**
in
**½ cup lukewarm water (100°F.)**
Over this, sprinkle
**1 envelope active dry yeast**
Let stand for 10 minutes. Then stir briskly with a fork. Add softened yeast to lukewarm milk mixture. Stir.
Beat in
**2¾ cups PURITY Flour**
Beat vigorously by hand or with electric

mixer for 3 minutes or until smooth. Then gradually beat in with a spoon an additional

**½ cup PURITY Flour**

Cover with greased wax paper and a damp cloth and let rise until doubled (about 1 hour). Keep in a warm place. Stir down risen dough and let stand 10 minutes. Fill greased muffin cups ¾ full of dough. Let rise until doubled in bulk (about ¾ hour).

Bake in preheated 375° oven for 20 to 25 minutes.

Makes 16 to 18 rolls.

ONION BATTER ROLLS: Prepare Batter Rolls following basic recipe and add ⅓ cup dried onion flakes to milk before scalding.

## HOT CROSS BUNS

Scald
**1 cup milk**
Pour into a large bowl and add
**⅔ cup granulated sugar**
**2 teaspoons salt**
**⅓ cup butter**
Stir until butter melts. Cool to lukewarm. Meanwhile, dissolve
**1 teaspoon sugar**
in
**½ cup lukewarm water (100°F.)**
Over this, sprinkle
**1 envelope active dry yeast**
Let stand for 10 minutes. Then stir briskly with a fork. Add softened yeast to lukewarm milk mixture together with
**1 egg, beaten**
**1 egg yolk**
**1 to 1½ teaspoons cinnamon**
**½ teaspoon nutmeg**
**¼ teaspoon mace**
**¼ teaspoon ginger**
Beat in
**2½ cups PURITY Flour**
Beat vigorously by hand or with electric mixer.
Then beat in
**⅔ cup raisins or currants**
**½ cup cut mixed peel**
Then gradually beat in with a spoon an additional
**2½ to 3 cups PURITY Flour**
Work in last of flour with a rotating motion of the hand. Turn dough onto a

lightly floured surface and knead 8 to 10 minutes.
Shape into a smooth ball and place in a greased bowl, rotating dough to grease surface. Cover with a damp cloth and let rise until doubled (about 1½ hours). Punch down and shape into 18 to 20 buns. Arrange 2-inches apart on greased baking sheets. Cover and let rise until doubled in bulk (about 45 minutes).
Combine
**1 egg white, slightly beaten**
**1 tablespoon water**
Brush risen buns with egg-white mixture. Slash top of bun in the form of a cross. Bake in preheated 400° oven for 15 to 18 minutes.
If desired, drizzle with Icing Sugar Glaze. (Blend together ¾ cup sifted icing sugar, 1 tablespoon milk and ¼ teaspoon vanilla.)
Makes 18 to 20 buns.

## ENGLISH MUFFINS

Scald
**2 cups milk**
Pour into a large bowl and add
**¼ cup granulated sugar**
**1 tablespoon salt**
**¼ cup shortening**
Stir until shortening melts. Cool to lukewarm and stir in
**1 egg, slightly beaten**
Meanwhile, dissolve
**1 teaspoon sugar**
in
**½ cup lukewarm water (100°F.)**
Over this, sprinkle
**1 envelope active dry yeast**
Let stand for 10 minutes. Then stir briskly with a fork. Add softened yeast to lukewarm milk mixture. Stir.
Beat in
**3¼ cups PURITY Flour**
Beat vigorously by hand or with electric mixer.
Then gradually beat in with a spoon an additional
**3 to 3¼ cups PURITY Flour**
Work in last of flour with a rotating motion of the hand. Turn dough onto a floured surface and knead 8 to 10 minutes. Shape into a smooth ball and place in a greased bowl, rotating dough to grease surface. Cover with a damp cloth

and let rise until doubled (about 1½ hours). Keep in a warm place. Punch down, divide into 3 portions, and roll out each ¼-inch thick. Cut in 3-inch circles. Place on cornmeal sprinkled baking sheet, brush tops with water and sprinkle with cornmeal. Cover with greased wax paper and damp cloth and let rise until doubled.
Cook on medium hot ungreased griddle for about 6 minutes a side.
Makes about 3½ dozen.

## CRUSTY FRENCH ROLLS

Pour into a large bowl
**¾ cup boiling water**
Add
**1 tablespoon sugar**
**1 teaspoon salt**
**2 tablespoons shortening**
Stir until shortening melts. Cool to luke-warm.
Meanwhile, dissolve
**1 teaspoon sugar**
in
**½ cup lukewarm water (100°F.)**
Over this, sprinkle
**1 envelope active dry yeast**
Let stand for 10 minutes. Then stir briskly with a fork. Add softened yeast to luke-warm mixture together with
**2 egg whites, stiffly beaten**
Mix thoroughly.
Beat in
**1½ cups PURITY Flour**
Beat vigorously by hand or with electric mixer.
Then gradually beat in with a spoon an additional
**1½ to 2 cups PURITY Flour**
Work in last of flour with a rotating mo-tion of the hand. Turn dough on a floured surface and knead 8 to 10 min-utes. Shape into a smooth ball and place in a greased bowl, rotating dough to grease surface. Cover with a damp cloth and let rise until doubled (about 1½ hours). Keep in a warm place.
Punch down and divide into 24 pieces. Shape into round buns and place, well apart, on a greased baking sheet. Cover with greased wax paper and a damp cloth, and let rise until doubled in un-heated oven with a pan of boiling water. Brush lightly with water. (To improve

crustiness, if possible bathe loaves after second rising with steam. An electric kettle is ideal.)
With a pan of boiling water in the oven, bake in preheated 425° oven for 18 to 20 minutes.
Makes 24 rolls.

*To make Cinnamon Toast: cream to-gether 2 tablespoons butter or margarine, ¼ cup lightly-packed brown sugar and 1 teaspoon cinnamon. Spread over hot toast and place under broiler until bub-bly.*

## BASIC SWEET DOUGH

Scald
**1 cup milk**
Pour into a large bowl and add
**⅓ cup granulated sugar**
**2 teaspoons salt**
**½ cup shortening**
Stir until shortening melts. Cool to luke-warm.
Meanwhile, dissolve
**1 teaspoon sugar**
in
**½ cup lukewarm water (100°F.)**
Over this, sprinkle
**1 envelope active dry yeast**
Let stand for 10 minutes. Then stir briskly with a fork. Add softened yeast to luke-warm milk mixture together with
**1 egg, slightly beaten**
Stir.
Beat in
**2 cups PURITY Flour**
Beat vigorously by hand or with electric mixer.
Then gradually beat in with a spoon an additional
**2½ to 3 cups PURITY Flour**
Work in last of flour with a rotating mo-tion of the hand. Turn dough onto a floured surface and knead 8 to 10 min-utes. Shape into a smooth ball and place in a greased bowl, rotating dough to grease surface. Cover with a damp cloth and let rise until doubled (about 1¼ hours). Keep in a warm place. Punch down, divide into half and use one por-tion to prepare any of these sweet dough variations: Swedish Tea Ring, Pecan Cin-namon Buns, Doughnuts, Crullers and Poteca.

## SWEDISH TEA RING

(Use ½ Basic Sweet Dough recipe.)
Roll the punched dough on a lightly
floured surface into a 9 x 16-inch rectangle.
Brush to within ½-inch of edges with
**1 tablespoon butter or margarine,
melted**
Sprinkle with mixture of
**¼ cup lightly packed brown sugar
⅓ cup chopped nuts
⅓ cup raisins
½ teaspoon cinnamon
¼ teaspoon nutmeg**
Roll up like a jelly roll starting at longer
side.

Seal edges firmly and place on a greased
baking sheet bringing ends together to
form a ring. Dampen and seal these ends
carefully. Slash with scissors, ¾ of the
way through the dough in 1-inch slices.
Turn each slice on its side (see picture).
Cover and let rise until doubled (about
¾ hour).
Bake in preheated 400° oven for 20 to
25 minutes. Partially cool the ring.
Drizzle with a mixture of
**¾ cup sifted icing sugar
1 tablespoon milk
¼ teaspoon almond flavouring**

## PECAN CINNAMON BUNS

(Use ½ Basic Sweet Dough recipe.)
Roll the punched dough on a lightly
floured surface into a 9 × 12-inch rectangle.
Brush with
**1 tablespoon butter or margarine,
melted**
Sprinkle with mixture of
**¼ cup granulated sugar**

**1 teaspoon cinnamon
½ cup chopped pecans**
Roll up like a jelly roll starting at longer
side. Cut into twelve 1-inch slices.

Combine
**¼ cup butter or margarine,
melted
½ cup lightly packed brown sugar**
Spread in the bottom of an 8 or 9-inch
square pan. Dot with
**½ cup pecan halves**
Place slices, cut side down, in the prepared pan.
Cover and let rise until doubled (about
¾ hour).
Bake in preheated 400° oven for 20 to
25 minutes.
Invert at once on a serving plate.

## DOUGHNUTS

(Use ½ Basic Sweet Dough recipe.)
Roll the punched dough on a lightly
floured surface to ½-inch thickness. Cut
with floured doughnut cutter. Cover and
let rise until doubled (about ¾ hour).
Meanwhile, preheat deep fat to 375°F.
Lift doughnuts with wide spatula and
slide into hot fat. Then fry until golden
brown on both sides.
Drain on absorbent paper.
Dip warm doughnuts into glaze.
Cool on wire rack.

## GLAZE

Blend together until smooth
**¼ cup milk
2 cups sifted icing sugar
1 teaspoon vanilla**
Makes about 10 doughnuts.

# CRULLERS

(Use ½ Basic Sweet Dough recipe.)
Roll the punched dough on a lightly floured surface to ½-inch thickness. Cut in strips and shape into figure 8's or cut with doughnut cutter and twist (see picture). Cover and let rise until doubled (about ¾ hour).
Meanwhile, preheat deep fat to 375°F. Drop crullers into hot fat. Then fry until golden brown on both sides. Drain on absorbent paper. Cool on wire rack.
Makes about 2 dozen crullers.

# POTECA

(Use ½ Basic Sweet Dough recipe.)
Turn the punched dough on a lightly floured cloth, roll out and stretch into a 25 × 15-inch rectangle.
Spread with a mixture of
   ¼ cup soft butter or margarine
   ½ cup lightly packed brown sugar
   1 egg
   ¼ cup milk
   ½ teaspoon vanilla
   ½ teaspoon cinnamon
   2 cups chopped walnuts
Roll up like a jelly roll by lifting cloth. Seal seam.
Place on greased baking sheet, curling into a spiral.
Let rise until almost doubled (about 1 hour).
Bake in preheated 375° oven for 30 to 35 minutes or until golden brown.

*If you have a gas range, the warmth from the pilot light makes the oven an ideal place to keep a yeast dough warm during rising.*

# ITALIAN PANETTONI

Scald
   **2 cups milk**
Cool to lukewarm.
Meanwhile, dissolve
   **1 teaspoon sugar**
in
   **½ cup lukewarm water (100°F.)**
Over this, sprinkle
   **1 envelope active dry yeast**
Let stand for 10 minutes. Then stir briskly with a fork. Add softened yeast to lukewarm milk. Stir.

Beat in
   **3 cups PURITY Flour**
Cover bowl. Let stand in warm place until light and full of bubbles (about 1 hour). Stir in
   **1 cup granulated sugar**
   **½ teaspoon salt**
   **½ cup butter or margarine,**
      **melted**
   **1 tablespoon grated lemon rind**
Beat with a fork
   **4 whole eggs**
Stir into batter.

Beat in
   **2 cups PURITY Flour**
Beat virgorously by hand or with electric mixer.

Stir in
   **1 cup raisins**
   **1 cup chopped citron peel**
Then gradually beat in with a spoon an additional
   **4½ to 5 cups PURITY FLour**
Work in last of flour with a rotating motion of the hand. Turn dough onto a floured surface and knead 8 to 10 minutes. Shape into a smooth ball and place in a greased bowl, rotating dough to grease surface. Cover with a damp cloth and let rise until doubled (about 2 hours). Punch down and divide into 3 parts. Shape into round loaves and place on greased cookie sheets. Cover and let rise in warm place until doubled (about 1¼ hours).
Brush with
   **cream**
Bake in preheated 375° oven for 30 to 35 minutes.
Makes 3 loaves.

# RUM SAUCE

In a saucepan, combine **1 cup granulated sugar, 1 cup water.** Bring to boiling point and cook over medium heat for 5 minutes. Remove from heat and stir in **2 to 3 tablespoons rum.** Pour over warm baba. Makes 1½ cups.

# CHOP SUEY LOAF

Scald
   **1 cup milk**
Mix together
   **⅓ cup granulated sugar**
   **1½ teaspoons salt**
   **½ teaspoon cinnamon**
   **¼ teaspoon nutmeg**
Pour hot milk into a large bowl with sugar mixture and add
   **¼ cup shortening**
   **¼ cup corn syrup**
Stir until shortening melts. Cool to lukewarm. Meanwhile, mix to dissolve
   **2 teaspoons sugar**
   **1 cup lukewarm water (100°F.)**
Over this, sprinkle
   **2 envelopes active dry yeast**
Let stand for 10 minutes. Then stir briskly with a fork. Add softened yeast to lukewarm milk mixture. Blend in, in turn
   **3 eggs slightly beaten**
   **3½ cups PURITY Flour**
Beat vigorously by hand or with mixer. Mix in
   **1 cup raisins**
   **½ cup chopped glacé cherries**
   **½ cup chopped mixed fruit**
Beat in with a spoon an additional
   **4 to 4½ cups PURITY Flour**
Work in last of flour with a rotating motion of the hand. Turn dough onto a floured surface and knead 8 to 10 minutes. Shape into a smooth ball and place in a greased bowl, rotating dough to grease surface. Cover with a damp cloth and let rise until doubled (about 2 hours). Keep in a warm place. Punch down and shape into 3 loaves. Place in greased 8½ × 4½-inch loaf pans, grease tops slightly and let rise again until doubled (about 1¼ hours).
Bake in preheated 400° oven for 30 to 35 minutes.
Makes 3 loaves.

# BABA AU RHUM

Scald and cool to lukewarm
   **½ cup milk**
Thoroughly grease an 8-cup ring mould.
Dissolve
   **1 teaspoon sugar**
in
   **½ cup lukewarm water (100°F.)**
Over this sprinkle
   **1 envelope active dry yeast**
Let stand for 10 minutes. Then stir briskly with a fork.
In a large bowl, cream together until fluffy
   **½ cup butter**
   **¼ cup granulated sugar**
   **½ teaspoon salt**
Gradually blend in
   **2 eggs**
Alternately beat in softened yeast and lukewarm milk with
   **2¾ cups PURITY Flour**
Work in last of flour with a spoon. (Dough should be softer than a bread dough.)
Cover with a damp cloth and let rise in a warm place until doubled (about 1¼ hours).
Stir down and blend in
   **3 tablespoons raisins**
   **3 tablespoons currants**
Half fill the prepared mould, cover and keep in a warm place until dough almost reaches top of mould (about ¾ hour).
Bake in preheated 400° oven for about 25 to 30 minutes or until brown. Loosen edges with sharp knife and unmould immediately.
Serve warm with Rum Sauce.
Makes 8 servings.

# QUICK BREADS

## TEA BISCUITS

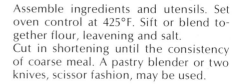

Assemble ingredients and utensils. Set oven control at 425°F. Sift or blend together flour, leavening and salt.
Cut in shortening until the consistency of coarse meal. A pastry blender or two knives, scissor fashion, may be used.

With a fork, stir in milk to make a soft dough.

Turn dough on lightly floured surface and knead gently 8 to 10 times. To knead, lift dough with fingertips to overlap to a double thickness. Press down with heels of the hands.

Roll out dough to desired thickness (biscuits double during baking). Cut with floured cookie cutter and place on ungreased pan. Have biscuits almost touching for soft sided biscuits and 1 inch apart for crusty sided biscuits.

## TEA BISCUITS

Preheat oven to 425°F.
Sift together
**2 cups PURITY Flour**
**4 teaspoons baking powder**
**1 teaspoon salt**
With a pastry blender or two knives cut in finely
**½ cup shortening**
Add
**1 cup milk**
Stir with a fork to make a soft dough. Turn dough onto a lightly floured surface and knead gently 8 to 10 times. Roll or pat to desired thickness (biscuits will double in height when baked). Cut with a floured 1¾-inch cookie cutter. Place biscuits on an ungreased baking sheet, close together for soft-sided biscuits or about 1 inch apart for crusty-sided biscuits. Bake in preheated 425° oven for 12 to 15 minutes. Makes 20 biscuits.

**CHEESE BISCUITS:** Prepare Tea Biscuit dough following basic recipe but stir ¾ cup grated cheese into shortening-flour mixture before adding milk.

**QUICKIE CROISSANTS:** Prepare Tea Biscuit dough as in basic recipe. Roll into a circle ¼ inch thick and cut into wedges 2½ inches wide. Spread each with softened butter and roll up towards tip and bend into a crescent. Bake on ungreased baking sheet in preheated 425° oven for 15 to 17 minutes or until golden. Makes 36 crescents.

**ZIPPY CROUTONS:** Prepare half of basic recipe of Tea Biscuit dough. Roll out ¼ inch thick and cut into ½-inch cubes. Melt ⅓ cup butter and season with ¼ teaspoon garlic powder. Dip cubes in melted butter and then in Parmesan cheese. Bake on greased baking sheet in preheated 400° oven for 8 to 10 minutes. Makes 3½ cups croutons.

**QUICK FRENCH STICK:** Prepare Tea Biscuit dough as in basic recipe. Shape into 6 small loaves 4 inches long and 1½ inches in diameter, tapering ends. Brush with slightly beaten egg white, sprinkle with sesame seeds and slash tops. Bake on ungreased baking sheet in preheated 350° oven for 35 to 40 minutes or until golden brown. Serve hot. Makes 6 individual loaves.

**CINNAMON BLOSSOMS:** Prepare Tea Biscuit dough as in basic recipe. Cut into biscuits and then snip each biscuit almost to centre to give 5 petals. Dip tops in melted butter and then in a mixture of sugar and cinnamon (⅓ cup sugar, ½ teaspoon cinnamon, ¼ teaspoon nutmeg). Place a quarter of a maraschino or candied cherry in the centre of each. Bake on ungreased baking sheet in preheated 400° oven for 12 to 14 minutes. Makes 20 blossoms.

**LITTLE DIPPERS:** Prepare Tea Biscuit dough following basic recipe but stir 2 tablespoons dried onion flakes into shortening-flour mixture before adding milk. Roll out ½ inch thick and cut into diamonds 2 inches long and 1 inch wide. Bake on ungreased baking sheet in preheated 425° oven for 8 to 10 minutes. Serve hot with fondue or cold with dips. Makes 6 dozen dippers.

**BISCUIT NIBBLERS:** Prepare Tea Biscuit dough as in basic recipe. With scissors snip into peanut-size pieces. Bake in ungreased 15 × 10 × 1-inch jelly roll pan in preheated 400° oven for 6 to 8 minutes. Meanwhile, melt ½ cup butter and combine with 1 teaspoon Tabasco sauce, 1 teaspoon Worcestershire sauce, 1 teaspoon garlic salt, 1 teaspoon garlic powder and 2 teaspoons celery salt. Pour over baked nibblers stirring to coat well. Bake in 200° oven for about 3½ hours or until crisp. Makes 6 cups nibblers.

**SOUR CREAM BISCUITS:** Prepare Tea Biscuit dough following basic recipe but substituting 1 teaspoon baking powder and ½ teaspoon baking soda for baking powder, and reducing shortening to ¼ cup. Use 1⅓ cups thick dairy sour cream instead of milk. Bake as directed.

*A tea biscuit dough should be soft and slightly sticky. A little kneading improves the quality of the biscuits, but should be done with a gentle touch as too much handling tends to make them tough.*

## CHEESE POCKETS

Preheat oven to 425°F.
Prepare Tea Biscuit dough as in basic recipe and roll out 1/8 inch thick. Cut into 4-inch squares and put a heaping teaspoon of processed cheese spread in the centre of each. Lift 4 corners to centre and seal seams.
Bake in preheated 425° oven for 13 to 15 minutes or until golden brown.
Makes 12 pockets.

## CHEESE PINWHEELS

Preheat oven to 425°F.
Prepare Tea Biscuit dough as in basic recipe and roll out into a 9-inch square. Cover with about ¾ cup processed cheese spread. Roll up as for jelly roll, sealing edge.
Cut into twelve ¾-inch slices. Place close together on greased baking sheet.
Bake in preheated 425° oven for 12 to 15 minutes or until golden brown.
Makes 12 pinwheels.

## BUTTERMILK BISCUITS

Preheat oven to 425°F.
Sift together
   **2 cups PURITY Flour**
   **2½ teaspoons baking powder**
   **½ teaspoon baking soda**
   **1 teaspoon salt**
With a pastry blender or two knives, cut in finely
   **½ cup shortening**
Add
   **1 cup buttermilk**
Stir with a fork to make a soft dough.
Turn dough onto a lightly floured surface and knead gently 8 to 10 times.
Roll or pat to desired thickness, (biscuits will double in height when baked). Cut with a floured 1¾-inch cookie cutter.
Place on an ungreased baking sheet, close together for soft-sided biscuits or about 1-inch apart for crusty-sided biscuits.
Bake in preheated 425° oven for 12 to 15 minutes.
Makes 20 biscuits.

---

*Muffins may be baked in paper baking cups, placed in ungreased muffin cups. Remove the papers before serving.*

## BUTTERSCOTCH PINWHEELS

Preheat oven to 425°F.
Grease 12 medium-sized muffin cups.
Cream until soft
   **⅓ cup butter**
Gradually blend in
   **⅔ cup lightly packed brown sugar**
Set aside.
Sift together
   **2 cups PURITY Flour**
   **4 teaspoons baking powder**
   **1 teaspoon salt**
With a pastry blender or two knives, cut in finely
   **½ cup shortening**
Add
   **1 cup milk**
Stir with a fork to make a soft dough.
Turn dough onto a lightly floured surface and knead gently 8 to 10 times.
Roll out into 9-inch square; spread with brown sugar mixture. Roll up as for jelly roll, sealing edge.
Cut into twelve ¾-inch thick slices and arrange cut side down, in prepared muffin pans.
Bake in preheated 425° oven for 14 to 16 minutes. Remove from pans immediately.
Makes 12 pinwheels.

## SHORTCAKE BISCUITS

Preheat oven to 425°F.
Sift together
   **2 cups PURITY Flour**
   **⅓ cup granulated sugar**
   **3½ teaspoons baking powder**
   **1 teaspoon salt**
With a pastry blender or two knives, cut in finely
   **½ cup shortening**
Add
   **1 cup milk**
Stir with a fork to make a soft dough.
Turn dough onto a lightly floured surface and knead gently 8 to 10 times.
Roll or pat ¾ inch thick. Cut with a floured 2½-inch cookie cutter.
Place about 1-inch apart on ungreased baking sheet.
Bake in preheated 425° oven for 14 to 16 minutes. Split, fill and top with sweetened fruit. Serve with whipped cream.
Makes 12 biscuits.

APPLE POCKETS: Prepare Shortcake Biscuit dough as in basic recipe. Roll out ⅓ inch thick and cut with floured 3-inch cookie cutter. Brush circle with melted butter, sprinkle with brown sugar and a dash of cinnamon. Place a heaping teaspoonful of sweetened applesauce or apple pie filling in centre, fold over into semicircle and seal edges. Bake on ungreased baking sheet in preheated 425° oven for 15 to 18 minutes. Makes 15 pockets.

STREUSEL-TOPPED BISCUITS: Prepare Shortcake Biscuit dough as in basic recipe. Cut with cookie cutter, spread with butter and sprinkle with a crumb mixture prepared by combining ⅓ cup butter, 1¼ cups lightly packed brown sugar and ¾ cup PURITY Flour. Bake on ungreased baking sheet in preheated 425° oven for 15 to 18 minutes. Split and fill with sliced fresh or canned peaches.

APPLE MINCEMEAT SHORTCAKE: Prepare Shortcake Biscuits following basic recipe but increasing baking powder to 4 teaspoons and substituting ½ cup canned mincemeat and ¾ cup milk for 1 cup milk. Bake as directed in basic recipe. Split hot biscuits, fill with sweetened applesauce, and serve with cream.

## BUTTERFLAKE BISCUIT RING

Preheat oven to 375°F.
Grease a 9-inch ring mould and sprinkle bottom and halfway up sides with
    **¼ cup corn flake crumbs**
Sift together
    **3 cups PURITY Flour**
    **5 teaspoons baking powder**
    **1½ teaspoons salt**
With a pastry blender or two knives, cut in finely
    **¾ cup shortening**
Stir in
    **¾ cup grated cheddar cheese**
Add
    **1½ cups milk**
Stir with a fork to make a soft dough.
Turn dough onto a lightly floured surface and knead gently 8 to 10 times.
Roll out ¾ inch thick. Cut with floured 2-inch cookie cutter.
Dip circles in
    **¼ cup butter or margarine, melted**

Place almost touching in prepared mould with edges down.
Sprinkle with
    **¼ cup corn flake crumbs**
Bake in preheated 375° oven for 40 to 50 minutes. Unmould and serve hot.
Makes 1 ring.

## OATMEAL MUFFINS

Preheat oven to 400°F.
Grease 12 medium-sized muffin cups.
Sift together
    **1 cup PURITY Flour**
    **3½ teaspoons baking powder**
    **½ teaspoon salt**
    **½ teaspoon cinnamon**
    **Pinch of nutmeg**
Stir in
    **¾ cup PURITY Rolled Oats**
    **½ cup lightly packed brown sugar**
Beat together
    **1 egg**
    **1 cup milk**
    **¼ cup vegetable oil or**
    **melted shortening**
Add liquid to dry ingredients and stir only until combined. (Batter will be lumpy). Fill prepared muffin cups ⅔ full. Bake in preheated 400° oven for 20 to 25 minutes.
Makes 12 muffins.

## BRAN MUFFINS

Preheat oven to 400°F.
Grease 12 medium-sized muffin cups.
Sift together
    **1½ cups PURITY Flour**
    **1 teaspoon baking soda**
    **1 teaspoon baking powder**
    **½ teaspoon salt**
Stir in
    **2 cups bran**
Cream
    **⅓ cup shortening**
Gradually blend in
    **2 tablespoons brown sugar**
    **1 egg**
    **½ cup molasses**
Beat until light and fluffy.
Add dry ingredients to creamed mixture alternately with
    **¾ cup buttermilk**
Combine lightly after each addition.
Fill prepared muffin cups ⅔ full.
Bake in preheated 400° oven for 15 to 18 minutes.
Makes 12 muffins.

## MUFFINS AND LOAVES

Assemble ingredients and utensils. Set oven control at 400°F. Blend or sift dry ingredients together.

Beat together egg, milk, vanilla and liquid shortening.

Add liquids to dry ingredients and stir only until moistened. Mixture is lumpy.

Fill greased muffin cups ⅔ full.

Bake in preheated 400° oven for 18 to 20 minutes or until golden.

For Loaves, follow muffin method but beat dough by hand for about half a minute. Turn into greased loaf pan. Bake as directed in recipe.

## MUFFINS

Preheat oven to 400°F.
Grease 12 medium-sized muffin cups.
Sift together
**2 cups PURITY Flour**
**¼ cup granulated sugar***
**3½ teaspoons baking powder**
**½ teaspoon salt**
Beat together
**1 egg**
**1 cup milk**
**¼ cup vegetable oil or melted shortening**
Add liquid to dry ingredients and stir only until combined. (Batter will be lumpy.) Fill prepared muffin cups ⅔ full. Bake in preheated 400° oven for 18 to 20 minutes or until golden brown.
*For a sweeter dessert muffin increase sugar to ½ cup.
Makes 12 muffins.

**CHEESE MUFFINS:** Prepare Muffins following basic recipe but adding ¾ cup grated cheddar cheese to dry ingredients before adding liquid. Combine and bake as directed.

**WHEAT GERM MUFFINS:** Prepare Muffins following basic recipe but reducing flour to 1½ cups and milk to ½ cup. Stir in with liquid ingredients a mixture of ½ cup wheat germ and ¾ cup boiling water. Bake as directed.

**CHOCOLATE CHIP MUFFINS:** Prepare Muffins following basic recipe for sweeter dessert muffin (½ cup sugar). Fold 1 cup chocolate chips into batter. Bake as directed.

**PEANUT BUTTER MUFFINS:** Prepare Muffins as in basic recipe and spoon half of batter into greased muffin cups, top with 1 teaspoon peanut butter and cover with remaining batter. Bake as directed.

**POTATO CHEESE PUFFS:** Prepare Muffins following basic recipe but reducing flour to 1¼ cups and stirring into dry ingredients ¾ cup instant potato flakes. Sprinkle muffin batter in pans with a mixture of ½ cup grated cheddar cheese and ¼ cup potato flakes. Bake as directed.

**BACON MUFFINS:** Chop and fry until crisp 5 strips side bacon. Cool. Prepare Muffin batter following basic recipe but substituting bacon and drippings for vegetable oil or melted shortening.

**PUMPKIN MUFFINS:** Prepare Muffins following basic recipe but adding 1 teaspoon cinnamon and ½ teaspoon nutmeg to dry ingredients and adding ⅔ cup canned pumpkin with milk. Bake as directed.

---

*To keep muffins hot for serving, loosen them and tilt slightly in the pans. Place them in a warm oven until needed.*

---

## APPLE CRUNCH MUFFINS

Preheat oven to 400°F.
Grease 12 medium-sized muffin cups.
Mix together until crumbly and set aside for topping
**⅔ cup lightly packed brown sugar**
**⅓ cup PURITY Flour**
**2 tablespoons butter or margarine**
Sift together
**1½ cups PURITY Flour**
**¼ cup granulated sugar**
**3 teaspoons baking powder**
**½ teaspoon salt**
**½ teaspoon cinnamon**
Beat together
**1 egg**
**¾ cup milk**
**3 tablespoons vegetable oil or melted shortening**
Add liquid to dry ingredients and stir only until combined. (Batter will be lumpy.) Fill prepared muffin cups ⅔ full.
Top each muffin with
**1 teaspoon applesauce**
Sprinkle with reserved crumbs.
Bake in preheated 400° oven for 18 to 20 minutes or until golden brown.
Makes 12 muffins.

---

*To serve day-old tea biscuits or muffins, split, butter and toast them, or wrap in foil and heat in a 400°F. oven for about 10 minutes.*

---

## CORNMEAL MUFFINS

Preheat oven to 400°F.
Grease 12 medium-sized muffin cups.
Mix together and allow to stand for 5 minutes
    **¾ cup PURITY Cornmeal**
    **1¼ cups milk**
Sift together
    **1 cup PURITY Flour**
    **⅓ cup granulated sugar**
    **3 teaspoons baking powder**
    **1 teaspoon salt**
Beat with a fork
    **1 egg**
Stir into cornmeal mixture with
    **¼ cup vegetable oil or**
      **melted shortening**
Add to dry ingredients and stir only until combined. (Batter will be lumpy).
Fill prepared muffin cups ⅔ full.
Bake in preheated 400° oven for 20 to 25 minutes or until golden brown.
Makes 12 muffins.

## CHOCOLATE NUT MUFFINS

Preheat oven to 400°F.
Grease 12 medium-sized muffin cups.
Sift together
    **1⅔ cups PURITY Flour**
    **¾ cup granulated sugar**
    **⅓ cup cocoa**
    **3½ teaspoons baking powder**
    **½ teaspoon salt**
Stir in
    **½ cup chopped walnuts**
Beat together
    **1 egg**
    **1 cup milk**
    **¼ cup vegetable oil or**
      **melted shortening**
Add liquid to dry ingredients and stir only until combined. (Batter will be lumpy). Fill prepared muffin cups ⅔ full.
Bake in preheated 400° oven for 20 to 25 minutes.
Makes 12 muffins.

## FRESH ORANGE PRUNE NUT LOAF

Preheat oven to 350°F.
Grease a 9 × 5 × 3-inch loaf pan.
In a meat grinder or blender, coarsely chop
    **1 medium unpeeled orange**

Measure ⅔ cup (including liquid) and combine with
    **½ cup orange juice**
Sift together
    **2 cups PURITY Flour**
    **⅔ cup granulated sugar**
    **2½ teaspoons baking powder**
    **½ teaspoon baking soda**
    **½ teaspoon salt**
Stir in
    **1 cup chopped, cooked prunes,**
      **drained**
    **1 cup chopped walnuts**
Beat together orange mixture and
    **1 egg**
    **2 tablespoons butter or margarine,**
      **melted**
    **½ teaspoon vanilla**
Add liquid to dry ingredients and beat for about half a minute. (Batter will be lumpy.)

Turn into prepared pan.
Bake in preheated 350° oven for 60 to 65 minutes or until toothpick inserted in centre comes out clean.
Wrap tightly in plastic wrap and store overnight to "ripen".

## PINEAPPLE CHEESE BREAD

Preheat oven to 350°F.
Grease a 9 × 5 × 3-inch loaf pan.
Sift together
    **2¼ cups PURITY Flour**
    **½ cup granulated sugar**
    **2½ teaspoons baking powder**
    **½ teaspoon baking soda**
    **½ teaspoon salt**
Stir in
    **1 cup grated cheddar cheese**
Beat together
    **1 egg**
    **¾ cup milk**
    **¼ cup vegetable oil or melted**
      **shortening**
    **1 cup canned crushed pineapple,**
      **undrained**
Add liquid to dry ingredients and beat for about half a minute. (Batter will be lumpy.)
Turn into prepared pan.
Bake in preheated 350° oven for 65 to 70 minutes or until toothpick inserted in centre comes out clean.

## DATE AND NUT BREAD

Preheat oven to 350°F.
Grease a 9 × 5 × 3-inch loaf pan.
Combine and cook, stirring constantly until thickened
   **¾ cup boiling water**
   **1½ cups chopped dates**
Cool.
Sift together
   **2 cups PURITY Flour**
   **½ cup granulated sugar**
   **2½ teaspoons baking powder**
   **½ teaspoon baking soda**
   **½ teaspoon salt**
Stir in
   **½ cup finely chopped nuts**
Beat together
   **1 egg**
   **1 cup milk**
   **¼ cup vegetable oil or**
   **melted shortening**
Add date mixture and liquid to dry ingredients and beat for about half a minute. (Batter will be lumpy).
Turn into prepared pan.
Bake in preheated 350° oven for 65 to 70 minutes or until toothpick inserted in centre comes out clean.

## PINEAPPLE DATE BREAD

Preheat oven to 350°F.
Grease a 9 × 5 × 3-inch loaf pan.
Sift together
   **2 cups PURITY Flour**
   **¾ cup granulated sugar**
   **3 teaspoons baking powder**
   **¼ teaspoon baking soda**
   **¾ teaspoon salt**
Stir in
   **1 cup crushed pineapple,**
   **undrained**
   **1 cup chopped walnuts**
   **1 cup chopped dates**
Beat together
   **1 egg**
   **⅓ cup milk**
   **⅓ cup vegetable oil or melted**
   **shortening**
Add liquid to dry ingredients and beat for about half a minute. (Batter will be lumpy).
Turn into prepared pan.
Bake in preheated 350° oven for 60 to 65 minutes or until toothpick inserted in centre comes out clean.

## NUT BREAD

Preheat oven to 350°F.
Grease a 9 × 5 × 3-inch loaf pan.
Sift together
   **1¾ cups PURITY Flour**
   **½ cup granulated sugar**
   **3 teaspoons baking powder**
   **½ teaspoon salt**
Stir in
   **1 cup finely chopped nuts**
Beat together
   **1 egg**
   **1¼ cups milk**
   **¼ cup vegetable oil or**
   **melted shortening**
Add liquid to dry ingredients and beat for about half a minute. (Batter will be lumpy).
Turn into prepared pan.
Bake in preheated 350° oven for 60 to 65 minutes or until toothpick inserted in centre comes out clean.

*Many tea bread loaves will slice more easily the second day, and the flavour often improves as well. This is especially true when the loaves contain dried fruit.*

## BANANA NUT BREAD

Preheat oven to 350°F.
Grease a 9 × 5 × 3-inch loaf pan.
Sift together
   **2 cups PURITY Flour**
   **½ cup granulated sugar**
   **3 teaspoons baking powder**
   **½ teaspoon baking soda**
   **½ teaspoon salt**
Stir in
   **½ cup finely chopped nuts**
Beat together
   **1 egg**
   **¾ cup milk**
   **¼ cup vegetable oil or melted**
   **shortening**
   **1½ cups mashed ripe bananas**
Add liquid to dry ingredients and beat for about half a minute. (Batter will be lumpy).
Turn into prepared pan.
Bake in preheated 350° oven for 65 to 70 minutes or until toothpick inserted in centre comes out clean.

## GLAZED LEMON LOAF

Preheat oven to 350°F.
Grease a 9 × 5 × 3-inch loaf pan.
Sift together
  **1½ cups PURITY Flour**
  **1 teaspoon baking powder**
  **½ teaspoon salt**
Stir in
  **½ cup chopped walnuts**
  **2 teaspoons grated lemon rind**
Cream
  **½ cup butter or margarine**
Beat in
  **1 cup granulated sugar**
Blend in, beating until light and fluffy
  **2 eggs**
Add sifted dry ingredients to creamed
mixture alternately with
  **½ cup milk**
Make 3 dry and 2 liquid additions, combining lightly after each.
Turn into prepared pan.
Bake in preheated 350° oven for 65 to
70 minutes or until toothpick inserted in
centre comes out clean.
Cool 5 minutes, then drizzle over top a
mixture of
  **¼ cup granulated sugar**
  **2 tablespoons lemon juice**
Cool, and then remove from pan.

## APRICOT LOAF

Preheat oven to 350°F.
Grease a 9 × 5 × 3-inch loaf pan.
Cover with tepid water
  **½ cup dried apricots**
Soak for 30 minutes. Drain and chop in
meat grinder or blender.
Sift together
  **2 cups PURITY Flour**
  **1 teaspoon baking powder**
  **½ teaspoon baking soda**
  **½ teaspoon salt**
Blend together
  **1 egg, beaten**
  **1 cup granulated sugar**
  **2 tablespoons butter or margarine,**
    **melted**
Blend in dry ingredients with
  **¾ cup orange juice**
Fold in apricot pulp and
  **1 tablespoon grated orange rind**

Turn into prepared pan.
Bake in preheated 350° oven for 65 to
70 minutes or until toothpick inserted in
centre comes out clean.

## JOHNNY CAKE

Preheat oven to 350°F.
Grease an 8-inch square cake pan.
Combine and set aside
  **1 cup PURITY cornmeal**
  **½ cup milk**
Sift together
  **1¼ cups PURITY Flour**
  **2½ teaspoons baking powder**
  **1 teaspoon salt**
Cream
  **½ cup shortening**
Beat in
  **½ cup granulated sugar**
Add sifted dry ingredients alternately
with a mixture of
  **1 egg**
  **1 cup milk**
Blend in cornmeal mixture.
Turn into prepared pan.
Bake in preheated 350° oven for 40 to
45 minutes or until cake springs back
when lightly touched. Cool 5 minutes,
then remove from pan.
Serve hot with maple syrup.

## STEAMED BROWN BREAD

Grease three empty 19-ounce cans.
Sift together
  **1½ cups PURITY Flour**
  **1 teaspoon baking powder**
  **1 teaspoon baking soda**
  **1½ teaspoons salt**
Blend in
  **1½ cups whole wheat flour**
  **2 tablespoons brown sugar**
Beat together with a fork
  **1¼ cups water**
  **¾ cup molasses**
  **2 tablespoons melted shortening**
Add liquid to dry ingredients and stir
only until combined. (Batter will be
lumpy.)
Fill prepared cans ⅔ full. Cover with wax
paper and foil, tying in place.
Steam for 2 hours on rack in pan filled
with water to half the height of tins.
Serve with butter.
Makes 3 loaves.

## CRANBERRY BREAD

Preheat oven to 350°F.
Grease an 8½ × 4½ × 3-inch loaf pan.
In a blender or chopper, coarsely chop
  **1 cup cranberries**
Sift together
  **1¾ cups PURITY Flour**
  **1 cup granulated sugar**
  **1½ teaspoons baking powder**
  **½ teaspoon baking soda**
  **½ teaspoon salt**
Stir in cranberries.
Beat together
  **1 egg**
  **¾ cup orange juice**
  **¼ cup vegetable oil or melted
    shortening**
Add liquid to dry ingredients and beat
for about half a minute. (Batter will be
lumpy.)
Turn into prepared pan.
Bake in preheated 350° oven for 60 to
65 minutes or until toothpick inserted in
centre comes out clean.

## COFFEE CAKE

Preheat oven to 350°F.
Grease a 9-inch square cake pan.
Cream together
  **⅓ cup shortening**
  **1 cup granulated sugar**
Beat in
  **1 egg**
  **1 teaspoon vanilla**
Beat until light and fluffy.
Sift together
  **1½ cups PURITY Flour**
  **2 teaspoons baking powder**
  **½ teaspoon salt**
Add sifted dry ingredients to creamed
mixture alternately with
  **1 cup milk**
Make 3 dry and 2 liquid additions combining lightly after each.
Turn into prepared pan.
Mix together
  **½ cup lightly packed brown sugar**
  **2 tablespoons PURITY Flour**
  **1 teaspoon cinnamon**
  **½ cup chopped walnuts**
  **3 tablespoons melted butter or
    margarine**
Sprinkle over batter.
Bake in preheated 350° oven for 45 to
50 minutes or until golden brown.

**FRUIT STREUSEL:** Prepare Coffee Cake
batter as in basic recipe and turn into
greased 9-inch square pan. Bake in preheated 350° oven for 40 minutes. Quickly
spread hot cake with 1 cup canned pie
filling and sprinkle with crumb mixture.
Return to oven and broil an additional
5 minutes. Use apple, cherry, blueberry
or peach pie filling.

**CHOCOLATE   TOPPED   COFFEE
CAKE:** Prepare Coffee Cake as in basic
recipe but sprinkle batter with 1 cup (6
ounces) semi-sweet chocolate chips
before sprinkling with crumbs.

**APPLE CRUNCH COFFEE CAKE:** Prepare Coffee Cake as in basic recipe but
insert unpeeled thinly sliced apple
wedges into batter before sprinkling with
crumbs.

**APRICOT BUBBLE CAKE:** Cook 1 cup
chopped apricots in 2 cups water until
tender and then cool. Prepare Coffee
Cake as in basic recipe but spread batter
with apricot mixture before sprinkling
with crumbs. Bake as directed.

**ZINGY LEMON CAKE:** Prepare Coffee
Cake batter following basic recipe but
substituting 1 tablespoon lemon juice for
the vanilla. Pour batter into a greased
deep 9-inch round pan. Instead of
crumbs, sprinkle batter with a mixture of
½ cup PURITY Flour, ½ cup granulated
sugar, pinch of nutmeg, 1½ tablespoons
grated lemon rind and 2 tablespoons
melted butter or margarine. Bake 55 to
60 minutes.

**PINEAPPLE CRUNCH COFFEE CAKE:**
Prepare Coffee Cake following basic
recipe but substituting ½ cup milk and
½ cup juice drained from canned crushed
pineapple for the milk. Sprinkle half of
crumbs on batter, top with 1 (10-ounce)
can crushed pineapple, drained. Sprinkle
with remaining crumbs. Bake as directed.

**BUTTERSCOTCH   SWIRL   COFFEE
CAKE:** Melt over hot but not boiling
water 1 cup (6 ounces) butterscotch
chips and cool slightly. Prepare Coffee
Cake batter as in basic recipe and spoon
into pan with swirls of butterscotch
sauce. Top with crumbs and bake as
directed.

**CHEESE JELLY CAKE:** Prepare Coffee Cake following basic recipe, but make only half the crumb mixture. Sprinkle batter with 1 cup grated old cheddar cheese before sprinkling with crumbs. Bake as directed and when still hot spread with ¼ cup apple, grape, or red currant jelly.

**PEACH MELBA CAKE:** Prepare Coffee Cake as in basic recipe but cover top with drained canned peach slices, dot with red currant jelly or raspberry jam and then sprinkle with crumbs. Bake as directed.

**POTATO SPOON BREAD:** Prepare Coffee Cake following basic recipe but reducing flour to 1 cup and adding ½ cup instant potato flakes, 1 tablespoon dried onion flakes, and omitting vanilla. Instead of crumb mixture sprinkle batter with 1 cup grated old cheddar cheese and ¾ cup cornflake crumbs. Bake as directed and serve hot as a vegetable.

**ORANGE YUMMY CAKE:** In a saucepan combine ½ cup frozen orange concentrate, thawed, and 1 cup granulated sugar. Cook and stir until mixture comes to a boil and boil for 1 minute. Pour into greased 9-inch square pan. Prepare Coffee Cake batter as in basic recipe (without crumbs) and spread in prepared pan. Bake as directed, invert, cool 10 minutes and then remove pan. Sprinkle with chopped nuts.

**LEMON YUMMY CAKE:** Substitute ⅓ cup frozen lemonade concentrate, thawed, for orange concentrate in Orange Yummy Cake variation.

## PRUNE APRICOT COFFEE CAKE

Preheat oven to 350°F.
Grease an 8-inch tube pan. Dust lightly with flour.
In a saucepan, combine
   **¾ cup chopped dried prunes**
   **¾ cup chopped dried apricots**
   **¾ cup water**
Cook 5 minutes or until tender and thickened. Allow to cool.
Sift together
   **2⅓ cups PURITY Flour**
   **3 teaspoons baking powder**
   **1 teaspoon salt**

Cream
   **⅔ cup shortening**
Beat in
   **1 cup granulated sugar**
Blend in, beating until light and fluffy
   **2 eggs**
   **1 teaspoon vanilla**
Add sifted dry ingredients to creamed mixture alternately with
   **¾ cup milk**
Make 3 dry and 2 liquid additions, combining lightly after each. Fold in prune mixture.
Turn ⅓ of batter into prepared pan.
Spoon over top ⅓ of a mixture of
   **⅔ cup lightly packed brown sugar**
   **1 tablespoon PURITY Flour**
   **1 tablespoon cinnamon**
   **⅓ cup melted butter or margarine**
Repeat layering twice. Top with
   **⅓ cup chopped walnuts**
Bake in preheated 350° oven for 55 to 60 minutes, or until cake springs back when lightly touched. Cool 5 minutes, then remove from pan.

## DUMPLINGS

Sift or blend together
   **1 cup PURITY Flour**
   **2 teaspoons baking powder**
   **½ teaspoon salt**
Stir in
   **½ cup milk (approx.)**
Drop by spoonfuls over hot stew. (Dough should be just soft enough to be dropped from spoon.)
Cover, and simmer 15 minutes without lifting lid.
Serve immediately.
Makes 6 to 7 dumplings.

## GRANDS-PÈRES

Prepare dumpling batter following basic recipe but add 2 teaspoons granulated sugar to flour mixture and mix in with milk, ¼ cup shortening, melted.
Drop batter by spoonfuls into boiling diluted maple syrup. Baste, cover tightly and simmer for 15 to 20 minutes without lifting the lid. Serve hot, spooning maple sauce over dumplings. If desired, sprinkle with walnuts.
Makes 4 servings.

# PANCAKES

Assemble ingredients and utensils. Preheat griddle or heavy frypan. Blend or sift dry ingredients together. Beat together egg, milk and liquid shortening.

Blend liquid into dry ingredients and beat until almost smooth.

Allowing about ¼ cup batter for each pancake, pour on preheated pan. Turn when bubbles break on surface. Brown other side.

## PANCAKES

Sift together
**1½ cups PURITY Flour**
**1-2 tablespoons sugar**
**3 teaspoons baking powder**
**½ teaspoon salt**
Combine
**1 egg, beaten**
**1¾ cups milk**
**2 tablespoons vegetable oil or melted shortening**

Add liquid to dry ingredients. Beat only until combined.
Heat a griddle or frypan to 380°F. (drops of cold water will dance across it).
Grease lightly with unsalted fat.
Use ¼ cup batter for each pancake.
Bake pancakes until surface is covered with bubbles and edges lose their gloss.
Turn and bake until golden brown.
Serve hot, with butter and syrup.
Makes about 12 (4-inch) pancakes.
NOTE: If batter thickens, add more milk.

CORN PANCAKES: Prepare Pancake batter following basic recipe and add ½ teaspoon celery salt to the dry ingredients. Fold in 1 cup drained whole kernel corn. Bake as directed. Serve with butter and molasses.

MAIN DISH PANCAKES: Prepare Pancake batter following basic recipe and add ¾ cup finely chopped ham, wieners or luncheon meat. Bake as directed. Serve with syrup or a raisin sauce.

FILLED PANCAKES: Combine 1 cup finely chopped cooked ham and 1 cup thick dairy sour cream. Set aside. Prepare and bake Pancakes as directed in basic recipe. Spread each hot pancake with about 3 tablespoons of sour cream mixture; fold over. Serve at once.

BLUEBERRY PANCAKES: Prepare Pancake batter following basic recipe and add ¾ cup fresh blueberries. Bake as directed.

DESSERT PANCAKES: Prepare Pancake batter following basic recipe but increasing sugar to ¼ cup. Use about 2 or 3 tablespoons of batter for each pancake and bake as directed. Keep hot. To serve, spread with jam, applesauce or cream filling. Roll up and sprinkle with icing sugar.

## FRENCH PANCAKES

Preheat a heavy 5-inch frypan and brush with butter.
Blend together
**¾ cup PURITY Flour**
**1 tablespoon granulated sugar**
Beat
**3 eggs**
Stir in
**1¾ cups milk**
Gradually stir liquid into dry ingredients, beating until smooth.
Blend in
**2 tablespoons melted butter**
Cover and chill for 1 hour.
Pour about 2 tablespoons of batter in preheated pan and tip to coat with a thin layer. When brown, turn to brown other side.
Makes 24 (5-inch) pancakes.

## BUTTERMILK PANCAKES

Sift together
**1½ cups PURITY Flour**
**1 to 2 tablespoons granulated sugar**
**1 teaspoon baking powder**
**½ teaspoon baking soda**
**½ teaspoon salt**
Combine
**1 egg, beaten**
**1¾ cups buttermilk**
**2 tablespoons vegetable oil or melted shortening**
Add liquid to dry ingredients. Beat only until combined. Heat a griddle or frypan to 380°F. (drops of cold water will dance across it). Grease lightly with unsalted fat.
Use ¼ cup batter for each pancake. Bake pancakes until surface is covered with bubbles and edges lose their gloss. Turn and bake until golden brown.
Serve hot with butter and syrup.
Makes about 12 (4-inch) pancakes.

## WAFFLES

Sift together
**1½ cups PURITY Flour**
**2 tablespoons granulated sugar**
**3 teaspoons baking powder**
**½ teaspoon salt**
Combine
**2 eggs, beaten**
**1½ cups milk**
**¼ cup butter or margarine, melted**
Add liquid to dry ingredients. Beat only until smooth.
Heat waffle iron as directed by the manufacturer. Pour batter onto hot waffle iron. (About 1 cup for a 9-inch square iron, and ½ cup for a 7-inch round pan.) Bake until the waffle stops steaming.
Makes 3 (9-inch) waffles or 6 (7-inch) waffles.

BUTTERMILK WAFFLES: Prepare waffle batter following basic recipe but reduce the baking powder to 1 teaspoon, and add ½ teaspoon baking soda. Substitute sour milk or buttermilk for milk. Bake as directed.

# Accompaniments

The finishing touch to any meal consists of those little extras that demonstrate flair. In this section we include soups to set the stage for what is to follow, sauces to blend with savoury dishes, candy to satisfy the sweet tooth and beverages to round out the whole. However, one accompaniment that deserves special mention is cheese, a standby for entertaining on all occasions.

## CHEESE

There is a wide assortment of Canadian and imported cheeses in our food stores: hard and soft, sharp and mild, natural and process. Do serve new flavours and include different varieties in your cooking. Cheese should be stored in the refrigerator, tightly wrapped in wax paper or plastic wrap. Small portions of firm cheeses, such as Cheddar and Swiss, may be kept in this way for 2 to 3 weeks. For larger portions, such as the rounds of cheese, seal the cut edge with cheesecloth dipped in melted paraffin and keep the wrapped cheese covered with a cloth dampened with water to which a little vinegar has been added. The soft cheeses such as Roquefort, Blue and Camembert should be kept well covered and used within a few days. Purchase cream cheese and cottage cheese as needed as they do not improve with age.

Cheese should be melted and cooked at low temperatures to prevent toughness and stringiness. Either natural Cheddar or process cheese may be used in main dishes. Process cheese melts more uniformly than the Cheddar and gives a milder flavour.

*Cheese is best when served at room temperature. Remove it from the refrigerator at least an hour before serving (except for cottage cheese).*

## SOUPS

### RASPBERRY SOUP

In a large saucepan, combine
**1 quart fresh raspberries**
**2 tablespoons lemon juice**
**2 cups water**
Simmer for 10 minutes.
Drain, reserving juice and set berries aside to cool.
Mix juice with
**¼ cup granulated sugar**
Blend in a mixture of
**2 tablespoons PURITY Flour**
**2 tablespoons cold water**
Cook, stirring constantly, until thickened.
Stir in berries and
**1½ teaspoons almond flavouring**
Chill.
Serve in chilled cups garnished with toasted almonds and whipped cream.
Makes 6 to 8 servings.

STRAWBERRY SOUP: Prepare Raspberry Soup following basic recipe but substituting strawberries for raspberries.

**Lime garnished Easy Party Punch, Canadian Wine Punch topped with a twist of lemon, chilled Gazpacho with a lemon slice float and Modern Pea Soup frame an array of sauces to depict menu accompaniments▶**

## SHERRIED CONSOMMÉ

In a saucepan, heat together
**2 (10-ounce) cans undiluted
consommé
2 cups water**
Stir in
**1 cup dry sherry**
Bring just to boil.
Serve piping hot garnished with
**lemon slices**
Makes 8 servings.

## GAZPACHO

In a bowl, combine
**1 (10-ounce) can condensed
tomato soup
1 soup can water
1 cup thinly sliced and quartered
cucumber
½ cup finely chopped green pepper
¼ cup finely chopped onion
¼ cup olive oil
2 tablespoons white wine vinegar
1 clove garlic, finely chopped
2 -3 drops Tabasco sauce
Pinch of salt
Pinch of pepper**
Cover and refrigerate at least 4 hours.
Stir and serve cold in chilled dishes.
Garnish with
**lemon or lime slices**
Makes 4 servings.

## OYSTER VICHYSSOISE

**Blender method:**
Pour into shallow pan and freeze until
crystals form around edge
**1 (10-ounce) can undiluted
consommé**
Peel and seed
**1 large ripe avocado**
In electric blender, combine with
**¼ cup cold water
2 tablespoons lemon juice
1 teaspoon salt
2 teaspoons grated lemon rind**
Cover. Blend on low then high speed
until smooth.
Gradually add iced consommé alternately
with
**1 cup thick dairy sour cream**
Blend smooth after each addition.
Rinse in cold water

**1 pint oysters, fresh or frozen
(thawed)**
To serve, pour soup into chilled dishes,
add 2 to 3 oysters per serving.
Garnish with
**lemon slices
chopped parsley**

**Rotary Beater or Mixer Method:**
Follow above recipe but mash avocado
and press through sieve.
Makes 4 to 6 servings.

*Most soups, like stews, improve in flavour
the second day of using. When reheating,
thin with vegetable liquids, soup stock,
milk or water depending upon the type
of soup.*

## TURKEY SOUP

Break apart carcass of leftover turkey or
chicken and place in large kettle along
with skin and trimmings.
Add
**6 cups cold water
1 cup celery leaves
2 sprigs parsley
1 large onion, sliced
1 large carrot, sliced
2 teaspoons salt
3 peppercorns
1 bay leaf
1 teaspoon poultry seasoning**
Bring to boil, cover, reduce heat and
simmer for 3 hours. Remove bones. Strain
broth through fine sieve or cheesecloth
in a colander. Cool quickly and refrigerate. Remove fat.
Measure and make up volume to 6 cups
with water or vegetable stock.
Add
**1 (12-ounce) package frozen mixed
vegetables
⅓ cup packaged precooked rice
Any diced leftover poultry**
Bring to boil, cover, reduce heat and
simmer 15 minutes.
Season to taste.
Makes 6 cups.
NOTE: **1.** For large turkey carcass, allow
8 or more cups water.
**2.** Pressure cook if desired, using
4 to 6 cups water depending
upon size of bird. Process at 15
pounds pressure for 20 minutes.
Proceed as directed in recipe.

## VICHYSSOISE

In a covered saucepan, bring to boil and simmer until tender
**1½ cups peeled, sliced potato**
**1½ cups thinly sliced leeks** or **Spanish onions**
**4 cups chicken stock** or **broth**
Purée in electric blender or colander. Return to saucepan. Mix together and stir in
**¼ cup PURITY Flour**
**⅓ cup cold water**
Cook, stirring constantly, until thickened. Cool slightly and stir in
**½ cup light cream (18%)**
Season to taste with
**salt**
**white pepper**
Fit a piece of waxed paper on top, touching surface. Chill.
Serve cold in soup cups sprinkled with chopped chives.
Makes 4 to 6 servings.

## MODERN PEA SOUP

In a large saucepan, put
**1 ham bone (trim off fat)**
**1 cup finely chopped onion**
**1 cup finely chopped celery**
Add
**8 cups water**
Bring to boil, cover, reduce heat and simmer about 1 hour or until ham scraps pull away from bone, readily.
Remove ham bone, cutting off any meat. Dice meat and return to saucepan. Skim off fat.
Drain, reserving ⅔ cup liquid, and mash

**3 (19-ounce) cans whole peas**
Blend peas into ham stock and beat thoroughly.
Stir in a mixture of
**1 cup PURITY Flour**
**⅔ cup reserved liquid**
**1½ teaspoons salt**
**Pinch of pepper**
**Pinch of thyme**
Cook, stirring constantly, until thickened.
Serve piping hot.
Makes 12 servings.

## SALMON BISQUE

In a saucepan, heat until foamy
**2 tablespoons butter or margarine**
Stir in and cook until transparent
**¼ cup finely chopped onion**
Blend in
**2 (10-ounce) cans condensed cream of celery soup**
**1 soup can milk**
**1 soup can water**
**1 (7¾-ounce) can salmon, drained and crumbled**
**2 tablespoons chopped parsley**
**1 tablespoon catsup**
**Pinch of pepper**
Heat thoroughly, then beat smooth with rotary beater.
Serve piping hot garnished with
**paprika**
Makes 6 to 8 servings.

**SEAFOOD BISQUES:** Prepare Salmon Bisque following basic recipe but substituting 1 (6-ounce) can crabmeat OR 2 (3-ounce) cans lobster paste OR 2 (4¼-ounce) cans shrimp instead of salmon.

# BEVERAGES

## CANADIAN WINE PUNCH

In a saucepan, combine
**¾ cup granulated sugar**
**⅓ cup water**
**6 thin strips lemon rind (cut corkscrew fashion)**
**⅔ cup lemon juice**
Bring to boil, cover, reduce heat and simmer for 5 minutes. Cool.
At serving time, put large chunk of ice

in punch bowl. Pour lemon syrup over top.
Stir in
**2 bottles claret, chilled**
**2 bottles sauterne, chilled**
**2 quarts soda water**
Thinly slice
**1 lemon**
Float lemon slices on punch.
Garnish with
**mint sprigs**
Makes 25 servings.

## CAFÉ BRÛLOT

In a chafing dish, combine
  **1 thin slice lemon rind (cut
    corkscrew fashion)
  1 thin slice orange rind (cut
    corkscrew fashion)
  4 cubes sugar
  2 whole cloves
  ¼ teaspoon cinnamon
  ¼ teaspoon vanilla**
Stir in
  **1½ cups brandy**
Heat and then flame.
Very gradually blend in
  **2 cups very strong black coffee**
When flame burns out serve coffee in
demitasse cups.
Makes 8 servings.

## FESTIVE EGGNOG

Beat together until very thick and lemon-coloured
  **4 whole eggs
  2 egg yolks
  ¾ cup granulated sugar
  ¼ teaspoon butterscotch flavouring**
Gradually beat in
  **2 cups Cognac or brandy**
Set aside for several hours to mellow.
At serving time, stir in
  **1 cup milk**
Beat to form stiff but moist peaks
  **2 egg whites**
Gradually beat in
  **¼ cup granulated sugar**
Beat until very stiff and shiny.
Fold into egg yolk mixture together with
  **1¼ cups heavy cream, whipped**
Pour into punch bowl and sprinkle generously with
  **nutmeg**
Makes 8 servings.

## CITRUS TEA PUNCH

Pour
  **6 cups boiling water**
over
  **8 teaspoons tea OR 3 tea bags**
Brew tea for 5 minutes. Strain.
Add
  **3 cups granulated sugar**
Stir until sugar is completely dissolved.
Add
  **6 cups orange juice
  3 cups lemon juice
  6 cups pineapple juice**
Just before serving, pour over ice in a
punch bowl and add
  **2 large bottles gingerale**
Garnish with slices of orange and lemon.
Makes approximately 50 (4-ounce) servings.

---

*For Mulled Apple Juice: heat a 48-ounce
can of apple juice in double boiler with
6 to 8 whole cloves and a 4 or 5-inch
piece of stick cinnamon. Remove spices
after 30 minutes. Serve moderately hot,
but not scalding. This makes eight 6-
ounce servings.*

---

## EASY PARTY PUNCH

In a large punch bowl, combine
  **1 (48-ounce) can pineapple juice,
    chilled
  1 (48-ounce) can orange juice,
    chilled
  1 (48-ounce) can apple juice,
    chilled**
Just before serving, add
  **2 large bottles gingerale**
Top with scoops of firmly frozen sherbet
(about 4 pints).
Makes approximately 50 (4-ounce) servings.

# SAUCES

## RAISIN SAUCE

In a saucepan, combine
  **⅓ cup PURITY Flour
  ½ cup lightly packed brown sugar
  ¼ teaspoon salt
  ¼ teaspoon cloves**
  **¼ teaspoon cinnamon**
Gradually stir in
  **2 cups apple juice or cider
  ½ cup raisins**
Cook over low heat, stirring occasionally
for 10 minutes.
Makes 2½ cups.

## CREAM SAUCE

In a saucepan, melt
**2 tablespoons butter or margarine**
Blend in
**2 tablespoons PURITY Flour**
**½ teaspoon salt**
**Few grains of pepper**
Gradually stir in
**1 cup milk**
Cook, stirring constantly, until thickened. For a thin cream sauce, decrease butter and flour to 1 tablespoon each. For a thick cream sauce, increase the butter and flour to ¼ cup each.
Use with vegetables, chicken, seafood or in casserole dishes. To keep hot, cover and place over simmering water.
Makes 1 cup.

CHEESE SAUCE: Prepare Cream Sauce following basic recipe and blend in ¾ cup grated cheddar cheese and 1 teaspoon Worcestershire sauce.

CURRY SAUCE: Add 2 tablespoons finely chopped onion and ½ to 1 teaspoon curry powder to melted butter in basic recipe. Cook, stirring constantly, for 2 to 3 minutes then follow basic recipe for Cream Sauce. Use with seafood, rice or hard cooked eggs.

EGG SAUCE: Prepare Cream Sauce following basic recipe and increase milk·to 1¼ cups and add 2 chopped or sliced hard cooked eggs and 1 teaspoon Worcestershire sauce. Serve with poached fresh or smoked fish, croquettes or toast.

SAUCE FINES HERBES: Prepare Cream Sauce following basic recipe and stir in ¼ cup finely chopped fresh herbs (chives, tarragon, chervil, green onion, dill).

MUSHROOM SAUCE: Prepare Cream Sauce following basic recipe and stir in ½ cup chopped or sliced cooked mushrooms.

MUSTARD SAUCE: Prepare Cream Sauce as in basic recipe and blend in 1 tablespoon prepared mustard and ½ teaspoon onion powder. Serve with green or wax beans.

PARSLEY SAUCE: Prepare Cream Sauce following basic recipe and stir in ¼ cup finely chopped parsley and ½ teaspoon celery salt. Serve with new boiled potatoes, fish or croquettes.

PIMIENTO SAUCE: Prepare Cream Sauce following basic recipe and stir in 2 tablespoons finely chopped onion and ⅓ cup chopped pimiento.

SHRIMP SAUCE: Prepare Cream Sauce following basic recipe and stir in 1 teaspoon Worcestershire sauce, ¼ teaspoon paprika and ½ cup diced cooked shrimps. Cooked crabmeat, lobster or oysters may also be used. Serve with poached or broiled fish.

TOMATO SAUCE: Prepare Cream Sauce following basic recipe and stir in 1 tablespoon tomato paste or 2 tablespoons tomato sauce.

## BROWN SAUCE

In a frypan, heat until foamy
**2 tablespoons butter or margarine**
Blend in
**2 tablespoons PURITY Flour**
Cook over medium heat, stirring constantly, until a rich brown.
Remove from heat.
Gradually stir in
**1 cup undiluted consommé**
**or beef bouillon**
**½ teaspoon dried onion flakes**
Cook over medium heat, stirring constantly, until thickened.
Season to taste with salt and pepper.
Makes 1 cup.

PIQUANT SAUCE: Prepare Brown Sauce following basic recipe. Combine 2 tablespoons vinegar, 1 teaspoon sugar and 1 tablespoon each of finely chopped onion and green pepper. Simmer together for 5 minutes. Blend into Brown Sauce with 2 tablespoons chopped sweet gherkins. Use with hot tongue, ham or game.

MUSHROOM SAUCE: Cook ½ cup sliced fresh mushrooms in butter before adding flour and browning. Prepare Brown Sauce following basic recipe and stir in mushrooms, 1 teaspoon Worcestershire sauce and a dash of nutmeg. Serve with lamb, veal chops, or hamburgers.

## BLENDER HOLLANDAISE SAUCE

Combine in blender jar
**3 egg yolks**
**2 tablespoons lemon juice**
**¼ teaspoon salt**
**Pinch of pepper**
In a small saucepan, heat until foamy
**½ cup butter or margarine**
Cover jar and blend at top speed for 2 seconds. Uncover, and continuing to blend at top speed, very gradually pour in hot butter. Do not add milky residue at bottom of butter pan. Cover and place in warm water until ready to serve.
Serve with fish dishes, asparagus, cauliflower or broccoli.
Makes 1 cup.

## CUCUMBER SAUCE

Peel, cut in quarters and remove seedy portion from a small cucumber.
Finely chop the firm portion and measure
**⅔ cup chopped cucumber**
Drain well.
Combine with
**½ cup thick dairy sour cream**
**1 teaspoon onion salt**
**Pinch of paprika**
Blend thoroughly and chill.
Serve with seafood or cold meats.
Makes 1⅓ cups.

## CREAMY HORSERADISH SAUCE

Whip until stiff
**½ cup heavy cream**
Fold in
**½ teaspoon salt**
**¼ cup horseradish**
Serve chilled with steaks, roast beef or ham.
Makes 1 cup.

## TARTAR SAUCE

Combine
**1 cup mayonnaise**
**1 tablespoon chopped stuffed olives**
**2 tablespoons finely chopped pickles**
**1 tablespoon chopped parsley or chives**
**1 tablespoon chopped green onion**
**¼ teaspoon tarragon**

Serve chilled with cooked fish, cold salmon or shellfish.
Makes 1¼ cups.

## TOMATO MEAT SAUCE

In a saucepan, heat thoroughly
**¼ cup butter or margarine**
**¼ cup olive oil**
Add and cook until onion is transparent
**1 onion, finely chopped**
**1 stalk celery, finely chopped**
**2 cloves garlic, finely chopped**
Stir in
**½ pound ground veal**
**¾ pound ground beef**
Cook until meat is lightly browned.
Blend in
**1 (28-ounce) can plum tomatoes**
**½ teaspoon salt**
**Pinch of pepper**
Bring to boil, reduce heat and simmer for two hours or until desired consistency. Skim fat from surface. Serve hot with cooked spaghetti.
Makes about 4 cups.

---

*Since the chief purpose of sauce is to impart flavour to foods, it is preferable to use butter to contribute to richness of flavour.*

---

## TOMATO BARBECUE SAUCE

In a small saucepan, heat until foamy
**2 tablespoons butter or margarine**
Add and cook until onion is transparent
**1 onion, finely chopped**
**2 cloves garlic, finely chopped**
**½ cup finely chopped celery**
Stir in
**2 cups tomato juice**
**¼ cup lemon juice**
**¼ cup lightly packed brown sugar**
**1 teaspoon salt**
**1 teaspoon dry mustard**
**2 tablespoons Worcestershire sauce**
**Pinch of cayenne**
Bring to boil, reduce heat and simmer uncovered for 25 minutes.
May be used for basting chicken, hamburgers and ribs while barbecuing or as sauce with baked spareribs.
Makes 2 cups.

## TOMATO MUSHROOM SAUCE

In a frypan, heat until foamy
**2 tablespoons butter or margarine**
Add and cook until onion is transparent
**1 onion, thinly sliced**
Blend in a mixture of
**1 tablespoon PURITY Flour**
**1 teaspoon salt**
**1 teaspoon Italian seasoning**
**Pinch of pepper**
Gradually, stir in
**1 (19-ounce) can tomatoes**
Cook, stirring constantly, until thickened.
Mix in
**1 (10-ounce) can sliced**
**mushrooms, drained**
**15 to 20 stuffed olives, sliced**
Heat thoroughly.
Serve with Italian Meat Loaf (See page 24).
Makes about 2 cups.

## BARBECUE SAUCE

In a small saucepan, heat until foamy
**2 tablespoons butter or margarine**
Add and cook until transparent
**1 onion, finely chopped**
Stir in
**1 cup chicken broth**
**1 cup gravy**
**2 tablespoons catsup**
**1 teaspoon parsley flakes**
**1 teaspoon Worcestershire sauce**
**½ teaspoon poultry seasoning**
**Dash of cayenne**

Bring to boil, reduce heat and simmer uncovered for 25 minutes.
Pour over sliced cooked chicken and heat thoroughly. May also be served with barbecued chicken or pork chops.
Makes 1½ cups.

# CANDY

It is always best to use a thermometer when making candy so the syrup is cooked to an exact temperature. However, if you do not have a thermometer it is possible to get satisfactory results with the "cold water test". To do this, fill a small bowl with cold water and allow syrup to drop from a spoon into the water. The following chart explains what happens at each stage:

| Temperature | Cold Water Test | Characteristics |
|---|---|---|
| 230° to 234°F. | Thread | Mixture will spin a fine thread, about 2 inches long, from a fork. This will disperse in water, sinking to bottom of the bowl. |
| 235° to 240°F. | Soft Ball | Mixture forms a soft ball in water which gradually disappears when rubbed. |
| 246° to 250°F. | Firm Ball | Mixture forms a firm ball in water which flattens when rubbed but will not disappear. |
| 250° to 265°F. | Hard Ball | Mixture forms a hard ball in water which holds its shape when rubbed. |
| 270° to 290°F. | Soft Crack | Mixture forms fine threads in water. These threads break when rubbed. |
| 300° to 310°F. | Hard Crack | Mixture is very brittle in the air and in the water. |

Always remove candy from the heat while doing the cold water test to prevent over-cooking. When using a candy thermometer, make sure the bulb is completely immersed in the syrup.

Cooked fudges and fondants are made up of tiny crystals—the smaller the crystals the smoother the candy. If the crystals start to form early, they will be large and the candy will be "sugary". Therefore, avoid too much stirring while cooking the candy, and allow it to cool without stirring until it reaches the correct temperature for beating.

## MAPLE CREAM FUDGE

Grease a 9-inch square pan.
In a saucepan, combine
**3 cups lightly packed brown sugar**
**1 cup granulated sugar**
**½ teaspoon salt**
**1 cup undiluted evaporated milk**
**OR cream**
**2 tablespoons butter**
Stir over medium heat until the sugar dissolves. Continue cooking the mixture until it reaches the soft ball stage (236°F.) Stir occasionally to prevent sticking.
Remove from heat and cool, without stirring, until bottom of the pan is luke-warm (110°F).
Beat until the fudge loses its gloss.
Then quickly stir in
**½ cup chopped nuts**
**1 teaspoon vanilla**
Pour into prepared pan.
When cool, cut into squares.
Makes about 1½ pounds.

## CHOCOLATE FUDGE

Grease a 9-inch square pan.
In a saucepan, combine
**2 cups granulated sugar**
**¾ cup undiluted evaporated milk**
**OR cream**
**2 squares unsweetened chocolate**
**2 tablespoons corn syrup**
**2 tablespoons butter**
**¼ teaspoon salt**
Stir over medium heat until the sugar is dissolved and the chocolate melted. Continue cooking the mixture until it reaches the soft ball stage (236°F.). Stir occasionally to prevent sticking.
Remove from the heat and let stand, without stirring, until bottom of the pan is lukewarm (110°F.).
Beat until the candy loses its gloss.
Then quickly stir in
**½ cup chopped nuts**

**1 teaspoon vanilla**
Pour into prepared pan.
When cool, cut into squares.
Makes 1¼ pounds.
NOTE: If desired, use ⅓ cup cocoa in place of the unsweetened chocolate. Increase the butter to 3 tablespoons.

## TAFFY APPLES

Lightly grease a baking sheet.
Wash and dry
**12 medium-sized red apples**
Firmly insert in stem end
**wooden meat skewer or stick**
In a saucepan, combine
**3 cups granulated sugar**
**1 cup corn syrup**
**1 cup water**
Heat, stirring constantly, until sugar dissolves. Cover and bring to boil. Boil, uncovered and without stirring, until a few drops in cold water separate into threads (300°F. on candy thermometer).
Blend in
**½ teaspoon cinnamon**
**¼ teaspoon red food colouring**
Remove from heat. Tip saucepan and dip apples in syrup turning to coat evenly. Place, stick up, on prepared baking sheet to harden.
Makes 12.

## PRALINE

Oil a 15 × 10-inch jelly roll pan.
In a small heavy saucepan, combine
**1¼ cups granulated sugar**
**1 cup unblanched almonds**
**¼ teaspoon cream of tartar**
Cook over medium heat, stirring occasionally with a metal spoon, until caramel coloured liquid.
Pour onto oiled jelly roll pan. Cool and break into pieces.

## QUICK FUDGE

Grease a 9-inch square pan.
In a saucepan, combine
**1⅔ cups granulated sugar**
**⅔ cup undiluted evaporated milk**
Simmer together for 5 minutes, stirring constantly.
Remove from heat and blend in
**1½ cups miniature marshmallows**
**OR 16 marshmallows, quartered**
**1½ cups chocolate chips**
**½ cup chopped nuts**
**1 teaspoon vanilla**
**¼ teaspoon salt**
Stir until smooth.
Pour into prepared pan.
When cool, cut into squares.
Makes about 1¼ pounds.

## PEANUT BRITTLE

Lightly grease a baking sheet or shallow metal pan.
In a saucepan, combine
**1½ cups granulated sugar**
**¾ cup corn syrup**
**½ cup water**
Heat, stirring constantly, until sugar dissolves. Then, bring to boil and continue cooking to hard crack stage (300°F. on candy thermometer) or until a few drops in cold water separate into hard, brittle threads.
Remove from heat and stir in
**2 tablespoons butter OR margarine**
**½ teaspoon salt**
**1½ cups salted peanuts**
Quickly pour onto prepared baking sheet. Cool and then break into pieces.

## CRYSTAL CITRUS PEEL

Wash and remove peel from
**\*4-5 oranges**
Cut peel into uniform strips about 3/8 inch wide. Measure 3 cups.
In a saucepan, combine peel with
**6 cups cold water**
Bring to boil and cook uncovered for 10 minutes. Drain and rinse in cold water.
Repeat cooking with a fresh
**6 cups cold water**
In a saucepan, combine
**1½ cups granulated sugar**

**½ cup honey**
**1¾ cups boiling water**
Bring to boil and boil 1 minute. Add cooked, drained peel. Simmer uncovered until almost all of syrup has been absorbed, about 30 to 40 minutes. Stir frequently to prevent sticking. Drain well in colander, about 10 minutes.
In a large bowl toss with
**1 cup granulated sugar**
Spread out on wax paper to dry. Store in tightly covered container.
Makes about 1 pound.
* Or cut peel from 6 lemons, OR 2 grapefruit OR 9 tangerines. Cook as above except tangerine peel does not need second boiling.

## STUFFED DATES

Mix together
**1 egg white**
**2 teaspoons butter or margarine**
**½ teaspoon vanilla**
Gradually add
**2 cups sifted icing sugar**
Beat until smooth and creamy.
If desired, tint with a few drops of food colouring. Stuff whole dates with about a teaspoon of the creamy mixture, then roll in granulated or fruit sugar.

## PULLED TAFFY

Grease a jelly roll pan.
In a large saucepan combine
**2 cups lightly packed brown sugar**
**2 cups molasses**
**½ cup water**
**2 tablespoons vinegar**
**1 tablespoon butter**
Bring to a boil, stirring constantly, until sugar dissolves. Continue cooking, without stirring, to soft crack stage (270°F. on a candy thermometer) or until a few drops in cold water separate into threads.
Remove from heat and stir in
**½ teaspoon baking soda**
Quickly pour onto prepared jelly roll pan. With a metal spatula, fold over from edges until cool enough to handle. With buttered hands, pull taffy, folding it back on itself. When colour starts to lighten, twist and pull as long as possible. Twist into lengths and cut into pieces. Wrap individually in wax paper.

# INDEX

# INDEX

# INDEX

# MAKE THIS A "GIFT" BOOK

As a birthday present, bridal "shower" gift, Christmas re-membrance, or bridge prize, what could be more accept-able than a copy of the Purity Cook Book! The coupons below are provided for your convenience when remitting, or for the use of your friends and neighbors who may desire to possess a copy of their own.

---

Enclosed is $1.25, *cash or money order* (Canada only) for which please send to the address shown below, postpaid, one copy of the Purity Cook Book.

NAME . . . . . . . . . . . . . . . . . .
(Please Print)
ADDRESS . . . . . . . . . . . . . . . .
(Please Print)
TOWN . . . . . . . . . . . . . . . . . .
Cash enclosed ☐    Money Order enclosed ☐
For prompt attention address your coupons and remittance to: **Purity Cook Book, Box 52, Toronto 9, Canada**

Enclosed is $1.25, *cash or money order* (Canada only) for which please send to the address shown below, postpaid, one copy of the Purity Cook Book.

NAME . . . . . . . . . . . . . . . . . .
(Please Print)
ADDRESS . . . . . . . . . . . . . . . .
(Please Print)
TOWN . . . . . . . . . . . . . . . . . .
Cash enclosed ☐    Money Order enclosed ☐
For prompt attention address your coupons and remittance to: **Purity Cook Book, Box 52, Toronto 9, Canada**

---

Enclosed is $1.25, *cash or money order* (Canada only) for which please send to the address shown below, postpaid, one copy of the Purity Cook Book.

NAME . . . . . . . . . . . . . . . . . .
(Please Print)
ADDRESS . . . . . . . . . . . . . . . .
(Please Print)
TOWN . . . . . . . . . . . . . . . . . .
Cash enclosed ☐    Money Order enclosed ☐
For prompt attention address your coupons and remittance to: **Purity Cook Book, Box 52, Toronto 9, Canada**

Enclosed is $1.25, *cash or money order* (Canada only) for which please send to the address shown below, postpaid, one copy of the Purity Cook Book.

NAME . . . . . . . . . . . . . . . . . .
(Please Print)
ADDRESS . . . . . . . . . . . . . . . .
(Please Print)
TOWN . . . . . . . . . . . . . . . . . .
Cash enclosed ☐    Money Order enclosed ☐
For prompt attention address your coupons and remittance to: **Purity Cook Book, Box 52, Toronto 9, Canada**

---

Enclosed is $1.25, *cash or money order* (Canada only) for which please send to the address shown below, postpaid, one copy of the Purity Cook Book.

NAME . . . . . . . . . . . . . . . . . .
(Please Print)
ADDRESS . . . . . . . . . . . . . . . .
(Please Print)
TOWN . . . . . . . . . . . . . . . . . .
Cash enclosed ☐    Money Order enclosed ☐
For prompt attention address your coupons and remittance to: **Purity Cook Book, Box 52, Toronto 9, Canada**

Enclosed is $1.25, *cash or money order* (Canada only) for which please send to the address shown below, postpaid, one copy of the Purity Cook Book.

NAME . . . . . . . . . . . . . . . . . .
(Please Print)
ADDRESS . . . . . . . . . . . . . . . .
(Please Print)
TOWN . . . . . . . . . . . . . . . . . .
Cash enclosed ☐    Money Order enclosed ☐
For prompt attention address your coupons and remittance to: **Purity Cook Book, Box 52, Toronto 9, Canada**

To secure additional copies of the

**COOK BOOK**
use the handy order coupons provided below.
*(Details on reverse side)*

**COOK BOOK**
**ORDER COUPON**

**COOK BOOK**
**ORDER COUPON**

**COOK BOOK**
**ORDER COUPON**

**COOK BOOK**
**ORDER COUPON**

**COOK BOOK**
**ORDER COUPON**

**COOK BOOK**
**ORDER COUPON**